MARXISM AND THE FRENCH LEFT

MARXISM
AND THE
FRENCH LEFT

*Studies in labour and politics
in France, 1830–1981*

TONY JUDT

CLARENDON PRESS · OXFORD

Oxford University Press, Walton Street, Oxford OX2 6

Oxford New York Toronto
Delhi Bombay Calcutta Madras Karachi
Petaling Jaya Singapore Hong Kong Tokyo
Nairobi Dar es Salaam Cape Town
Melbourne Auckland

and associated companies in
Berlin Ibadan

Oxford is a trade mark of Oxford University Press

Published in the United States
by Oxford University Press, New York

© Tony Judt 1986

First published 1986
First issued in paperback 1989

British Library Cataloguing in Publication Data
Judt, Tony
Marxism and the French left: studies on labour
and politics in France 1830-1981.
1. Socialism—France—History 2. Communism
—France—History
I. Title
320.944 HX261.5
ISBN 0-19-821929-6
ISBN 0-19-821578-9 (pbk)

Printed in Great Britain
by Courier International Ltd
Tiptree, Essex

TO THE MEMORY OF
GEORGE LICHTHEIM

Acknowledgements

DURING the preparation of this book I have been most generously served by institutional support on both sides of the Atlantic. In the USA I was the recipient of a Fellowship from the American Council of Learned Societies, and of a grant from the Hoover Institution to study there in the summer of 1981. In Britain I have received assistance from the Nuffield Foundation, the British Academy, the Twenty Seven Foundation and the Politics Department of Oxford University. Much of this support has been for essential travel to libraries and archives, and fellow historians and others will know just how invaluable that sort of help can be. In some instances the research thus facilitated was divided between the present work and a future, quite different project. I hope that in both cases those who have thus supported my research will not be too disappointed with the result.

Foundations exist to help scholars, but individuals have other calls upon their time and resources. I am thus especially indebted to all those friends and colleagues who have discussed some of the themes of this book and thereby contributed to my own education, if not to the improvement of the end-product, whose inadequacies are my responsibility alone. I owe special thanks to Jan Gross, Gareth Stedman Jones, Dave Travis, David Levy, Tim Mason, and Eric Foner. Rich Mitten has confirmed my belief that there are still people around who take arguments about marxism (as distinct from arguments *within* marxism) seriously. I always enjoy our discussions—I hope he will not despair upon reading this, their interim product. Colleagues in the Oxford Politics department, notably David Goldey and Vincent Wright, have tried in vain to save me from an obsessive interest in theory; I am grateful for their efforts and stand in awe of their encyclopaedic acquaintance with the practice of politics in France. As to what it is really all about, only the subjects of our mutual interest would suppose it was necessary or possible ever to know.

My debts to the work of many others will be clear from text and notes alike, but to John Dunn I remain particularly grateful for the reiterated reminder that the history of ideas must above all be *historically* intelligible. The 'Cambridge' school of intellectual history is now so well established that the work of Dunn and Skinner is occasionally downplayed as 'obvious'. No one who has kept abreast of the historiography of socialism and 'popular culture' would be so optimistic—the obvious can take a long time to penetrate. To Leszek Kolakowski I owe particular thanks. This is in part because of his generosity in reading some of my work, but chiefly through the stimulus of his many writings. It is not necessary to agree with a book, nor even to share its intellectual approach, to recognize the immensity of its achievement.

Kolakowski's *Main Currents of Marxism,* with his earlier essays, forms part of the upheaval in the European radical consciousness which has contributed so much to the subject-matter (and, doubtless, the perspective) of this book.

I also owe thanks to my College, St. Anne's, which provides so pleasant a working environment, and to my colleagues there who have generously allowed me ample leave to prepare and complete this book. My editors at the Press, Ivon Asquith and Nancy Lane, have been tolerant and patient and very understanding in the face of a book which is rather different from the one we first discussed. They should know that their forbearance is much appreciated.

I owe thanks, appreciation, and much else to Patricia Hilden, without whom this book would not have happened, and other things besides. Nor is this the extent of my acknowledgement to her, since her own work has greatly influenced mine. Her research on the working women of French Flanders and their experience of French socialism in its early years has taught me a lot that I did not know, and encouraged me to look afresh at old subjects. I have also learnt from her, sometimes by example, a lot more about radical politics. I know that this book has benefited enormously thereby. I hope it shows.

The book is dedicated to the memory of George Lichtheim. He died more than a decade ago and some of his work has been overtaken by new research. But Lichtheim is still quite unmatched in his ability to capture, in taut and succinct prose, the essential features of the history of the Left in Europe. Reading him now is as much a pleasure, above all a pleasure, as it was when it first stimulated my interest in the 1960s. Nobody, as the jingle goes, does it better. Lichtheim was unique among those writing in English in his thoroughly European grasp of the importance of the history of ideas in the history of social movements, and was magnificently gifted in his ability to illustrate and elucidate the point.

Although his interests were encyclopaedic (his *Europe in the Twentieth Century* is a masterpiece of its kind, witty, allusive, and the best textbook in its field), he had a special interest in France. His essays on the elucubrations of the French intellectual Left in the 1960s should be required reading for all those who discovered marxism in the 1970s and disillusion a decade later. His commentary on the history of the socialist idea in France, *Marxism in Modern France,* is still, twenty years after its appearance, the best place to acquire an *understanding* of what was going on, though like all Lichtheim's work it presumed a curious intelligence in the reader and made no concessions to intellectual indolence.

What Lichtheim did not write, though he frequently alluded both to the desirability of such an undertaking and its extraordinary difficulty, was a social account of left-wing thought and its political practice in France. This book is in no way an attempt to meet that need. Instead, it treats a number of themes illuminated in passing by Lichtheim's own work, and takes as its premiss and justification his own emphasis: the impossibility of saying anything intelligible about the history of the popular movement in France since 1789 without a well-founded grasp of the history of socialist thought. If I have succeeded at all in conflating the two in some way which illuminates them both, the credit is his, and I am glad of the opportunity to say how and why this is so.

Contents

List of Maps and Figures

I

The Left in France

IN 1970, while doing some research in the city of Toulon, I was invited for lunch to the home of a family all of whose members were active in the local Socialist movement. It was a time of upheaval in the Socialist Party, the period between the death of the old SFIO and Mitterrand's final seizure of control, and lunch was dominated by heated debate on the subject. Afterwards, sitting on the balcony looking out to the Mediterranean islands, we talked about the socialist tradition in the region and I asked whether anyone knew when the tradition of being 'on the Left' in this family had begun. There was some confusion on the husband's side because of an Italian ancestry dating from the annexation of Nice, but his wife had no hesitation. We have been 'à gauche' since the 1790s, she announced, when an ancestor stood out against Toulon's 'treason' with the English. But as to *why* they had always stood so firmly on one side of the great divide in France, for this there was no ready answer.

Two reflections struck me at the time. The first was how much this family (of schoolteachers, incidentally) stood in contrast to some others I had known elsewhere in France, despite sharing similarities of occupation, income, taste, and sometimes even opinion. I had often supposed that the difference was simply political, and of course it is. But it is more, and deeper. There is a *culture* of the Left in France, whose profound historical significance lies precisely in the frequent inability of those who share it to say just what it is that accounts for and describes their views. Those French acquaintances of mine who are not on the Left cannot be so readily identified, nor are they so quick to locate themselves in that way. Deep in the Sarthe, the Vendée, or the Morbihan, of course, one still can (or could, until quite recently) meet people for whom the events of 1793 are as yesterday, and whose whole social vision is dominated by the experiences of their forebears. But even though this not infrequently has the political consequence of benefiting the Right at election time, it does not by any means entail a consistent political conservatism. And it certainly does not give the

Breton anything very positive in common with similarly inclined voters
from Alsace, the eastern foothills of the Massif, or the people of the
Béarn and Basque departments of the far south-west.

In short, there is not a culture of Right, or 'Centre' in the same way
that there is one of the Left. It is the Left which provides its opponents
with their common ground, without which regional, religious, and
personal antagonisms would divide them deeply.

The second reflection concerns the sheer longevity of radical
political traditions in France. It is customary, at a time of Labour's
decline in Britain, to speak of it as retreating to its heartlands, its long-
held and impregnable bases in the industrial communities of the north
and the 'celtic fringe'. Yet by comparison with France, these are
footholds only recently established. Before the rise of industrial cities,
with the revolution in textiles and the growing importance of coal, most
of today's Labour strongholds were villages, and when they had a local
political tradition it was quite different in kind, dating to the old
politics of the restricted suffrage. Even its most sympathetic historian
does not propose the existence of a working-class political tradition in
Britain before the 1820s, and as for some more formal expression of
that tradition and its interests, we must wait at least until the 1880s for
firm evidence. There was a history of radical opposition, of course,
from Wilkes to Cobbett and beyond, but the extent to which it can be
said to have linked with and contributed directly to the rise of the
modern Left in Britain is, to say the least, a matter of heated debate.

No such controversies surround the history of the Left in France.
(There are, of course, others.) To be 'à gauche' in France, whether in
Lille, Paris, Toulon, or a thousand tiny villages, was to be Republican,
Radical, Socialist, or Communist at different times (or at the same
time in different places). All, however, were related in some very
ancient way, and indeed that relationship and its complexities and
contradictions were a source of strength, often in the apparent absence
of more determinate political characteristics and programmes. And my
friends in Toulon were remarkably representative of their half of
France in the confidence with which they averred their political
identity, the antiquity of their claim to it—and the uncertainty
surrounding the exact meaning to be attached to the tradition to which
they were so unwaveringly faithful.

Tracing the ancestry of the geological cleavage in French political
culture may not be the most profitable way to proceed, even though
everything points to history and memory as the most important

ingredient in the division. The vocabulary of the Left certainly encourages such an undertaking: workers/bourgeoisie, *peuple/exploit-ants* (in the pejorative sense acquired after 1830 in the towns), patriots/traitors, *travailleurs/oisifs*, us/them. And there are other, sometimes older oppositions which intersect with more recent divisions: order/movement, Catholic/anti-clerical, provinces/Paris, periphery/centre, north/south, urban/rural. These cast us back to the great domestic conflicts of the monarchical centuries and beyond—the Wars of Religion and the Albigensian Crusade. To bind all of these together in some tidy manner is a profound error, of course, a mistake in causality at the least, crude reductionism at worst. But the Manichean character of political argument in France does point towards one very relevant aspect of the question, that of vocabulary. To be on the Left in France is before all else to share a style of discourse, a way of talking about politics, present and past. When Georges Clemenceau announced that one is either 'for' or 'against' the Revolution, he was appealing directly to a rich, or 'thick' complex of beliefs on which he and his audience could rely for communication and identification.

It is the French Revolution which supplies the form for much of this discourse, both in the vocabulary itself, but also in the resonances produced by that vocabulary in popular memory. The very scale of national political mobilization in the decade after 1789 ensured that certain phrases would retain their force and emphasis well into the twentieth century (indeed until at least the late 1960s, in the hands of the educated élite). This is especially the case for certain particularly contentious matters, such as the problem of legitimacy. Who might rule, and on what terms? It is worth noting that from St Just to Blum, the Left in France was consistently more interested in the grounds on which a person or party could claim to inherit authority, than the ends to which that authority was to be used. This is why political programmes in France always seem, to the Anglo-Saxon eye, so extraordinarily vapid (and are thus erroneously dismissed as so much flannel, as though cynicism were a more truly human characteristic than faith). The *locus classicus* here is the Bonapartist inheritance. Only a thoroughgoing Revolution could produce Napoleon, whose claim to power resided more completely in the putative support of the people than did that of the clubs or the Assembly. Hence the ease with which both Bonapartes, Grand and Petit alike, could invoke, successfully, a populist and revolutionary legitimacy. What they *did* might horrify the

Left, then and since, but the only effective barrier was institutional—in ideological terms, their claim was embarrassingly plausible.

Formally, then, the history of the French Left begins with the French Revolution, and many of its problems arise from this source. But some of the key motifs in left-wing discourse breach the Revolutionary barrier reef and are rooted in earlier national concerns. The discussion of power, and more specifically the powers of the state, are rather different in France from elsewhere, in that they are manifestly more inclined to a sympathy for the central authority. This is frequently and erroneously held to be the unfortunate result of the French Left's failure to impose strict quotas upon the importation of ideas. If only the indigenous socialist movement had kept German marxism at a distance, it is suggested, the modern Left would not be saddled with such a misplaced enthusiasm for planning, control, and central authority in general.

In truth, however, it was the early modern French philosophers, and their enlightenment heirs, who first drafted the maps onto which the socialists have superimposed their own topography of political authority. From the sixteenth century, critical observers in France were far more apprehensive (and for good reason) of the over-mighty individual subject than of the sovereign, individual, or institutional. And while they did not themselves universally propose or approve the historical solution to this—the melding of state and society into something at times resembling a unity—their instincts, like those of their successors in the 1790s, where to favour the state as the fountainhead of authority, even at the cost of a steady diminution of the powers of the localities. As to the rights of individuals, these had never been estimated very highly by critics of absolutism, much less by its apologists; in so far as they were identified as a subject for consideration, they were thought best protected by the disinterested powers of a well-founded and powerful authority. It was the Fronde, not Hegel, that supplied this instinct to radical political theory in France, and it is still there today.[1]

A side-effect of this unbalanced concern with social security, so to speak, has been the inability of the French Left ever to theorize very convincingly about the state. Not that they have not tried. From St Simon to Poulantzas the history of socialist thought in France is permeated with a concern to *define* the nature of authority, a concern

[1] See Nannerl Keohane, *Philosophy and the State in France* (Princeton, 1980), esp. pp. 453–61.

which became the more urgent after 1880 when the marxists faced the problem, then as now, that Marx himself had never satisfactorily explained where the modern state stood in a system of social intercourse determined by production relations. But even here one notes a curious absence of interest in what it is that the state may properly *do* (the abiding focus of Anglo-American writings on the subject). The French socialists have tried mightily to *account* for the state, and in particular to show how the state just must be the servant of a given social group (for good or evil). As to what it might *do* with its power, this is assumed to be entailed in the description of its origins and not to merit discussion.[2]

A different perspective, surfacing in the Proudhonian tradition and in the work of radicals such as Alain, *appears* to offer an alternative branch of left thinking in France, emphasizing popular initiative and a diminution of the state's powers. It has sometimes been supposed that this is *the* socialist tradition in France, overpowered by foreign competition but indigenous to radical thought there and unjustly underestimated.

Yet of the two strands in socialist thinking it was the 'anti-state' position which was the more recent—indeed, it was a direct response to the dominant emphasis in the French Revolution upon administration and regulation. As such it was always tinged with 'reaction', however unfair the charge, and was at one point accused of being the 'objective' collaborator of the enemies of Revolutionary government. At only two moments during the nineteenth century did those who doubted the efficacy or desirability of the paternal state gain a firm foothold in popular sentiment: in sections of the workers' movement under the Second Empire, with political and sectional reasons for seeking a reduction in the regulatory powers of government, and in the partial re-emergence of provincial consciousness towards the end of the century.

[2] This preference for the abstracted theoretical premiss over the empirical outcome seems to be deeply rooted in French thought. De Tocqueville tells a story of an eminent French engineer who was sent to study the Liverpool–Manchester railway shortly after its opening. After a cursory observation of the railway itself, Monsieur Navier, the engineer in question, made some theoretical calculations of a complicated nature to test certain information he had been given about the workings of the railway. His conclusion was, 'The thing is impossible, it does not fit at all with the theory'. Whereupon he returned to France. It is a pity that M. Navier made his career at *Ponts et Chaussées*—he would have been a wild success at the *Ecole Normale Supérieure*. See A. de Tocqueville, *Journeys to England and Ireland*, ed. J. P. Mayer (London, 1958), p. 113 (quoted in Jack Simmons, *The Railway in England and Wales 1830–1914* (Leicester, 1978)), p. 22.

One can go further. The 'alternative Left' in France founded its thinking about power and authority upon the same central premiss as that which underpinned the dominant strand. This was the common assumption that the people retained the final power to confer legitimacy upon those who governed them, and to withdraw it when the need arose. Disagreement (in so far as it was not merely a matter of personality) concerned the optimum way to guarantee this power to the citizenry and the extent to which the services owed them by those in office could be provided with or without the further enhancement of the capacities of the state. In other words the area of disagreement was formal and practical. It was thus of secondary significance (for a discussion of this point see chapter four in this book).

As a result of the way in which the debate over power and government was thus cast in the French socialist tradition, the minority tradition (whether we call it *autogestionnaire*, decentralizing, or simply anarchist) has always been wrong-footed. Its strongest suit has been the defence of vested interests, whether those of Proudhon's privileged property-owning artisans or Alain's suspicious villagers, fearful of taxation, conscription, and Paris. The Left, especially the Radicals and more recently the Parti Socialiste, have had good electoral grounds for incorporating elements of the anti-state vocabulary into their own programmes, but the historial sentiments behind such promises as decentralization or workers' control have never sat comfortably with the political culture of the mainstream Left, and it is Michel Rocard's identification with these and other iconoclastic preferences, for example, which have isolated him today in his political family.

The Left, then, is fairly clearly and closely associated with a particular sense of the state in France (which does *not* mean that it is, or always has been, a friend of the authority vested in Paris—but its opposition has never hinged upon a questioning of the powers of government, only their source). On other matters it is much less determinate, which is a reminder of just how much the problem of institutions has dominated political debate in French history. Indeed, much of what passes for radical political thought in France might better be understood once again as variations upon a mode of discourse. For all its many continuities with and from the Old Regime, contemporary France is above all the first European nation to have been constructed around a self-consciously revolutionary doctrine. Loyalty to such a doctrine is thus an integral part of the meaning of being Left in France. This was much clearer in the years from 1815 to

1945 than it is today. In that period the institutional form of revolutionary sympathy, the Republic, was under constant threat, or at least in question, and the institutional problem thus uppermost in left-wing concerns (this was true for the Socialists during most of these years and even for the Communists from 1934–8 and again from 1941).

Since 1945 loyalty to the revolutionary doctrine has taken on a rather anachronistic air, in keeping with the rapidity of social change in the country over the past generation. But it has been rather easily replaced by a no less compelling loyalty to certain residual tenets of the marxist tradition. This tradition was facilitated by a long period of overlap during which the socialism of Jaurès and Blum combined marxist social analysis and final goals with democratic or republican methods drawn from the earlier tradition. So long as political marxism itself *had* no methods of its own this peculiar combination worked rather well. After 1917 it was no longer plausible as a *revolutionary* practice, and there followed two decades of ideological confusion. The difficulty was sorted out by the experience of fascism, and the new orthodoxy of the Left from 1945–75 emerged thence.

Beyond doctrine, there is the importance of *debate.* The French are notoriously slow to join national organizations (unions, political parties, social or charitable associations), but the history of radical politics in France has none the less been a story of collective activity grouped around incessant discussion. From the clubs of the Revolution to the clubs of 1848, from the *chambrées* and *cercles* of the 1840s to the clubs (again) of the 1960s, public engagement in political argument has been a vital part of the action of the Left in modern France. The peculiar force of this way of mobilizing support and establishing programmes and tactics is that it derives from the way in which *power* was broked at the moment of the creation. In the high months of the Great Revolution, in Paris but also in some provincial cities, the right to rule could depend upon the government's ability to claim that it spoke for the men of the clubs. This in turn gave the debates of the latter a special interest, as the *de facto* source of political legitimacy.

From this feature of the history of the Revolution (a moment at best, but a terribly important one) there has emerged the peculiarly French relationship between theoretical debate and radical political action. In other countries this is frequently seen as a fine example of the hubris of intellectuals, unable to act but given to proclaiming that their very words are action incarnate. But here again, history has served France differently. For those Revolutionary clubs were also the source of a certain popular legitimacy—given the impossibility (and the undesirability) of testing national opinion before embarking on revolutionary acts, the radicals of the 1790s adapted constitutional writings of an earlier era (including those republican philosophies grounded in an Italian or Dutch history of which the French had no experience), and invented a style of direct democracy by acclamation. And thus the French Left is heir to a double tradition, public doctrinal debate and political legitimacy deriving from direct democracy, but conflated into a single historical experience.

This has two consequences for the historian of the Left in France. The first is that intellectual debate about politics is taken very seriously and takes itself seriously, as participant. The second, of more immediate concern here, is that the distinction between left-wing argument and popular mass politics simply never existed. In Britain or the USA it is not prima facie absurd to treat of the history of the labouring population and the history of socialism in separate compartments, so long as due recognition is made of the ways in which they came into contact and influenced one another. In Germany, the union movement and the Socialists were united in a single party from 1891, but in practice they went their separate ways until 1914, joined only by a common defensive interest in opposing the Wilhelminian state. But in France, where unions had few members and where they were anyway hostile to the political Socialists (who also lacked mass support), unions, workers, and Socialists alike were in fact much more closely bound together by the experience of Revolution and the terms in which that experienced was couched, than in any other European land.

The relation between labour and socialism in France is camouflaged by the terms and the power of the republican tradition, and by the slow emergence of industrial society. It is heightened by the precocious advent of manhood suffrage, which drove politics into the experience of every community in France long before railways, newspapers, and parties had achieved a similar end in other nations. The slightly misleading picture bequeathed us of the 'utopian' socialists can sometimes seem to suggest that in so far as left-wing politics other than republicanism appealed to the masses it was only to *remove* them from the actual political conflicts of early nineteenth-century France. But this was not quite the case. Most of the 'utopians' were not utopian at all (we have Engels and his gift for polemic to thank for seeing them thus!), and some of those who were had an interest in cosmology, astrology, and 'moral reform' which far outweighed their political or social analyses in importance or impact. And where the pre-1848 socialists did establish links with the working population it was through a common concern with very mundane contemporary matters, and in a vocabulary familiar to workers and theorists alike.

Even if there was still doubt before 1848 as to whether socialism and the concerns of workers might share common ground (and I argue in chapter two that this was not the case), from 1851 the question was moot. No radical movement in France after that date could establish enduring credentials without a firm social base among the working population in town and country alike—or, more precisely, it was *felt* by the Left that this must be the case, which within twenty years had made it so. The radical bourgeoisie (republican since the 1840s if not before) might continue to proclaim its membership in the family of the Left, but it was seriously discredited in the eyes of its plebeian allies by the experiences of 1848–51. Only the Napoleonic interlude and the Commune and post-Commune repression enabled the republicans to renew their claim for a further half-century.

If the Left by mid-century was constrained to describe itself in increasingly *social* terms, thus providing itself with a proletarian identity even before the full emergence of the actual proletariat onto the industrial scene, the history of labour in France, *mutatis mutandis,* is suffused from about the same time with a vocabulary which drew increasingly on socialist sources. The groundwork for this was provided by notions of legitimacy and rights deriving from the Revolutionary experience and from trade traditions in equal parts, but what the socialists provided, and what could not have been disinterred from the Revolutionary traditions of the 1790s, was a discourse adapted to fighting *against* other republicans who happened to be employers, landowners, or *rentiers.* At this point the working class in France simply ceased to have a history distinct from that of the socialist idea, since both were crucially dependent upon the other for their strength and their credibility as actors in French life and affairs.

The result of the effective monopoly, by socialism and its hypothetical base in the interests and identity of the working class, was progressively to exclude as claimants upon the tradition of the Left considerable segments of French society, notably the rural population and the *radicalisant* fringe of the old republican movement. Something similar took place in other countries, but the consequences in France were more serious because of the unusually slow shift to an urban and industrial society, and the enduring plausibility of republican ideals in the face of a still-powerful strain of political reaction, continuing into the 1930s to deny that the Revolution of 1789 should ever have occurred.

These difficulties were overcome, but at a price. Rural France was finally incorporated into the Left via the ballot box, thus conferring a respectability upon that tradition of rural radicalism which in 1851 had been thought either atavistic or at best very unusual. As to the old Radicals of the small provincial towns, the sense in which they remained 'à gauche', as the issues which had once moved them (the church's role in education, the threat of monarchy) were resolved, is hard to define. It is certainly an error to capitalize upon the obvious contradictions of their position and assume that the Radical electors of 1936 (or even 1914) were a mere residue, voting left by habit but squarely situated with the conservative sentiment on all social issues. For we are back again with vocabulary, and the Radicals, party and supporters alike, spoke to themselves and to each other as members of the Left. Indeed, so they were, since nothing in the French tradition of radical discourse required a consistently critical attitude towards capitalism, nor one that presupposed the essential iniquities of government under capitalist economic arrangements. These were secondary positions, which only became fundamental with the final socialist monopoly of radical politics in the years following the Second World War. And even so their hegemony has been brief; in the 1980s it is again no longer a requirement of the Left that it condemn profit, economic exploitation, and wealth. The salient achievements of Mitterrand's presidency have been in the areas of civil and economic rights, justice, institutional reform—classic themes all of them, but which once again open up the traditions of the Left to a wider, less sociologically determined (and less reliable) audience.

The consequences are well known. Every time the Left in France restricts its political vision in order to give clarity to its social goals, it reduces its ability to influence affairs. When it makes itself available to a wider audience and places the emphasis upon the very indeterminacy, the nebulous catholicism of its inheritance, it gains voters, members, and sometimes even power. But all it can bring to office under such circumstances is . . . discourse. For it is the form of the appeal, rather than its advertised content, which unites women textile workers of Roubaix with male printers in Lyons, farmers from the Allier with schoolteachers in Lyons, wine-growers in Burgundy with Parisian metaphysicians. Nothing would dispel that unity quicker than too sharp an emphasis upon *either* the particular interests of any one of them alone, *or* some hypothetical general interest of the whole nation (including, that is, their political opponents).

*

The chapters which follow deal with these and other aspects of the history of the Left in France in greater detail. They do not, of course, represent in themselves a history of the Left or of Socialism, much less of the French labour movement. It is to be regretted that such a history does not yet exist in English. To be serviceable as well as comprehensive, however, it would need to concern itself with the whole of the experience of political, social, and intellectual movements of the Left in France since the great Revolution. The balance and brevity which such an undertaking would entail are no doubt virtues in themselves, but they would necessarily exclude detailed consideration of underlying themes or peripheral developments whose significance can only be disinterred through close argument. The purpose of this book is to cast some new light upon the understanding of the Left in France by way of just such a thematic approach.

That is not to claim that the chapters form a cohesive whole in every respect. At first glance their subject-matter is very varied indeed. The second chapter is the only one which deals directly with the history of labour in France, and that only for the nineteenth century. It is followed by a survey of the impact of the birth of Communism upon the non-Communist Left between the wars, and thence by a discussion of the rise and decline of marxist thought in France in its heyday after the Second World War. Only the final chapter is concerned with a major turning-point in the modern history of the French Left, and even there the focus is upon the historical context and the longer-term significance of the 1981 elections, rather than the events themselves. There are considerable chronological gaps and a number of participants in French political life most notable for their absence.[3] What, then, constitutes the common thread in these pages?

---

[3] Most obviously, there is no direct discussion of the PCF, and only passing reference is made to the years 1880–1914, during which the French Left came to maturity. For the PCF, see the bibliography, and Judt, 'Une historiographie pas comme les autres', in *European Studies Review* (1982). For the earlier period there are many excellent monographs, notably that of Michelle Perrot, *Les Ouvriers en grève,* 2 vols., (Paris, 1974),

The clue, it seems to me, lies in the very subject spread itself. During the past generation the historiography of the Left has been fractured and splintered into a dozen professional shards: labour history, social history, women's history, history of ideas, political history, political sociology, political theory. Most recently it has been further stretched to accommodate the needs of post-structuralist literary criticism, for whom Althusser on the one hand and radical French feminist thought on the other have been figures of the first importance. Today, everyone has a little bit of the culture of the French Left in his or her intellectual arsenal.

Whether or not the newly-acquired material can be made to serve depends in some measure on the skill of the person who has acquired it. There are some very good social histories of nineteenth-century French artisans and some appalling misappropriations of Parisian intellectual jargon. The converse is just as true. But *caveat emptor!* Applying sociological theory to mid-nineteenth-century Toulouse, or wallowing contentedly in the miasmic marsh of Parisian signifiers requires abstracting the material or the method from the only setting in which it makes historical sense. And *historical* sense is what needs to be made of it. This is especially true of the history of the Left in France in view of its own propensity, discussed above, to collapse into metahistorical discourse. Taken at face value, as it so often is by bemused cohorts of foreign admirers, it has a very low tolerance threshold for reality, and floats quite free of restraints, epistemological, social, or historical.

Oddly enough, the problems with monographic approaches to

as well as the general works cited in the bibliography. The best English-language texts covering that period are now R. D. Anderson, *France 1870–1914* (London, 1977), and J.-M. Mayeur and M. Rebérioux, *The Third Republic from its Origins to the Great War, 1870–1914* (Cambridge, 1984). I have not included in these chapters any extended consideration of the relations between the Left and the peasantry, but those interested in the subject are referred to Judt, *Socialism in Provence 1871–1914: a study in the origins of the modern French Left* (Cambridge, 1979); also Yves Lequin, *Histoire des français: XIX–XXᵉ siècles*, 3 vols. (Paris, 1983–4), esp. vol. 3; G. Duby and H. Wallon, *Histoire de la France rurale*, vol. 3 (Paris, 1976); Eugen Weber, *Peasants into Frenchmen* (Stanford, 1976). See also A. Compère-Morel, *Le Socialisme aux champs* (Paris, 1906): René Cabannes, *Le Parti socialiste et les Paysans* (Bayonne, 1907); Yves Rinaudo, 'Syndicalisme agricole de base: l'exemple du Var au début du XX siècle' in *Mouvement social no. 112 (1979)*; P.M. Jones, 'An Improbable Democracy: nineteenth-century elections in the Massif Central', in *English Historical Review*, vol. 97 (July 1982); Eugen Weber, 'Comment la politique vint aux paysans: a Second look at Peasant politicisation', in *American Historical Review*, vol. 87, no. ii (1982); Edward Berenson, 'Socialism in the Countryside?', in *Comparative Studies in Society and History*, vol. 23, no. ii.

French labour history are basically analogous. Unable to see just how or why French working men and women *should* have been attached to the doctrines and goals of marxism, historians trained either as functionalists *or* as neo-marxists assume the absence of such attachments. This results in a hermetic engagement with Labour as a socially unattached phenomenon, a self-creating and self-sufficient object of historical dissection. Where a connection between life and thought leaps unavoidably to the eye, it is recast in one of two ways. Traditionally the political affiliations of working men and women were described in variously modified reflection theories of consciousness, an intellectual tradition among left historians stretching back at least to Lenin and still in considerable vogue among historians of the work experience in industrial America. More recently, and in oblique acknowledgement of the intellectual preferences of the descendants of their protagonists, historians have taken to treating the political ideas of working people in the last century as the cultural equivalent of a sealed cooling system, with the same basic materials ('language', 'discourse', 'belief') circulating and re-circulating into infinity. Nothing is ever new, workers just recycle their old vocabulary and myths to adapt to changing external circumstances (one author actually writes as though it were the same workers being recycled, and in his terms the inference is perhaps legitimate!).[4]

What this historiographical diaspora points towards is the need for some gathering in of the wanderers. In this book I am proposing two ways in which to set about such a task. In the first place it seems reasonably urgent to impose some sort of historical control on the subject-matter. It is not simply the case that most modern accounts, however competent, however thorough, make too restricted a sense of the history of the Left in modern France. In any serious meaning of the word they do not actually make *sense* of it at all. It is not only that the frequently reiterated suggestion that marxism was an alien import on the French scene does not square with the facts; it is not intuitively plausible, when one knows just how deep and abiding has been the romance between working men and women and the avowedly marxist movements to which they gave their allegiance, especially in the years 1880–1940 (it is the besetting crime of the PCF in particular that it has so often and so cynically betrayed this trust). Or, to take another example, it is a major error of judgement by students of French politics

[4] See Bernard Moss, *The Origins of the French Labor Movement. The Socialism of skilled workers 1830–1914* (Berkeley, 1976).

today to discount ideology and dogma as so much cynical verbiage, pap for the militants and grist to the mill of marxist ephemera from Berkeley to Bloomsbury. There just is so much more behind these 'mere words' than the most sensitively calibrated political science can hope to capture, especially when it abandons the struggle in advance.

The dimension whose case I wish to press is of course that of history. It is remarkable how little the study of the Left in France has been touched by developments in the techniques of historians of ideas (or of science). Perhaps this is because the sort of close contextual attention which brings its rewards in the study of Locke, or Machiavelli, or the Scottish Enlightenment seems altogether too overmighty a tool for application in the investigation of lesser thinkers and their followers. Perhaps. But it is a very great pity, for the way in which the history of socialism, the history of revolutionary politics, and the experience of the working population come together in the creation of 'the Left' in France makes of it a uniquely historical instance of the interplay of ideas and actions with their context, its restrictions and possibilities.

In each of the chapters that follow I have tried to approach the material with these considerations in mind. Although I have on occasion invoked the interpretations of others as pegs on which to hang alternative accounts of my own, the starting-point has in each case been an interrogation of the commonplace. In the following chapter three assumptions are questioned: is there a causal relationship between modern French economic history and the attitudes and choices of workers' organizations? In what ways can we accept the view that marxism and 'French' socialism diverged significantly and exactly when did this divergence emerge? Just because labour and socialism are inextricably intertwined throughout these years, does this mean that we can thereby infer some explanation for the later weaknesses of the latter from the divisions of the former? My contention is not that such questions lend themselves to tidy alternative responses, but that an insensitivity to their very particular history leads to students of the subject posing them in radically misleading ways.

The chapter on inter-war socialism is in response to a different debate but with similar underlying concerns. The enormous literature on the French Communist Party, its history and nature, tended for many years to cast a shadow over the socialist movement, which seemed (as Communists said it was) to be a mere footnote to the history of revolutionary politics in France after 1917, an epilogue that stubbornly refused to end. There has of course been renewed interest in socialism as a result of the rise of the PS since 1971, but rather than transforming our understanding of the twentieth-century history of the non-Communist Left this last generation of studies has simply adopted the myths for its own and built upon them. Annie Kriegel and others have long since opened up the terrain of Communist history itself—Professor Kriegel's massive study of the way in which Communism was born in France is a model of a historically sensitive telling of a story which too readily invites the functional mode. But there is no remotely satisfactory account of what the historical accident of the birth of Communism meant for *Socialists*. I am thus proposing a line of argument to the effect that the schism of 1920, far from casting the SFIO into a void, actually renewed its ideological commitment, modified its sociological constitution less than one is led to believe, and reinforced those very characteristics of dogmatic rigidity and tactical flexibility which are more commonly associated with Communism. If we thus see the inter-war SFIO as it really was, and not as it might have become (or is inferred in retrospect to have become), we can begin to make sense not only of the Popular Front débâcle, but also the ambiguities of the non-Communist Left in France up to and including the present (which thus introduces one of the themes of the final chapter in the book).

The most blatant attempt to attach the experience of the Left in France to its time and place occurs in chapter four, on modern French marxism. Independently of one's assessment of the arguments of the chapter, there are two respects in which the subject and approach are open to controversy. In the first place, the chapter is selective and critical, and its very approach entails denying to its subjects that intellectual autonomy and meta-historical credibility which was and has to be *their* first claim upon our attention. For those who take Sartre, Althusser, and his followers very seriously, then, this chapter is in part beside the point. For it is my contention that they were listened to at the time for very circumstantial and largely political reasons, and if we persist in asserting that they can be listened to independently of those conditions we are not making very much sense of them.

On the other hand, I do think we should pay these persons some close attention. They are not of mere passing interest, nor are they the property of a handful of left intellectuals passionately engaged in conversation amongst themselves. Long after Henri Lefebvre, André Gorz, Cornelius Castoriadis, and even Althusser have ceased to weigh very much in the intellectual balance and have passed from fashion along with MM Lacan and Derrida, they will still matter quite a lot to historians of the Left in their country, both for what they said, for why they said it, and for the nature of the response their way of saying such things elicited from the radical community in France, inside the universities and beyond. Those who find such concerns of marginal or perhaps élitist interest may be accurately recording the quality of the subject-matter, but they are sadly misreading the history of the Left in France.

One common thread in these chapters, then, is the desire to recast our understanding of a number of areas of social, political, and intellectual history in France, via a rather aggressively historical reformulating of the questions and the evidence. It remains clear, however, that the areas in question are very selective indeed. They clearly would benefit from some more tangible link. This role is served, I believe, by the emphasis upon marxism in the life and ideas of the French Left. Because the history of History in France is unrelentingly political, all histories of the Left written by French historians engage the problem of marxism directly. In doing so, however, they unfailingly distort it. It is, after all, just as misleading to suggest that marxism never really happened in France as it is to assert that the whole history of the social movement in that country is that of the self-fulfilment of marxism as politics and prophecy. The same lack of discrimination can be found in the proposal that marxism 'ruined' socialism in France or in the idea that it 'saved' it, by grafting Leninism onto the broken stem of the indigenous plant.

Yet trailing coats do mark a path. The historiography of the subject in French at least makes very clear that the problem of marxism lies at the very heart of the experience of the Left in France. For the point surely is that from the moment at which marxism became the lens through which French socialists saw and understood their own circumstances and behaviour (a moment fairly precisely situated between 1881 and 1900), distinguishing between 'French socialism' and 'marxism' is either theology or bad faith. If the SFIO lacked a Kautsky or even a Bernstein, this was in part attributable to the differences between living in the Third Republic and negotiating one's political existence in the Second Reich. It was a lot harder to be a political marxist (the other kind achieved prominence only once revolution in Europe disappeared from the realistic political agenda, which was not until 1922 at the earliest) when you had to situate yourself inside and against the republican tradition. This and the cultural preferences fashionable at the Ecole Normale Supérieure after 1870 militated against a high level of intellectual engagement with Marx's own writings before 1930, but none of that has *anything* to do with whether or not marxism permeated the French socialist and labour movements in France after 1880.

This is because marxism in France moved with great ease into and out of the varieties of intellectual and social explanation and criticism which formed the ideological nucleus of radical thought in France (compare the very real difficulty in assimilating Marx to the British radical tradition in the same years). As I argue in chapter two, the relation was even closer than this until 1848, at which point it was French circumstances rather than socialist thinking which created a division within the radical tradition. Moreover, marxism in later years had so thoroughly penetrated the popular consciousness that it took the Communist Party near twenty years to train and adapt its membership to the idea that Communists and Socialists were truly distinct, so accustomed were working men and women to seeing in the avowedly marxist PCF a mere tactical variation upon the programme of the (equally marxist) Socialists. Indeed, were this not so, much of the recent history of Socialists and Communists alike would be utterly incomprehensible (see chapter five).[5]

It is a weakness in these chapters that they do not sufficiently bring to the fore the extent to which a suitably popularized marxist discourse captured the hearts and minds of the French working population for two generations after 1880 (and in less admirable and more etiolated form retained that hold well into the 1960s[6]). I have argued elsewhere that the underlying assumptions of the late nineteenth-century marxist vocabulary had penetrated deep into rural society in some parts of France; how much more so was this the case in those districts of the north, the centre, and the industrial south where twenty years of organization and education by Jules Guesde's underestimated Parti

---

[5] The difficulties experienced by the PCF in extricating itself from the circumstances of French socialist history were notorious in its early years. For representative foreign Communist opinion, see Togliatti's speech at the 6th Comintern Congress (in *'Classe contre classe'. La Question française au IXᵉ Exécutif et au VIᵉ Congrès de l'Internationale Communiste, 1928* (Paris, 1929) p. 30); also Jules Humbert-Droz, *l'Œil de Moscou à Paris* (Paris, 1964).

[6] See for example a poll taken in the mid-1960s showing that 68 per cent of Communist *electors* had a 'good opinion' of Stalin (*Sondages*, no. 1, 1966, pp. 57–73).

Ouvrier Français paid off in the form of a political and ideological commitment which has spanned four generations and more.[7] It is no accident that the history of the implantation of the Communist Party sometimes follows these earlier popular bases, sometimes not. For the trajectory of the PCF and that of marxism as the mobilizing ideology of the labour movement in France are not synonymous, for all they overlap.

The Communist experience, if anything, throws into particular relief the importance of the history of marxism in France just because it sits in a slightly tangential relation to that history. Whereas the history of the labour movement in France from 1840 had been one of difficult and incomplete separation from the republican umbrella, the Communists were released from the mortgage of republicanism by Lenin's peculiar combination of ideological rigour and tactical flexibility. Marxism under the PCF ceased to be a form of political affiliation and was declared to be a political method in its own right. This had the virtue of sharpening the emphasis upon the working class (indeed it *had* to do this in order to give sociological plausibility to the ideological shift) in a country where marxism had for rather obvious reasons never placed too great an emphasis upon its exclusively proletarian constituency; but it also invited the comment that those for whom these changes were either intolerable or simply unwise were just not real marxists. In due course the wish became father to the thought (in large part as a result of the SFIO's unhappy experience of government in 1936 and the Communists' heroic posture in the Resistance) and Communists and non-Communists alike agreed that the language and practices of the (mainstream) socialist and labour traditions in France could not comfortably be labelled 'marxist'. This is an interesting history in its own right, but it is parasitic upon the real history of marxism in France and should not be given heuristic priority.

In placing the history of marxism at the centre of an account of the Left in France I am of course implicitly proposing a further emphatic shift in our understanding of that account. Coming as we do at the tail end of the history of marxism as a living idea, we quite reasonably think of it *as* an idea. In Europe, that is to say, marxism's final resting place is university courses and micro-circulation journals of the unenfranchized

---

[7] For the Nord, see the study by Patricia Hilden, *Working Women and Socialist Politics in France, 1880–1914* (Oxford, 1986). For other areas of Guesdist penetration see Claude Willard's hugely informative but ideologically tendentious study, *Les Guesdistes* (Paris, 1965).

intellectual Left. But it was not always so, and we should not forget that there was once a time when marxism was important not because it stretched the mind but because it exercised the body. Before Althusser there was Gramsci, before him there was Trotsky and before him and of infinitely greater social significance there were the hundreds of marxist popularizers, the Guesdes and the Mincks, the Paul Faures and the Jean Longuets, who may not have had access to much of the marxist canon but who knew exactly how and where to tie marxist theory to popular practice. Marxism, in short, was politics, and politics at the grass roots. If it had not been thus, if it had not been so very adaptable to local political and industrial practices and perceptions (especially in France), we should not now still be negotiating with its heirs.

Some of the confusion surrounding the history of socialism in general concerns the issues raised here. It might be argued that until the 1880s, the language and practices of socialism were still heir to the moral idealism of an earlier age, a body of aspirations and ethical preferences on to which had been grafted the mundane needs of a growing industrial labour movement. But from the last years of the century it became quickly clear that nowhere on the Continent of Europe had organized radical movements survived unscathed the encounter with marxism as a popular teleology. Whether one proposes that this encounter resulted in a botched union of opposites, or was on the contrary a successful reunion of forms of social criticism which had been separated by forty years in the Restoration desert, it is indisputably the case that by 1914 the commonplaces of a popularized marxism formed the unquestioned foundations of left-wing thought *everywhere*. The fact that this involved accepting some radically contradictory propositions is neither here nor there. People *did* accept them—indeed it was the very certainties of Second International marxism which provided the long perspective in which short-term 'neo-Kantian' compromises and exhortations could thrive. Deprived of the latter, socialism would have been nothing but a (marxist) utopia, and sadly lacking in moral appeal at that. Shorn of the guarantees provided by the labour theory of value and the 'laws of history', socialism could never have aspired to an independent existence distinct from that of middle-class radicalism. This is what Bernstein, for example, simply never grasped.

Marxism and socialism only parted company as a result of Lenin's reformulating of the terms of marxist *practice*. But even this shift did not take place in the aftermath of 1917, but was delayed some forty or more years by the highly implausible nature of Lenin's tactics when imposed upon the labour movement west of the Elbe. From 1880 until very recently, therefore, marxism *was* socialism. The cut-off point varied only according to context: in Scandinavia it came in the 1930s, in West Germany in the late 1950s, in France and Italy it remains unclear as to how far it has yet occurred.

All of this would be much more straightforward were we not accustomed to thinking of marxism as something altogether more complicated than the political vocabulary and practices of organized labour and socialist parties. But that is actually what marxism was for much of its active life. This point frequently fails to emerge in histories of the subject because even the most finely-tuned of tracking systems cannot pick up signals emitted on alien frequencies. When Kolakowski devotes three volumes to a history of marxism, he is in practice confining his attention to the fortunes of an idea and its advocates. But there is another history of marxism which is the story of those who were both on the receiving end of Kolakowski's protagonists, but who also contributed the material conditions for the production of their ideas. The two are thus interwoven. On the one hand marxism has failed because it has failed in its aspiration to change the world. Whether this is because it has not described the world correctly, or has been unable to convince others of its case is interesting but beside the point—its inability to convince is prima facie evidence of some fault in the construction of its description (in the long run this may or may not be true, but then in the long run . . .).

On the other hand, marxism is the history of a success story in a *political* key, a success story which actually weighs rather heavily on the consciences of marxists—it would be better if some marxist achievements had not happened. Even the undoubted success of marxism in mobilizing the enthusiasms of generations of voters and workers is not an unambiguous benefit—it has transformed marxism in ways which work against its more rigorous claims on our attention, by incorporating it into the political superstructure of capitalism in spite of itself. And all of this—the Russian Revolution, the crimes of Stalin, the assimilation of what Marx wrote into what politicians say and people unreflectingly believe (about their own condition or future changes in it)—all of this now just *is* the history of marxism. And because of the sort of political theory that marxism is, this means that all of this now is part of marxism itself. It cannot slough off its identity on the grounds that there has been an error in comprehension and that what marxism *really* is, or what Marx *really* meant is something somehow different and thus distinct from everything that has been said or done in the name of the idea.

That is why one can write of marxism as integral to the history of socialism, in France as elsewhere. It is also the reason why to be a marxist in the modern world is either to accept the burden of the history of socialism, its compromises, failures, and achievements; to claim that this history is somehow the result of a cognitive error and can thus be separated from the still-living body of 'marxism'; or to treat marxism *ab initio* as nothing more than the quest for ontological certainty quite divorced from the consistently erroneous efforts to relate it to experience and circumstance. We are all familar with the flourishing condition of the literature in the last two categories, but it is only the former which could have made any sense to the millions of people who thought they were marxists in the history of European politics after 1880. It is the history of the role played by marxism and marxists in that *context*—its own context—which is at issue in this book.

To say that one cannot make any historical sense of the history of the Left in France unless one has grasped just how much of that history is a very serious, if subterranean, debate between marxism and French history itself, is also therefore to assert that politics lies at the heart of the popular experience in modern France. It is to propose that public political engagement was from its earliest days the very essence of what it was to be on the Left in France, and that the political imperative in marxism is what gave it such close ties to the revolutionary tradition in a land where politics always took precedence over economics in determining collective behaviour. The final theme of this book, then, 'politique d'abord' as it were, does not in the least entail a denial of the multifarious differences of opinion as to the nature of politics and political action which permeated unions, clubs, and parties alike ever since 1830. But in even the most resolutely syndicalist of organizations, these were still, after all, political disagreements, rather than disagreements over the importance of politics. It is a mistake to infer from the late nineteenth-century artisan distaste for parliamentary leadership and direction some sort of apoliticism which is then read back into the French labour movement as a whole and invoked thereafter as grounds for treating of labour and socialism as separate universes.

In the conversation to which I referred at the outset, my hosts asked me what I thought of the results of the 1969 presidential election in France, the most recent national election at the time. I replied to the effect that it had had the virtue of precipitating a necessary and overdue crisis in the affairs of the SFIO. This, they agreed, could not be denied, but the derisory turn-out for the Socialist candidate (5.1 per cent of the vote) seemed to them something very worrying indeed. For they took it as a sign that socialists in France had lost interest in the electoral process and had retreated to cultivate their garden. This, they said, would be a disaster.

As it happened, their fears were exaggerated. But the emphasis they placed upon the significance of voting was striking. They were on the left of their party, and thus heirs to that tradition which always preferred to treat elections as exercises in agitprop rather than as a means to alter social conditions, and yet even so they could seriously claim that the popular propensity to turn out at elections was perhaps *the* fundamental achievement of the radical tradition in France. Yet they were right. Part of what it is to be on the Left in France is to take very, very seriously the business of politics, including and especially the act of voting. This is in some part a consequence of the fact that the struggle for accession to the political realm via the ballot box was the necessary first condition for radical politics in a country like France, which overthrew the hereditary monarchy and proclaimed the people as the source of legitimate authority long before the coming of the railways, much less industrial capitalism. It is also linked to rural conditions, where voting is not only a collective public act but one of the few forms of political participation open in isolated parts of the country. The sons and daughters of the politicized peasants have maintained the practice and the commitment.

For this reason, the history of socialists and workers in France is political history, or else it is not their history at all. This does not require that one accept that politics was *all* that mattered to such people. But in their capacity as members of the political family of the Left, the artisans, workers, peasants, teachers, journalists, and professors who composed and compose this family had precisely this in common, that they saw their world in political (and for much of our period marxist) terms and took extraordinarily seriously the forms of political expression open to them, including abstract and recondite language of no immediate application to their own circumstances. To write their history as though elections, the selection of candidates, the organization of the union, arguments over doctrine, the great issues of the moment, were somehow ancillary to other matters would be to do them a grave disservice. In one sense, then, the chapters in this book are indeed about the everyday world of many people in modern France. For politics and the private world of work, education, entertainment, and family were totally intermeshed, for the autodidacts of 1840 no less than for the militant schoolteachers of the 1970s. That, in France, is what it has meant, in the past century and a half, to be of 'the Left'.

2

The French Labour Movement in the Nineteenth Century

THE history of the labour movement in the nineteenth-century France rests uncomfortably between two powerful and opposed poles of attraction. It is in the first place the historical and historiographical preface to the story of the French Left. The latter is itself in thrall to the ambivalent history of modern French marxism, with its deep divisions, its eschatological appeal and mundane achievements, its enduring moral magnetism and diminutive political legacy. With the history of the modern Left commonly dated from the last third of the nineteenth century, the accompanying account of French labour serves as an overture to the main performance, a context in which to describe and explain the origins of the numerical insufficiency and doctrinal confusion of the mature socialist (and Communist) Movements. It is inherent in this sort of approach that the French working population acquires a causal agency: a weak and divided labour force produces a similarly fragmented labour movement which in its turn contributes to the difficulties of those who would speak for it in the political arena. Yet while thus attaching a primacy to the socio-economic context, such accounts are closely dependent upon the specifically political history of France—and thus begin with the emergence of open political debate in the Third Republic of the late 1870s.

The opposite pole of attraction is of course the French Revolution. Here the concern is less with origins than with outcome (at least so far as the history of political radicalism is concerned[1]). In order to trace satisfactorily the loose ends of the 1790s—the residual if defeated Jacobinism of the clubs, the heirs to the forlorn Babouvist conspiracy of 1796, the descendants of the provincial *fédérés* and the small-town *sans culottes* with their enthusiasm for popular dictatorship and economic controls—much effort has gone into the reconstruction of

---

[1] See the discussion in François Furet, *Interpreting the French Revolution*, (Cambridge, 1981), Part 1; also William Doyle, *Origins of the French Revolution* (Oxford, 1980), pp. 7-41.

semantic and ideological continuities between eighteenth-century organizations of apprentices, craftsmen, confraternities, and the disparate and occasional expressions of discontent and opposition that surfaced after 1815.

As a result, the re-emergence of a nation-wide workers' 'presence' after 1830, and with growing significance in the prelude to 1848, makes some sense as a recognizable outgrowth of traditional radical concerns of which the conflicts of the French Revolution itself were in part a concentrated expression. In this case, however, the history of labour in France becomes not so much a factor in the origins of other matters, but rather the residual consequence of an alternative account of eighteenth-century French history. Where in the first example there is an air of economic determinism, recent accounts of the historical roots of the French labour movement find continuity in language and infer from this an unbroken chain of concerns and ways of expressing them. In both instances the history of labour benefits from light cast upon it, but the real interest lies elsewhere.

In this chapter, instead of emphasizing the origins or the outcome of the history of labour in France, I am concerned with the history of the labour movement and its constituency *between* 1830 and the 1880s. This is not a stunningly original undertaking, but precisely because I am *also* interested in the movement's origins and (especially) its heirs, it may offer a new way of thinking about old questions. The usual first-order concerns remain: why was the labour movement weak? Why was 'revolutionary syndicalism' so prominent? Why has French socialism been so perennially unsuccessful in even its most modest aspirations? What did the experience of Revolution bequeath by way of practice and understanding to nineteenth-century radicals and protesters? But my more immediate interest is in investigating the assumptions usually adopted as a condition for answering such concerns. For example, in what precise ways did the economic history of France contribute to the character of labour and its organizations in France? Were artisans so important, in what ways? Was marxism weak and the utopian socialist inheritance strong, and what does that distinction mean and did it matter? And even more fundamental, are the commonplace assumptions of a link between economic identity and social aspiration, between what was lived and what was spoken (or written), worth retaining? Or are they not themselves the intellectual legacy of the very same political tradition whose history we are writing, and self-sustaining myths on that account?

In the face of such an ambitious undertaking, it may help to set out with greater precision the difficulties that face students of the nineteenth-century labour movement.[2] The first consists of defining the object of study. It is not sufficient to answer: 'workers', nor is the problem resolved by a redescription in sub-categories: artisans, skilled workers, proletarians, women workers, etc. Not merely do these overlap constantly with one another and with other social groups (most obviously 'peasants', itself a hopelessly collapsed category), but to aspire merely to describe the condition and opinion of workers is to engage in fruitless antiquarianism. It is not for nothing that the subject is usually refracted through the history of the workers' *movement*; that is how the sources speak to us. Deconstructing the historical text by shifting the emphasis to 'silences'—or the unvoiced expression of a silent majority—adds nothing to our understanding, and deprives us of a proper appreciation of what material we have.[3] It is not just a future-oriented obsession which directs our attention to the labour movement —the latter simply does occupy a prominent place in the sort of historical understanding of the period to which we have access.

It follows, then, that the question is not how to ignore or 'get beyond' the public and organized minority of French workers, but how to make sensible use of our knowledge of it. In this task we might begin by abandoning two seductive fallacies. The first is that there is something to be learned by inference from a movement's form to its 'real' content.[4]That the organizations of working people in early nineteenth-century France emphasized protection and exclusivity, often in a vocabulary reminiscent of the previous century, is an interesting observation. The same is true of the greater concern with political and outward-looking demands in the next generation. But to suppose that this change necessarily points to some other and profound alteration in the economic fabric of France is to indulge a view of the history of opinion and action no less mechanical and banal

---

[2] These remarks are, of course, addressed to the French experience, but in principle their application is broader than this.

[3] Thus Jacques Rançière: 'Que signifie cette fuite en avant qui tend à disqualifier le verbiage de toute parole proferée au profit de l'éloquence muette de celle qui ne s'entend pas?' (Jacques Rancière, *La Nuit des proletaires* (Paris, 1981), p. 23). By way of contrast, William Sewell wishes to attain an understanding of workers' consciousness by 'searching out . . . the symbolic forms through which they experienced their world' (William Sewell, *Work and Revolution in France* (Cambridge, 1980), p. 11).

[4] On this see Gareth Steadman Jones, 'The Language of Chartism', in Thompson and Epstein (eds.) *The Chartist Experience* (London, 1982), p. 6.

for being clothed in a subtlety of reading and expression. Once we cease to suppose such correspondences, we shall avoid all manner of 'paradoxes'—notably that which finds something problematic about a 'radical revolution carried out in corporate terms', or which is troubled by the idea of a 'modern' socialist doctrine being espoused by the artisan representatives of a retarded economy.[5]

The second fallacy derives from this misconceived urge to tie manifested formal behaviour to 'real' social content. The laudable wish for greater precision in the identification of the protagonists of mass protest in nineteenth-century France has placed 'artisans' at the centre of the historical stage, replacing the more ideologically convenient but sociologically marginal proletarians who peopled early socialist histories of the period (this has had the parenthetical consequence of producing a neglect of the *idea* of a proletariat, a concept much debated in the early part of the century and which provided a vital conceptual alternative to the eighteenth-century *'peuple'*. The fact that most of those who used the terms were not themselves proletarians is irrelevant—the elective preference of some for the identity of proletarian is important in its own right as a clue to the way the world looked to many after 1840.[6]) Because many prominent persons in the labour movement *were* artisans, for rather banal reasons of education and convenience, and because artisans are too readily assumed to be on the defensive, in the face of deskilling, factories, and industrial capitalism generally, all sorts of theories about the defensive, corporatist, and 'pre-modern' nature of the movement achieve currency.

This approach involves finding artisans active in organizations, noting certain characteristics of the artisan work-experience, and then relating the two. Yet it neither follows in principle that the two need be related, nor was it the case that either element was constant. The

---

[5] See Sewell, op. cit. p. 3. As Ansart puts it, 'Rien n'indique que les expériences et les actions d'un groupe social soient, à priori, homogènes et que, par exemple, ses pratiques religieuses soient en rapport d'adéquation rigoureuse avec ses pratiques économiques' (Pierre Ansart, *Naissance de l'Anarchisme, esquisse d'une explication sociologique du proudhonnisme* (Paris, 1970), p. 152). For a nice instance of the most obtuse sort of tunnel vision, we have Michael Hanagan: 'Because of the marked slowness of the French economy to industrialise, the history of the French labour movement is *par excellence* the history of the strategies used by artisanal workers struggling with employers armed with machines and new methods of work organisation.' (Michael Hanagan, *The Logic of Solidarity* (Urbana, Ill. 1980), p. 13).

[6] On this general point see Steadman Jones, loc. cit., and the Introduction to his collection of essays, *The Languages of Class* (Cambridge, 1982).

artisan work-experience varied enormously over time (the very term
'artisan' is grossly unhelpful, especially when so defined as to include
any skilled occupation—in the hands of one author miners are artisans
too, which may be taxonomically convenient but is intuitively
nonsense[7]), and far from declining, small-scale operations actually
increased in number and importance in mid-century, as we shall see.
As to their activity in strikes or political debate, the character and
intensity of artisan participation varied enormously, and reflects with
considerably greater accuracy changes in external constraints and
opportunity than conditions of work or threats to skill-related status.
Furthermore, talk of artisans evokes misleading notions of continuity;
although some mid-century skilled occupations are contiguous with
those of an earlier period (master-carpenters, locksmiths, artisan-
blacksmiths, master-roofers, etc.) other significant categories of artisan
were wholly new, themselves a product of industrial change. This
included many ironworking specialists for the new giant forges, and of
course the many tiny sub-branches of the clothing and textile
industries. The latter in particular included many women workers,
who were not classified as artisans—nor were they often welcome in
the artisan organizations. Writing of the labour movement of the time
as though it were little more than the public expression of the needs
and the economic role of artisans entails excluding women from the
story—as we shall shortly see.

Freed from such distortions, we can set the labour movement back
in the real world of France, and take seriously its expressed concerns
and ambitions. Here two further and final notes of caution should be
sounded. The history of labour is by no means the history of socialism.
In France (as in Britain or Germany) there is an identifiably distinct
story of the development of the socialist idea. But just as the latter
makes only limited historical sense divorced from the story of those
who espoused it, so the history of labour is inextricably intertwined
with the emergence of notions of a socialist sort. This much can be
readily demonstrated. But in order that this demonstration not impede
our understanding of the history of the labour movement in its own
right, we must divest ourselves of certain commonplace assertions
about the peculiar nature of French socialism. Michelle Perrot's claim
that 'le marxisme n'avait pas vraiment pénétré en France', or Hugues
Portelli's description of the 'nature particulière du socialisme français'

[7] Hanagan, again, op. cit., p. 49 and Table 2.

as one embodying a 'developpement tardif, un faible enracinement ouvrier' are in their different ways representative of some French thinking in this matter.[8] Directed, like so much of the writing on the subject, to the errors and weaknesses of the twentieth-century Left, they cast a light on the pre-history of their subject, and tend to preclude investigation of questions long since begged.

No less misleading is the habit of studying the French labour movement by reference to workers and organizations in other countries. This is not just because comparative history, like comparative politics, is always problematic.[9] It is because the comparison is often with the British experience, and that is especially misleading. It is not clear why Michael Hanagan, for example, should think it important to spend time identifying differences between the two trade-union movements, since at best this results in a litany of distinctions. The exercise loses even this virtue when it is recalled that recent work in British labour history casts doubt on much hitherto thought secure— the contrast between old and new forms of protest, the distinction between artisan/skilled worker/proletarian, the readily-assumed relationship between Britain's precocious industrialization and the character there of labour and protest. If traditional ways of explaining Chartism and its decline, or theories of a labour 'aristocracy', no longer function as ready keys to British labour history, then the latter can hardly stand as a plumb-line by which to calculate the deviations of the French variety. In short, the very concepts of 'normal' and 'peculiar' are best abandoned. The identity of labour in France can only be ascertained by the inadequately mapped route through its own experience, and its experience alone.[10]

*

We must first consider the nature of the economic background to the emergence of French labour, and how the economic history of France

---

[8] See Michelle Perrot, 'Les Guesdistes: controverse sur l'introduction du marxisme en France', p. 702, in *Annales ESC* (mai–juin 1967); Hugues Portelli, *Le Socialisme Français, tel qu'il est* (Paris, 1980), p. 8. Even J.-P. Brunet, in his sensitive and exemplary study of St Denis (*St Denis la ville Rouge, 1890–1939*, Paris, 1980) falls into the error of seeing the 'absolute separation of socialism and the workers' movement as the special characteristic of the French Left' (p. 97).

[9] On this point see Alasdair MacIntyre, 'Is a science of comparative politics possible?' in Alan Ryan (ed.), *The Philosophy of Social Explanation* (Oxford, 1978), pp. 171–89.

[10] See Hanagan, op. cit., ch. 1; Sewell, op. cit., p. 154; on the historiography of Chartism, see Steadman Jones, 'The language of Chartism', loc. cit.

coloured the latter's experience. The traditional account of the French economy, though much revised in detail over the past generation, remains broadly thus: a thriving eighteenth-century economy suffered considerably through Revolution and war, and the industrialization of France thus proceeded piecemeal after 1815, in large part because of the survival of a flourishing rural society. France was overtaken by various other nations in the course of the century, despite spurts of growth during the July Monarchy and (especially) the Second Empire. Taken together with France's particular strengths in certain labour-intensive sectors (e.g. textiles) and its weaknesses in raw materials and labour, this relative industrial 'retardation' both corresponded with and favoured the survival of a small-scale and artisan sector, with, among other results, the delay in the emergence of a large urban proletariat.[11]

Taken at face value, this account naturally favours a view of the French work-force as predominantly artisan and (by implication) skilled, frightened at the prospect of its own decline, and made socially and politically marginal by a large and thriving agricultural sector. With due allowance for exceptions and regional special cases it provides the premiss for descriptions of the nature and limitations of early organizations of labour in France.

The true picture is somewhat messier and less heuristically convenient. In the first place, there is a case for placing more emphasis upon the advanced character of *some* areas of French industry. The works at Le Creusot were smelting coke on a large scale from 1785, and steam machines were in use there even earlier (1781). The mines at Anzin had twelve pumping machines in action on the eve of the Revolution, and the Oberkampf printing rollers were also steam-powered at that time. Nor was it just a matter of motorpower. The *scale* of eighteenth-century industry in France was often quite considerable: as early as 1760, the textile industry centred in Le Mans, in the Sarthe, was providing work for some 35,000 spinners and weavers in the region and out into adjacent departments. Where such work was concentrated into single centres, the specialized division of labour had already begun—a visitor to Aix-la-Chapelle in 1795 (at that date a part of France) noted the continuing simplification of the work process:

[11] Among many economic histories of modern France, see e.g. François Caron, *An Economic History of Modern France* (New York, 1979); Roger Price, *The Economic Modernisation of France* (London, 1975); T. J. Markovitch, *l'Industrie française de 1789 à 1964* (Paris, 1967).

'l'ouvrier ne doit faire qu'une chose, afin d'acquérir habitude, certitude, précision'.[12]

This process may have been slowed down and distorted by the costs of war and the depredations of blockade, but France during the Restoration and the July Monarchy was still a major industrial nation and growing rapidly. Certain specialized parts of the textile industry, such as silk, grew very fast in the first half of the century: from a pre-1789 annual average of 900 metric tonnes, output in the decade after 1815 reached 1,200 tonnes, expanding to 24,000 annually in the years 1835–44.[13] These were also the years of the opening of the mines in Commentry, in the Allier, significant contributors to the tripling of national coal output in the two decades from 1828 to the February Revolution.[14]

In general, French industrial performance for the early nineteenth-century was not at all poor. The gross national product measured per capita rose steadily from 1825 to the onset of depression in the mid-1870s, the average rate of increase oscillating between 10 and 18 per cent. By mid-century 30 per cent of the active population was engaged in industry or construction, and 55 per cent of the active population was wage-earning.[15]

Within this otherwise plausible account of a steady industrial development there are, however, certain pointers in a different direction. The textile industry in France, for example, was not just an important element in the *early* stages of French industrialization, an unremarkable cliché of European economic history, but remained dominant *throughout* our period, and indeed until the First World War. In 1861 it was the second largest employer of women (19.6 per cent of working women were in textiles, 21.4 per cent in clothing manufacture and the work of laundering/cleaning); more surprisingly perhaps, it was the second largest employer of *men*, with 16 per cent of the male work-force.[16] Because technical development in the textile industry

[12] For the examples cited, see P. Kessel, *Le Prolétariat français* (Paris, 1968); vol. 1, pp. 50, 187; F. A. Isambert, *Christianisme et classe ouvrière* (Paris, 1961), p. 131.

[13] See Price, *Economic Modernisation*, p. 107.

[14] For Commentry, see Pierre Couderc, *La Région urbaine de Montluçon-Commentry* (Clermont Ferrand, 1971), *passim*.

[15] For per capita growth see Price, op. cit., p. 171; other data from B. R. Mitchell, *European Historical Statistics, 1750–1970* (New York, 1978), p. 72. These figures certainly underestimate the industrial population.

[16] *Statistique de la France. Résultats Généraux du Dénombrement de 1861* (Paris, 1864). The construction industry was the largest employer of men, with 22 per cent of the male industrial work-force. But note that women, too, were unusually prominent in the

was progressive (unlike that of metallurgy, where it was discontinuous, with sharp breaks and high rates of obsolescence in machines and skills alike), old and new machinery often worked side by side. Thus the 5,000 mechanical looms of 1830 rose to 31,000 by 1846 (in the country as a whole), while the Lyons Fabrique, an area of traditional and intensive textile output which even exported 78 per cent of its output by 1870, still had 100,000 handlooms in active use as late as 1880. Technical change and traditional skills were contemporary, rather than consecutive, bases for the survival of France's major industry.

At the same time, significant areas of the textile and other industries were in trouble from very early in the century, whether from competition or the social consequences of innovation. For all that the number of handlooms in Lyons grew from 11,000 in 1812 to nearly 30,000 by the middle of the July Monarchy, weavers there as in England were peculiarly vulnerable, and by 1846 some 75 per cent of the looms lay idle. All over France, but especially in areas of concentrated textile manufacture (the Lyonnais, Normandy), the wartime blockade had hit rural textile workers by limiting the supply of cotton, and they had hardly recovered before urban competition struck them an even heavier blow. That they survived at all was due to the regional variations and rural nature of production (see below), but also to the preferences of the French *patronat* for dispersed and less socially disruptive manufacture.[17] Thus the crisis-prone textile industry both proletarianized skills, with the decline in use of handlooms, but also slowed down the rate of urban industrialization. By 1850 spinning (a predominantly female occupation) was mechanized and on the way to concentrated industrial organization, while the more male-dominated weaving did not keep pace in either respect. This helps to account for some of the differences in work experience between men and women at the time, and also for the ambivalent nature of France's largest industry, an ambivalence of identity in equipment, location, and scale which cast long shadows over the character of French industrial development in general.

The nature of the textile industry, together with the uncompetitive

building trades—16.9 per cent of them worked in construction, making it the third largest employer of female labour.

[17] On the Lyons Fabrique, see the work of Yves Lequin *Les Ouvriers de la région lyonnaise*, 2 vols. (Lyons, 1977); on the number of looms, see E. Levasseur, *Histoire des classes ouvrières et de l'industrie en France de 1789 à 1870*, vol. 2 (Paris, 1904), p. 178.

costs of raw material extraction and transporation (in the 1820s British coal was already competitive even after a 1 fr. 50 per ton excise duty[18]), imposed on the French economy the strains which became more apparent after 1860.[19] True, construction maintained its position as a major employer of labour, but it functioned chiefly to circulate capital invested by the state for urban renewal and did little for national growth. Moreover, the building industry contributed to the continuing predominance of the rural in French life (many of the construction workers coming to town on a seasonal basis) and to the illusion of a skilled and predominantly artisan work-force (the construction industry employed people with traditional skills, organized in small groups). Yet at the same time one should record the rapid emergence of industrial centres: the textile city of Roubaix grew from 25,000 to 75,000 inhabitants during the Second Empire, the industrial town of Le Creusot from 9,000 to 24,000. By 1861 nearly eleven million people (29 per cent of the population) lived in towns.[20] France was an industrial society with all the characteristic industrial landscaping— massive conurbations (Lille-Roubaix-Tourcoing, St Etienne), fast-growing metropolitan cities (Paris, of course, but also Marseilles, which grew from 185,000 to 315,000 during Louis Napoléon's reign), gross extremes of wealth and poverty.[21] Yet there subsisted, incongruously, a France where 60 per cent of all non-Parisian horsepower in industrial establishments was generated by water in the early 1860s, where coal output was actually falling in some hitherto important mining districts, and where shoemaking was still the second most important urban occupation in the middle years of the Second Empire.[22]

---

[18] See Jean Vidalenc, *La Société française, vol. 2: le peuple des villes et des bourgs* (Paris, 1973), p. 134.

[19] The falling birth-rate was a further handicap, after 1850. In 1809 the birth-rate had exceeded the death-rate by 28 per cent, and was 32 per thousand. In 1829 it was 30 per thousand, and still 20 per cent ahead of the death-rate. But by 1859 births were just 27.9 per thousand, while deaths had risen to 26.8 per thousand. By the end of the century the birth-rate stood at 21.8 per thousand and the population was no longer growing. See Mitchell, op. cit., pp. 18–21.

[20] On urban population see Jean Bron, *Histoire du mouvement ouvrier français* (Paris, 1968), vol. 1, p. 151. Overall population figures are from the census quoted in note 16.

[21] In the 1850s, 91 per cent of the textile workers in Lille died without leaving anything. At the end of the century the gap between the average patrimony of industrialists and workers in the city was 20,541: 1. See F.-P. Codaccioni, *De l'Inégalite sociale dans une grande ville industrielle* (Lille, 1976), pp. 88, 430.

[22] For details of horsepower, see Caron, *Economic History of Modern France*, p. 139.

A degree of clarity and precision can be established in the midst of the anarchy of French economic data by identifying two pieces of information regarding the organization of French economic life between 1830 and 1880: on what sort of scale was French industrial activity organized, and how far was it rural or urban in character? More succinctly, how big were French factories and where were they located?

Regarding the size of industrial establishments one must insert a caveat: when an employer, for example a tailor, is said to have thirty workers, it is quite unclear whether this means that all thirty were in one place, under one roof, or were spread out across a tract of countryside and linked to their employer only in the sense that the latter provided them with work and materials and marketed the finished product. This is especially a problem with data from the first half of the century. There is also the illusion born of averages: in the Troyes region in 1820, for example, there were 34 spinning shops employing 1,700 workers; in 1846 the number of shops had fallen to 16, while the workers now numbered 1,900. This appears to point to an increase in the average size of this sort of textile establishment, bespeaking a more industrial level of activity. But note the very small increase in the absolute number of people employed in the industry in this vital period of growth. Allowing for the crisis of the 1840s which probably accounted for the disappearance of many of the smaller shops, the situation *may* not have altered significantly at all.[23]

With this thought in mind, what can we learn from the data available? Before 1848, very little. In isolated instances, such as the tanning industry, we find that tanneries in the city of Marseilles varied from one establishment with twenty-six workers to seven with less than five (there were nineteen tanneries in the city). In the small industrial town of Montluçon during the July Monarchy there were three tanneries with just four workers between them. A very small-scale activity, then, but susceptible of considerable variation even in one city.[24] Conversely, the much more highly-skilled work of glass-making often took place in very large establishments. At the beginning of the July Monarchy, in the years 1832–3, the average number of employees in the glassworks of north-east France was high: 133 per factory in the Aisne, 179 in the Moselle, 244 in the Meurthe. It was even substantial

On falling coal output in e.g. Commentry, see Couderc, op. cit., pp. 4–5. On the number of shoemakers in the Second Empire, see Levasseur, op. cit., p. 213.

[23] For Troyes, see Vidalenc, *La Société française*, p. 101.   [24] Ibid., p. 156.

in Paris, with 825 workers in just three establishments. In the rural valleys of the upper Loire there were smaller glass manufactures, some 22 of them, but even there the average number employed exceeded 45 in these years.[25]

So far as Paris itself was concerned, the 1848 enquiry revealed the following: 7,117 *patrons* (11 per cent of the total) employed eleven or more workers and thus had 'large' establishments. It is interesting to note that by 1861 this percentage had fallen to 7.5, while the proportion of *patrons* working for themselves or with just one employee had risen from 50 per cent to 62 per cent of the total. This need not suggest a 're-artisanalization' of Paris, since most of these small businesses did not thrive, but it certainly points away from industrial concentration.[26]

The Parisian experience mirrored that of the country as a whole, where the average number of workers per establishment appears to have fallen between the censuses of 1841–5 and 1861–5. In only sixteen departments did the number of workers per establishment rise significantly (by a factor of 50 per cent or more) and in only two of these (Bouches-du-Rhône and Somme) was the percentage of the active population engaged in industry above the national average for 1861. Put differently, the increase in size of factory or workshop in mid-century France was most marked in departments which were otherwise predominantly agricultural. In the Corrèze, the Creuse, Cantal, Ardèche, Tarn, Allier, Sarthe, and elsewhere, rural-based industry was increasing in concentration, with ever-larger factories or factory-villages sharing the countryside with the farmers. In the truly industrial regions, such as the departments of the Nord and Pas de Calais, Alsace, or the mining districts of the Loire, the average size of factory was actually falling in these years.[27]

By the end of the century one can trace these developments with more precision, and a pattern begins to emerge in retrospect. The average number of workers per establishment had risen quite sharply in certain industries—from 7 to 22 in textile manufacture in the thirty years after 1866, from 7 to 32 in mining, from 6 to 18 in the chemical

[25] Levasseur, op. cit., p. 194.
[26] See Isambert, op. cit., p. 130 n. 33 (quoting Augustin Cochin, *Paris sa population, son industrie* (Paris, 1864), p. 63). See also Levasseur, op. cit., p. 211.
[27] See Statistique de la France: Industrie 1841–1845, 4 vols. (Paris, 1847–52); *Statistique de la France, Résultats Généraux du Dénombrement de 1861* (Paris, 1864), also *Statistique de la France, Industrie. Résultats Généraux de l'Enquête effectuée dans les années 1861–1865* (Paris, 1873).

industry. The increases are noteworthy (and most came about after 1880), but the absolute figures for the later date (1896) are still not very high. In the building trades the average number of workers per unit remained low (7 in 1896, having risen from 3 in the late Second Empire), and lower still in the food industry (excluding agriculture), where it was just 4.5.

As to the work-force as a whole, fully 49 per cent of industrial establishments in 1896 still occupied no workers or just one, and a further 39 per cent employed from 2 to 5 persons. All told, tiny workshops employed 36 per cent of the industrial labour force. At the other extreme, a further 36 per cent of the work-force was in factories or work units of 50 or more people. The hitherto dominant middle-sized establishments were being progressively squeezed out.

In geographical terms, the interesting disparities of the mid-century were beginning to disappear. The heavily industrial departments of the north and centre were now areas of rapidly intensifying concentration —of the twelve departments with the largest number of workers in very large factories, eight were north of the Loire and only one, the Aveyron, still overwhelmingly rural in aspect. Notwithstanding this, echoes of the past remained strong: among those departments with a degree of industrial concentration *below* the national average were the Somme, the Oise, and the Rhône, all overwhelmingly industrial by any other measure.[28]

The tentative conclusion seems to be this. Until the middle of the last century, French industry was not unusually dispersed or small-scale. There were large factories and there were small workshops and these varied with the industry and the location. In the case of textiles they also reflected a very special sort of work-force, much of which was both dispersed (in that it worked at home) and large-scale (being frequently dependent on a single agent or middleman). In mid-century we thus find the rate of industrial concentration higher in the predominantly rural departments of the centre and south. Elsewhere, in industrial France, growing labour shortages and the nature of the Second Empire boom encouraged a discernible shift towards smaller units of production (or, perhaps, an expansion in those sectors where smaller units had always predominated). The slump of the 1880s knocked out many of the small producers and encouraged larger work units, thus picking up, so to speak, from the pattern of the 1830s and

---

[28] See *France. Ministère du Commerce et de l'Industrie. Résultats Statistiques du Recensement des Industries et Professions, 1896* (Paris, 1901).

1840s. And although this uncertain rate of industrial concentration meant that France was left in the last years of the century with an industrial base both dispersed and apparently under-capitalized, we should note that in 1901 the number of French workers engaged in *industrie à domicile* was just 12.5 per cent of the total, while in neighbouring Belgium, continental paragon of rapid industrialization and already with a substantial union-based social democratic party, the figure for home-workers was . . . 20 per cent![29]

This suggests that whatever pattern can be discerned in the changing scale of nineteenth-century French industry, it is not one conducive to a linear account of the process of proletarianization and a declining *artisanat*. Two uncomfortable facts obtrude. One is the marked hiccup which seems to have occurred in the years 1848–75 (the very moment, supposedly, of France's industrial and commercial transformation), the other is the omnipresence of rural (and perforce agricultural) France in all accounts of French industrialization. The significance of the Imperial hiccup will be considered later; we have first to look a little closer at the rural roots of industrial work in France.

The importance of the rural context was twofold. It determined the location and character of much of French industry, and it provided in various ways the chief source of labour. That early nineteenth-century industry should be located mostly in the countryside was hardly surprising—with water power predominant until the 1860s at least, the rural departments abutting the major rivers of France were natural sites for factories, and the greater the need for motor power, the higher the likelihood of a factory being sited in the countryside.

There was a further important reason for this. The year-round availability of wood was vital for industry until French coal could be produced and moved on a competitive scale and at a reasonable price. In France these conditions were frequently not met before 1870. Moreover, the wood that was burnt, together with the product for whose manufacture the water or steam power was required, had to be transported as cheaply as possible, and south of the Beauce this meant by river or canal. If only for this reason, French industry was at the mercy of the rural calendar. In many parts of France the flow of water in the summer months was insufficient to power a mill or carry a barge, and what water there was the peasant farmers claimed for irrigation.

As a result of this, large-scale industry, such as the giant forges at

[29] On Belgium, see M. Bourguin, *Les Systèmes socialistes et l'évolution économique* (Paris, 1913), p. 177. Other data from source cited in note 28.

Fourchambault in the Nièvre, or the iron mines along the Cher, both depended upon their relationship to the countrsyside but were also a victim of it. Some rural industries were better adapted to this circumstance than others, of course. The mines of the Allier and the Gard, the ironworks of the Cher, were eventually overtaken by competition from the coal basins of the Nord and the steelworks of St Etienne. But large-scale leather-working (as in Millau, where 780 women and 130 men, 9 per cent of the total population, were employed in the tanneries in 1848) or the huge domestic-based textile industries of Normandy and the Lyonnais, could survive not just because they were less immediately vulnerable to competition, but precisely because their very existence was predicated upon the agricultural economy itself: the pastoral farming of the Cevennes in the case of Millau, seasonally available labour in the textile instance.

The human resources of the countryside took various forms. In the Creuse the tradition of migrant masons lingered on, with some 20,000 every year travelling seasonally for work in the urban building trades well into the 1890s. Elsewhere, in the Languedoc for example, the big rural spinning factories worked only six or seven months per year, employing the women and children who were available after the completion of the silk harvest in early July. In the Normandy countryside, early nineteenth-century weavers were often migrants, travelling each week from the countryside and bringing with them rural produce in part-payment of the rent owed to their landlord in the textile towns of Louviers or Rouen. And everywhere the overlap between peasant and industrial worker was intricate and complete, despite the best attempts of government officials to sort out who was an *ouvrier*, who a *journalier agricole*, who a *fileuse* and not a *ménagère*. In so far as there *was* an answer it depended upon the season and on the market—sometimes the chestnut harvest of the southern Cevennes was profitable for those engaged in it, but when it was not, they returned to iron mining. The implications for popular economic protest were legion, of course. The worker with land or agricultural employment on which to fall back could afford a degree of militancy not available to the *ouvrière* in a Roubaix mill. As late as 1911 the director of an aluminium factory in St Michel en Maurienne conceded a wage demand in August, '. . . vû qu'en ce moment il y a pénurie d'ouvriers en raison des travaux des champs'.[30]

[30] Quoted in Lequin, op. cit., vol. 1, p. 153. Other examples from Vidalenc, *La Société française*, p. 157; Jean Vidalenc, *Le Département de l'Eure sous la monarchie*

This symbiosis of industry and countryside was not timeless, of course, nor was it unchanging. The crisis in rural handloom weaving, although it came later in France than Britain, came none the less, striking many regions in the 1850s and 1860s, following a doubling in the number of looms between 1815 and 1852. The former (male) weavers switched initially to agricultural labour, but given the necessarily periodic and seasonal character of such work they soon sought more permanent employment in factories, leaving parts of the countryside predominantly female, a fact reflected in the growing number of women recorded as having a primary role as sharecropper or smallholder in the later years of the century.

In the same period that saw the onset of the crisis in rural textiles, the progressive shift to coal as a combustible fuel put out of work many woodcutters, carters, and carbon-burners, seriously distorting the balance of employment in the departments of the northern Massif Central in particular. In this instance factory work was less readily available, and the decline in the wood trade marked the first in a number of instances of de-industrialization in France, where both the land and its inhabitants returned to agriculture—or else emigrated for good. Many of the woodcutters and their families entered upon a marginal, semi-legal existence, returning to the public eye two generations later as one of the earliest and most radical of rural unions.[31] The levelling off of population growth from mid-century alleviated some of the problems of rural unemployment, but changed nothing in the fundamental character of rural industry where it had survived. As a result the rural factory of the second half of the century was not necessarily an anachronism, but on the contrary had survived precisely because it formed part of a local or regional social economy which continued to run smoothly. The mines of the Tarn, Allier, and Gard could not compete nationally, but they and the small metalworks of the Ariège or the Corrèze (often specializing in arms manufacture) contributed directly to the rural economy as well as drawing on it. All that happened was that a different France grew up alongside, represented by single-industry cities or old commercial centres with a huge accretion of occasionally employed casual labour.

These parallel worlds of rural and urban industry (reflected openly

constitutionelle, 1814–1848 (Paris, 1952), p. 438; Michel Pigenet, 'l'Usine et le village—Rosières 1869–1914, in *Mouvement social*, no. 119 (avril–juin 1982), p. 35.

[31] On the woodcutters, see Philippe Gratton, *Les Luttes de classes dans les campagnes* (Paris, 1971), pp. 59–107.

in the *Enquête* of 1848, where factories are classed as situated 'en ville' or 'en campagne') created and were in part the creation of very different strands in the formation of the French working class. But although it is reasonable to emphasize the manner in which French peasants could be eased into the industrial work-force, this was not always the way in which the latter was recruited, and there were considerable variations.

Miners come closest to conforming to type in this respect. The men who worked the mines at Carmaux, in Commentry, at La Machine in the Nièvre, were drawn overwhelmingly from the local peasant community. In the case of the Nièvre they were often former woodcutters, moving logically into coal-digging. As woodcutters, incidentally, they introduced into the mines their own traditions of teamwork and payment as a team. As the children of peasants (and this pattern can be traced from the 1820s through to the end of the century, in tandem with the development of mining traditions within families), miners in many parts of France, even in the big pits of the Calaisis, kept their links to agriculture. They frequently maintained their own fields, or at least a sizeable working garden, and raised domestic animals. Their children worked with the animals, their daughters sometimes as domestic servants in neighbouring areas, and the whole family turned out for the harvest, with the mines often closed for the duration. In 1862, two-thirds of the Carmaux miners came from families of smallholders and had not abandoned the ambition of retiring to the family property (with which they were in constant touch). In Commentry, work in the fields was a permanent if inadequate safety net for times of unemployment, and all over the country miners were assiduous in opposing all attempts to lengthen the workday (e.g. by the introduction of piece-work) because of their second occupation, often pursued upon completion of their shift.[32]

But however widespread, the experience of the miners was not representative. From very early in the century, most French industrial workers were recruited from among industrial workers. In the Nîmes area mid-century weavers were usually from long-established local weaving families, and glassworkers everywhere were likely to be the children of glassworkers. In the latter case social mobility was replaced

---

[32] On the foregoing, see Couderc, op. cit., *passim.;* Lequin, op. cit., vol. 1, pp. 221–70; Rolande Trempé, *Les Mineurs de Carmaux*, 2 vols., (Paris, 1971), p. 176 n. 1, and p. 219; Guy Thuillier, *Aspects de l'économie nivernaise au dix-neuvième siècle* (Paris, 1966), p. 341.

by geographical disperson, with glassworkers following employment all over the country. Metalworkers, too, were itinerant, sometimes following an employer, as in the case of those forge workers who moved in the wake of their *patron* from the Saône-et-Loire to Montluçon, in the neighbouring Allier. In this case, too, occupational continuity within families was achieved at the price of geographical rootlessness, and metalworkers in particular became 'outsiders', not to urban life or factory work, but to the local community. As a result they early on lost any very close sense of identity (though not necessarily the accompanying skills), married outside their trade (though not their class) and became, like the railway-workers, more receptive to cross-occupational solidarity and organization, whether in big cities or small, semi-rural towns.

This continuity within certain industrial occupations meant that the nineteenth-century French work-force, although embedded in a routine often conditioned by agricultural requirements, was not on that account without any sense of its industrial identity. Even the tens of thousands of textile workers, men and women alike, who contributed through the spinning and working of lace, silk, and flax to the manufacturing centres of Rouen, Le Mans, Lyons, Nîmes, and St Etienne, while working in their villages and at home, were no less dependent upon industry for their living. Where they differed was in their limited capacity for organization and defence, both because of their occupational vulnerability and their geographical isolation. From the onset of depression in the 1870s they had increasingly to choose between a rural and an urban existence—the penurious condition of the domestic outworker having fallen well below the merely unenviable one of the urban factory worker—and by the end of the century the distinction between rural (and primarily agricultural) work and urban employment had at last become more marked.

*

The theme of overlapping or even simultaneous forms of work can be pursued from the countryside into the towns, where the distinction between artisans, skilled workers, and proletarians is remarkably difficult to trace with clarity. In general terms the mid-century revival of small-scale production is reflected in national statistics: in 1860–5, 58.9 per cent of total industrial production in France was the work of 'craftsmen'.[33] But this hides two intersecting processes, one of survival,

[33] See T. J. Markovitch, 'Salaires et profits industriels en France sous la Monarchie de Juillet et le Second Empire', in *Cahiers de l'INSEA*, série AF, 8 (1967).

the other of innovation. The survivals are perhaps better known. They include team-working in mines, among railway navvies, in the spinning factories of Reims, the dye-works of Rouen and even in printing. This was not always or necessarily 'craft' work, of course, but it was work organized on a small scale, with payment by group and dependent upon the competitive skills and mutual organization of small numbers of people. In the July Monarchy it could also impede occupational solidarity, as in the case of the Rancie miners of the Ariège who each worked a seam and kept their coal separate from each other at the gallery entrance.[34]

Other long standing manufactures included the specialized metal-workers of the east, in the Ardennes or Haute-Marne, where some villages made knife handles, others knife blades, and so forth, or the pin-makers of the lower Seine valley (although these were from the later eighteenth century totally dependent upon urban *négociants* who provided the material and purchased the end-product). In this sort of work piece-rates and traditional skills predominated, and their survival indicates that such dispersed manufacture was still economically realistic (in part, no doubt, because of the level at which wages were pegged in these trades). It is impossible to know the share of manufacturing output contributed by these older occupations and work systems, whether as cottage industry or within larger units. What *is* clear is that the men and women thus employed constituted, in a purely economic sense, a large part of the real proletariat of nineteenth-century France.

By contrast, many of the truly skilled and artisan occupations were not old at all, but were themselves the by-product of industrialization. In the early steam forges of the Nièvre, studied by Thuillier, it was precisely the difficulties of adapting to new and large-scale machinery, and exploiting it to the full, which provided opportunities for specialists to gather around the new metallurgical complexes and capitalize upon the reliability and quality of their work, initially indispensable. A giant complex such as Le Creusot in the July Monarchy consisted not only of coal-miners, furnace and foundry workers, but also of some 300 more specialized trades: wheelwrights, coopers, fitters, boiler-makers, turners, etc. These had been rendered essential not in spite of modern industry but because of it. Shipbuilding, the railways, the chemical industry, all created *new*

---

[34] See Vidalenc, *La Société française*, p. 129.

needs and skills. The contribution of urban development to the revivification of specialized skills in the building industry has been noted, but the clothing and food-processing industries also had new markets and needs which, initially at least, required a return to or the creation of skilled labour. This process can be traced in the Isère region as late as the 1880s, with the old weaving and glove manufacturing giving way to more specialized work for preparers and finishers, lace-braiders, and many others. In the industrial complex of the Lyonnais, which took in rural manufacture in the Isère as well as the hill towns of the Vivarais, constant shifts in occupational specialization meant that industrial growth and the concentration of capital went hand in hand with the dispersion of production and the generation of whole new orders of skilled work.[35]

In Paris this process was even more visible. Here it was precisely in the new heavy industries of metallurgy, chemicals, ceramics, that a 'rejuvenation' of the *artisanat* was most marked.[36] There was certainly an increasing division of labour of the kind associated with industrialization and 'de-skilling' (and which dated back before the French Revolution), but it was as much a feature of small, specialized production as of large enterprise: artificial flower making, for instance, which flourished during the Second Empire, encompassed up to twelve different operations per product, with work done in very small and highly specialized units. The same was true for the manufacture of costume jewellery, broken up into twenty-two different special operations.

Similar observations apply in the newer, less 'typically' Parisian industries. The late nineteenth-century metalworkers of St Denis may have been classic 'proletarians', but the chemical works of Aubervilliers were composed of numerous small units of workers, a few skilled, many not at all. In St Ouen, where food-processing was concentrated, or in the clothing manufacture of Boulogne, small workshops were the norm, with many of the employees engaged in activities unknown to their parents.[37] The increase in output from many of these industries

[35] For the Lyonnais, see Lequin, op. cit., vol. 1, pp. 189–97. Worthy of note is the remarkable continuity in the number of textile workers in the Rhône department who lived and worked in isolated rural and domestic conditions: far from declining, the number of outworkers actually rose in 60 per cent of the rural cantons of the Lyons arrondissement between 1851 and 1891 (Lequin, p. 131).

[36] For what follows see the important (and rather neglected) work of Jeanne Gaillard, *Paris, la Ville (1852–1870)*, Univ. of Paris Doctoral thesis, 1976, esp. pp. 438 ff.

[37] See J.-P. Brunet, *St Denis*, p. 28.

derived less from their size, or the benefits of mechanization, than from the centralization of control and the co-ordinating advantages of specialization. Seen from the point of view of the worker, this need not have implied a reduction in either status or skill and expertise. Those genuinely engaged in unskilled proletarian labour in Paris, Lille, or elsewhere were unlikely themselves to have been artisans at *any* earlier stage. It was more probable that most French workers, especially in the larger cities, were neither independent artisans nor modern factory proletarians. If the categories would have been misleading to contemporaries, implying a process of evolution rather than adaptation and flux, then perhaps we too should set them aside. In that they carry suggestions of dichotomies in French industrial history between old/new, skilled/unskilled, workshop/factory, they lead too readily to characterizations of belief and opinion which may seriously confuse the history of labour.[38]

One rather obvious division can not be set aside, however. There were male workers and there were female workers. It is well known that many women worked as domestic servants, and that the vast majority of women who lived in the countryside were *de facto* agricultural workers of one sort or another, whether day-labourers or peasant proprietors. More contentious is the role played by women in the industrial labour force. No sketch of the working population in nineteenth-century France is complete without some account of the latter, if only because of the conclusions so readily and erroneously derived from the absence of such an account.

One leading authority gives women industrial workers as 35 per cent of the total industrial work-force in 1856, and 31 per cent of the active population.[39] Allowing for regional variation (women were 41 per cent of all *ouvriers* in Paris in 1847[40]) this seems a reasonable estimate. By 1896, women were still 36 per cent of the industrial work-force, and 34 per cent of the active population—very little had changed. Only in their share of agricultural work had women advanced, from just under 30 per cent of the agricultural working population in 1856 to 35 per cent in the last census before the War.

Two aspects of women's employment stand out. The first, of course, is their omnipresence in certain major industries, notably textiles and

---

[38] A glance at most books purporting to study women's work in nineteenth-century France will establish the point. A representative example is Louise Tilly and Joan Scott, *Women, Work and Family* (New York, 1978).

[39] Mitchell, *European Historical Statistics*, p. 53.   [40] Gaillard, op. cit., p. 406.

clothing. Whether one takes the industrial mills of Lille, the long-established semi-domestic industry of Normandy, the glove makers of the Isère, the ribbon industry in and around St Etienne or the fashion tailoring of the big cities, one finds women workers ever present. In 1872, 66 per cent of the industrial work-force of the Isère department was female; in the major local city of Grenoble, 20,000 seamstresses worked in the neighbouring countryside, semi-rural outworkers for the 4,150 male glove cutters in the town itself.[41] This was an old division of tasks—in the glove manufacture of the 1840s, nearly 9,000 of the 12,800 workers in Grenoble manufacture had been women working *extra muros*.

While textiles and clothing were the chief employers of women, however, they were far from unique. The paper manufacture of Vienne in 1840 employed mostly women workers; a few years later the highest concentration of female workers in Lyons itself was in the Perrache district processing of tobacco (819 out of 916 workers). The 1851 census revealed women as 45 per cent of the work-force in paper manufacturing establishments employing more than ten persons, and 51 per cent of the workers in large factories handling the preparing and transformation of leather and skins. By 1896 there were 125 women in the box and packaging materials industry for every 100 men. One mid-century census gives women as 45 per cent of the chemical industry work-force.[42] Nor were women only active in traditional occupations or semi-skilled work: in 1861 they comprised 47 per cent of the workers in luxury goods manufacture and 46 per cent of those employed in arms manufacture. Indeed, there was *no* major sector of industrial activity, skilled or unskilled, from which women were substantially absent.

The second feature of women's employment was its concentration in the larger industrial units. This is not particularly surprising: textile factories, urban and rural alike, were among the largest undertakings of the period, and the mid-century expansion of rural industry in particular favoured the employment of peasant women and girls, though usually on a seasonal basis (in the case of tailoring, March for the summer fashions, September for the winter ones). None the less, this tendency for women to be found more frequently in larger work

[41] Lequin, op. cit., vol. 1, p. 136. Note that these figures confirm Olwen Hufton's observation for the eighteenth century, that the ratio of (female) spinners to (usually male) weavers was remarkably stable, at around 4:1 (private communication).

[42] See *Dénombrement de 1861*. For Lyons and Vienne, see Lequin, op. cit., vol. 1, pp. 21, 176. For 1896, see *Dénombrement Général de la Population. 1896*.

units *is* significant, even if we discount those cases where an enquiry defined as one unit large numbers of dispersed workers employed by a single patron.

In 1851 in the Lyonnais there were 75,068 *femmes salariées*, some 51 per cent of the total waged work-force. In smaller industry however (units with 0–10 employees) the proportion was 44 per cent. The same indications emerged from an enquiry in Rouen three years earlier, covering 3,474 workers of both sexes in twenty-one enterprises. There the investigator found that the larger the factory, the higher the percentage of female workers (most of the factories were mills of one sort or another).[43] Conversely, in Second Empire Paris, where the drift to smaller work units was most marked, female employment dropped sharply: 41 per cent of all *ouvriers* in the city had been female in 1847, whereas in 1861 the figure was just 16 per cent. By 1896 it had risen again to 46 per cent, with the expansion of food-processing, chemical industries, and metalworks.

If there *is* any generalization to be made about women workers in nineteenth-century France, it might be this. They were an integral part of the industrial work-force, but especially in evidence at the more concentrated end of the spectrum. The more industrialized the department, the more clearly was this the case. In the Pas de Calais in 1911 women were 44 per cent of unskilled labourers, but only 19 per cent of metalworkers and 16 per cent of shoemakers, for example.[44] They do *not* appear to have left the work-force upon getting married.[45] In Rouen in 1848 women worked on average to the age of forty-five, rarely past fifty, while men stayed on about five years longer.[46] Because they were particularly concentrated in old industrial jobs, they were vulnerable to pressures born of mechanization, competition and locally-abundant labour. In France, at least, industrialization often meant feminization, and women were in many industries the true proletariat (as well as constituting a *de facto* industrial reserve army in the poorer rural areas) for much of the century.

---

[43] Lequin, op. cit., pp. 9, 10, on the Lyonnais. Also François Denier, 'Les Ouvriers de Rouen parlent à un économiste en juillet 1848', in *Mouvement social* no.119, p. 15. On the problem of periodic unemployment, with women in the clothing trades unable to find work between January and March, and again from July to September, see Paul Leroy-Beaulieu, *Le Travail des Femmes au XIXe siècle* (Paris, 1873), p. 123.

[44] See *Statistique Générale de la France: Résultats Statistiques du Recensement de la Population, 1911* (Paris, 1915).

[45] Notwithstanding claims to the contrary. Thus Hanagan: 'The concentration of the trade (textiles) into large factories excluded most mothers . . . from the textile workforce.' *Logic of Solidarity*, p. 144.   [46] See Denier, loc. cit., p. 10.

That this is indeed the case, and not just a tidy transposition of the old categories, is borne out by what we know of industrial wages in this period. Such information is particularly problematic, however. In the first place, all the usual difficulties of regional variation are exacerbated by time-lags in technical change, with resulting differences in forms and levels of payment. Just when cotton production in mid-century Mulhouse, for example, was undergoing rapid technical modernization, an 'archaic' wool industry was emerging in the Verdon valley of Provence, protected in its local monopoly by poor regional communications.[47] Equally important were sharp differences in the price of basic commodities—the average price of a hectolitre of wheat in 1835 varied from 10 fr. 95 in the Meuse to 20 fr. 73 in the Var, and local wages naturally reflected this sort of disparity, inherited in only slightly modified form from Ancien Régime conditions.[48]

There were other complications. Subsistence crises brought about in part by steep variations in bread prices remained common until the middle of the Second Empire, albeit localized, and they were accompanied by long periods of unemployment in many industries: building workers in the winter, clothing workers in the summer were frequently underemployed if occupied at all, and it was rare even in the early years of the Third Republic for women in clothing, textile or paper manufacture to be employed more than two-thirds of the year. On the eve of the First World War, a dressmaker in Boulogne-sur-Mer could not expect more than an average of 200 working days per year, in Montluçon (in the Allier) at best 280 days. Even skilled male workers faced this problem—the average number of days worked by a metal turner in Bâpaume in 1910 was just 260 per annum.[49]

Finally, the very notion of a 'wage' was indeterminate. In the mining communities in the first half of the century, it was common for much payment to be in kind, with miners also responsible for maintaining their equipment. With averages based on reports which were themselves estimates of piece-work output, the money wage of the

[47] See Vidalenc, *La Société française*, p. 97. Note the comments of Thuillier (*Aspects*, p. 193): 'jusqu'à la fin du dix-neuvième siècle, il existait un cloisonnement technique très grand, et le niveau technique était fort différent d'une province à l'autre'.

[48] See *France. Statistique du Territoire et de la Population. Rapport au Roi, 1837 (Paris, 1837)*. In 1797 the variations in wheat prices had been from 72 to 170 (French average = 100). In 1835 they were still 72–136, a quite remarkable persistence of Ancien Régime characteristics. As a rule, prices were much lower north of the Loire, highest in Provence and the lower Rhône valley.

[49] Data from *France. Office du Travail. Salaires et Coût de l'Existence à diverses époques, jusqu'en 1910* (Paris, 1911).

more complex industries is an exercise in faith and guesswork. As for the real wage, the zigzag progress of bread prices (falling from 1817 to 1826, rising until 1829, steady for the next four years then falling to 1835, rising slowly to 1840, steady for the first half of the decade, and rising sharply thereafter) vitiates any precise calculation of what workers' wages could buy. Subject, however, to such caveats, what do we know of workers' earnings in nineteenth-century France?

In the 1820s there was probably a very substantial gap between the earnings of the poorest textile worker and those of a skilled industrial artisan. Even within one factory, such as the Fourchambault works, wages in 1820 ranged from 1 franc per day for a young puddler's assistant to about 4 fr. 50 for experienced forge workers. But the puddler's assistant was doing well when compared with women who spun flax into linen thread at home for the merchants of Roanne, and whose earnings ranged from 20 to 25 centimes per day. Most wages lay somewhere between these extremes.[50]

From the mid–1820s real wages in France began to fall steadily, an observation confirmed by contemporaries and historians alike.[51] By the 1850s the range of payments at Fourchambault had narrowed down to a scale of from one franc up to 2 fr. 75, but even these were better earnings than most. Although higher wages continued to be paid in the expanding and skilled sectors of industries like mining or glassworking, there was a clear drop in those sectors which had undergone rapid mechanization or where piece-rates were the norm. Where these factors were combined, as in the rural textile industry, the fall was catastrophic. Domestic weavers in the Cambrésis, such as those of Bertincourt, earned about 45 centimes per day in 1848—when they could find work. The ribbon makers of Bernay (Eure) had suffered a drop of 25 per cent in their wages during the July Monarchy, and those who survived were located exclusively in agricultural villages where they had ancillary resources. The rest had gone to the cities in search of employment.[52]

---

[50] Thuillier, op. cit., p. 283; Bron, op. cit., p. 39.

[51] As an example of contemporary opinion, see Charles Noiret writing in 1836: 'Il y a environ douze ans que le bénéfice des ouvriers a commencé à être insuffisant.' (Ch. Noiret, *Mémoires d'un ouvrier rouennais* (Rouen, 1836), p. 3.)

[52] For Fourchambault, see Thuillier, op. cit., p. 283. On the Cambrésis, see Y.-M. Hilaire, Les ouvriers du Nord devant l'Eglise Catholique, in *Christianisme et monde ouvrier* (Cahiers du mouvement social, no. 1, Paris, 1975), p. 227. On the Eure, see Vidalenc, *Département de l'Eure*, p. 484. Leroy-Beaulieu gives copious details of the wages of women working in the textile industry, op. cit., pp. 58 ff.

Migration to the towns certainly made sense, if there were jobs to be had. Rural glove makers (mostly women) in the Eure on the eve of the 1848 Revolution earned about 70 centimes per day; in the town they could expect 30 per cent more for the same work. At the bottom end there was a certain national homogeneity: silk winders in St Etienne earned 60–90 centimes per day, ribbon makers about 10 centimes less (a day at this time was normally sixteen hours long). Local *ourdisseuses* (warp-winders) in the same area could earn 1 fr. 40 per day— comparatively good work, when available. But women who worked the mechanical spinning looms in the countryside around Abbéville, in the Somme, were reduced to as little as 25 centimes per day at the trough of the depression. Had they been able to find work as handspinners they would have doubled that wage, although this would still have left them earning less than almost anyone else in employment.[53]

The sheer scale of misery in the late 1840s generated a spate of enquiries, private and public. From these we can establish some idea of the ratio of women's earnings to those of men. In Rouen, in 1848, female spinners earned between 49 per cent of their male counterpart's wage (at the top of the scale) to 56 per cent (at the lowest levels). These calculations are based upon data supplied by the workers themselves, but it is interesting that the figures supplied by the *patronat*, although higher absolutely, retain the same relative proportions. More significant still is the variation in these proportions according to factory size. Rouen spinning was concentrated into very large units, and one investigator divided his material into three categories: factories with less than 100 workers, those with between 101 and 500 workers, and those with over 500. In the first category women's wages were higher, about 62 per cent of the average male wage in the same factory. In the largest mills, women's wages were at most only 49 per cent that of men's. The implications for women workers, grouped disproportion-ately in the most concentrated manufacture, are obvious.

These figures were borne out by those from St Quentin, taken from the local cotton industry, where women's earnings oscillated between 33 per cent and 60 per cent of those of men. Note that these figures pertain only to cotton mills in the town itself—in the countryside wages were lower but the gap smaller, women's wages often rising to 70 per cent of those of men similarly employed. The crisis in rural textiles had

---

[53] For Abbéville, see Levasseur, op. cit., pp. 253–4, and note 3. On the Eure see Vidalenc, *Département de l'Eure*, pp. 485–6. For St Etienne, see Pétrus Faure, *Histoire du mouvement ouvrier dans le Département de la Loire* (St Etienne, 1956), p. 113.

left men and women sharing a common fate, whereas women in urban industry were at a real disadvantage. In 1849 even a navvy could earn two francs per day, more than double the wage a woman cotton spinner in St Quentin could expect for a thirteen-hour day.[54]

Although the second half of the century brought some important changes, an end to bread price fluctuations, and some general wage increases (especially at the end of the Second Empire), industrial wages at the end of the century reveal remarkable continuity with some of the earlier patterns. The gap between skilled and unskilled in a given industry had opened up again (the range on the railways was 5.5:1 for drivers and linemen respectively), and the male:female proportions had stayed consistent. Only in certain skilled trades where women were under-represented did women's wages approach those of men for similar work. In the Pas de Calais in 1910, women employed making shoes earned 79 per cent of the wages of their male counterparts. But in the industrial suburbs of Paris women earned between 40 and 60 per cent of the wages of men, and had some of the worst jobs—handling phosphorous in the match factories of Aubervilliers, or working with dyes in St Denis. In the Calaisis male cotton spinners in 1894 earned 2 fr. 85 per day on average, women just 1 fr. 95; in lace manufacture men earned 4 fr. 95 per day, women 2 fr. 40—68 per cent and 48 per cent respectively. In the giant sugar refineries of Flanders, men were paid a daily rate of 3 fr. 30, women 1 fr. 55, just 46 per cent of the male wage for technically similar work.[55]

Taken overall, men's wages for comparable work had increased by something between 75–110 per cent in the period from the 1840s to the 1890s, women's by a similar amount (with the exception of the building trades, where men's wages had risen by 80 per cent, women's by just 35 per cent). As a result, women's average daily wage (expressed as a percentage of that of men), varying between 42 and 55 per cent in 1845, lay in the range 32–61 per cent by the end of the century. The widest gaps were no longer in textiles but in chemicals and food-processing, which were emerging as primary industrial activities.[56]

Differences in work experience between men and women were thus

[54] For Rouen, see Denier, loc. cit., *passim;* details on St Quentin in Levasseur, op. cit., pp. 252–3.

[55] See *France. Office du Travail. Salaires et Durée du Travail dans l'Industrie Française* (Paris, 1894), vol. 2. On the railways, see E. Fruit, *Les Syndicats dans les chemins de fer en France (1890–1910)* (Paris, 1976) pp. 74–5.

[56] See Bourguin, *Les Systèmes socialistes*, Annexe IX.

characteristic of life in French factories and workshops throughout the century—and it must be emphasized that these differences took shape *within* the experience of industrial employment, rather than between a male labour force and non-working women. Furthermore, if there is any sense in desporting ourselves amidst the taxonomic flora of categories such as 'artisan', 'skilled worker', 'proletarian' and the like, it might be to emphasize again the extent to which the division of labour in France saw women much the more susceptible to pro-letarianization. We need not assume that in itself this constitutes an explanation of their relative absence from the organized labour movement, or their low membership of such traditional organizations as mutual-aid societies, although that absence was noticeable and appears to have been most marked in areas of intensive industrial development.[57] What we *can* safely infer, I believe, is that attempts to explain the aspirations and divisions of the labour movement in France through the conditions of work are made peculiarly troublesome by the extent to which some of the *male* labour force was marginal to precisely those developments on which rest certain influential theories of mass class consciousness.

This observation, then, extends to the wider difficulty of relating the labour movement to its economic experience in general, as we have seen. There *are* themes, directions, discernible continuities in the history of French labour's response to its industrial experience, but these are only contingently identifiable with the overall pattern of employment and industrialization as I have sketched it here. Why this is so, what those themes were and why they can so much better be understood as a response to the *political* history of France is the question to which attention must now be directed.

*

The Restoration years are commonly seen as a hiatus between the turbulence of the Revolutionary generation and the re-emergence of popular movements in the 1830s. They are also regarded as a preface to the development of socialist ideas, with the term 'socialism' itself not used before 1831.[58] There is much truth in this picture. Suzanne

---

[57] For some details on the membership of the *sociétés de secours mutuels*, see the *Annuaire Statistique* for certain years after 1878. In 1886, for example, women were 16 per cent of the total membership of the *sociétes*. In the Var department they were 22 per cent of the membership, in the Allier, 19 per cent, but in a heavily industrialized department like the Pas de Calais only 9 per cent of the societies' members were women.

[58] Pierre Leroux is normally credited with having first employed the word in its modern sense. See Jacques Viard, *Pierre Leroux et les socialistes européens* (Paris, 1983).

Voilquin was not alone in experiencing the Restoration period as 'pénible', a time when the gap between the condition of the working people and the wealth of the upper classes was as yet hardly articulated, much less protested.[59]

Behind this silence lay both the political repression of the Restoration governments, and the legislative impact of the Revolution and the Empire. The new laws affected more people than their drafters might have supposed. The migration into towns which characterized much of the late eighteenth- and early nineteenth-century France meant that the abolition of guilds and the ban on coalitions, for example, had an exacerbated impact upon an urban work-force now facing much greater competition. This work-force was also subject to *political* controls of a more stringent nature: the re-establishment of workers' *livrets* in the laws of 22 Germinal XI and 9 Primaire XII combined with the effect of Article 291 of the Penal Code (requiring permission for any gathering of twenty persons or more, and on such terms as might please the authorities) to make public activity or unconventional opinions truly hazardous for a person seeking employment.[60]

Not surprisingly, then, such organizations of working people as existed before 1830 were confined to forms of collective activity acceptable to the authorities and to employers— acceptable either because they posed no intrinsic threat or, even if potentially disruptive, fell so very obviously into traditional forms of labour organization that contemporaries could find little in principle against which to object, whatever the annoying consequences.

Three forms of collective activity predominated at this time: the *compagnonnages*, the workers' corporations and the mutual-aid societies (*sociétés de secours mutuels*). The *compagnonnages* reached their apogee in the second half of the 1820s, when they could still exercise sufficient control over the employment market to make membership of their society advantageous, sometimes essential, to a worker in a skilled trade. It is significant that as early as 1807 a prefect used the term *syndicat* as synonymous with *compagnonnage*, because the latter certainly existed to fulfil one of the prime functions of an early trade organization: limit entry to a skill, through apprenticeship and

---

[59] Quoted in Jacques Rancière, *La Nuit des prolétaires* (Paris, 1981), pp. 38–9.
[60] On migration patterns, see Furet, *Interpreting the French Revolution*, p. 124.

membership requirements, and thus exercise, however indirectly, some control of qualifications and wages.[61]

As journeyman rather than masters, *compagnons* were male, young, and unmarried. Not all of them aspired to a career in the skill to which they were apprenticed, and a good part of their attention had historically been directed towards violent competition with members of rival *compagnonnages* (there were usually two per trade). Partly for this reason, partly because the societies were ritualistic, exclusivist, and separatist, they posed little threat to public order (except in their occasional brawls), and in their rather conservative influence on young workers they were passively favoured by the authorities.[62] They could, however, exercise themselves in defence of their interests in ways which were potentially in conflict with the spirit of the law. Thus the two orders of stonemasons, the Tour de France and the Devoir de Liberté, occasionally, as in 1821, united to oppose the employment of any *un*organized masons. In Toulon, in 1828, the *compagnon-boulangers* tried the opposite tactic, visiting bakeries in the town to mobilize non-members into demands for higher wages. In the previous year the prefect of the Charente complained that workers in paper manufacture were establishing fines and fixing wage-rates, while excluding as beneficiaries all who were not themselves the *children* of *compagnons*.[63]

In general, however, the government looked benevolently upon such activities. Probably more representative were the events at Tournus in 1825, when the stonemasons of the Devoir de Salomon refused a certain rate for the job. The master masons called in members of the Compagnonnages de Maître Jacques who readily accepted the money offered. The result was a *rixe*—a minor outbreak of gang warfare— which, whether one regards it as a 'traditional' occurrence or a recognizably modern conflict in anachronistic guise, hardly posed the sort of united threat to employers that might have prompted repressive action.[64]

The *compagnonnages* survived well into the 1860s, and in the special case of the Limousin masons even into the 1890s.[65] But both the

[61] Kessel, *Le Prolétariat français*, pp. 189, 199.

[62] See Ronald Aminzade, *Class, Politics and early Industrial Capitalism* (Albany, NY, 1981), pp. 71–2; Olwen Hufton, *The Poor of eighteenth-century France* (Oxford, 1974), pp. 34–5; Maurice Agulhon, *Une ville ouvrière au temps du socialisme utopique: Toulon de 1815 à 1851* (Paris, 1977), pp. 119–29 where he notes the conservatism of *compagnon* practice.

[63] See Agulhon, op. cit., pp. 119 ff; Vidalenc, *La Société française*, p. 205.

[64] See Bron, op. cit., p. 47.

[65] Remi Gossez, *Les Ouvriers de Paris. 1. l'Organisation 1848–1851* (La Roche sur Yonne, 1967), p. 127.

economic and the political climate were inhospitable to them long before then, and they were already marginal to the concerns of many workers even as they flourished in the 1820s. Much the same was true of the corporations, though for a different reason. The corporations were a true anachronism, organizations of master craftsmen inherited directly from the eighteenth-century urban networks of the same name. They served chiefly to control the supply of materials to and from the workers they took on, and to oversee work methods, quality, and markets. They were as exclusive as the *compagnonnages* (when *compagnons* were permitted to join a corporation it was normally as a separately organized sub-group), and of course kept out manufacturing workers. They did not have the bitter sectarian conflicts of the *compagnonnages*, since ritual and pride in an acquired skill mattered less than control of the market in a particular product. And thus, while confined to master artisans, they were actually less divisive than the *compagnons*. But what they were united upon was a distinctively limited angle of vision. They were still organizing mass action in their own defence in the 1830s (e.g. in the case of the shoemakers in 1833, who co-ordinated strikes against middlemen in Paris, Châlon, Toulon, Dijon, Beaune, and Marseilles), and in one respect the great Lyons uprisings of 1831 and 1834 were the last gasp of the *corporations ouvrières* (the slightly misleading contemporary term). But the very power of the corporation depended upon the inherited sense of its collective strength as a group of skilled craftsmen with rights and expectations *within* a particular occupation. The idea of unity across occupational lines was not encompassed in its vision, and if corporations threatened businessmen and local authorities it was with the prospect of a return to the power of the guilds, and the danger of locally effective economic bargaining power, not as a potential source of social disruption or mass mobilization.[66]

The corporations withered and died with the political changes after 1830 and the ever-growing migration to Paris in particular, which

[66] See Agulhon, op. cit., p. 130; Isambert, op. cit., pp. 141 ff. Sewell, in *Work and Revolution*, argues that the *métier*-based *corporations* provided the 'idiom' in which workers' consciousness could emerge. But note Rancière's comment on these organizations: 'Il n'y a pas d'ouvriers moins irremplaçables que les tailleurs. Tous pourtant l'attestent: il n'est pas de corporation plus susceptible, plus soucieuse des égards qu'on lui doit, plus prompte à entrainer dans sa révolte l'ensemble des ouvriers. C'est que la dignité ouvrière dont ils se posent en premiers representants n'a rien à voir avec la fierté du métier. Celle-ci est bien plutôt, au sein du monde ouvrier, un facteur de divisions qui vont jusqu'à la lutte à mort.' (*Nuit des prolétaires*, p. 49.)

smothered the informal organizations of craftsmen which had survived revolutionary legislation. But long before then they were being overtaken by the mutual-aid societies, much the more representative form of worker organization of the period. The 'Mutuels' differed from the other two forms of society in being open, in principle, to any member of the trade in which they were established. They were as they described themselves, mutual assistance societies for workers, intended to provide help and financial support for those incapacitated through illness, accident, or (in some cases) death. Although organizations of this sort can be traced back to the Revolution (the Parisian joiners had founded a Société fraternelle de secours in 1792), they came into their own in the 1820s, when they presented an appealing alternative to the restrictive and exclusivist older movements, while still falling within the approved range of public and collective activity. In Paris in 1819 there were 45 societies. In 1823 there were 132, with some 11,000 members. In 1828 there were 184 such societies in the city, with a total membership of 17,000.[67] Whereas the *compagnons* recruited most successfully among itinerant masons, woodcutters, or metalworkers, where they offered support in the perennial problems of seasonal travel, mutual-aid societies flourished among more sedentary workers—the upper end of the textile trade, or artisan shoe-makers—and they frequently set minimum age requirements (forty, in the case of one society of weavers). They also had religious overtones, in their names and in their preference for the patronage of popular saints.[68]

It should be stressed that these early mutual societies differed from the *compagnonnages* chiefly through their reduced exclusivity. They did not entail any very high level of collective solidarity, and took pains to keep their formal activities well within the legally-defined limits. They were actually less aggressive than the corporations, for obvious reasons (one of which was that the immediate economic interests of their members were often at variance). But what they offered was the beginnings of a looser and more heterogeneous approach to the defence of workers' interests. The emphasis, however, *was* on defence, and still on protection through collective self-insurance.

---

[67] See Bron, op. cit., p. 51; Kessel, op. cit., p. 205 (and note). For 1792, see Ernest Labrousse, *Le Mouvement ouvrier et les théories sociales en France de 1815 à 1848* (Cours de la Sorbonne, Paris, 1964), p. 79.

[68] For the age requirements in a society in Louviers, see Vidalenc, *Le Département de l'Eure*, p. 495.

Protest before 1830, therefore, in so far as it was not the direct representation of corporate demands, continued to take other forms. These, like so much else at the time, were often muted but recognizable continuations of pre-Revolutionary activity. This is hardly surprising when we consider how much the social context of protest and the response to it had remained the same. Le Chapelier notwithstanding, the Emperor had restored the bakers' corporations in the towns after the famine of 1812, and bread prices and supply in every major town were regulated by municipal subvention, taxation, and oversight. The price fluctuations of the late 1820s saw many instances of country-dwellers coming to town to buy bread; the habit of walking from Boulogne (in the Seine-et-Oise) to St Cloud, for example, to buy bread at a controlled price endured into the Second Empire. The corollary to this was the ever-present threat of the bread riot, of far greater concern to Restoration governments than the survival of semi-legal corporations or their occasional strikes.[69]

With popular expectations on bread prices went traditional claims to common rights. Although chiefly rural (mostly in the south, where disputes over peasant access to common lands endured into the 1920s) these spilled over into industry, especially in the case of mining, where the collective defence of those rights (as for example by the Ariège miners in the early 1820s) was as indistinguishable from a traditional rural 'riot' as were the violently asserted claims of the Savenay peat-cutters in 1822.[70] The vocabulary that informed and accompanied such actions was unmistakably that of eighteenth-century radical rebellion, where the notion of 'fairness' and established claims counted above all else. This helped to cement solidarity within protesting communities, but not between them. It was also deprived of a wider frame of reference by the fear of attaching political significance to collective interest (an area in which contemporary British radicalism, also the beneficiary of an older tradition, was altogether less inhibited).

Perhaps the only instance in which mass protest before 1830 could adopt a distinctive tone was in the most atavistic activity of all: machine-breaking. Here, at least, there was a hidden vocabulary of protest which did implicitly transcend corporatist boundaries (even if,

[69] See Vidalenc, *La Société française*, pp. 242–7, and Agulhon, op. cit., p. 63.

[70] Vidalenc, *La Société française*, p. 135. A propos tradition, note the statutes of the Nantes Association Typographique of 1833. Article 13 required that all members agree to support anyone sacked from his work for refusing to accept 'des usages contraires à ceux qui existent'. Quoted in Ansart, *Naissance de l'anarchisme*, p. 123.

paradoxically, dependent upon corporate interest for its success). There are numerous documented instances of machine-breaking in early nineteenth-century France, from the attacks on new machinery in the Normandy spinning factories in 1788, through similar acts during the Revolution in St Etienne, Rouen, and Lille (where a whole series of wool-carding and spinning machines were attacked in 1790) to the destruction of new equipment for the manufacture of rifle barrels in St Etienne in 1831.[71] Even where machines were not actually attacked and damaged, their very presence served to mobilize interested parties. In 1819 the *maîtres-ouvriers* of the Eure pin-making industry agreed among themselves to break the equipment of any pin-maker who used the greater output capacity of new machines to accept lower rates for work. For all that this was a restriction upon trade (and thus illegal) and against the immediate interests of any one producer, the agreement appears to have held. The forms of occupational solidarity thus confirmed can be traced forward to the mid-1840s, when wool-sorting machinery in Elbeuf was threatened by the women it stood to replace. But by then there were alternative organizational avenues to register discontent (though not, perhaps, for the women of Elbeuf).[72]

Of properly political popular protest there was little, however. At best there endured a certain popular Bonapartism (in the west and south-west), where it was identified with a preference for the Imperial bureaucracy over its successors among the local *notables*,[73] and the occasional conflation of anti-patronal shouts with seditious cries, as in the streets of Tarare in 1828, when some strikers chanted, 'Vive la République! A bas les fabricants! La liberté des ouvriers!'[74] In retrospect, given the rapid emergence a few years later of a popular and working-class consciousness, we may assume a significant subterranean political education, not least through the circulation of literature by the hundreds of wandering salesmen active in these years, systematically collecting and distributing books, pamphlets, and songs from their bases in major provincial (and foreign) cities. But before 1830 the expression of overt popular political opinion was rare, and in

---

[71] See Bron, op. cit., p. 54; Pétrus Faure, op. cit., p. 109.

[72] See Vidalenc, *Eure*, p. 479, and Vidalenc, *La Société française*, p. 106.

[73] See Yannik Guin, *Le Mouvement ouvrier nantais. Essai sur le syndicalisme d'action directe à Nantes et à St Nazaire* (Paris, 1976), p. 43.

[74] See Gossez, op. cit., p. 8.

any case and more to the point, not at all associated with the distinctive (and divided) interests of the working population as such.[75]

It follows that the very earliest signs of socialism in France, such as the nascent St Simonian groups of the 1820s, were not even of marginal significance to the workers' organizations described above. Socialism at this point was at least partly religious in character—certainly many early socialists thought of their system of beliefs in deist terms—and what distinguished them from one another, before 1830 as after, were often rather recondite issues of religious and philosophical definition (a fact in part accounted for by the intellectual context and the overwhelming presence of students in the socialist sects). But there was another reason why socialism remained of small relevance to workers at this stage. The problem of politics in France, in the aftermath of Revolution and Empire, was a problem of government, of institutions. Like the Republicans and even the moderate royalists, theoretical socialists in the first thirty years of the century were obsessed with the question of the *form* of government. It is not that its content was a matter of indifference, but it was the formal institutional problem that posed the immediate hurdle. In this respect the French political opposition (like French political theory) differed sharply from their British contemporaries.

So far as the workers' societies of the 1820s were concerned, this political obsession (with its accompanying concern with the threat of clerical power, and its desire for political action) was not one they could readily share, both because of the risks to their legal status, and because such formal considerations of constitutional structure placed in the shade those more urgent concerns around which workers' societies had coalesced. Socialism, like the secret societies of the 1820s, nostalgic for terror and dictatorship, developed not in conflict with nor in opposition to the general lines of popular sentiment (in that case 1830 would have been impossible) but in parallel, in a quite different world. It is important to grasp this distinction, since the different origins of socialism and labour movement in France are sometimes read forward through the mid-century to account for other sorts of divergences which emerged later. This is wrong—the next generation, that of the July Monarchy, would see a convergence of the initially separate movements. There was nothing essentially antithetical

[75] Note, too, that the printing industry which helped furnish and spread these writings was active on a large scale in these years. Many of the Parisian establishments had 200+ workers (246 in one instance). See Vidalenc, *La Société française*, pp. 207–17.

about socialist and worker concerns. But nor did they share common roots, and much less did the French labouring classes themselves provide either the clientele or the rationale for early elaborations of socialist thought.[76]

In the light of what was to come, then, the labour movement of the 1820s was literally 'old-fashioned', and the experience of 1830 therefore constitutes a crucial moment of change. It is not that there were not intimations—and continuities. Strikes both before and after the July Revolution can be found calling for higher wages, but also for the exclusion of undesirable (because unincorporated) workers. The concept of a 'tarif' for work hovered uncertainly between its old meaning in the context of collective rate-setting by autonomous worker corporations, and the new claim to an adequate wage. An organization like the Société de l'Union des Travailleurs du Tour de France, born in the 1830s of a *compagnonnage* scission, was a half-way house between an organization of *compagnons* and an attempt at a General Union.[77] At least one authority has identified the workers' struggles of the July Monarchy as the unbroken continuation of conflicts dating back before the Revolution, but in an aggravated economic setting.[78]

But in spite of this temptation to seek a continuous line of development, it has to be acknowledged that the revolution of 1830 brought immediate and important changes to the circumstances of the labour movement, the most obvious of which was the relative political freedom in which it could operate, at least until 1834. And the result of *this* was an outburst of self-assertion, a search to identify *the* working population with unique and common interests. Whereas the ephemeral *Journal des Ouvriers*, published in the aftermath of the *Trois Glorieuses*, could still assert that 'nos patrons sont ouvriers comme nous: plus nous travaillons, plus ils gagnent, et leur intérêt particulier est un sur garant du nôtre', it was still in 1830, in September, that *L'Artisan* ('journal de la classe ouvrière') was forcefully advocating the principle of association and writing that it was 'la classe ouvrière . . . qui donne de la valeur aux capitaux en les exploitant'. The road to an emergent working-class consciousness lay open.[79]

[76] See Rancière, *La Nuit des prolétaires*, p. 220; Isambert, op. cit., pp. 135–54; Maxime Leroy, *Les Précurseurs français du socialisme*, pp. 8–12.

[77] See Agulhon, op. cit., p. 131.

[78] J.-P. Aguet, *Les Grèves sous la Monarchie de Juillet* (Geneva, 1954), p. 394.

[79] Quoted in A. Cuvillier, *Hommes et idéologies de 1840* (Paris, 1956), p. 89. See also Emile Coornaert, 'La Pensée ouvrière et la conscience de classe en France de 1830 à 1848', in *Studi in onore di Gino Luzzatto* (Milan, Giuffre, 1950), p. 13.

Given that nothing had altered overnight in the varied nature of French industrial life, it follows that it was the specifically political experience (and lessons) of 1830 which lay behind the rapid growth in collective identification. It is a cliché to note that the events of July 1830 aroused great optimism and hopes which were almost immediately dampened down, first by the acquisition of power by the Orleanist dynasty, then by the ensuing vigorous repression of the popular movement. Yet as such clichés go, it is remarkably to the point. Every where in the worker press of the 1830s there was reference to the disappointments of those years and the realization that the working population must now act alone, and on its own behalf. And many of the early leaders acquired both their ideas and their authority through years spent in prison as activists in, for example, the Ligue des Droits de l'Homme.[80]

The first stage in this process was the adoption of the concept of economic exploitation, and its implications. The New Republican Catechism, widely circulated among Lyons weavers in 1833, placed exploitation at the centre of the division between two antagonistic classes, and saw the resolution of this exploitation in a pact of association to place the instruments of labour in the hands of those who used them. This call for a pact of association was not just a platitude, for all that it ran counter to the deepest traditions of separate and intraverted French *organisation de métiers*. In the same year the newspaper of the silkworkers, the *Echo de la Fabrique*, supported the claims of the stonemasons when the latter were on trial for coalition, and the two groups established thereafter various links of mutual support.[81] In Paris the Union des Doreurs of 1832 spoke in its regulations of the primacy of 'l'industriel prolétaire, l'homme le plus utile', thus adopting an altogether novel justification (and terminology) for its claim to fix rates and hours of work.[82]

From a sharpened focus upon the 'worker', defined by contrast with those who exploit, it was a natural step to the adoption of the general category *ouvrier* in progressive replacement of an earlier emphasis upon particular trades and skills. This change implied no devaluation of the skill or standing of the working person—quite the contrary. Like the German journeymen of the 1830s who were abandoning craft-

[80] Rancière, *La Nuit des prolétaires*, p. 111.
[81] See R. J. Bezucha, *The Lyon Uprising of 1834* (Cambridge, Mass., 1974), pp. 85–6; Kessel, op. cit., pp. 274–5.
[82] See Labrousse, op. cit., p. 169.

specific titles in favour of the more solidarist *Arbeiter*, the French derived considerable strength and pride from the growing singularity of reference. Thus there was no longer just a problem of pauperism, but one of worker-pauperism; but whereas the first had been seen as a moral and social problem of a general nature, the new definition here as elsewhere allowed for a more precise account of the causes of poverty, and thus greater concentration upon the necessary conditions for its removal. This was not in conflict with the older concerns of trade control, protection, and improvement of work conditions—it went along with the new form in which these were cast: the reassertion of the power of property after 1830 (including the more assiduous enforcing of laws against coalition after 1834) drove a growing minority of workers to the view that collective control of their trades, the necessary condition for protecting their livelihood, required collective ownership of the relevant property—the means of production.[83]

It was thus that we find, as early as 1832, calls for a worker party (and a worker *Chambre*), with representation of and *by* workers as the only way to secure their economic rights. It is fruitless to try to assess which category of workers was involved here, other than to note the obvious, that all prominent participants in such contemporary discussions were of necessity from the educated minority of wage-earners. The point is that calls for a united class of workers long anteceded the existence of any such class—hence the rather odd use of the term 'proletariat', which shifted only gradually after 1830 from its St Simonian signification of 'those who suffer under present arrangements' to its eve-of-1848 meaning of 'those who earn their living by work'. In neither case did it nor could it refer to the mass factory proletariat of later times. For the first self-conscious workers' leaders in France, as for the Marx of 1848, the political wish fathered the economic thought.[84]

What brought into being this sense of self, and an emerging vocabulary to articulate it, was the quite remarkably fast growth of anti-bourgeois sentiment in French popular milieux. The French working

[83] See J. Kocka, 'The study of social mobility and the formation of the working class in the nineteenth century', in *Mouvement social* no. 111, pp. 97–112; also William Sewell, 'Property, Labor and the Emergence of Socialism in France, 1789–1848', in Merriman (ed.), *Consciousness and Class Experience in Nineteenth-Century Europe* (New York, 1979), p. 58.

[84] On some uses of the term 'proletariat', see M. L. Macdougall, 'Consciousness and Community', in *Journal of Social History*, vol. 12, no. 1 (1978), p. 132.

class achieved consciousness, that is, by the act of distinguishing itself from the selfsame middle class whom it had so enthusiastically endorsed at the start of the decade. As *Le Semeur* noted, in 1833, 'La guerre des classes ouvrières contre la bourgeoisie, des ouvriers contre les maîtres, dure depuis trois ans.' For the working men and women who began to join the Parisian St Simonist circles of these years, the determining concern was the social and economic opposition between the rich who gave work and the poor who sought it.[85]

What is interesting about these early expressions of class sentiment, however, is how little emphasis they place upon the producers or workers 'saving' themselves from below. Although there was much rhetoric surrounding the desire to own the means of production, and in collective form, the specific solution to the rule of the bourgeoisie was overwhelmingly seen as a political one—domination must end. For A. Ott in 1838, the root cause of the workers' troubles was the monopoly of work instruments and capital in the hands of the bourgeoisie, but the way to put an end to this monopoly was through the *political* act of abolishing free competition. A year later Gustave Biard developed this analysis one step further: 'l'Abaissement du cens ou l'extension indéfinie du droit éléctoral (la société demeurant ce qu'elle est) aboutit à néant.' In other words, solutions attempted from within the framework of existing institutions were doomed. Only complete social upheaval would achieve anything. The lesson of 1830 was already being grafted onto the idealized memory of 1789.[86]

By the 1840s the machine question—the fear that exploitation and loss of autonomy were not passing threats but endemic to capitalism—had begun to replace the political dimension as the focus of concern, although the effect of this was only to deepen further the gulf between workers and 'capitalists' (whether employers or middlemen). From 1840 the distinctiveness of the 'working class' was a received truth in all worker circles; the economic analysis which underpinned that faith is readily traced in the contemporary literature. The term 'capitalist' was being refined to describe the more successful and exploitative

---

[85] Le Semeur quoted in Coornaert loc. cit., p. 16. The quote continues, '(Since July 1830) les ouvriers ont eu conscience de leur force . . . ils ont confusément senti, de plus, que la bourgeoisie allait séparer son drapeau de leur, parce qu'elle cessait d'avoir besoin d'eux-pour lutter contre les castes privilegiées'. Quoted in Hilda Rigaudias-Weiss, *Les Enquêtes ouvrières en France entre 1830 et 1848* (Paris, 1936), p. 10. For St Simonien *professions de foi*, see Rancière, *La Nuit de prolétaires*, p. 167.

[86] August Ott, *Des Associations d'ouvrier* (Paris, 1838), pp. 7, 8. Gustave Biard, *De la Réforme Electorale selon les Libéraux et selon les Travailleurs* (Paris, 1839), p. 11.

employer, in the face of whom workers and small masters alike were doomed. Merely being the immediate source of economic authority did not place a man among the enemy. This resolved a dilemma of the 1830s: the links between workers and their immediate employers were very close in the smaller workshops, and identifying the *patron* with the (politically-defined) bourgeoisie was difficult. Hence the frequent protestations of good faith and the desire for conciliation expressed in earlier writings. Once the *maîtres-ouvriers* were themselves defined as victims of a squeeze exerted by big (and mostly absent) capitalists, verbal intransigence was easier.[87]

With remarkable speed there then disappeared the idea that a successful journeyman might become a master, a master a flourishing bourgeois. Obviously the repeated emphasis on the collectivity and on collective action, itself heir to older corporate traditions, helped here, but the struggle was anyway one-sided. From its first polemical use, 'bourgeois' implied the Other. Manichean categories—privilege/ equality, party of exploitation/party of revolution, status quo/complete change, 'l'exploitation du prolétaire ou la fraternité des travailleurs'— captured the popular imagination within half a generation, and here again part of the explanation lies in the political origins of the experience and the vocabulary. The absolute division was given, only the explanation and the solution remained to seek.[88]

There was, of course, a further strand in the explanation of the rapid emergence of a popular consciousness of class. This is the efflorescence of workers' organizations in the July Monarchy, because there is little doubt that whatever the origins of the leaders of the contemporary workers' movement, the rank and file of French labour was politicized, where this was the case, through membership of such organizations.

Although they survived through this period, the *compagnonnages* were increasingly marginal to most workers' experience after 1830. The labouring community was for the most part grouped into two overlapping forms of sociability: the mutual-aid societies and the *cercles* or clubs. Although it was the latter (in the south especially) which fed more directly into future political action, because of their open membership, it was the *mutuels* which now dominated the scene, at least until the late 1840s.

The July Monarchy saw the founding of over a thousand more mutual-aid and benefit societies (a prefectoral enquiry of 1852

---

[87] Ott, op. cit., *passim*.   [88] See Gossez, op. cit., p. 303.

established that 1088 had been founded in the eighteen-year period, compared to 337 for the years 1814–30, but these are low estimates based on incomplete returns). Most were district-based, rather than linked to the workplace, and their membership was not always confined to a single occupation, though in practice it would be dominated by a prominent local trade. There seems to have been no pattern of motive or circumstance for the creation of such societies, though it was not uncommon for one to emerge from a strike, as with the Paris printers in 1830. Because of their avowedly non-political and protective nature, the societies normally had prefectoral backing, though this changed in the 1840s.[89]

A representative mutual-aid society would have an upper limit of between eighty and one hundred members, with a monthly membership charge of about one franc in the 1840s. Members were entitled to free medical care and some payment during illness and convalescence. Rules of eligibility and behaviour were strictly maintained, and all illness and loss of work due to drink, venereal disease, debauchery, fighting (if the member was the aggressor), and the like were not recompensed. Political (and usually religious) discussion was banned. Most societies excluded women—who in many cases would anyway have had difficulty meeting the payments—but there were some women—only societies, notably in the *Dauphiné* (Lyons, too, had an Association Fraternelle des Femmes Ouvrières). It is particularly ironic that the feeling among printers, for example, should have been so strongly against women in their trade just at the moment (1845) when the *livret* was being extended to women workers.[90]

Although the *mutuels* performed a significant function in enrolling the upper echelon of workers into collective organizations, and occasionally acted as the spring-board for defensive actions (against wage-cuts, for example), their very attractions constituted limitations upon their range of activity. Unlike the editorial boards of the worker press, they could never become the cutting edge of protest precisely because they precluded a political role for themselves. And they could not hope to provide the organizational link between old trades and new

[89] On the printers' strike, see Vidalenc, *La Société française*, p. 210. On the importance of the *cercles*, see Maurice Agulhon, *Le Cercle dans la France bourgeoise, 1810–1848* (Paris, 1977).

[90] For the example quoted, see Agulhon, *Une ville ouvrière*, p. 148. For the Dauphiné, see Bron, op. cit., p. 67, and Labrousse, op. cit., p. 167. For Lyons in 1848, details in Gossez, op. cit., p. 81. The attitude of the printers is documented in A. Cuvillier, *Un journal d'ouvriers: l'Atelier, 1840–1850* (Paris, 1954), p. 105, p. 107 n. 5.

because the latter (as in the case of railwaymen, for example) of necessity used the workplace rather than the community for their focus and as a place to meet and talk.

It was this as much as anything which provoked the emergence of the social groups, whether *cercles*, musical societies, or early 'unions'. These were more vulnerable to prefectoral interference, but they were also more likely to be the place where an articulate leadership could hope to find an audience among a labouring population, meeting in the workshop, at a café, or in the dingy offices of a news-sheet. Many of the men (though not the women) who took part in such meetings would also be members of a mutual-aid society, so that their various activities all served to reinforce, in differing ways, the importance of the community and of collective action.

But collective action to what end? It is not sufficient to note that the dominant ethos of the labour movement in France before 1848 was anti-bourgeois, nor that the origin of that sentiment was in part political. For the fact is that the workers' movement, as it emerged in the Second Republic, had certain characteristics which could not readily be inferred from these observations, and was making demands of a kind and in language which suggest a fairly widely-shared and sophisticated critique of its condition. Despite the obvious sociological divisions there had emerged both a unity, and an awareness of that unity, which is the reason why socialism, hitherto independent of the history of labour, now became so much a part of its vocabulary and ideas. Of what did this complex of attitudes and hopes consist?

At the centre of workers' discourse in the 1830s and (especially) 1840s lay the concept of 'work', and the values attached to it. Work, whether the activity itself or the resulting product, provided the basis for the self-identification and assertion of the labouring classes. Part of the origins of this outlook are to be found in the divorce between popular belief and the official Church which the Revolution had done so much to hasten and the Restoration failed fully to reverse. As a consequence, the system of popular values had a distinctly earthly identity by the 1840s: salvation was to be found in life and on earth, and in one's own world. For those whose world was bounded by work and the workshop, this translated readily into a search for salvation through effort and struggle.[91]

The religious impulse, often found in contemporary language, not to

[91] See Rancière, *La Nuit des prolétaires*, esp. pp. 68 ff.

speak of the rituals and forms of labour activities, posed a dilemma. Was work a duty or a right? The implications were considerable (and remain so): if work was a duty, then the generalized distaste for the liberal bourgeoisie could be reduced to an altogether more specific rejection of its way of life and its *rentier* sources of wealth. From this to an overtly political critique of the whole social system was then an easy step. As a popular epigraph of the 1840s had it: 'Celui qui ne veut pas travailler ne doit pas manger.'[92] Punishment of the lazy would take the form of depriving them both of their present power and of any future opportunity to remain socially inert. The instinctive affinity of working men and women for such a point of view explains the breadth of the St Simonian appeal in this period, especially when adopted in more moral and ambivalent a form by other socialist schools, such as that of Cabet.[93]

The idea that work might be something to which one had *a right*, although not in any necessary conflict with the idea of work as duty, had different roots and carried alternative implications. Its derivation, of course, is to be found in the vocabulary of eighteenth-century radicalism and in the latter's elective preference for the individual's claims against the collectivity. But it had the special virtue of being readily translated into a claim on behalf of one community against the rest. It also dovetailed with the more mundane concerns both of those threatened with unemployment and of those who had hitherto assumed certain rights to be inalienably theirs through membership of a given trade, skill, or society. Hence the emphasis of the *Atelier* group of the early 1840s, for example, upon the 'right' to control of placement, control of wage rates, abolition of *marchandage*, all necessary conditions for the protection of a right not merely to employment, but to employment in keeping with certain legitimate expectations.[94]

The notion of 'dignity' provided a common theme for advocates of rights and duties alike. The *producteur réel, the véritable producteur* as *L'Atelier* described the worker, should have control of the conditions of work because work, being a duty, conferred dignity and dignity was

---

[92] See, for example, the anonymous *Dialogue sur l'Association Ouvrière* (Paris, 1841).
[93] See Jean-Christian Petitfils, *Les Socialismes utopiques* (Paris, 1977), p. 140.
[94] For details on the *Atelier* group, see Cuvillier, *Un journal d'ouvriers, passim*. Note that the Atelier newspaper used the terms 'producteur réel', 'véritable producteur', as synonyms for 'ouvrier' throughout the 1840s. See also Rancière, *La Nuit des prolétaires*, ch. 10.

something to which one just did have a right. The dignity in question was not the wounded *amour propre* of the hypothetically déclassé artisan, but precisely that pride in work and in the thing produced to which all might aspire, and which was forever alien to the isolated, unproductive bourgeois.[95] Nor should we misread as some sort of submission to the dominant ideology of respectability contemporary workers' obsession with being respectable, with respect for property and so forth. This too was part of a process of self-assertion, a way of claiming attention on equal terms. Spokesmen for the working people claimed their share of freedom not in order to enter into the way of life of others, but the more fully to be and become themselves: 'Qu'est-ce que la liberté? Le droit dont chaque homme est investi de développer ses facultés à sa convenance.'[96]

There is a paradox here, in that it was the very desire to abolish the condition of *prolétaire* which led to the forging of a vocabulary and politics which precisely identified and took pride in the fact of being a worker. It was from this that the *ouvriérisme* of the French labour movement was born. But seeking justice in a hostile political environment meant mobilizing large numbers of people. To do this it was necessary to abandon the emphasis on secrecy which had characterized opposition in France since 1795, and this could only be done by finding a common identity which spoke to the feelings and needs of the widest possible community. The moral emphasis upon the duty to work thus gave way to the demand for rights, whether in work or simply to have work, and this in turn collapsed progressively into the 'question of proletarism', a widely-adopted shorthand for the complex of fears and difficulties that was exacerbated by the crisis of the mid–1840s.[97] There were occasional tangential concerns of a related

---

[95] 'Bourgeois' was already a term of opprobrium, surpassed in its scorn only by the despised 'petit bourgeois'. Here is the tailor Desplanches, writing in *La Ruche Populaire* in July 1841: 'Si dans le peuple chaque individu pouvait se dire bourgeois et propriétaire, ce serait fini pour lui de toute gloire, de toute nationalité. Qu'aurait en effet à attendre l'avenir d'un peuple composé de petits-bourgeois? d'un peuple où chaque individu se ferait centre, aurait à défendre sa petite propriété, sa petite boutique, son petit atelier, ses petits droits politiques, car tout alors serait infiniment petit.' Quoted in Rancière, *La Nuit des prolétaires*, pp. 258–9.

[96] Richard Lahautière, *Petit catéchisme de la Réforme sociale* (Paris, 1839), p. 5.

[97] 'Il y a quelques années, une question ardue, périlleuse, occupait tous les esprits, celui du pauperisme. Depuis, elle a changé de nom, en se compliquant de difficultés nouvelles. Il ne s'agit plus seulement de donner les moyens de vivre à ceux qui manquent de tout: avec la liberté si féconde en résultats pour les classes moyennes, le sentiment de l'égalité est descendu jusqu'au fond des classes inférieures, on y parle de droits et de

nature, such as the demand for a full and free system of education, widely voiced in the replies to the 1848 enquiry, or an interest in labour legislation (such as the ineffective child labour law of 1841). But the broader issues never left the centre of popular debate, and writers and speakers always returned to the central problem: if work was a right, and therefore a condition of liberation and autonomy, how should it be organized in France to this end?

I use the term 'organized' advisedly. For it was implicit in the importance accorded the notion of dignity, of respectability, and of rights, that whatever changes were necessary to remove both the moral stigma and the economic risk attaching to work could not simply be sought in political upheaval, however violent. On this there was a remarkable concurrence. All the various socialist sects, whatever the degree of their interest in the working people as *means* to a better world (by 1848 most now saw the improved condition of the working classes as part of their avowed ends), had by now abandoned direct political action as a vehicle for radical change. Only Blanqui and the radical Jacobin fringe of the republican movement still saw immediate constitutional change as an overwhelming priority. For the rest of the heterogenous opposition crowding around the embattled Orleanist regime and its successor Republic, the plots and uprisings of the 1830s had exhausted the plausibility of assaults on power for their own sake. Moral dignity was the new watchword, and moral dignity could not be legislated, but only asserted and created, and then only at the base. The idea of 'base' and 'superstructure' had entered popular political literature in France well before Marx endowed it with metaphysical legitimacy, and changing matters at the base meant that the hitherto random and anarchic forms of work and production (regarded as all the more irrational by those whose trades had once and not so long ago been so very well and effectively regulated) must be organized to a more rational (and therefore worthy) end.

There were two distinct views on how to 'organize' work. One emphasized autonomy, the other the role and involvement of the state. This important difference of opinion emerged surprisingly early: in a paper read to a meeting in London in 1839, the speaker emphasized the need for government to play the role of 'premier manufacturier, directeur suprême de tous les industries', while opposition to the very idea of a providential state was the driving force behind the faith of the *Atelier* workers' paper from 1840 onwards.[98] There was no fixed relationship between the opinion held and the social identity of the speaker—workers, like socialists (and socialist workers too) were divided sharply on the role, if any, that the state should play in the emancipation of labour.

The division was unequal, however. Contemporaries had a clear preference for the active, interventionist state. The free-market economy was associated with just that 'egoist' liberty and individualism to which the popular writers opposed the ideal of 'association'. Hence the calls for the 'Abolition de la Libre Concurrence!', or Noiret's view, stated in 1840, that the only reform which could work was 'l'organisation du travail, de l'industrie et du commerce, l'association des ouvriers, travaillant en commun et pour leur propre compte'. He had no illusions that such an ambitious programme could be implemented except by and through the state.[99]

Part of the point of imagining association as a process involving workers and government alike was precisely to distinguish it from any nostalgic preference for the old workers' corporations, described by one writer as 'la continuation du mal présent et de plus le retour du privilège'. The master artisans, after all, had been a certain sort of capitalist in their own right, and the whole point of association was to abolish capitalists and the system which favoured them. The point could not simply be to advocate conditions of prosperity in which a few more impoverished workers would become *maîtres'*—'toujours la différence fondamentale subsistera entre les propriétaires et les non-propriétaires, entre les exploiteurs et les exploités'. The object was to end competition, not to benefit from it, and this would require legislation.[100]

It is in this context that one must understand the significance of the idea of organizing work, as advocated most prominently by Louis

---

[98] *Rapport sur les mesures à prendre et les moyens à employer pour mettre la France dans une voie Révolutionnaire le lendemain d'une insurrection victorieuse* (read to the Société Démocratique Française in London, 18 Nov. 1839), London, 1840, p. 4. Also Cuvillier, *Un journal d'ouvriers*, p. 141.

[99] See the toast by Citoyen Duval (hairdresser), 'A l'Abolition de la Libre Concurrence!', quoted in a pamphlet reporting the speeches at the *Premier Banquet Communiste, 1ᵉʳ juillet, 1840* (Paris, n.d.). Noiret's views can be found in Ch. Noiret, *Aux Travailleurs* (Rouen, 1840), p. 16.

[100] Auguste Ott, *Des Associations d'ouvrier* (Paris, 1838), p. 7.

Blanc. Not only did it take up what was in any case a well-established public function in France (charity workshops, for example, had been a way of employing the poor in state-financed undertakings ever since the fifteenth century[101]), but it provided a scaffolding of economic theory. There was nothing wrong with political rights and extensions of the franchise, but these would always be insufficient protection so long as workers could be forced by their masters to abuse their rights, or not use them at all. Free competition was thus detrimental to the political freedoms of the people. But it was also (Blanc would argue) economically unsound. Not only did competition force down wages, but it led inevitably to monopoly (an old target for popular resentment, of course), and monopolies could control (and thus raise) prices. Since low prices were the hypothetical benefit of competition, the system was radically unworkable.[102]

So much was common to the analyses of autonomists and *étatists* alike. Then why the preference for strong government? Part of the answer lies in wider aspects of French political culture to be taken up in later chapters, and part, too, came from a sense of urgency: genuine workers' autonomy, in the sense of co-operative workshops, not to speak of the ending of capitalist competition and the wage system, were utopian nostrums in the real world of politics in the 1840s, or at best nostalgic references to the incorporated trades of minority artisan memory. It made political sense to think first of controlling the state, rather than imagining that it might eventually be ignored. But most important, I believe, was the simple and evident truth that there was an overwhelming popular preference for an interventionist state, a preference to which the press and pamphleteers were responding.

So far as the more truly proletarian work-force was concerned, such a preference made sense. Employees in the newer industries, those at the bottom of the wage-scale, those who were geographically and socially uprooted, had few grounds for supposing they could construct autonomous work units, much less protect them against competition. For them the immediate need was for an ally in their unequal struggle with the *patronat*, and the state, whatever its identity, was the natural choice. Hence, for example, the unambiguous emphasis in the feminist worker press for collective social forms as the necessary condition for an improvement in working women's condition. This included demands for the collective control of certain occupations through the

---

[101] Hufton, *The Poor*, p. 182.
[102] Louis Blanc, *Organisation du travail* (English edn., Oxford, 1913), pp. 76–9.

nationalization of the medical and culinary trades (and the establishment of *restaurants nationaux*). At the other end of the labouring
spectrum we find the railwaymen of 1848, in the person of the
spokesman for the employees of the Chemin de Fer du Nord,
announcing that they would prefer to work for half their salaries and be
employed by the state, than have their wages doubled but remain at the
mercy of the companies.[103]

If women were a special case (though hardly an insignificant one)
and railwaymen a new element in the labour movement, the same
cannot be said of coal-miners or construction workers. Yet the former
were aggressive advocates of a governmental 'organisation du travail'
long before 1848 as well as during the Second Republic, while the
masons' wages were largely determined by the continuing practice of
marchandage, where a contractor would offer a fee for a job and then
force workers to accept low wages if they wanted the work. Hence the
plethora of appeals by building workers to the provisional government
of 1848 to end the practice and introduce state regulation and
oversight of the organization of work practices on site.[104] There were
195 petitions in 1848 for state intervention or legislative regulation of
industrial practices, representing the view of workers in 100 different
trades (mostly Parisian, and thus predominantly skilled and artisan in
character).[105]

When socialists such as Blanc or Buchez advocated conquering the
state in order to render it sympathetic to workers' needs (for cheap
credit facilities, for example, as well as legislation on conditions at
work) they were thus tapping a rich vein of popular feeling, as much
among those who saw the state as a bulwark against selfishness
(whether the selfishness of corporations or of capitalists) as among
those who saw it as the only way in which those selfsame selfish
interests could be protected. It was, however, almost certainly the
preferences of the former, that is to say of the manufacturing working
class, which were of growing importance, especially outside Paris. As
the prefect of the Rhône observed in 1849, 'Une assez grand nombre
d'entre eux ont admis comme une vérité qu'ils sont les victimes du
capital; ils voient leur bien-être futur dans l'association, et pour

---

[103] See Evelyne Sullerot, 'Journaux féminins et lutte ouvrière (1848–1849)', in
J. Godechot *et al.*, *La Presse Ouvrière* (Paris, 1966), pp. 107, 109–10. Also Gossez,
op. cit., pp. 216, 308.
[104] Pétrus Faure, op. cit., p. 139; Vidalenc, *La Société française*, p. 289.
[105] Gossez, op.cit., p. 65.

s'affranchir de ce qu'ils appellent les servitudes individuelles, ils réclament le concours de l'Etat.'[106]

Clearly, the state of popular imagining was a providential and essentially economic one. It had little in common with the actual one, feared and often despised by people in town and country alike. *L'état flic/l'état providence* is an enduring dichotomy in French popular thinking (and French political theory). It has its roots in a dual inheritance from the Ancien Régime. On the one hand French republicans, like British radicals, saw the state as a predatory, monopolizing and coercive force, a limit upon freedom and rights. But on the other, and unlike the British instance, there was in France a well-founded awareness of the importance of the central government, whatever its colour, in everyday life. What is more, the particular forms of revolutionary organization in France had idealized the absence of mediating or representative institutions, inculcating an enduring preference for direct links between individual and state, unbroken by intermediary organs, whether economic or political.

By extruding from the debate any concern with *l'état-flic*, advocates of worker organization in the 1840s could cast the state in a central role in their theories without having to engage the specifically political problem of how to ensure that the state in question would be theirs to organize. Thus *Le Peuple* in 1847: 'La science économique nous enseigne qu'organiser le travail et organiser le gouvernement, c'est une seule et même chose.' Even writers such as Dezamy, one of many in the early 1840s who idealized the notion of 'community', were very clear that what they envisaged was a society of egalitarian communes, with common workshops, equality of the sexes, and so forth, but sharing a single (national) direction. An important part of the task of this direction, under whatever name, was to ensure the medium-term financial stability of the workers' own communities. This was Louis Blanc's vision too: 'Ce qui manque aux prolétaires pour s'affranchir, ce sont les instruments de travail; la fonction du gouvernement est de les leur fournir. Si nous avions à définir l'Etat, nous répondrions: l'Etat est le banquier des pauvres.'[107]

That the financial support in question *need* only be for the medium term was an important article of popular faith. Memories of 1830 (and, after 19 June 1848, of the suspension of the recently granted freedom

---

[106] Quoted in Rancière, *La Nuit des prolétaires*, p. 317.
[107] See *Le Peuple*, 1847 (n.d.); T. Dezamy *et al.*, *Almanach de la Communauté, 1843* (Paris, 1843). Also Blanc, *Organisation du travail*, p. 14.

of association) were still fresh, and none of those who looked to the state supposed that it was in any sense neutral (*that* view was more likely to be held by extreme autonomists, and even there not until the next generation); the long-term ambition remained a rather hazily articulated image of a community of self-governing production co-operatives, not threatened by capitalist competition or patronal exploitation and thus not in need of a sympathetic ally or arbiter. Noiret, for example, in his preference for national over local 'association', saw such an arrangement as submerging all separate interests into an 'être collectif appelé l'Etat'. None the less, 'l'Association nationale industrielle ne serait encore qu'une belle transition, qu'un heureux passage à un état meilleur.' Even for Louis Blanc, the point of a strong state was to 'contrebalancer les injustices qui naissent de la société'—a defensive stage on the road to a better future for all.[108]

The political state, then, had to be conquered *in order* to establish the providential economic state which in its turn would help to ensure the emergence of conditions in which neither would be needed. There was thus much sympathy for the general aims of Proudhon or Cabet, and probably even for Considérant with his insistence that social reform begin at home, so to speak. The difficulty had to do with means, not ends. If workers' troubles arose, as was generally agreed, from their non-possession of property and tools, then the collective organization of work and its conditions was the only answer. But as the experience of the evanescent workers' co-operatives before and during the Second Republic was revealing, the artificial generation of utopian conditions in one corner of the market (or the country) was no protection against the combination of economic and political barriers to progress all round. Only the acquisition of political power could change this, a view held even by those for whom political or social considerations for their own sake were peripheral to the needs of workers. Hence the force of Henri Celliez's condemnation in 1840 of those who wanted just to 'organiser le travail': 'Ils veulent organiser le travail pour la société comme elle est constituée, sur la base de l'inégalité.' It is ironic that this council of logical utopianism was directed *against* the ideas of Blanc and his followers, for the tactical conclusions drawn were identical, and were shared on the eve of 1848 by a whole generation of workers' leaders: *politique d'abord.*[109]

[108] Alain Faure and Jacques Rancière, *La Parole ouvrière 1830–1851. Textes rassemblés* (Paris, 1976), quoting Noiret, pp. 134–6. On Louis Blanc, see the comments of François Furet in *Le Debat*, no. 13 (juin 1981), p. 44.
[109] Henri Celliez, *Devoir des Révolutionnaires* (Paris, 1840), pp. 15–17.

This, above all, explains the growing importance to the labour movement of socialist ideas in the latter part of the July Monarchy. Although it is of course true that the organizational *practice* of workers itself contributed to the formation of French socialism, the systems of the French theorists had an independent origin and existence, with wide support.[110] From the very first, socialism was a critique of individual appropriation, a doctrine of the oppressed which was drawn by its own logic to support for collective ownership. The three-part historical argument which was common to most schools of socialist thought at this time was also independent of any necessary link to the labouring classes, though naturally of special interest to them. History was seen as a process of movement from the authoritarian, through the individual, towards the collective, the fraternity, with 1789 the moment of change from the first to the second, and with a future stage to herald the final transition. All that was needed for socialist theory to acquire popular support was for the moral prescriptivism of the historical analysis to be organically tied to an economic critique of capitalism, a process which actually came to fruition rather earlier in the writings of French socialists than in the mature thought of Marx.[111]

This was true not only of the working-class St Simonist circles, but also in the writings of Leroux, for example, who described class struggle as simply the battle for power between those who owned the means of production and those who had none, or Pecqueur, whose *Théorie Nouvelle d'économie social et politique* concluded that socialization of the means of production was the only way for the worker to get the full value of his labour. It is no accident that it was these opinions, together with those of St Simon and Robert Owen, which were singled out by *L'Egalitaire* in 1840 as the leading contemporary socialist systems.[112]

The other side of the socialists' appeal was that (after 1833) theirs was the only doctrine of protest which offered an alternative to the paths of violence and failure. Hence the marginality of Blanqui and the Babouvist inheritance, despite being widely known. Hence, too, the limited appeal of the contemporary *Communistes*, whose doctrines constituted an active protest against existing conditions only in the most abstract and ideal sense. As for the Jacobins and their heirs (e.g.

---

[110] Sewell (*Work and Revolution*) is perhaps a little misleading on this theme, insisting as he does upon the workers' practices as the primary contributor to the content and vocabulary of revolutionary discourse in this period.

[111] Leroy, *Les Précurseurs français du Socialisme*, p. 14; Jean Bruhat, ch. 2 of *Histoire générale du socialisme*, vol. 1, ed. J. Droz (Paris, 1972), pp. 375–82.

[112] *L'Egalitaire* (mai 1840), no. 1.

the Société des Droits de l'Homme of the early 1830s), their appeal was restricted by their continued concern with the construction of a 'virtuous élite' to guide the people. The habit of accepting authority and leadership *within* the workers' associations remained strong, but advice and direction from outside was no longer so sure of a welcoming response.

That socialists were better received is beyond doubt. Contemporaries such as Heine even went so far as to state that subversive doctrines had quite taken over the lower classes in France by 1841. In Lyons a workers' paper of the time hammered insistently away at the theme of property as the source of all oppression—common property was the solution and no political programme was satisfactory which neglected this fact.[113] It was this congruence between the primary concerns of workers and the *common* premisses of most of the socialist schools which explains why the same social milieu, that of the Lyons master artisans, could provide support for the ideas of Proudhon and Cabet alike, in spite of their many differences and disagreements.[114]

Socialist literature was in wide circulation at this time: it is estimated that more than 400 different Fourierist brochures were available before 1846, and works by Cabet, Proudhon, and Leroux were frequently found in popular districts of Toulouse during the Second Republic. Socialist libraries were a feature of many towns on the eve of the 1848 Revolution, and if Adolphe Blanqui's claim that 'radical' sheets were widely read during mealtimes in Rouen is accepted, then it comes as no surprise to learn that the prefect of the Seine–Inférieure was worried in 1848 by the eight thousand workers in the *chantiers de travail* overlooking the city, '[qui] discutent sur le salaire et le profit du travail'.[115]

As to the social basis of socialist support, we are of course substantially in ignorance. Cabet's Icarian movement was dominated by old trades like tailors and shoemakers, a predictable response to its separatist and utopian aspirations. The St Simonians of the 1830s, on

---

[113] *Le Travail: Organe de la Renovation Sociale*, no. 2 (juillet 1841). Heine is quoted by Kessel, op. cit., p. 345.

[114] Here I disagree with the views of Madeleine Rebérioux, who finds it incongruous that the same social milieu should have received with sympathy such radically differing ideologies. See Rebérioux's review of books on utopian socialism in *Mouvement social*, no. 106 (1979), pp. 119–30.

[115] See Bruhat in Droz, *Histoire générale*, vol. 1, p. 373; Aminzade, *Class, Politics and early Industrial Capitalism*, p. 84; Denier, 'Les Ouvriers de Rouen', loc. cit., p. 27. Blanc was another author who was widely read in these years.

the other hand, seem to have corresponded rather better, in age and occupation, to the working population as a whole, and were a reasonably faithful anticipation of the crowds of Second Republic Paris. They were also less likely to exclude women, an important part of their appeal in some industrial regions. Even in Paris one list of St Simonians for the very early 1830s gives 100 women of a total of 280 members. At about the same time a St Simonist meeting held in a popular district of Nantes attracted a mixed audience of one thousand persons. In general it was old towns such as Nantes (or Vienne, where Cabet's party had 62 subscribers in 1846) that favoured a socialist appeal to the working population. In the newer industrial centres lower literacy, greater poverty, and the effective exercise of patronal control rather restricted the possibilities for political participation.[116]

In the end, however, neither membership nor even readership mattered that much, because the substance of socialist doctrines already constituted the basic vocabulary of protest of most working people. When the Arsenal workers of Toulon invited Flora Tristan down to speak to them in 1844, they already knew what she would say. As one blacksmith puts it '. . . faîtes-nous entendre ces vérités touchantes que vous dites si bien'. It was the results of her visit that mattered—in this case a major strike in the Arsenal the following year and what Maurice Agulhon calls the definitive moment in the making of a working class in the city.[117] Socialist propaganda and the activists who carried it all over France in these years were catalysts for sentiments which already existed across a wide spectrum of opinion.

That socialism could thus so completely achieve identification with the working population was also, in part, a consequence of the failure of republicanism to set down deep roots among the newer industrial workers. Armand Carrel might claim that the republican faith of the Ligue des Droits de l'Homme had widespread backing in the working people of Paris during the 1830s, but Paris was a special case. Elsewhere, militant popular republicanism was either confined to the politicized peasantry (an observation confirmed by the nature of the 1851 uprising) or else supported by traditional artisans, as in the Gard, where shoemakers were prominent among the republican societies but

---

[116] On the Icarians, see Christopher Johnson, *Utopian Communism in France: Cabet and the Icarians, 1839–1851* (Ithaca, NY, 1974), esp. Appendix 2; for St Simonians, see Rancière, *La Nuit des prolétaires*, pp. 154 ff., and Labrousse, *Le Mouvement ouvrier*, p. 113. For Nantes, see Guin, op. cit., p. 73.

[117] Agulhon, *Une ville ouvrière*, p. 179.

the textile proletariat was conspicuously absent.[118] In general, political republicanism was associated with the radical bourgeoisie, and this alone would increasingly restrict its appeal at a time when the middle classes were ceasing to be regarded by the workers as their 'natural' allies.

Nor did republicanism benefit from popular anti-clericalism, as one might suppose by analogy with a later period. The church was certainly resented, especially in areas where the religious orders served as adjunct foremen in factories and factory dormitories. This was the case in Lyons and its region, where nuns were widely employed as overseers and 'spiritual directors', and there the news of the February Revolution was the occasion for anti-clerical and anti-patronal demonstrations that were virtually indistinguishable. In St Etienne too, the church was unpopular, in this case because of the employment of cheap labour in convents—in April 1849 four women were killed during a demonstration by two hundred lace-making women against such threats to their own jobs.[119]

Yet in spite of such dislike for the formal role of the church, the neo-religious vocabulary of many of the socialists did not work to their disadvantage. Perhaps this had to do with the rather particular meaning attached to 'religion' in popular parlance. Being idealistic in an almost millenarian sense did not preclude identification with the far Left: in 1841 the editorial prospectus of one socialist paper in Lyons announced its desire to see 'tous les hommes réligieusement unis dans une œuvre d'amour et de félicité commune: nous sommes communistes'. This same paper would sell shares in itself only to bona fide workers and maintained a consistent line in favour of 'true' religion.[120] In later years the socialist movement would take considerable pains to distance itself from the aggressive anti-clericalism of the Radical Party, and this caution clearly derived not just from a concern with the 'fundamentals' (i.e. economic matters), but also from an early appreciation that the mass of the French working population was far from sympathetic to the free-thinking Voltairian approach of the radical middle class. Whether this lack of sympathy derived in turn from earlier and more basic

---

[118] Armand Carrel, *Extrait du dossier d'un prevenu de complicité morale dans l'attentat du 28ᵉ juillet* (Paris, 1835), p. 6; on the Gard, see Raymond Huard, *Le Mouvement républicain en Bas-Languedoc, 1848–1881* (Paris, 1982), pp. 94–5. The best work on the 1851 uprising is now that of Ted Margadant, *French Peasants in revolt* (Princeton, 1979).

[119] Lequin, *Les Ouvriers de la région lyonnaise*, vol. 2, pp. 158–60; Pétrus Faure, op. cit., pp. 143–4.

[120] *Le Travail*, no. 1 (juin 1841, published in Lyons).

cultural differences, or was itself a corollary to the growing scission between the republican élite and the working class remains unclear.

What *is* clear is that the experience of the Second Republic was itself decisive in widening and solidifying this antipathy. Not the least of the reasons for this was the spurt of growth in the number and scope of exclusively workers' associations. This, rather than the romantic contemporary idealism, was the most important popular experience of the short-lived regime, at least in the cities. In Paris alone, some three thousand producer co-operatives were founded between 1848 and 1851, many of them along explicitly socialist lines. Few survived long, and many soon abandoned their principles, losing their exclusively working-class identity and even employing outsiders. But for a time Paris and other cities were full of co-operatives of joiners, stone-masons, plasterers, carpenters, ironworkers, locksmiths, and the like. Many of these were formed from existing mutual-aid societies, or emerged from established workshops, but the urge to create was also strong. The movement 'trickled down' to smaller communities as well, although it was not until the end of the first year that towns like Sedan saw their first workers' production associations. The vast majority, in Paris and province alike, included in their declaration of aims the duty to strive for the abolition of 'man's exploitation by man' (a phrase employed and popularized by Louis Blanc).[121]

Spontaneous organizational combustion was one feature of the popular experience in the Second Republic. A second, equally important, was the use of the briefly-held political authority to create communal institutions through the state. The Luxemburg Commission, for example, in addition to its better-known innovations, also established a *Bureau de Placement* in every town hall in Paris. This both met an immediate need (unemployment, and the continuing influx of provincial workers in search of jobs) and also corresponded to a popular and long-established desire to see public control of hiring and selection. It was not enough to set up national workshops, nor even to propose the nationalization of mines, railways, insurance companies, and the Banque de France (all of which the Commission re-commended); the organization of work also meant seeking an end to the arbitrary anarchy of the market in employment, no less than in

[121] See Bron, op. cit., p. 109; Gossez, *Les Ouvriers de Paris;* Lequin, op. cit., vol. 2, pp. 184–6. For Sédan, see Armand Audiganne, *Les Populations ouvrières et les industries de la France dans le mouvement social du dix-neuvième siècle,* 2 vols. (Paris, 1854), vol. 1, pp. 56–7.

commodities. The roots of one strand of a later syndicalist movement were emerging.[122]

As yet, this 'proto-syndicalism' implied no divorce from the socialist movement—quite the reverse. But it is possible to detect during the Second Republic a rather sharper definition in the meanings attached to socialism, association, organization, and the like. Until 1848, as we have seen, they overlapped to the point of synonymy, and even during the Second Republic itself it was rare to find such distinctions openly drawn. Only very occasionally was there conflict, as when the editorial collective of *L'Atelier* opposed the June insurrection and specifically limited its concerns to association as an end in itself. But then as Cabet observed, *L'Atelier* was run by the 'bourgeoisie et l'aristocratie de la classe ouvrière', with 30 per cent of its members also adherents of the printers' society, and most of the rest jewellery workers, tailors, craftsmen in wood, and the like.[123] Cabet had a polemical interest, but his general observation was valid—by mid-1848 a small section of the *artisanat* was progressively divorcing itself from the concerns of other workers and retreating from politics altogether.

As to the majority of the workers, *their* differences from the socialists, and especially from the politically-engaged *démocrates-socialistes*, were harder to articulate, since they were not inherently a function of class or sectional interest. What the workers' delegates in the clubs and the Commission had sought was to abolish the *salariat*, by organizing, by nationalizing, by ending competition. The tone was egalitarian, and thus excluded reference to *compagnonnages* or *corporations*, but it was potentially apolitical, and became the more so as republican politics lost their meaning for the poor, with the defeat of the republicans and the loss of unrestricted male suffrage. Socialists, on the other hand, remained by definition political, in their ambition to abolish property, the very foundation of politics. They thus pursued an emphasis on rights and needs which could only be met by fundamental political upheaval, while in the meantime it was control of the existing state which was the end to be sought.

This slow process of implicit disassociation between the workers' organizations and the aims of avowed socialists was partially compensated by the fact that many of the socialists in public life were now themselves working men. But since they were united by political aims

---

[122] See, for a general account of this process, Bruhat, in Droz, op. cit., Part 3, ch. 2, pp. 502 ff.

[123] Quoted in Cuvillier, *Un journal d'ouvriers*, p. 51.

above all, they were naturally more occupationally heterogeneous than the co-operatives and trade associations which were still identified by *métier* rather than by purpose. It would be wrong to assign excessive sociological significance to this observation, but it was a difference which would become more important after 1849, once political activity diminished with the onset of serious repression.

The effects of this repression on the labour movement were 'catastrophic' (Emile Coornaert[124]). The June Days of 1848 and the steady process of arrest, surveillance, or exile which culminated in the coup in December 1851 destroyed twenty years of patient effort. It was not that reaction had come as a surprise—the crowds of February 1848 stayed in the streets for a whole week precisely in order to recover the opportunities lost in the naïve credulity of the July Days eighteen years before. That is why so many initial reforms were achieved, and why the early months of the Republic saw such a flowering of working-class activity. But the ending of all hope of 'reform from above', the abolition of the Luxemburg Commission, and the evident refusal of the new assembly to engage in the regulation of work (as witness the unwillingness to ratify a decree stipulating a right to employment) not only reinforced distrust of the bourgeoisie. It also ended for good the political leadership exercised by an old working-class élite, which now retreated to what would later be identified as a Proudhonian position: nothing by the state, everything by the worker himself, a socialist gloss upon possessive individualism: 'à chaque travailleur la propriété individuelle d'une valeur de richesses consommables égale à celle qu'il a produite'.[125]

To the rest of the labour movement, thus deprived of leadership and vulnerable as ever to economic pressures which the higher-paid skills could to some extent avoid, it was clear by 1850 that the Republic, whatever else it stood for, was not going to be the 'Republic of work'. For the time being (indeed, for twenty years) this lesson had no practical significance, but it would eventually weigh heavily upon the *kind* of political and ideological appeals to which the French proletariat would be receptive.

The experience of the Second Republic was thus absolutely central to the creation of working-class consciousness in France. It was an end, not a beginning. Only the minority current of self-regulating trade organization survived the experience intact. It had been a

[124] Coornaert, loc. cit., p. 33.
[125] *L'Atelier*, quoted in Cuvillier, *Un journal d'ouvriers*, p. 137.

minority, moreover, not only because it represented a small section of the work-force, but also and more importantly because even *within* that section there had been frequently articulated preferences for the 'non-autonomous' road. The Second Empire, as we shall see, served the autonomists well enough. But for the others, it represented a generation of hiatus during which the relationship between economically conditioned hopes and politically attainable ends had radically to be recast.

The importance of this break makes the overthrow of the Second Republic a useful vantage point from which to offer an interim response to one of my initial questions: was marxist socialism weak in France, and why? There are wider issues at stake here, and they are discussed later. Here it is pertinent to make one or two observations.

The first is that nothing in the French circumstances *before* 1848 precluded the successful application of marxist categories to the local labour movement. If anything, the opposite is true, which is no surprise when we recall how much Marx himself relied on France for his contemporary political writings. The idea that a totally depressed class, with no experience of possession, might generalize its experience and demand community of goods was a perfectly plausible way of describing the feelings of a majority of the French work-force in the July Monarchy. It even speaks to the attitude of that minority which *did* have experience of possession, at least until 1848. There was no more reason in France than in Germany or Britain why the experience of labour need have rendered it refractory to the political message of marxist socialism.

That this was indeed so may be seen in the character of the socialist movement in these years, polemically dubbed 'utopian' by Engels in a later decade. From the St Simonian emphasis upon the 'essentially' material origins of social conditions, through the determinist economic perspectives of Blanc and his circle, to a woman like Jeanne Derouin who confessed to having appreciated as early as 1831 people's capacity to mislead themselves as to their 'true' interests, there were many indications that the fundamental articles of faith, and the grounds on which they were held, had more than a passing resemblance to the style of argument and critique associated with Marx in those years. This was also true of contemporary historiographical fashion, where the primary themes of a positivist and materially grounded theory of history were laid down well before 1848. The popular histories of the period laid particular emphasis upon just that historicist reading of the

French Revolution which was and has remained the linchpin of marxist history from the Manifesto to the present. When Louis Blanc wrote that the extreme left of the 1790s 'ne périrent à la tâche que parce qu'ils etaient venus trop tôt', he was not merely explaining the failures of his audiences' grandparents, nor proposing a manifesto for future action. He was also mapping out a *way* of seeing their place in the scheme of things which became very much a part of popular discourse in the 1840s. And, of course, he was saying the same things as the Marx of his generation and the marxists of a generation to come.[126]

Louis Blanc might be thought a rather unusual instance (though his work was widely read and his ideas readily assimilated into popular nostrums). But he was not alone. In his *Devoir des Révolutionnaires* (1840), Henri Celliez wrote the following:

La Révolution n'est jamais fini—chaque génération a dans l'œuvre révolution-naire une tâche déterminée et circonscrite à remplir. (Depuis 1830) . . . la Bourgeoisie,maîtresse de la société, a pu contenir son expérience politique. Et pour n'en point être détournée, elle a toujours arreté l'expansion des idées révolutionnaires.[127]

Even a rudimentary theory of ideological hegemony can be identified in the worker press—witness this example, from a piece by a weaver written in 1840: '. . . tout en nous menaçant, on a peur de nous. Aussi, pour nous captiver, on tâche de faire naître en nous des considérations qui nous enchaînent.'[128]

Further examples would be otiose, though they could be multiplied infinitely. The point is not to propose that in some absurdly anachronistic sense the French socialists and their working-class supporters were 'marxists'. It is to suggest that the peculiarly utopian emphasis upon 'fraternity' of which Marx was so scornful hides from the historian's eye the wider intellectual context in which socialism was being forged. What distinguishes marxism as it came later to be

---

[126] Louis Blanc, *Organisation du travail*, p. 13. Jeanne Derouin is quoted by Rancière in *La Nuit des prolétaires*, p. 119.

[127] Henri Celliez, *Devoir des Révolutionnaires*.

[128] Ch. Noiret, *Aux Travailleurs*, quoted in Faure et Rancière, op. cit., p. 106. Note, too, Théophile Thore, *La Vérité sur le Parti Démocratique* (Bruxelles, 1840), on what divides contemporary Communists: [p. 28] 'Il y a parmi eux deux groupes bien distincts: ceux qui sont fermes révolutionnaires en vue de leur théorie communiste; et ceux qui, préoccupés exclusivement de la doctrine, négligent ou nient le sentiment révolutionnaire.' During debates held in the summer of 1841 between the journals *L'Humanitaire*, *Le Travail*, and *L'Atelier*, *L'Humanitaire* especially chose to emphasize its rational, non-religious, 'scientific' approach.

recognized was important with respect to the intellectual history of socialist thought. But it is secondary when compared to the common ground on which 'utopian' socialism and marxism alike were being constructed. And such first-order differences as there were between marxism and popular French socialism were not important at the time. For example, the *Atelier* group had an under-consumptionist argument at the heart of their attack on *laissez-faire* capitalism. This was not at all the same as the altogether more complex economic analysis with which Marx would later be associated. The underlying moral problematic was similar, however, and in the eye of the labouring beholders the differences hard to distinguish.

In sum, there was nothing about the specifically French socialism which precluded it a priori from sharing in the more superficial (and thus politically marketable) sort of marxism which emerged as the dominant strand in European socialism after 1880. Nor, indeed even less so, was there anything about the local market for socialist ideas which suggests that marxism would have had a reception less friendly than that accorded to socialist thought in general. The *de facto* premises of a popular marxism were *already* the common verbal currency of socialist and worker parlance in mid-century France. Taking one's starting-point in, say, June 1848, one would have little ground for supposing that the history of marxist socialism in France would *necessarily* develop very differently from elsewhere. And if the industrial sociology of France threatened to produce a labour movement divided between skilled and unskilled workers, with radical implications for a socialist theory predicated upon assumptions regarding their unity, then this was at least as true for any other country one cared to name.

If we are to accept that political marxism in France *did* eventually undergo an etiolating experience peculiar to that country, it follows from the story so far that we cannot attribute this to the 'nature' of French socialism, or the 'peculiarities' of French industrialization, without doing violence both to the course of French history in the first half of the nineteenth century *and*, in some measure, to marxism itself. The latter, after all, provides us with no analytical criteria for excluding France from the range of nations of which much might have been expected. We are thus forced to conclude that something of considerable significance for labour history in France must have taken place at some point between the class struggles of 1848 and the emergence of the labour movement in recognizably modern garb after

1880. That 'something' was the Second Empire, to which we now turn.

*

The significance of the Second Empire in the making of the French working class movement is consistently underestimated, yet it was unequalled in importance. Where in 1848 the old labour organizations and socialist groups were still recognizably heir to a half-century of mobilization and self-education, with 1848 itself providing the impetus for a qualitative leap in political consciousness, the movements which surfaced in the 1880s were altogether different. After the Empire, not only was the dominant strand in working-class sentiment recognizably 'syndicalist', but socialism too was henceforth divided into two general schools of thought soon to be seen as, broadly, marxist and 'reformist'. Neither in the case of nascent syndicalism nor in that of the post–1880 socialist divisions can the lines of cleavage or their determinants be traced smoothly back to 1848 and beyond.

The role played in this by the government and laws of the Second Empire was crucial. Building upon massive popular disillusion with the Republic in its declining months, the Imperial government forbade, for many years, all overt displays of opposition opinion and labour organization. But at the same time it held out the promise of the rudiments of a providential state, and from 1860 came progressively to allow and even encourage a very limited and exclusively economic self-organization of workers. As a result it gave sustenance and justification to what had hitherto been a minority strand among the labour movement, the belief that the autonomous organization of work *at* the workplace might become an end in itself, rather than the means to some more ambitious objective. The emergence of such a view had very little to do with struggling or even successful artisans *opting* for the archaic preferences of their corporate heritage; it was just that this sort of workers' activity and vocabulary was permitted—and this alone.

Thus whereas the artisan press of 1848 had occasionally been critical of someone like Proudhon for his insistence upon reducing the 'Revolution' to a problem of circulation and distribution, this was precisely what talking about politics *was* reduced to in the early Second Empire. Ironically (in view of the later importance of Proudhon's ideas for anarchist thinkers), the Imperial elevation of the powers of the state and the executive assisted in the popularization of Proudhonism at this time: if the state *could* no longer be captured, there was even less reason to waste time discussing how to seize it. But it could *serve* the workers' interests notwithstanding, either in specific legislative acts, or merely by holding the ring while the avowedly non-political labour organizations beavered away at the economic foundations of capitalism in their own lives.[129]

The social legislation of the Empire certainly confirmed this diagnosis. Two examples will serve, because they illustrate the point from opposite angles. On 22 June 1854, the workers' *livret* ceased to be a basis for patronal control and retribution (so that factory owners could no longer refuse to release it—and thus enable the worker to find alternative employment—until all debts were met, etc.). It became instead a purely police tool, a means of exercising political surveillance over the dangerous classes. Ten years later, on 25 May 1864, the law against coalitions was revoked. Workers' organizations as such ceased to be a crime—instead the law was restricted to the punishment of any 'atteinte à la liberté du travail'. What both these laws, the one restrictive the other notionally permissive, sought to achieve was the removal, so far as practicable, of government and legislative oversight of economic conflicts. This was less from any abstract preference for the minimal state (!) or for the market mechanism, but rather the result of a distaste on the part of executive and chamber alike for the need to make policy and write laws for the complicated and fluid problems of wage-rates, hours, and conditions of work. The risks of open, collective action were less than those of the political unpopularity such interference might court.

This approach was not an unmitigated success—witness the surge of opposition in the last three years of Louis Napoléon's reign. The appeal of political republicanism did not go unheard. But now more than ever it was losing its idealistic sheen—for most working-class activists republicanism was only the expression of the obvious: if you wished to work for a better society and to convince others of the need to do so, only a republic could offer the minimal institutional framework for such activity. But even this restricted appeal would not always find an audience: revolutionary socialists and anti-political workers alike remembered all too well the republicans' failure in 1848.

It was thus from 1851 that the experience of the French labour movement took on certain peculiar characteristics. Where the decline

---

[129] See Faure and Rancière, op. cit., e.g. p. 379; on the general impact of the experience of the Second Republic upon the working population in Paris, see Gossez, op. cit., p. 31.

of Chartism in Britain might be attributed to the steady advance of liberalism and the diminished rationale in radical rhetoric for attacks on the repressive state, no such observation applied to France. Where Britain and British capitalism advanced in unsteady but recognizable symbiosis with political reform and a modicum of social legislation, the French experienced a searing tear in the 'logic' of change: with manhood suffrage and economic development there came—a *return* to the oppressive state. If the British and German labour movements responded to the defeats of 1848 by beginning a process of structural, if not semantic, integration, the French experienced a twenty-year gap during which, in effect, they *could* not respond. By the time the French Left re-emerged as an unrestricted participant in bourgeois politics, it had a very different account to offer of the prospects for integration and improvement. And given its particular experience, it had good rational grounds for such an account.

The nature of economic change in the years 1850–70 favoured the emergence of two sorts of collective action by the working population: the development of the associational traditions of the mutual-aid societies and workers' co-operatives on the one hand, collective economic protest (strikes) on the other. This was because the combination of rapid industralization and the flowering of the skilled sector provided sometimes contradictory stimulants. Thus while the number of establishments employing steam power rose more than threefold during the two decades, and numbers employed on the railways rose from 31,693 to 138,213, an artisan élite in both production and commerce was reconstructing itself, especially in politically sensitive Paris.[130] For the former, the withdrawal of labour (and a direct appeal to the government) was the only effective way of drawing attention to their demands, both before and (especially) after the rescinding of the ban on coalitions. For the latter, this was a time of organizational opportunity and professional vulnerability alike.

Most of the associations which flourished under the Emperor's approving eye were composed of skilled workers (whether in small workshops or the craft sections of industries like shipbuilding and construction). There were, first, the old mutual-aid societies: in 1851 these numbered just 2,737, but by 1869 there were over 6,180 of them, with a membership which had grown from 255,000 to 794,000. They were joined by a growing number of worker' credit and savings

---

[130] See Georges Duveau, *La Vie ouvrière en France sous le Second Empire* (Paris, 1946), p. 105; Codaccioni, *De l'inégalité sociale*, p. 128; Gaillard, *Paris la Ville*, pp. 404–11.

societies, whose function was more directly economic and which lacked the benevolent society overtones of the older *mutuels*. The point of the credit associations was only partly to provide a savings bank for individuals. The other call upon their resources and services came from the predominant form of skilled-worker organization in these years, the co-operatives.[131]

The *association de production*, or *atelier coopératif*, or *syndicat coopératif* (the names signified subtle differences in function, rather than origin or membership) were the natural heir to the *associations ouvrières* of the 1840s. They were predictably concentrated in Paris, with only a few provincial strongholds, notably in the Rhône department. Most of those which were still going at the end of the Empire dated from the period 1855–66. Only 39 per cent of those in existence in 1869 had been founded before the 1851 coup. Moreover, what had begun as a tradition of collective production (the *atelier social* of the Luxemburg enthusiasts) was sliding unmistakably into consumption-oriented co-operation by the late 1860s. In a pamphlet of 1867 written for the co-operative movement, P. Malardier used the terms 'coopératif', 'mouvement coopératif' as synonymous with the collective concerns of his audience in those years: mutual credit funds, savings societies, producer and consumer co-operatives. Although there was still a number of genuine societies of producers in the highest skilled trades (such as jewellery-makers), with rules of behaviour and performance similar to those of contemporary factories, these were in a minority.[132]

Many of the members of these societies were also active in the Conseils des Prudhommes. From 1853 the latter, whose historical function was to arbitrate between master and employees in craft and workshop, were composed of 50 per cent patrons and 50 per cent representatives from wage-earners, foremen, and overseers. The minimum age for eligibility was thirty. They thus reinforced the social pattern of the skilled élite: male, stable, and, where possible, self-governing. The last was important—the Prudhommes helped reinforce the assumptions of certain artisan trades about the nature and limits of collective action. There was a markedly defensive air to the discussions in the associations and even more to the disputes which came to the Prudhommes. Printers, jewellery-makers, bronzesmiths, even drivers, were all worried about the wave of unskilled labourers arriving in the towns of mid-century France and offering their services

---

[131] Data on the *sociétés de secours mutuels* are from Bron, op. cit., pp. 181–3.
[132] See Levasseur, *Histoire des classes ouvrières*, vol. 2, p. 638.

at cheap and unprotected rates. The apprenticeship system was being replaced by the male (and, increasingly, female) labourer, who cost less, did not represent for the employer a long-term commitment and who could not resort to the collective support of an organization in case of dispute.[133]

The associations of skilled workers and their various activities thus came increasingly to represent a point of division rather than unity in the labour market. The promise they held out of a world of self-governing workshops was almost from its inception a veiled replica of the old demand for protection against competition, rather than an invocation to an egalitarian community of producers. They were certainly active enough in their *own* interest, and in the *Manifeste des Soixante* of 1864 they articulated a list of complaints and claims which succinctly expressed the concerns of their class.[134] What they could not do, and here the change from the 1840s is remarkable, was hold out the promise of leadership to the working community as a whole. Their 'syndicalism', as it was beginning to be called, was reactionary, in a literal sense.

It would be an oversimplification to say that the response of the industrial proletariat to this changing attitude on the part of their higher-paid peers was to turn to strikes as *their* method of organization and expression. Strikes were not uncommon in the skilled trades, and in any case we have seen that the distinction between skilled and unskilled was blurred in economic practice.[135] Textile workers, furthermore, had never looked to printers, for example, for advice or leadership even in the past. But the point contains an important truth: for those to whom savings societies or producer co-operatives, not to speak of self-governing industrial communities, were always at best a utopian ideal of emancipation, united mass action on the shop-floor was the *only* form of collective expression open in these years—and even then a strike was a risk in the period before 1864.

It is hard to be sure just how many strikes there were in the Second Empire, not least because until 1864 it depends upon inference from the number of prosecutions for *coalition*. The number of recorded

---

[133] Ibid., p. 786; Gaillard, op. cit., p. 404. On the Prud'hommes, see Duveau, op. cit., p. 15, and Edouard Dolléans, *Histoire du travail en France* (Paris, 1953), vol. 1., p. 257.

[134] Details of the Manifeste des Soixante can be found in Bron, op. cit., p. 185, and Levasseur, op. cit., vol. 2, p. 644.

[135] Thus a (skilled) bricklayer would employ by his side an (unskilled) bricklayer's labourer, both of them then subsumed into the general category of 'construction workers'.

strikes in that period varied from a high of 168 per year in 1855 to a low of 21 in 1864 (but the earlier record is inflated by a higher likelihood of prosecution). The five-year average for 1850–4 was 73 per annum, based on prosecutions, or just 10 if one relies on confirmed reports. For 1855–9 the average was 81 and then fell to 43 for the quinquennium preceding the change in the law. In the later years of the Empire data are more reliable, with the annual number of recorded strikes peaking at 116 in 1870. Of greater significance is the average number of recorded participants, which was already quite high (never less than 270 in the years after 1864) and rising sharply in the last months of the regime.[136]

These averages are a little misleading; the point about a strike in this period was that it served above all as the form of collective action of a particular working community. What mattered was whether a whole factory or network of shops struck, not just the absolute number of persons involved. In this respect, for example, a strike of 150 embroiderers in Alès in December 1858 was just as significant as that of the spinners of Vigan (also in the Gard), some 600 of whom struck in June 1853 and again in October of the following year (this is an interesting instance of the peculiar propensity of women in the proletarianized industries to express their demands through strike action: in the Gard, again, the spinners of Alès struck in October 1852 and July 1870, and at points in between, and they were emulated at various times by spinners in Uzès, St Ambroix, and Ganges, and lace-workers in Nîmes. At the end of the period, two-thirds of those arrested after strikes in the cotton mills of St Etienne de Rouvray in the Seine-Inférieure were women.)[137]

Strikes by unorganized workers, whether in old industries or among newly-arrived labourers, were sufficiently frequent to have acquired *de facto* legality in advance of the recognition of the right to unite for economic demands. It has been proposed that there was a detectable shift from the defensive focus of strikers' demands in the first half of the period to a more offensive focus after about 1860, but this is a little arbitrary[138] and misleading in that it encourages the drawing of a distinction of which contemporaries would have been unaware. The

---

[136] For details, see Edward Shorter and Charles Tilly, *Strikes in France 1830–1968* (Cambridge, 1974), Appendix B.

[137] Details on the Gard strikes are in Huard, op. cit., pp. 31, 157–9, also in F. L'Huillier, *La Lutte ouvrière à la fin du Second Empire* (Paris, 1957), pp. 25 ff. See also Claire Auzias and Annik Houel, *La Grève des ovalistes, Lyon juin–juillet 1869* (Paris, 1982). [138] Huard, op. cit., pp. 160 ff. argues this case.

four dominant themes in strikes were maintenance and increase of wages, limitation of work hours, workers' control of the insurance fund, and, especially, opposition to the introduction of piece-work. These were closely interwoven issues, and only the demand for supervision of the administration of funds drawn from workers' pay can be directly related to the questions of control and autonomy which had been the priorities of an earlier decade and which continued to be of significance chiefly for the higher-paid trades.

There certainly *was* variation in emphasis: where the Alès spinners in October 1852 struck *against* a reduction in their wages in the event of a shortened workday, the 1869 Loire strike of silk-working women, led by Marguerite Fabry, was over a demand *for* a reduction in hours (from 13 to 11) *and* a 20 centimes per day increase. But there was no secular pattern and the nature of strike demands varied not only with place and industry, but also according to the economic situation, to which textile workers in particular were highly sensitive. The pattern of miners' strikes was perhaps a little clearer, but this was because the battle over piece-work and piece-rates, a live and bitter issue in the 1852 Rive de Gier strike, for example, when the company tried to introduce piece-rates instead of the old day-rate, had been lost by the end of the Empire. In Carmaux too this was a major cause of conflict between 1857 and 1869, but by the beginning of the 1870s only the coal-haulers were still holding out. In the Le Creusot metalworkers, however, the workers were still fighting back on the piece-rate issue in the strikes of January 1870, and in general the idea of measuring income by performance was bitterly opposed wherever it was attempted (to the extent of provoking an unsuccessful forty-nine-day strike in the winter of 1866 in the mills of Lille).[139]

One theme in particular aroused considerable feeling, and may serve as a symbol for the essential differences between the syndicalism of the older trades and the more expansive and outward-looking concerns of the rest. This was the much-debated problem of women workers which, unlike the demands discussed above (whether 'offensive' or 'defensive') does bring out sharp and *new* divisions.

The 'problem' of the female labour force, as the subject rose to prominence at the end of the Empire, was essentially the problem of competition. As such, it was one instance of the general difficulty that

[139] See Huard, op. cit., p. 31; L'Huillier, op. cit., p. 25; Pétrus Faure, op. cit., p. 147; Rolande Trempé, *Les Mineurs de Carmaux 1848–1914*, 2 vols. (Paris, 1971), vol. 2, p. 236; Auzias and Houel, op. cit. *passim*.

the specialized occupations were facing in retaining the advantages of exclusivity. There were, of course, ancillary considerations in the case of women—the desire to see them at home rather than competing for work, the fear expressed by Fribourg of the First International in 1869 that women working destroyed the family and thus paved the way to 'Communism' (he was a Proudhonian)—these were in some measure the popular dimension of a general nineteenth-century response to the higher visibility of women. But economic considerations proper were undoubtedly uppermost in such men's minds. The *Manifeste des Soixante* pressed for the 'regulation' of women's work, explicitly locating it in that category of complaints which dealt with threats to wage-levels and qualifications in the organized occupations. The men of such trades—hatmakers, shoemakers, printers, master masons and others—feared competition above all; only a few of their leaders, such as Tolain, actually voiced objections *in principle* to women taking paid employment.[140] In the Enquiry of 1867 they were united in seeing no objection to women working at home, but complained of their growing presence in the workshops themselves.

From the point of view of the male *industrial* workers, on the other hand, the 'woman' problem was quite different. For them, the low wages paid to women were a threat, but a threat best resolved by the *upward* equalization of all wages. No one who worked in textiles, clothing, paper, packing, tobacco-processing, or, increasingly, chemicals, dyes, and the food industry could plausibly have talked of removing women from the work-force. Nor did they. The wages of both men and women in most of these industries were vital to the survival of the proletarian family. Even in the mines it was still not uncommon to find women (and of course children) employed in the pits, though at lower rates of pay; in Belgium and parts of the Pas de Calais the miners even insisted on the right to have work for their daughters in the mine. The exploitation of women workers was seen in these contexts not as a case for returning them to the home (where many of them already were, but as *travailleuses à domicile*, not housewives) but as the best argument for equal pay and for industrial organization.[141]

---

[140] For the views of Fribourg, see Alain Dalotel, Alain Faure and Jean-Claude Freiermuth, *Aux origines de la commune: le mouvement des réunions publiques à Paris 1868–1870* (Paris, 1980), p. 172; for the Manifeste des Soixante see sources cited in note 134; On the opinions of Tolain, see Gaillard, op. cit., p. 411.

[141] On the miners, see Trempé, op. cit., vol. 1, p. 133, and note 1.

This threat posed by cheap female labour to the working conditions of both sexes explains the frequency with which the problem was raised in public meetings when these were organized on a regular basis in Paris during the 'Liberal Empire' after 1868. The very earliest of these gatherings, which fed directly into the pre-Commune mobilization of the Parisian population, were devoted exclusively to 'Le Travail des femmes', and the average audience was at least 20 per cent women, in marked and telling contrast to the male-only membership of the trade associations and their co-operatives. Because it was at public meetings, rather than in the private and non-political societies, that socialism was again beginning openly to be discussed, we should not be surprised to find a few years later that it was socialists, not syndicalists, who took up the matter again, while syndicalists until 1913 retained a firmly exclusivist attitude towards the whole question of women, whether at work or in their movement.

The socialists who surfaced at these meetings were not a homogeneous group. To the extent that socialism had been co-opted in name at least by the Proudhonians who helped form the early branches of the AIT (Association Internationale des Travailleurs—First International) there was a sharp division between them and the 'politicals', who occasionally took to calling themselves 'Communist' to accentuate the difference (the woman question in the years 1868–70 was one of the variables in this difference). The general political indifference of the French branches of the AIT (there were about 3,000 members in 1869) was blamed by Marx, characteristically if inconsistently, on the nefarious influence of Proudhon. In fact it arose quite naturally both from French circumstance and from the fact that many of those who joined the AIT had as their ideological baggage very little to declare—they favoured workers' organization and 'fraternity' and opposed violent or 'premature' acts. Small wonder then that the AIT in France (as elsewhere but more so) wished to 'confine women in the family and holds them to be inferior to men', as one woman speaker put it in 1869. Support for the emancipation of women came from those concerned with the emancipation of industrial workers in general, and hence by-passed the AIT as well as the co-operatives. It was thus an issue which served as something of a lightning-conductor for the desire to build a broader and necessarily more political movement of protest.[142]

[142] On the AIT, see Bron, op. cit., p. 180; J.-B. Dumay, *Mémoires d'un militant ouvrier du Creusot (1841–1905)* (Grenoble, 1976), p. 140. On the significance of the issue of

The results of all this activity at the end of the Empire were minimal, although the political liberalization which made it possible was itself a response to industrial discontent on a wide scale. Strikes occasionally led to the organization of a *Chambre Syndicale*, with the strike committee transformed into a *de facto* meeting place for the planning of future demands. Strikes and meetings alike thus helped form a new generation of popular leaders, many of them to be prominent in the Paris Commune. There was also an immediate link between economic demands and popular leadership, in that it was a reiterated theme of workers' meetings that their *own* representatives should stand for elections (on municipal councils, for example). But until 1871, this was as far as agitation could go.

For industrial workers, the concern with being represented by one of their own was a new one. By 1871, it had ceased to be possible to distinguish between a refusal to be led by the spokesmen of the republican bourgeoisie and a distinctive, class-conscious anti-patronal sentiment. Indeed, it was one of the achievements of the Second Empire inadvertently to educate the French proletariat into the idea that these sentiments could be collapsed into a single political position. When the workers of Thann, in Alsace, declared that they would be voting 'yes' in the 1871 plebiscite, 'parce que les fabricants votent non', they were expressing the most important outcome of a generation in which popular mass action and organization had been forced by political repression away from the republican societies, clubs, and cafés, and into the factories themselves. And, of course, nothing could have been further from such an outcome than the contemporary battle cry of the co-operative artisans: 'Rien par l'Etat, tout par l'individu'.[143]

In the light of this, it was particularly ironic that it should have been the Parisian workers who bore the brunt of the repression which followed the defeat of the Commune, considering how much the latter represented the institutionalized preferences of the skilled minority. Yet, if one can speak of strategy in these things, those who bore the brunt of repression in Paris and elsewhere after 1871 were clearly chosen for the threat they had begun to pose in the last years of the Empire. There had been the unmistakable beginnings of a widespread

women workers, see Gaillard, op. cit. pp. 409 ff., and Dalotel *et al.*, op. cit., where they quote a certain 'femme Randier', speaking in 1868: 'L'Association internationale des travailleurs nous confine dans la famille et nous déclare inférieures à l'homme . . . on veut transformer la femme en femme mécanique.' (p. 170.)

[143] See L'Huillier, op. cit., p. 62. The quotation is from P. Malardier, *Aux Ouvriers: la Coopération et la Politique* (Paris, 1867), epigraph.

popular socialism, with people like Paule Minck travelling the land and addressing large audiences on themes of press freedom, the workers' right to form unions, women's emancipation, and the abolition of property. What held these and other demands together was a newly-militant worker politics, the socialism of the barricades but divorced from either the radicals of earlier street battles ('ces vieux floueurs de la révolution' as one Blanquist called them) or the socialism of the workshop. And there was no question but that a distinctly class-oriented vocabulary had flowered in the industrial cities in the last years of the Imperial government. The latter having created a proletarian movement, it fell to the Republicans to repress it.[144]

This makes more sense when we appreciate that the people who dominated Parisian popular argument did not always represent the country as a whole. It used to be asked why the Paris Commune did not arouse a larger sympathetic echo in provincial France, with only spasmodic and forlorn efforts at communes in Lyons, Narbonne, Marseilles and Nantes, and nothing at all in the industrial north and east. One answer is that what the Commune spoke to were the municipal and professional concerns of a restricted class, especially concentrated in Paris, only occasionally prominent in the economy of provincial towns and absent from the new industrial conurbations. As a proud outburst of mutualist corporate sentiment it could still arouse echoes in popular memory, and in any case much of the Commune's legislation was of immediate benefit to a larger constituency. But it pointed in the direction of a municipal socialism and syndicalism which would oppose the state by ignoring it, and this limited its appeal. The Commune must thus be seen as the logical outcome of one strand of the bifurcated popular movement as it emerged from the Imperial

---

[144] The change in the later years of the Empire is worth emphasizing. Contrast, for example, the sociology of happiness underpinning a report from one of the workers' delegates to the 1861 London exhibition with a speech delivered by a worker in Belleville in 1869:

Par les associations, toutes les découvertes faites par le génie du travail, mises au profit des associations, seraient autant de sources fécondes pour la propriété publique . . . Les associations ne pouvant exister que sur des rapports fraternels, elles détruiraient bien vite les mauvaises passions engendrées par la misère . . . (1861).

La bourgeoisie est l'ennemi la plus dangereuse de la classe ouvrière . . . Qui est-ce qui produit le capital? C'est le peuple travailleur. Qui est-ce qui fait progresser? Toujours le peuple travailleur. Pourquoi et comment se fait-il que le peuple travailleur ne possède rien? . . . Puisque le capital, le progrès et la propriété sont des productions du travailleur, et bien! c'est notre propriété (1869).

Quoted in Levasseur, op. cit., vol. 2, pp. 627 n. 1, and p. 629.

shadow. This fact is blurred by the violence and the rhetoric which surround the story of the Commune and which were not at all part of the political aspirations and tactics of the majority of its leadership. And any accurate account of the true historical place of the Commune is further exposed to the need to remember the altogether unpredicted consequences of its rise and, especially, its fall.

However, that was the future. Placing the Commune back into the experience of the Empire offers us a vantage point from which to summarize the latter. In economic terms, the two decades of Empire were certainly vital for the development of an economic and urban infrastructure, and the clear emergence of modern commerce and industry on an unprecedented scale. But at the same time, small-scale operations also flourished, sometimes as never before. Accordingly, the Second Empire witnessed *both* the birth of an industrial proletariat *and* the last generation of a widespread and self-confident *artisanat*. This in itself was not so vital for French labour history. What was important was how these two parts of the labouring population were organized, and the central point is that they were organized for different ends and in very different ways. This marked a shift from both the social facts and the elective rhetoric of the 1840s (by 1869 few artisans would voluntarily have applied to themselves the sobriquet 'proletarian'), and was a product of the political circumstances and restrictions of the period.

It was the political character of the Empire which thus conditioned the divisions of the French labour movement. The organizations of skilled workers retreated into what one might in shorthand call 'Proudhonism', although the socialist connotations would not at the time have been acceptable to all. The industrial workers, with no obvious doctrine of their own, and unable until 1868 to meet and discuss openly, formed their demands and identity around economic action, primarily the strike. But this was a product of circumstance, and by the end of the Empire this economic focus was emerging as the basis for much wider claims against both the state and the ruling (capitalist) class, whereas for co-operatives and benefit societies economic concerns, however articulated, were becoming the very goals of collective action.

The divisions within socialism in part reflected the schism in the labour movement. The socialism of the 1840s did not simply disappear. But it could not function openly during most of the Empire, and was thus overshadowed by the 'trade socialism' of the workers' spokesmen in the International and in Parisian debates. The latter continued to emphasize the passive themes of an earlier generation of socialist thinkers—collective solidarity, class independence, a rudimentary theory of labour value as the source of exploitation—but these were now firmly attached to the disillusion born of the Second Republic and an apoliticism transformed from necessity into virtue by the political vacuum of the Empire. The two approaches to socialism shared, of course, a suspicion of the republicanism of the bourgeoisie, and spoke the same language of class and rights. They even conflated momentarily in the confused enthusiasm of the Commune. But they were fundamentally at odds over the problem of revolution—*how* to bring about a better society—and over what to do with the state, both before and after such a revolution. It is not very helpful to call the one utopian and the other Jacobin, or Blanquist; the former implies a Kantian moral idealism which one finds in every expression of socialist politics, while terms such as Jacobin or Blanquist suggest an obsession with power and action and control of the state as ends in themselves, a perspective not at all that of socialist activists like Minck. Like labour, socialism in France was divided, weakened, and altered by the experience of the Empire, but both sides of the division were recognizably heir to a common base.

The years 1851–70 thus gave the French Left, on the eve of the Third Republic, an inheritance unique to France. Because it was the formative moment for working class and socialism alike, the fact that the Empire both created a political hiatus and then ended in bloody conflict became the determining element in French labour history. The French never experienced that political liberalization which so confounded observers and protagonists after 1848 in other countries. Labour and socialism were divided both internally and from one another on the problem of how to respond to social change in the circumstances of a semi-benevolent dictatorship, and they would then be further divided on the lessons to be drawn from the effort in 1871 to overthow that state. On one thing, perhaps, there was agreement: that the political power which accompanied the rise of a capitalist bourgeoisie would *always* be used at the expense of the working population. For various reasons, this lesson proved difficult to convey in Britain, Germany, or the USA. In France, the evidence was not readily refuted. Accordingly the Empire may be credited with having forged that very special sense of internal exile, of deep class resentment combined with political frustration, which has ever since characterized the French working-class movement, even in its rare moments of optimism. Because a vigorous repression was pursued into the first decade of the Republic, and because the term 'republic' was anyway associated for many with the 'treason' of 1848, a liberal alliance of workers and radicals could not be forged. Workers and socialists were republicans, of course, but precisely because that went without saying it did not say very much.[145] Indeed, just as the mid-century saw the labour movement forced to define itself against the conditions of the Second Empire, so the post-Imperial generation of socialists and labour leaders had to define themselves both against one another (the heritage of the 1860s) *and* against the conservative Republic which ensued.

*

The decade which followed the defeat of the Commune saw the formal cementing of these divisions. Even if the most obvious lesson of the Commune's defeat had not been that violent confrontation with the state was no longer a serious option, the very effective repression of the next few years would have established the point beyond doubt. Even in the provinces, where the destruction wreaked upon the workers' organizations was not so extreme, very little survived the first half of the 1870s. The co-operative societies foundered in the onset of the depression, and only a handful of autonomous craft workshops, mostly in the luxury trades, were still intact as collective undertakings by 1875. What did endure, though in an uncertain semi-legal zone of tacit government approval, were the *Chambres Syndicales* of the provincial towns, strictly limited to their residual function as mutual-aid societies, with the ancillary ambition of regulating job placement where this was permitted them.

With the victories of the Republicans in 1875–7, and the definitive establishment of the new regime, the government began to look more favourably upon such activities, though still not according them formal status. Workers' delegations were allowed to attend a Universal Exhibition in Vienna in 1874, and again in Philadelphia in 1876, and in that year a national workers' Congress was held in Paris, composed strictly of approved delegates from the *Chambres Syndicales*. The Congress of 1876 was notably restrained in tone, even to the extent of decorating its rostrum with a bust of Marianne, shorn of her insurgent

---

[145] Trempé, for example, notes how short-lived was the 'phase républicaine des mineurs' (op. cit., vol. 2, p. 861).

cap and decorated instead with a star on her forehead. As for its demands, these were confined to a request for parliamentary legislation to allow the unrestricted growth of *Chambres Syndicales*, and a symptomatic enthusiasm for the encouragement of a renaissance in the co-operative movement.[146]

Even these two undemanding claims upon the attention of the world illustrated the resurfacing of the fundamental division of concerns within French labour. This became clearer still in the congresses held in 1878 and 1879. In the latter instance, the audience at Marseilles were treated to a much more overtly political case for working-class organization, and they voted in favour of the principle of a 'federation of socialist workers' to press for the legislation they sought. A large minority, however, continued to prefer an emphasis upon workers' associations based in industry and concerned primarily with conditions of work, and in the following year, at a Congress held in Le Havre, the latter, now dubbed 'moderates', broke away. Two years later the original majority subdivided over the issue of political strategy—the 'revolutionary' or the 'possibilist' option—and the divisions within the French Left were consummated for a generation.

The erstwhile moderates, known increasingly as syndicalists because of their preference for industrial over political organization, were themselves split over strategic issues. The tradition of *Chambres Syndicales* provided two alternative paths: locally organized 'horizontal' *Bourses du Travail* (with their origins in the earlier associations of the same name in the Second Republic), or vertically structured industrial federations. The former were usually favoured by craft trades and artisan militants, the latter by spokesmen for the factory workers, but the line was not rigid. When the two sides merged in 1895 to form a single Confédération Genérale du Travail, the industrial unions got their way—a fact somewhat obscured by the continuing predominance of advocates of *Bourses* in the leadership of the new confederation. The habit of referring to the ideas of the workers' leaders as 'revolutionary syndicalism' derived from this rather unwieldy conflation of craft union concerns and industrial labourers' organizational clout.

This point is worth emphasizing, since there was nothing in itself new or radical in the syndicalists' demands for freedom from political control, and the right to concern themselves exclusively with organizing a

---

[146] On the bust of Marianne, see Agulhon, *Marianne into Battle: Republican imagery and symbolism in France, 1789–1880* (Cambridge, 1981), p. 177. Three years later, at the 1879 Congress in Marseilles, Marianne was still there, but this time with a red cap!

labour movement to remake society from below by economic means. The difference lay in the scale of the movement and the freedom (after 1884) to organize openly. The depth of the gulf separating socialism from syndicalism was itself as much the product of personal and organizational antagonisms as of ideological disagreements, and would have mattered less had the numbers involved not become so large. The size of the labour movement in France after 1880 is normally measured by reference to the trade unions of Germany or Britain, against which it is small indeed. But it is more relevant to note that compared with French labour activity *before* 1880, unions such as those of the miners of the Pas de Calais (35,000 members by the end of the 1890s), or the Syndicat national des Travailleurs du Chemin der Fer (founded in 1890 and with over 42,000 members by the end of the decade) were very substantial indeed. Even the Paris-based Fédération des Travailleurs du Livre (printing workers), a rather conservative craft trade with 168 distinct local sub-unions, had 10,783 members by 1900.[147] The militancy of these and other unions was guaranteed by the continuing restrictions on collective action in France, with only the powerful mining federation based in Lens (Nord) able to force the granting of collective contracts (in 1891).

The formal divisions between syndicalists and socialists, and within each movement, did not actually last very long. 'Revolutionary' syndicalism had hardly united into a single body, in 1895, before it was on the decline. Abortive attempts at mass strikes culminated in a *de facto* recognition after 1906 that even purely economic action against the state was not going to succeed, and all that remained was the residual distaste for parliamentary socialism, given voice in the Charter of Amiens, published in the very year (1906) that its strategy was shown to be hopeless. Whatever remaining rationale there was for division was removed by the coming of war, when the ideological and structural foundations of both movements were destroyed and redrafted in altogether new circumstances.

The 'peculiar institutions' of French labour thus lasted for one generation at best. But it is none the less true that this generation has coloured both the political and the historical understanding of the subject ever since. I have tried to show how those divisions came into being, and why they emerged with such particular emphasis in the first years of the Third Republic. It remains now to return to the questions

---

[147] See M. Bourguin, *Les Systèmes socialistes*, Annexe VII.

posed at the outset and to see how far the account offered here
provides a basis from which to propose plausible answers.

*

The characteristic concerns of students of the French labour
movement can be collapsed into two sorts of questions: why has it
shown such a propensity for division, and why (in so far as this is not
just an inevitable outcome of division) has it been so unsuccessful in
moulding French society to its own ends? There is also a related but
distinct problem concerning the ideological identity of socialism in
France, and the hypothetical strength or weakness of the marxist strain
within it. This chapter is of course chiefly a discussion of the labour
movement proper, but it is inherent in the argument I am proposing
that the nature of French socialism is both dependent upon and
contributory to a proper understanding of how that labour movement
came into being.

Some 'explanations' are manifestly inadequate to the task. To say
that *ouvriérisme*, the rejection of leadership (or even members) from
outside the working class, was a widely-shared prejudice among
French workers, and that this limited the scope of mass action in a
society where political power and the reigning republican ideology
were in the hands of the middle class, is true but not very enlightening.
We have still to know why it *was* such a broadly accepted prejudice
within labour and socialist movements alike.

I have also noted that it is far from clear that there was any
distinction between marxism and an indigenously 'French' socialism.
That this is a rather odd account of the weaknesses of the Left can be
inferred from the ironic difference of opinion as to its significance.
While some have argued that marxism in France was so weak as to
inhibit an effective socialist organization and strategy of the kind
associated with the SPD, a case has also been made for the view that
French socialism was, on the contrary, a 'victim' of marxism, without
whose unwelcome but effective ideological attentions the indigenous
movement would have fared a lot better.[148] These positions stem from
the political stance of those who propose them, of course, but that in
itself is not grounds for ignoring them. They are both wrong because
they claim, incompatibly, to be correct on the basis of identical
evidence. It is the evidence itself which needs a second look.

---

[148] See e.g. *La Nef*, nos. 65–6 (1950), 'Le socialisme français victime du marxisme?'

Finally, one should note a third style of explanation which proposes the case that French labour became the unwilling battleground for a variety of essentially political doctrines, of whatever provenance, and that all of these were little more than shallow ideological glosses on what would otherwise have been the properly limited and interest-related concerns of real workers, concerns which were either ignored or misdirected into fruitless paths of revolutionary rhetoric (socialist or syndicalist), espoused by unrepresentative minorities and doomed, leaving the masses on whose behalf it was uttered leaderless and adrift in a hostile social environment. Even if the facts supported such a reading, we should still have to ask why such dead-end doctrines had so wide a circulation in *fin-de-siècle* France, and why the French labour movement was so uniquely masochistic as to organize itself behind them. Fortunately, we are spared the effort—the facts do not speak thus, and all that we can concede is that most French workers did not join these movements. We do not know what this means, taken in isolation, and we have no a priori grounds for inferring a distaste, or even a lack of sympathy for their ideas. Rather the contrary—revolutionary syndicalism and the various socialist schools certainly did speak accurately enough for the interests of the working population; they just did not offer any very realistic account of how to serve them. But that is a very different matter.

Of the more intrinsically plausible accounts offered, I have made frequent reference to that which emphasizes a deep and enduring division between the interests of artisans and skilled workers on one hand, factory proletarians on the other. Because the former imprinted their concerns on organized labour, because the French economy matured slowly enough for them to retain control, and because the mass of the working class could not recognize itself in a craft-based syndicalism, the labour movement, it is argued, remained divided and ineffectual.

One difficulty with this is that French economic history, as I have suggested, cannot provide the foundations for such an account. At no time between 1840 and the end of the century were the divisions of labour and skill sufficiently clear and steady for one to build upon them in this way. Even where a secular trend *can* be discerned, from craft worker decline to proletarianization and even de-industrialization with the rise of a tertiary sector, the rate of change, the degree to which it was experienced *as* change, varied enormously. As one writer has tersely observed:

Ce pouvait être un caractère permanent de la classe ouvrière que d'être toujours en formation, de présenter à chaque étape cet aspect d'un lieu de transit où l'œil se perd à vouloir distinguer le 'vrai' prolétaire de l'artisan attardé ou du tertiaire déqualifié.[149]

Yves Lequin makes the same point for the working population of the Lyonnais in the last third of the century.[150] Even if it could be shown that there was a tidy correlation between certain industrial activities and a particular style of organization and opinion, it would remain to show why the organizations and the opinions proved so durable even as the participants varied in every possible respect. It would be infinitely depressing to learn that people's elective social preferences could be calibrated from the shape of the tool they wielded and the time it took them to perfect its use. Fortunately, this is not what French labour history teaches.

A second difficulty is more subtle. No one denies that there were such people as artisans and proletarians, and that the world was a very different place according to which group you were in. Why should we not assume, then, that the ways in which they set about improving or protecting their condition might vary with the group in question? In theory one could sustain such a view, while agreeing that the general character of the opinions of the protagonists might vary with circumstances and not be subject to iron laws of occupational determinism. But the trouble is that artisans were frequently encountered in the political movements of socialist workers, and textile-working women might be prominent in syndicalist-led strikes. And it was common to find artisans, loosely defined, active in the industrial unions on behalf of the apparently conflicting interests of the proletarian masses who threatened their livelihood and status.

There is a tendency to explain this sort of solidarity as a function of the weakness of the unskilled, whose 'industrial work structure put serious obstacles in the way of worker organization'. Hence they turned to artisan workers, who, 'because of their artisanal work structure were able to develop a militant trade union movement'.[151] Yet why should we discount the possibility that there was a shared community of ideas, even of ideals, which transcended the conditions of the workplace? Why, indeed, are we mesmerized by the distinctly nineteenth-century idea that consciousness is a function of labour and circumscribed by that labour? Why, for example, should one believe

---

[149] Rancière, *La Nuit des prolétaires*, p. 40.   [150] Lequin, op. cit., p. 158.
[151] Hanagan, *Logic of Solidarity*, p. 89.

that women textile workers 'had little long-term commitment to the industry because they had no expectation of remaining at work for more than five or six years' (I pass over the factual inaccuracy)? These arguments are rendered unnecessarily complex and unwieldy by a concern to derive action and attitudes from economic circumstance alone. When textile workers strike, for example (if they are women), one is driven to construct elaborate rationales deriving from a presumed emotional atavism, or familial priorities spilling into the street, all because an alternative account of human behaviour—that people act out of moral or political preferences of a broader kind—has been dismissed *ab initio*.[152]

There were, after all, places other than factory or workshop in which to acquire views and learn to assert them. If anything, the routes by which the ideas associated with nineteenth-century labour reached their audience had very little to do with a workshop or skill, however much the ideas themselves spoke to the interests of the latter. This was true for all kinds of worker, but especially the case for those prevented from acting *en masse* in their occupational capacity. For them, politics was not just a way of expressing a preference, but represented an alternative form of united action. The workers in the ironworks at Rosières (Cher), whose *patron* in 1878 still forbade them control of the mutual fund, and who comprised highly-skilled workers and part-time migrant labourers alike, struck in May 1892 for a wage increase and a variety of 'old' and 'new' demands and complaints. Their first act was to telegraph the nearest socialist *député*, Eugene Baudin, and ask him to come down and 'guider le mouvement'. Six years later, at a socialist electoral meeting in the nearby town of Lunéry, a mere 150 persons turned up. Only ten hands were raised in support of the Socialist candidate, and no one would come forward to form a *bureau de séance*. The police reporter and the historian alike could be forgiven for concluding that the workers in the arrondissement were 'refractaires aux doctrines socialistes'. Yet a few weeks later 61.4 per cent of the electors, including the overwhelming majority of forge-workers, voted Socialist at the first round of the election. The vote for a Socialist, like the request that a Socialist representative take the lead in a difficult strike, was the best available expression of unity and belief, by artisans and labourers alike, under adverse circumstances.[153]

An interesting gloss on the difficulty with mechanical and inflexible

[152] Ibid., p. 142.   [153] Pigenet, 'L'usine et le village', loc. cit., p. 50.

accounts of labour consciousness in this period is that it applies as much to marxisant accounts as it does to those of the neo-functionalist school. The emphasis on 'artisan consciousness' in French labour history is, after all, little more than an ecologically adjusted application of the theory of the labour aristocracy once so favoured by British labour historians. The only significant difference is that in Britain the labour aristocracy was thought to be on the rise after 1850, thereby accounting for the loss of militancy on the left, whereas in France it is the very longevity of an *older artisanat* which is adduced to explain the peculiarities (and thus the failures) of the French. Yet in both cases this has the rather odd consequence of emphasizing status and income (whether rising or falling), with the risk of hinting that revolutionary capacity and its attendant consciousness are dependent to some degree upon such variables. This may offer a bolt-hole for conscientious apologists of the official Left, but the same (marxist) theory which imposes the burden of providing such an escape valve is also, of course, the basis for dismissing precisely the sort of argument upon which the explanation rests.

The occupational taxonomy of French labour is not, then, sufficient to answer our questions, although it is necessary to our understanding of what would serve as a sufficient account. What of the argument which places the history of *socialism* at the centre of the history of labour? I have already suggested that the divided nature of the former cannot itself be treated as a fixed 'given'. Nor, clearly, will it do merely to assert that the inadequacies of French socialism deprived the working class movement of a leadership and direction vital to its success. This begs one question (why the inadequacies?) and prompts another. Such accounts presume a Leninist labour history, of the sort proposed by the Communists in 1920 when they offered to provide the missing leadership. History has so far failed to proffer any additional evidence in support of the theory underlying the claim.

Beyond doubt, the history of French labour is incomprehensible without some resort to the history of French socialism, because socialism *was* the organizational channel for many workers after 1880, whether as an electoral force or (in the north) as the mobilizing ideology of the major unions of the textile and metallurgical industries. Earlier still, the ideas of the socialists between 1830 and 1850 were also those of the nascent workers' movement. But when casting back from the last decades of the century to measure the impact of socialism upon the labour movement, one has to disentangle three separate hypotheses, all entangled in the 'problem' of marxism.

The first hypothesis is simply that the imposition of marxism, in its narrow Guesdist form, restricted the appeal of socialism to a wider audience. Certainly, the Parti Ouvrier Français was always a tiny organization, and even when it merged with other socialist parties to form the SFIO in 1905 the resulting party could boast just 90,000 members on the eve of the First World War. Yet the syndicalist movement (in 1911) had only 700,000 members, so that the relative size of the political movement was not notably diminutive. Moreover, 20 per cent of the Guesdist membership in 1900–2 worked in textiles, and a further 18 per cent in metallurgy and 8 per cent in mining, a respectable representation from just those industrial activities to which the party's restricted marxist appeal was best directed.

Whether the appeal of socialism would have been significantly wider within the working class had it not been couched in the particular and, it is suggested, culturally alien vocabulary of marxism, one cannot know. But the SFIO drew 1,400,000 votes in the last pre-war elections, and even allowing for its electoral strength in the centre and south it could not have done this had it not won over 20 per cent of the vote in the industrial Calaisis, over 30 per cent in the textile and mining cities of the Nord, and in the industrial suburbs of Paris. If marxism in France limited the organic appeal to workers of the socialist movement, these votes would surely have been hard to win. It might be argued, of course, that there was nothing very marxist about the socialism for which the Lens miners voted, just as it is sometimes said for the large rural socialist vote in the south. Perhaps. But in that case the argument for French labour's weakness as a result of the reduced appeal born of a foreign ideology also falls.

Another view proposes that it was the deep theoretical inadequacy of what passed for marxism in France that weakened the labour movement by depriving it of a cogent doctrine and a workable strategy. This is how Michèlle Perrot approaches the problem, remarking in particular upon the superficiality of the marxism of a Paul Lafargue, for example. There is a pedigree for such a view: Engels certainly had scant respect for the level of analytical argument of the French socialists (in Lafargue's case he had other, more personal, grounds for disapproval), and haughty dismissals of the French forays into theory were common currency in certain circles of the Second International.

But true or no, the criticism is off the point. It was precisely what passed for marxism in the writings of Lafargue or Guesde, for all its manifest limitations, that was so very familiar to French ears from the socialist writings of an earlier generation, just *because* these men incorporated all of that contradictory moral optimism and social positivism which was *the* characteristic tone of the older French socialism and against which Marx had inveighed so harshly. Nor, it might be added, did the SPD attain a trade-union membership of 4.5 million by 1912 because Karl Kautsky was a 'better' marxist than Jules Guesde . . .[154]

This then directs attention to the third hypothesis, that marxism, whether doctrinally sound or not, was of itself a force for division in the French labour movement. The only sense in which this could be true in the century before 1914 (it is of course valid for the period since 1920, in a very particular way) would be if one could first establish what it was that was thereby divided. Yet we have seen how the basic intellectual scaffolding of French socialism was shared by Marx himself: the invocation of the laws of history by a '48er in Nîmes in support of his argument that the monarchy had 'epuisé toutes les formes sous lesquelles elle pouvait vivre', the many speeches in 1868 and 1869 in favour of expropriating the means of production, even the St Simonian preference for big business over landed capital, all these were no doubt planted in shallow intellectual soil, but at the receiving end—as read and heard in club and society, on the street and in the factory—they must have been quite indistinguishable from the self-consciously marxist variations on similar themes a few years later.[155] Even genuine differences—as when a self-educated worker such as Dumay is unclear as to the differences between the 'collective ownership of the means of production' and the traditional demands for workers' control ('la mine aux mineurs')—are themselves evidence of the ease with which distinctions of this sort could be elided.

In one sense, a suitably simplified marxism actually sat rather more comfortably with the history of radical politics in France than did the so-called 'French' socialism. Writers such as Fourier or St Simon had been deeply disappointed by the experience and outcome of the

---

[154] For Perrot's opinions, see her review of Willard's book cited in note 8.

[155] See Raymond Huard, 'La genèse des partis politiques démocratiques modernes en France. Y-a-t-il une spécificité populaire?', in M. Dion *et al.*, *La Classe ouvrière française et la politique* (Paris, 1980), pp. 9–40; Levasseur, op. cit., vo. 2, pp. 649 ff.

Revolution, and in particular with the dictatorial and repressive instincts of the Jacobins and Babouvists, instincts well preserved in the writings and speeches of their heirs. This helps to explain the preference of the early socialists for an analysis which both displaced political conflict from the centre of the historical stage *and* made a plausible case for changing society, but in a different way. For some, though not all, of the 'utopian' socialists, it was always a matter of secondary importance whether the political regime was a monarchy, an Empire, or a republic, and became a matter of complete unconcern as a result of the actual experience of Empire in mid-century. In this context, the unambiguously *political* obsessions of all sorts of marxists and their supporters thus fitted rather better into older traditions of protest and action, while still maintaining that healthy distance from republicanism which was the common legacy of the years 1849–71. Far from dividing the French labour movement, marxism after 1880 offered it the nearest thing to a common, if ideologically flaccid, dogma.

We are brought back, it seems, from the inadequacies of French marxism to the complexities of the revolutionary tradition, and thence to an allied set of questions. To what extent was the French labour movement, in its organization, its aims, its 'style' so to put it, heir to the revolutionary tradition in France? And with what consequences?

There was, of course, no unambiguous, uncontentious 'revolutionary tradition'. On the one hand there was the revolutionary model, the partially articulated sense that power is and can only be transferred at a single moment in time, and by a highly ritualized process of collective action. There were some very mundane reasons for the appeal of such a model. The centralized nature of power in France, the social geography of Paris, the consequent vulnerability of the executive power to concerted popular disaffection and so forth. But the force of the image of revolution as inherited from the *journées* of the 1790s cannot be diminished—it explains, for example, the very centrality of the idea of revolution even in the writings of those for whom the past specifically did *not* constitute a blueprint for the future. To the degree to which the utopian socialists distanced themselves from all this, by rejecting violence or by proposing the establishment of distant ideal communities, they cut themselves off from their natural constituency. *Only* the repeated defeats of the 1830s and 1840s, together with total political repression under Louis Napoléon, capped by the worst defeat of all, could undermine the plausibility, the legitimacy of revolution as act, to be replaced by the popular adoption of the idea of revolution as process.

The second meaning of the revolutionary tradition was that of power, the theory of popular dictatorship initially associated with the Jacobins but translated via the writings of Buonarotti and Blanqui into the prelude to the construction of an egalitarian society of producers. Taken together with the claim that equality necessarily entailed common property, this became the basic political platform for every socialist activist in France, from Blanqui himself, through Minck and Guesde to the working-class militants in Jean Allemane's breakaway *ouvriériste* branch of the collectivist movement in the 1890s. Dictatorship was no mere option on the path to a better world, it was a *necessary* means to freedom for the lower classes. This idea was to gain currency in socialist and labour movements elsewhere in Europe, it is true, but nowhere else did it ring so true (again, in part, courtesy of Louis Napoléon and Thiers). There is a direct line of affiliation from the Committee of Public Safety to the working-class advocates of popular dictatorship in 1871, and from them to the agonized soul-searchings of Jaurès and (especially) Blum, instinctively opposed to the violent establishment of dictatorial power, but no less instinctively attuned to its resonances in the popular ear. In one sense, the anti-socialist syndicalists of the 1880s were less offended by the socialists' claim to lead the labour movement than by the suggestion that the latter might be led along a path of parliamentary compromise.[156]

The third aspect of the revolutionary inheritance is perhaps the one which most directly affected the course of labour history in France. This is what François Furet has called the 'imaginary discourse of power',[157] the Jacobin invocation of the 'people' in defence of their political strategy and dictatorial tactics. For the far left ever since 1790, the imagined unity of a hypostacized 'people' has repeatedly provided the incantatory justification for restrictive authority and undemocratic practices. In that year the Convention asserted that 'le Gouvernement de la révolution est le despotisme de la liberté contre la tyrannie', an ontological transposition of meaning taken still further by the Jacobin

---

[156] Thus Guérard, the railway workers' leader, opposing Jaurès in 1900 on the question of the desirability of obtaining a majority for social change: 'Toujours les majorités restent passives. Le problème consiste donc à constituer une minorité assez puissante pour mettre en échec la minorité dominante. C'est à construire cette minorité opposante que les syndicats s'emploient.' Quoted in Fruit, *Les Syndicats dans les chemins de fer en France*, p. 127.

[157] Furet, *Interpreting the French Revolution*.

club in the Year II, when it introduced the censorship of journalists' reports of its meetings. In reply to the forlorn objection that this was a return to the practices of the old regime, the club leaders replied 'qu'une censure jacobine n'en est plus une'. The people was virtuous, therefore its representatives were no less so. Virtue excludes sin, so there could be nothing wrong with censorship or dictatorship given only that it is exercised on the people's behalf. The people being one and indivisible, all objections to such practice must *ex hypothesi* denote an *interested* (reactionary) party.[158]

This remarkable 'catechism' entered the political consciousness of the left in nineteenth-century France as a particular form of the general proposition that individualism, the emphasis upon the interests and protection of the individual (a radical territory of earlier days) was of necessity the enemy of the common interest, which it fragmented and weakened. Socialism (or, sometimes, Communism) was proposed as the true protector of the individual. All that was needed was for the eighteenth-century *peuple*, social in its definition, to be replaced by the more economically precise *ouvrier* for the basis of modern socialist discourse to be laid. Henceforth it was the workers who had claims upon society and whose generalized common interest could stand bail for a multitude of political sins.[159]

The twentieth-century implications of this are self-evident. What is less commonly noted is the effect upon the labour movement at an earlier date. It was the authority conferred by the revolutionary memory upon this way of engaging opposition which accounts for a lot of the anti-parliamentarianism of French popular organizations, including the workers' societies and the early syndicalist movement. Moreover, from 1831 until 1877, with the brief exception of February–June 1848, the manner in which the heirs of Thermidor divided the spoils confirmed everything the Revolution seemed to teach. And so far as socialism appealed to this way of understanding the world, thus far could it plunge roots into the organizations of

[158] Ibid., p. 51; Maxime Leroy, op. cit., quoting the Convention for 13 November 1790 (p. 25 n. 1); Mona Ozouf on the Jacobins in Ozouf, 'Fortunes et infortunes d'un mot', *Le Débat*, no. 13 (juin 1981), p. 31.

[159] Sewell is quite right to emphasize this shift, but he is perhaps mistaken in supposing it a secular and single, unreversed process—the French Communists have oscillated between 'peuple', 'ouvrier', 'travailleur' in their appeal over the past two generations in accordance with circumstance and tactic. The eighteenth-century vocabulary has never disappeared, but has instead been accompanied and (usually) overlaid with the occupational categories of the nineteenth century. See Sewell, 'La Confraternité des prolétaires', in *Annales, ESC*, no. iv (juillet–août 1981).

workers. Where it tried to invoke the bourgeoisie's own ideal of a representative democracy it found a less sympathetic audience and was a force for division.

The *ouvriérisme* of French workers, then, was no accident, although circumstances reinforced its appeal over the course of the century. In a country where the state had always shown an alarming propensity to swallow up civil society, both before and after the Revolution, representative institutions were something of a minority taste, a political luxury. Ruling the state meant controlling the executive, in contrast with the experience of other countries where the eighteenth-century revolutions had been characterized by an alliance of people and nobility against the crown, with a consequent preference by radicals for the institutionalization of power in the legislature. French circumstances, in this respect more like those of a later period in eastern Europe, rendered implausible the Panglossian resort to a theory of the eventual harmony of interests; the only hope for the inherently antagonistic social forces was to struggle for the control of the whole, not the representation of a part. Hence the natural congruity between the direct democracy of the club or union and the focus upon control and direction of the state. Anything in between was built upon sand.

Hence, too, the much-remarked interest of French workers in state control and control of the state, even as they took for their own the Proudhonian preference for autonomy and self-direction. This concern with the executive power and an accompanying lack of interest in intermediary institutions did not leave its stamp only upon French labour—it was no less marked in the politics of the French lower middle class, notoriously socially 'protectionist'. The state returned the compliment faithfully, adjusting economic policy in matters like banking, tariffs, and conflict arbitration on primarily political considerations of stability and the threat of civil conflict. Even at the end of the century, when syndicalist leaders criticized miners for placing their faith in the benevolent neutrality of an interventionist government, the dispute hinged on the particular character of the state at that time; that the state *as such* was not a proper locus for the attentions of an insurgent labour movement was only ever the view of a small minority, and even then not a proposition of which their supporters were genuinely convinced. In 1900 as in 1848, the socialist and syndicalist press was always more likely to address its attacks to the factory *patronat*, rarely criticizing the prefect or the state for which he spoke.

In so far as this pattern varied, it was usually in those cases where state and *patronat* were one and the same; hence the distinctly revolutionary aura surrounding the actions of the miners, the railway workers and, for example, the state employees at the Arsenal in Toulon.[160] We have here the makings of the apparent paradox of the Left in France: that peculiar combination of social militancy and political weakness which arose from the very special circumstances in which the labour movement came to maturity. And it is of course the *combination*, and the circumstances of its emergence between 1850 and 1880, which are peculiar to France.

In other respects, however, much of French labour history was duplicated elsewhere. To take but one example, there was much that linked the radical movements of France, Spain, and Italy: their lack of a strong industrial labour movement, and the accompanying divisions within the socialist Left and between socialism and its constituency in the working-class community. Hence the frequency of comments about a division between a social democratic northern Europe and an 'anarcho-syndicalist' south. But this is to draw the wrong conclusion. Anarchism in Andalusia or Italy was a response to an imperial state with uncertain local roots, and was in any case partly a rural phenomenon; in France anarchism as such was weak, and syndicalism had little to do with mass movements of landless labourers. What *was* common was the distinctly autonomous political realm in these countries—in all three the labour movement had little choice but to define itself in direct relation to the governing power. Intermediary institutions were weak or scorned, though for locally variable reasons, and it was this shrivelled civil sector, rather than the level of industrialization, which distinguished north from south in nineteenth-century Europe.

To conclude, then, the French socialist movement was not at all 'un parti si différent des autres sections de l'Internationale Socialiste'.[161] It differed no more from the SPD than did the latter from the PSI or either from the British Labour Party. Its relations with labour were certainly no more strained than those which characterized the history of socialism and labour in Italy (or Britain, come to that). What was unique was the context in which it had to function, the fraught problem of operating within a parliamentary republic as a revolutionary

---

[160] On the significance of employment in an industry closely bound to the state by legal relations and governmental interest, see Trempé, op. cit., vol. 2, p. 826.

[161] Hugues Portelli, *Les Socialisme français tel qu'il est*, p. 29.

party, a republic which gave parliamentary socialism its *raison d'être* but which had only the most tenuous of holds upon the loyalty and imagination of the socialist movement's primary constituency. This, rather than the ideological rigidity of the one or the sociological peculiarity of the other, is what made France unique and the French labour movement so vulnerable.

*

I argued at the beginning of this chapter that one of the constraints upon the historiography of French labour was the extent to which it has been co-opted into the history of other matters. I hope it is now a little clearer why this has been so, and with what consequences. Both in the historiography of the French Revolution and in the study of modern French socialism, the course of labour's history has been largely determined by concerns parasitic upon its experience. It may thus not be inappropriate to end with an observation deriving from an inversion of these concerns.

I have argued that whatever general patterns may be glimpsed in the history of the nineteenth-century labour movement in France, these derive not from economic change nor from occupational variations, but from the opportunities and constraints born of political experience. This political experience owed its emergence in large measure to the French Revolution and its aftermath, so that labour history and the interpretation of the Revolution are necessarily related concerns. The same is true for the relationship between labour and socialism in modern France, and for much the same reason. And what holds all three in some sort of relation is the explanatory tension provided by marxist historiography or its paler derivatives.

Yet the irony of the history of the labour movement in France is precisely that it offers little aid or comfort to marxism as a social theory. If my account is even partially plausible, then the class consciousness of the labouring population as it emerged in the 1840s and developed over two generations, for all that it was indeed acute and took frequent political and even revolutionary form, owed virtually nothing to identifiable shifts in the nature or organization of production. To use the redundant vocabulary of an earlier generation of marxists, the consciousness of the French working class emerged out of encounters with the political superstructure, with the economic infrastructure quite absent from the equation.

There is a further point. The French labour movement failed to deliver the revolutionary goods. And this in a country well suited by history and circumstance to a testing of the hypothesis of class-based political revolution (or so Marx believed, paying French politics very special attention on at least three major occasions between 1848 and 1871). This is especially problematic in that two of Marx's major prognoses, regarding the development of capitalism and the emergence of a political labour consciousness, were correct in the French instance. What the history of French labour thus illustrates is that they were *not* related by any causally secure chain of circumstance. Or, put differently, Marx was largely correct in his reading of the history of government and the state in nineteenth-century France, seeing the state as sitting in a very determinate relationship to the interests of the ruling class, and the working population reacting accordingly. But the selfsame evidence from France which thus endorses Marx's political analyses also makes nonsense of his theory of history and revolutionary process. Flaubert was perhaps wrong to imagine that the working class aspires only to disappear. The true difficulty seems to be that it has no particular teleological aspirations at all.

In this light, then, the history of French labour is of interest to historians of the French Revolution largely in so far as it can counsel them against certain sorts of macro-social interpretations. But if one looks forward to this century, the picture is rather different. If the history of the labour movement in its early years will not bear the marxist account of itself, then it most assuredly is ill-adapted to the use to which it has been put by French politicians of the far Left, whose own legitimacy an alternative history casts in question. One can (people do) adduce a multitude of Ptolemaic addenda to account for the oddities of the trajectory of the French labour movement. My contention is that there was nothing odd about it, unless one is seeking to retrieve a normative hypothesis about What Labour Movements Do. The French Left, however, burdened with an interpretation of its own past bequeathed to it by political theory and historical practice alike, has spent the last hundred years with an uneasy conscience born of an awareness of the gap between what a proletariat 'should' achieve and what has actually been done. This is what lies behind the related survival of a Stalinist PCF and the unwillingness of the non-Communist Left to adopt the forms of social democracy.

There are thus good political, as well as academic, reasons to call for a demythologized history of French labour. This would help to return that history to its protagonists who have for a long time now been silent participants in a non-stop theoretical shell game. The difficulty is that the removal of accreted layers of understanding, interpretation, and assumption risks revealing an aesthetically unpleasing muddle. There is much to be done. Marxists and anti-marxists alike are going to have to abandon their anachronistic obsession with the workplace and the shop-floor, with everything described in terms of its effect upon or as the result of work relations or work-related attitudes. Perhaps some Ranke-like antidote to the hitherto prevailing obsession with interpretation would be temporarily appropriate. French labour has fought honourably on a number of historiographical battle fronts. It has served its time, from Marx to Mitterrand. It deserves a rest.

3

The French Socialist Party 1920–1936

THE eighteenth national Congress of the Parti Socialiste, Section Française de l'Internationale Ouvrière (SFIO), held at Tours in December 1920, ended in the definitive division of the French socialist movement. The majority voted to join the Third International and thereby gave birth to the French Communist Party. For the minority of socialists left in the old party, no less than for the newly formed Parti Communiste, the scission at Tours was the central reference point in the twentieth-century history of the Left in France, and so it is still. My concern in this chapter is to trace the impact of this split upon the post-Tours socialist movement, from 1920 to the eve of the Popular Front; however, in order to set in relief the consequences of the scission for the history of socialism in France it is necessary to remind ourselves of the characteristic features of the united socialist movement in the years before Tours.

The first point to recall, and it is something of a paradox, is that the experience of political unity among socialists in France was of very recent origin. It was only in 1905, and then only through pressure from an international socialist movement frustrated with the endless internecine bickering of competing French parties, that the two major movements within French socialism joined to form a single party. These two movements, the Parti Socialiste de France and the Parti Socialiste Français (dominated respectively by the personalities of Jules Guesde and Jean Jaurès) were themselves of recent vintage, formed from alliances of the older French socialist parties which had come together during (and in part because of) the Dreyfus affair and the attendant political crisis in France.[1]

The paradox lies in the fact that socialism in France may have found national political unity long after the appearance of strong socialist and

---

[1] Among the more useful general histories of French socialism to 1905 are the following: Georges Lefranc, *Le Mouvement socialiste sous la Troisième République*, vol. 1 (Paris, 1977); Claude Willard, *Le Mouvement socialiste en France (1893–1905): les guesdistes* (Paris, 1965); Madeleine Rebérioux, 'Le Socialisme français de 1871 à 1914', in Jacques Droz (ed.), *Histoire générale du socialisme*, vol. 2, (Paris, 1974).

workers' parties in other European countries (notably Belgium and Germany), but the history of the socialist idea in France, and of attempts to embody it in practice, went back a very long way. The problem of separating the collective social interest of the working population from the organizations and aspirations of the republican bourgeoisie was already old when it took the form of bloody conflict in June 1848. This, taken together with the shattering defeat of the 1871 Commune and the frustrations and divisions of the Imperial decades, helps to account both for the proliferation of parties and organizations in late nineteenth-century France, each with its own ideas on how to organize within and combat the republican state, and for their separate and collective weakness when compared with other member parties of the Second International.

When unity was finally achieved in 1905, then, it was a unity which of necessity papered over certain very severe doctrinal and tactical differences within the SFIO. This is not to say that unity was not taken seriously. Quite the reverse: precisely *because* the foundations of socialist unification were so shaky, there was a tendency to make a fetish of the principle of unity and to regard with horror any actions or pronouncements liable to threaten it. Hence the rather unwieldy and ineffectual socialist policies of the pre-war years and the importance of Jaurès, with his unequalled capacity to hold together conflicting wings of his party. Hence, too, the older socialists' fury at the Communists after Tours for destroying the precarious achievement of an earlier generation.

The internal differences of opinion with the pre-war SFIO fall broadly into three areas. The first of these concerned the attitude to be adopted towards the organs of government. A central issue in the years before 1905 had been the entry into government in 1899 of Alexandre Millerand, a close associate of Jaurès and until then a leader of the 'right' tendency in French socialism. Millerand's supporters held that in the absence of any imminent revolution it was incumbent upon socialists to work in all ways possible for the improvement of the condition of their social constituency in the present. Since socialists accepted the republican form of government and strove for election to parliament, refusal to participate as ministers in a left-leaning republican administration was illogical and self-defeating.

The opponents of Millerand argued that in accepting Waldeck-Rousseau's invitation to join his government, he had acted without consulting other socialists and as an individual parliamentarian. This, they insisted, threatened the unity and discipline of a socialist movement in parliament, without which it would be unable to keep its distance from other Left parties of a non-socialist character. Further-more, it was precisely *because* revolution was not on the agenda that it was vital to make a distinction between participation within the political system, which was a tactic born of necessity, and participation in government, which meant accepting the role of caretaker in a system whose overthrow was the object of all socialists, however moderate.

The result of the Millerand crisis,[2] which lingered on as a point of dispute well into the early twentieth century, was an unhappy compromise. Millerand's supporters, notably Jaurès, accepted the view of many, including the leading foreign parties in the Second International, that it was wiser to adopt a principle of no participation in government except under extraordinary circumstances (not specified). This retreat was made easier by Millerand's own sharp swing to the right and away from socialism after 1905. Conversely Guesde and other opponents of participation came to accept *de facto* recognition of the need to operate into the indefinite future in a parliamentary system and to build a party equipped to succeed in such a system.

The second area of division came ever more sharply into focus as Europe approached war. Here the lines were drawn somewhat differently. The long tradition and experience of Jacobin nationalism, reinforced by the memory of the Commune, meant that Guesde and many like him were militant in their view that socialists must be ready to fight in defence of the French Republic, for all that such a fight might not be one of their choosing. For them, republican achievements were the prospective inheritance of the workers, who must thus defend them when necessary. Others, among them Jaurès but also some of Guesde's own marxist supporters, regarded war as an evil under any circumstances. Jaurès himself came increasingly to the radical and in some ways more properly marxist view that the socialist movement should oppose any war brought about by and fought in the interest of competing capitalist powers. Although never taking what would become the Leninist line of revolutionary pacifism, a substantial

[2] On the Millerand crisis and its implications, see in addition to sources cited in note 1, Leslie Derfler, *Alexandre Millerand, the Socialist Years* (Paris, 1977); Jean-Jacques Fiechter, *Le Socialisme français: de l'affaire Dreyfus à la Grande Guerre* (Geneva, 1965), esp. pp. 60–76. On the response of the Second International, see Annie Kriegel, 'La IIe Internationale (1889–1914)', in Droz, op. cit.; James Joll, *The Second International* (London, 1955); a discussion of the problem of power for French socialists appears in Michelle Perrot and Annie Kriegel, *Le Socialisme français et le pouvoir* (Paris, 1966).

minority of French socialists in the years after about 1908 devoted much time and energy to opposing military expenditure, colonial engagements, and alliances. In this they were aided by a growing anti-militarism in the country as a whole from around 1911. However, because a small minority of the party was taking a *completely* pacifist line, opposing support for France in any war for any reason, the 'Jacobin' and 'anti-militarist' strains within the SFIO tended to seek middle ground, to avoid the political costs of an extreme position on a sensitive issue. Nevertheless, the divisions of feeling ran deep, and surfaced in acute form once the war had actually begun.[3]

The third major area of divided opinion concerned the proper form of relations between the SFIO and the French syndicalist or trade-union movement, and was thus a peculiarly French problem. Ever since the 1830s, the French labour movement had grown up largely independent of political affiliation, though often sharing the policies and programmes of political movements, first republican, later socialist. The experience of the Second Empire, when political organization was forbidden, and then of the Paris Commune, where direct political opposition to the state had proven disastrous, convinced many of France's leading unionists, and theoreticians of the syndicalist movement, that it was wiser to keep their distance from political parties, whose involvement might hinder their own claims to legal existence and would loosen their control of their own movement.

This attitude helped form in France a syndicalist movement which self-consciously strove to keep at arm's length the 'bourgeois', parliamentary, and potentially domineering socialist parties that emerged in the last decades of the century. Such a policy achieved apotheosis in the resolution passed at the Amiens Congress of the Confédération Générale du Travail (CGT) in 1906, where the leading organization of French unions declared that, precisely because the working class was engaged in a 'class war' with the industrialists, and a war whose primary weapons were economic, union members should refrain from introducing politics of any kind into the syndicalist movement.

Many of the socialists accepted this demand that politics and syndicalism be kept separate. However, those who had come up through the more orthodox marxist channels, notably Guesde's Parti

---

[3] For a thorough study of the anti-militarist sentiment in France on the eve of the war, see Jean-Jacques Becker, *1914: Comment les français sont entrés dans la guerre* (Paris, 1977).

Ouvrier Français, saw the division as weakening the workers' movement in practice and anyway untenable in theory, given the inextricable links in a capitalist society between economic and political power. They thus preferred to continue the tradition of certain regions such as the north, and certain industries, among them textiles, where unions and socialist movement were closely intertwined. The resulting friction between syndicalist leaders (resentful at some socialists' claims to represent their interests) and the socialist movement on the one hand, and *within* the SFIO on the other, grew rather than subsided in the years after unification, and the question of socialist/syndicalist relations lay at the heart of the post-war schism. Few pre-war socialists were quite as blunt as Lenin in asserting the primacy of socialist (political) activity over mere unionism, but that in essence was what lay behind the arguments over syndicalist autonomy. Whereas in Germany, in Belgium, in Britain, these arguments were being pursued *within* labour movements which included political and economic elements, in France the division was deep-seated and institutional.[4]

It is clear, then, that the pre-war SFIO was a divided party, and moreover lacking a base in the union movement except in a very few regions. It was certainly seen thus by contemporaries, and was regarded by foreign socialists as a fragile and uncertain organism. None the less, this frail plant went on to survive a major schism. Before we turn to the analysis of that schism, it is worth noting certain features which gave the pre–1914 SFIO a hidden strength.

The first of these was the regional base of the socialist movement in France. In the national elections of 1914 the SFIO received 1,400,000 votes and 103 Socialists were elected to the Chambre des Députés. These socialist votes were concentrated in three areas of the country: the northern industrial departments of the north, the Pas de Calais, and the Ardennes; the northern and western borders of the Massif Central, from Limoges to the valley of the Saône; and the Mediterranean basin of southern France, from the Gard to the Var. Membership of the party was less impressive—some 93,000 persons in 1914—but the party daily newspaper *L'Humanité* was selling 90,000

---

[4] On the history of French syndicalism see, among many works, Georges Lefranc, *Le Mouvement syndical sous la Troisième République* (Paris, 1967); Jacques Julliard, *Fernand Pelloutier et les origines du syndicalisme d'action directe* (Paris, 1971); Edouard Dolléans, *Le Mouvement ouvrier*, vol. 2 (Paris, 1933); Georges Lefranc, *Essais sur les problèmes socialistes et syndicaux* (Paris, 1970); F. F. Ridley, *Revolutionary Syndicalism in France* (Ithaca, NY, 1970).

copies in 1913, and many more than that number must thus have been following party activities on a day-to-day basis.

Like the Socialist electorate, the membership were clearly concentrated in certain regions. The top twelve departmental federations in the SFIO, based on Socialist membership per thousand persons in 1913, comprised the Nord, the Pas de Calais, and the Ardennes; the Allier and the Haute Vienne in the centre, and the Gard, Pyrenées Orientales, Vaucluse, and Var in the south. The Aube, in the champagne region, and the Isère south-east of Lyons, were other areas of strong membership, but there the Socialist *electoral* support, though respectable, was lower than in the other departments. The Paris region also figured in a list of leading departments based on membership per head, but it never provided a solid electoral base for the SFIO, although it would prove fertile terrain for the Communists in later decades.

This regional specificity of the SFIO is what provided its stability. Moreover, although apparently spread across wide areas of provincial, rural France, the socialist strongholds were in fact quite well placed to benefit from the pattern of industrialization in the country. Not until the 1920s would Paris prove a major industrial and proletarian centre.[5] Before the war industry was concentrated in the north and north-east (coal, steel, textiles); in the centre (mining in the Allier, steelworks in the Saône et Loire, iron and steel in the Loire); and in the south and south-east (textiles in the Isère, mining in the Gard and contiguous departments, chemical and related industries in the Marseilles basin to take advantage of the volume of trade, increasingly in petrochemicals, passing through the port). Taken together with the depth of genuine rural support for Socialist candidates in departments like the Var and the Haute Vienne, this economic geography meant that the dispersion of Socialist support around the country seemed to be working to the long-term advantage of a would-be working-class party. Indeed, as early as 1908, some 53 per cent of Socialist Party members were located in departments of a predominantly industrial nature, and only 6 per cent in overwhelmingly agricultural areas.[6]

[5] The important changes came during the war, when establishments like Renault at Boulogne-Billancourt grew from 5,000 workers in 1914 to nearly 25,000 in 1918, or when Citroën at Quai Javel expanded from virtually nothing in 1914 to over 10,000 employees at the end of the war. See J.-L. Robert's contribution to the collective work *Le PCF: étapes et problèmes 1920–1972* (Paris, 1981), pp. 14–42.

[6] Social and economic data used in this article are drawn from the *Annuaire Statistique*, published annually in Paris from 1878; the *Résultats Statistiques du recensement*

Finally, it is worth observing that even the separation of socialism from organized syndicalism may not have been such a problem once one passes beyond the disputes of the leadership. Fourteen departments in France in January 1912 showed a percentage of the active population belonging to trade unions that exceeded the national average. These included the Nord, the Pas de Calais, the central departments of the Cher, the Nièvre, and the Loire, and the southern departments of the Var, the Tarn, the Gard, the Hérault, and the Bouches du Rhône. The correlation between areas of high unionization and departments of Socialist electoral success and strong membership is very marked.[7] It would seem, then, that political and 'economic' organizations of the Left were moving along parallel if separate lines. The only noticeable exception, once again, was the Paris region. Here, fully 18.4 per cent of the working population was in unions, making it the leading department in the country. The failure of the socialists to benefit from this would cost them heavily in the next generation.

There is not space here to recount the wartime history of the SFIO, nor is it necessary to do so.[8] For the purposes of an understanding of the nature of French socialism following the split from the Communists it is only essential to identify the changes that had overtaken the party between August 1914 and December 1920, and these can be understood under two headings: the change in the ideological balance within the socialist movement, and the renewed and altered character of its membership.

So far as the first is concerned, the prolonged experience of war had a markedly radicalizing effect upon socialists in France as elsewhere. At first united in the face of German aggression, they came increasingly after 1915 to adopt differing views on the nature of the

général de la population for various years between 1901 and 1936; the *Annuaire des Syndicats* for various years between 1913 and 1935. Criteria for urban and rural population are provided in these sources; I have made my own calculations from the data to establish regions of above or below average population density, and also the percentage of the working population engaged in industry or agriculture by department.

Sources for the history of socialism, its electorate, and membership are chiefly these: Parti Socialiste (SFIO), *congrès nationaux, comptes rendus sténographiques* and *rapports* for the years 1905 to 1938; Georges Lachapelle, *Elections législatives, Résultats officiels* (Paris, 1914–36).

[7] For union membership, see sources cited in note 6, especially the *Annuaire des Syndicats* for 1913.

[8] The best histories of the French Left during the war are Annie Kriegel, *Aux origines du communisme français*, 2 vols. (Paris, 1964), and Robert Wohl, *French Communism in the Making 1914–1924* (Stanford, 1966).

war and how to end it. Until the summer of 1918 the majority remained supporters of the war effort, although increasingly unhappy with the human and economic costs. A growing minority emerged, however, which favoured a negotiated peace and a 'reconstruction' of the shattered Second International along radical lines. The division between the majority and the 'reconstructers' did not follow pre-war lines, since many former Jaurèsists were led by their pacifist past to doubt the propriety of support for a belligerent government, and were joined in their misgivings by supporters of Guesde like Paul Faure from the Haute Vienne, no less opposed to war in principle, but also resolutely in favour of a post-war rebuilding of Europe along internationalist and socialist principles. Finally a third group, comprising the extreme Left of the party and in contact with sympathizers in the Italian and Russian socialist movements, was by 1917 moving towards a neo-Leninist stance of revolutionary opposition to its own government.

The decisive shifts in power within the party came in two stages. The first was at the SFIO national council of July 1918. There Jean Longuet, leader of the wartime minority, successfully opposed the party leadership on a number of votes, notably concerning the Russian Revolution. The 'reconstructers', led by Faure and Longuet amongst others, favoured international support for the revolutionary Russian government, while the hitherto ruling majority endorsed the government's plans to intervene on behalf of the Whites. As a result of these victories, the 'ex-minoritaries' became the party leadership, gaining control of the party newspaper, *L'Humanité*, and securing the direction of the party at every level.

The second, and ultimately more decisive break came during 1920, with the rapid emergence of the hitherto tiny group of wartime revolutionaries, now become a major force in the party. The appeal of the Russian Revolution as a model, the disillusion with parliamentary politics after the election of 1919 (see below), divisions within the new majority on the question of the reconstruction of a new International, the strikes and subsequent governmental repression of 1919 and spring 1920, all played a part in this evolution. By the last months of 1920 the balance within the SFIO had swung sharply to the left. Now the original wartime majority, led by Pierre Renaudel and Léon Blum, was a shrinking and ineffectual minority, while the post-1918 leadership had fallen out, split between those who wanted to continue the organization and tactics of the SFIO along pre-war lines and those who were partially convinced by the arguments of the far Left, believing that the time was ripe for a new and fundamental revision of socialist strategy. For them, such a revision must begin with adherence to the Moscow-based Third International and adoption of Lenin's ideas on party structure and revolutionary politics. In the end, the vote at Tours reflected the overwhelming success of the alliance of the Leninists and the left-leaning 'ex-reconstructers' against the more moderate reconstructers around Faure and Longuet, and their right-wing 'reformist' allies among the supporters of Blum.

In order to understand why these developments came about, it is necessary to cast a glance at the second major change that had overtaken the party since 1914, that concerning its social base. Although the SFIO had shrunk, by 1917, to under 40,000 members, demobilization saw a rapid recovery and unprecedented expansion. By December 1919 membership stood at 132,000 and at its peak, in the months before the Tours congress, it reached 180,000. More to the point, it has been estimated that more than two-thirds of the former membership had been lost, many of them killed. Three-quarters of the 1919 members were new men and women with no experience of the pre-war socialist movement. They were young, they were in many cases ex-soldiers, and they were galvanized by the image of the 1917 revolution in Russia and the promise of urgent changes upon the ending of the war. A slightly higher percentage of the membership now came from industrial departments (62 per cent in 1920) and a good number of these were also members of the expanded post-war unions.

This last point is significant. The increase in union membership in the two years following the armistice was staggering. Some examples: from a membership of 96,000, the metallurgical unions had grown to 235,000 in 1919, an increase of 144 per cent. Similar increases marked the textile industry (union membership there rose from 92,000 in 1913 to 174,000 in 1919, a rise of 88 per cent); the mining unions (73 per cent increase in membership) and nearly every occupation except agriculture, where the *syndicats* were hard hit by the extraordinary peasant casualties at the front. The union movement as a whole increased its membership by 54 per cent and female unionization reached 240,000, an increase of 149 per cent on pre-war figures and representing some 15 per cent of the total membership. These increases in union support were both cause and consequence of the strikes of 1919 (mostly local and spontaneous) and 1920 (when they were organized and led by the CGT).[9]

The failure of these strikes, particularly galling to strikers who had dreamt of them as the first step towards a revolution, led to a sharp disillusionment with the syndicalist leadership of the CGT; this in turn reinforced the growing political disillusion of the newly-enrolled socialists. The elections of November 1919 saw an increase in the Socialist vote to 1,700,000 but a fall in Socialist parliamentary representations to just 68, thanks to a new and visibly distorted electoral system. Accordingly, the pre-war concensus in favour of an electoral road to socialism collapsed, and socialist and syndicalist movements alike turned to advocates of more immediate and violent means to the overthrow of capitalist governments. Thus reinforced by wartime and post-war experience alike, and with mass backing for their views in all branches of the French labour movement, the pro-Moscow activists in the SFIO had little difficulty in engineering a decisive split from the old movement by the end of 1920.[10]

*

For analytical purposes it will be helpful to separate for discussion the various aspects of the socialist experience in France from Tours to the Popular Front. Thus I shall consider first the organization and resources of the party, then its membership, its representatives, and its electorate and how these altered over the period. Following this there will be an overview of the doctrinal positions of the socialists, the divisions of opinion these generated, relations with other movements of the Left, both in France and in the Socialist International. As a prelude to these necessarily artificial categories for investigation, however, there follows a brief survey of the state of the French Socialist Party at the beginning of 1921, on the morning following the departure of the Communists.

The situation was by any standards unpromising. If one accepts the

---

[9] On the history of the CGT after 1918, see in particular Annie Kriegel, *Le Croissance de la CGT 1918–1921* (Paris, 1966); J.-L. Robert, *La Scission syndicale de 1921, essai de reconnaissance des formes* (Paris, 1980); Antoine Prost, *La CGT à l'époque du Front Populaire* (Paris, 1964); D. J. Saposs, *The Labor Movement in Post-War France* (New York, 1931).

[10] For the history of the Tours congress, see Parti Socialiste (SFIO), *XVIIIᵉ congrès national à Tours, décembre 1920, compte rendu sténographique* (Paris, 1921); Annie Kriegel, *Le Congrès de Tours* (Paris, 1964); Jean Charles (*et al.*), *Le Congrès de Tours* (Paris, 1980), together with works cited in note 8.

view of the police experts, a mere 9,000 members remained with the SFIO, the rest of the 180,000 represented at Tours having stayed with the Communists or else retreated from active politics. Even the socialists themselves claimed no more than 'about' 40,000 members (they were for many months uncertain as to the exact figure), acknowledging the loss of the vast majority to the Communists. Because the latter had been in the majority at Tours, they retained control of the party funds, the party newspaper, the bulk of the party records, and, more seriously, a claim to the inheritance of the legitimate, official marxist movement in France. In many departments of the country it was not just a majority but the whole of the local federation which deserted the SFIO—as late as December 1922 there were still 24 departments without a single official socialist section, much less a properly-constituted federation. Among these were major industrial regions such as the Loire and the Moselle, as well as formerly powerful rural bastions such as the Yonne, the Jura, and the Drôme.[11]

The numerical depletion was exacerbated by the loss of the majority of the *younger* members. For all that they might have been recent recruits, and under the influence of the hopes raised by the revolutionary mood of the immediate past, it was these militants on whom any party would rely for much daily activity and for the mobilization of other support. Without them, and with few material resources, the SFIO was ill-equipped to begin the task of rebuilding itself. Moreover, the legitimacy of the SFIO was itself in question—if it asserted its distinctiveness of character *vis-à-vis* the Communists, in other words if it accepted and adopted the implications of Tours, then it risked sliding to the right and becoming an adjunct to the Radical Party, much of whose vocabulary at least echoed the preferred themes of the socialists' extreme 'right wing'. On the other hand, if the SFIO proceeded to compete with the Communists for the established terrain of anti-capitalist politics in France, it was likely to be outmanœuvred by an opponent who was younger, more extreme and still in 1921 a beneficiary of the reflected glow from a successful revolution. The question of whether there was now any place for a socialist movement in France was frequently asked, and it was not without substance.

On the other hand, the way in which the old Socialist Party had split was not completely without its advantages to the remaining members

---

[11] See *Archives Nationales, F⁷ 12893, rapport de police sur la SFIO, 25 avril 1921.* Also T. Judt, *La Reconstruction du Parti Socialiste 1921–1926* (Paris, 1976), chs. 1 and 2.

of the SFIO. To begin with, the older members, men and women of the pre-war generation, had mostly remained loyal to the party, and they had experience on their side. Moreover, they frequently held positions of some influence. In the Chambre, 55 of the 68 Socialist representatives stayed with the SFIO, ensuring it continued national political prominence. Many of the more experienced and prestigious Socialist leaders also refused to join the Third International, among them Faure, now the party secretary, Longuet, the grandson of Marx and who provided the party with a new daily paper, *Le Populaire,* and of course Léon Blum, emerging during the 1920s as the *de facto* leader and spokesman for the non-Communist Left in France.

In the provinces it emerged in the course of 1921 that a feature of the split had been the propensity for local organizers—federal secretaries and treasurers, for instance—to remain with the old party, thus facilitating the work of reconstruction. Finally, the scission in the departments seems frequently to have taken the form of a rural/urban division, with the members from small towns and villages going for the Communists, but the sections in the larger towns and cities, often the departmental capitals, remaining loyal. This happened in the Nièvre, where the socialist section in the town of Nevers was all that remained of the flourishing pre-Tours federation, and it was a pattern repeated in other places, including the important federations of the Cher and the Saône et Loire in the centre of the country. Since the local socialist press was usually printed and distributed from the regional capital, it transpired that the SFIO may have lost *L'Humanité,* but its control of the urban sections in the provinces had secured for it some important local newspapers, among them *Le Cri du Nord,* in Lille; *Le Droit du Peuple* (Grenoble); *Le Populaire du Centre* (Limoges, in the Haute Vienne), and *Le Midi Socialiste* (Toulouse). These were not inconsiderable assets, and they would enable the party to present itself nationwide as a continuing entity.

Organization

The system of authority and the internal power structure of the SFIO dated from pre-war years and had its origins in the highly centralized forms of Guesde's Parti Ouvrier Français. The party was arranged vertically, beginning with the individual member and moving to the apex at the national congress, usually an annual event. In between came the local group, the section (comprising two or more groups—in isolated rural areas, or regions of low membership, group and section sometimes collapsed into a single unit), the departmental federation. Members of each elected representatives to the meetings of the higher organ, culminating in the congress, which was expected to debate and determine policy.

Inevitably, power along this chain tended to emanate from above, despite the ostensibly democratic and local basis for decisions. The point was never reached, as in the Communist movement, whereby the party leadership instructed local groups on what to discuss and how to vote on resolutions due for congressional debate, but it was none the less rare for local groups, or even departmental federations, to initiate policy. This was because the inter-war years saw the continuation of a pre-war tendency, the reduction of annual congresses to formal events, best adapted to grand statements of intent and debates on abstract matters. Instead the national *council,* whose composition was determined at each congress and which comprised delegates from every federation, met on an occasional basis through the year to resolve practical matters and handle unforeseen developments.

Even the council proved too unwieldy for a party so active in daily politics, especially after 1924, and its authority steadily devolved to the Commission Administrative Permanente (CAP), a body which sat in Paris and effectively ran the SFIO under the guidance of the general secretary. Although elected at each congress, the members of the CAP remained remarkably unchanged through the inter-war years. Inevitably, too, they were predominantly Parisian, if only because they had to be available on a weekly basis for meetings in the capital. Although party regulations stipulated that no more than one-third of the CAP be parliamentary *députés,* there was continuous resentment at the predominance of elected representatives on the party's leading bodies, and much provincial grumbling at the disproportionate presence on the CAP of militants from the Seine Federation.[12]

The centralized character of power in the SFIO would have created problems at any time—it was the highly articulated and authoritarian nature of Guesdism which had been both its greatest asset and its most resented feature in the eyes of its early opponents—but it was especially contentious in the aftermath of Tours. Some of the provincial federations, and some, too, of the national leaders, saw the departure of the Communists as an opportunity to re-found the SFIO upon a looser, less centralized structure. They were to be disappointed:

[12] For examples of provincial suspicion of Paris and the parliamentary group, see Judt op. cit., ch. 4.

although the 1920s saw a number of conflicts between local federations and the CAP—over electoral alliances, over aspects of party policy, whether or not to admit as members people belonging to proscribed organizations—these disputes were consistently resolved in favour of the authority of the party hierarchy. Until 1924 this was because of the need to avoid any conflicts that might damage or weaken the still fragile socialist movement; thereafter and until the late 1930s it reflected the success of the leadership in re-establishing authority on a basis stronger, if anything, than that enjoyed by them before the war.

Part of the reason for the success of the central authority, largely in the person of the secretary-general, Paul Faure, lay in his exploitation of provincial and militant dislike for the parliamentary side of socialist activity. There was a strong, inherited suspicion of 'parliamentarism', and this provided a bond between leaders and militants within the party itself. Throughout the inter-war years it was common for a congress to hear a series of speeches against the dangers of compromise with the 'system', of 'easy living' at the party's expense, of 'Parisianism'—the failure of parliamentary Socialists to visit their provincial constituencies.[13]

One of the results of this mood in the party was the sense gained by the parliamentary leaders—notably Blum—that it was the better part of valour for socialists to stay out of government for as long as could be justified. By the early 1930s the SFIO was paying a price for this, in that many of its *'élus'* felt hamstrung and limited in their actions, notably in their growing desire to join the Radicals in a coalition government, in 1932 as in 1924 a crucial issue for both parties. The upshot was a series of individual departures culminating in a substantial split in November 1933. But this rigid control of the initiative of the parliamentary Socialist Party gave far-flung provincial members a sense that authority was being exercised on their behalf, and it compensated for the actual assumption of decision-making power within the party by a handful of permanent officials.

Within the constraints of such an arrangement, daily life in the SFIO remained flexible and even casual, when compared either to the PCF or to foreign parties like the SPD. Although each member was supposed to purchase a stamp for the party card every month, compliance with this rule was rare. In 1924 only nine departmental

[13] Many of the most vehemently critical speeches at Tours came from provincial militants expatiating on these themes. See sources cited in note 10.

federations reported an average of twelve stamps purchased per month, and in many federations the annual average often did not exceed six. The national ratio of stamps per card peaked at 9.5 in 1927, declining thereafter.[14] This lack of assiduity on the part of the membership had a consistently damaging effect on party funds (as did their failure to purchase the party daily paper, *Le Populaire*, in sufficient numbers to make it financially independent[15]), but was left unsanctioned. The CAP was more likely to take a disapproving view of local alliances with Radicals (or Communists) for electoral ends, where these did not coincide with national policy. This was an issue in the elections of 1924 and 1928, with some weaker socialist federations attempting pre-election agreements with other local parties. Even here the party was disinclined to take disciplinary action—usually because the costs of losing a disaffected federation far exceeded the benefits of a formal unity which could in any case readily be re-established after the election was over. In general, and in the name of unity and the rebuilding of the movement, the SFIO took a benign view of most breaches of discipline—except in matters of formal doctrine or political principle. But these caused little difficulty, at least so far as militants were concerned, since it was by 1936 well understood that such matters were the all-but-exclusive province of a handful of party leaders.

Membership[16]

The numbers of men and women belonging to the SFIO between the wars were never large. Having struggled back to 50,496 by 1923, the membership then rose steadily through to 1926, when it stood at 111,368. There was a brief drop the following year, to 98,000,

[14] See Judt, op. cit., Appendix 9, and the reports of national secretaries to congresses throughout the period in the *comptes-rendus* of these congresses.

[15] For much of the 1920s, *Le Populaire* failed to reach a daily sale of 10,000 copies and survived only through assistance from central party funds and loans from, among others, the Parti Ouvrier Belge. For part of the period after 1924 it was reduced to a bi-monthly, and even when it was revived as a daily paper it failed to achieve a large steady readership. Unable to compete economically with the plethora of local socialist papers in the provinces, it lacked the ability to capture the audience of 20,000 or more in the Paris region which it needed to meet its costs. In other words it was the weakness of the SFIO in Paris which contributed to the failure of its major publication—just as the strength of the PCF in the capital directly benefited the party paper *L'Humanité*. Most French socialists preferred to read a local socialist paper such as *Le Midi Socialiste*, and complement it (if at all) with a 'non-political' national daily.

[16] For detailed annual reports of SFIO membership, arranged by department, see the reports to congresses listed in note 6.

probably brought about by disillusionment and disappointment with the Cartel des Gauches and the socialists' role in it, but after that there began a further slow rise to 137,684 in the election year of 1932 (then as now membership was wont to rise in election periods, especially at moments when the Socialists' prospects were thought good). From 1932 until 1935 the membership stagnated, falling briefly in 1934 to some 110,000 as a result of the departure of the 'neo-socialists', advocates of governmental participation. The year 1936 of course saw a sharp increase in requests for membership, the figure for that year passing the 200,000 mark for the first time (202,000), while the following year saw a pre-war record number of enrolled Socialists, 286,604.

Within the party, these members were unevenly distributed. One quarter of them in 1926 were in four leading federations, those of the Nord, the Pas de Calais, the Seine, and the Gironde. Indeed, the Nord federation alone, with 13,000 members in 1926, represented 12 per cent of the party strength. Conversely, the twelve weakest federations in 1926 (concentrated heavily in the west and north-west and with membership ranging from 275 in the Orne to just eight persons in the Haute-Loire) together made up less than 2 per cent of the party.

It is instructive to compare the areas of high membership for the years before and after the Tours split. In 1920 the largest federation had been that of the Seine, with 21,200 members. There followed the Nord (at that time with 20,700 members), the Pas de Calais, the Moselle, and Bas Rhin departments in the newly-liberated region of Alsace-Lorraine, three more departments from the Paris basin (Seine-et-Oise, Seine-et-Marne, Seine-Inférieure), the Rhône and Isère departments from the south-east, and two socialist strongholds in the Massif Central, the Haute-Vienne and the Corrèze. In 1926 the whole of the Seine region with the exception of Paris itself had disappeared from among the leading socialist federations. The two giant northern industrial federations continued to predominate, but were joined now by a flurry of southern regions: the Bouches du Rhône, the Hérault, the Haute-Garonne from the far south, the Gironde from the south-west. The Rhône and the Haute-Vienne remained, but the Strasbourg region was now eclipsed by support in upper Alsace around Colmar. Also appearing on the list for the first time were the departments of Finistère, in Brittany, and the Saône-et-Loire in Burgundy.

A decade later, in 1936, the balance of power in the party had consolidated the changes just noted. The Nord and the Pas de Calais had been joined by the neighbouring industrial region of the Aisne, there was a slight recovery of membership in the suburban districts of the Seine-et-Oise, and a further addition to the southern emphasis within the party with the emergence of the Pyrenées Orientales as one of the twelve largest federations. Conversely, membership fell in the Alsace and Lyons areas.

These bald indications of the geography of socialist membership in absolute terms are a useful guide to the distribution of power *within* the party; it is thus clear that by 1936 the dual power bases of the industrial north and Mediterranean littoral were already in place (where they would remain into the 1980s). What they cannot reveal is the strength of the party in the *country*. To see this, we must turn to an analysis of the geography of socialist membership expressed as a percentage of the departmental population.

In 1920, by this measure, the five departments in which socialist membership was highest were, again, the Nord, the Moselle, the Pas de Calais, and the Seine-et-Oise and Seine-et-Marne. However the next seven departments in order include three from the central region (Corrèze, Nièvre, and Haute-Vienne) and four from various loci: the Vaucluse and the Drôme in the southern Rhône valley, the Aube to the east of Paris, and the Indre-et-Loire on the fringes of the recalcitrant west.

Six years later, the change is quite noticeable. Excepting the inevitable Nord and Calais regions, and the brief increase in support in the Haut-Rhin, the regions of *relative* socialist strength were all either in the centre (from the Haute-Vienne to the Saône-et-Loire), the south-west (Gironde and Lot), or the south (Haute-Garonne, Aude, Var, and Basses Alpes). By 1936, with the exception of the return of the Indre-et-Loire and the replacement of the Pas de Calais by the Aisne, the situation of the party reflected and reinforced the changes already in place in 1926.

On the other hand, while there was some movement among the areas of socialist strength, regions in which the SFIO signally *failed* to find members remained remarkably consistent. The southern massif, in an arc from the Ardèche to the Aveyron, the less-industralized east (Vosges, Meuse), the high Alps, and the Catholic regions of the west, all these were as conservative in 1936 as they had been before the war. The only exceptions to this rule appear to have been Finistère (already mentioned) and the Tarn-et-Garonne in the south-west (but there it was the Communists, rather than the SFIO, who benefited).

How is one to interpret this data? Does it suggest any secular patterns? Can one correlate socialist strength with predominance of industry or agriculture, with urban or rural regions of France? Did the Tours scission significantly alter the pattern of socialist allegiance?

If we take, as a crude but constant criterion of industrialization, the departments where 40 per cent or more of the working population was engaged in industry, we find that in 1913 five of the twelve leading socialist federations were in such areas (using here the measure of socialist membership as a percentage of the local population). Conversely, none of the socialist federations was among those departments where 65 per cent or more of the population was employed in agriculture. By the congress of Tours, in 1920, six of the leading federations were in industralized departments and one (the Corrèze) in a predominantly agricultural region.

By 1926 there had been a shift (or, more accurately, an accentuation of a pattern starting to emerge in 1920). Only three of the strong socialist departments were dominated by industrial occupations, while four of the top twelve were in agricultural areas. In 1936, however, although only two of the socialist strongholds were now in industrial areas (Nord and Aisne), the number of major federations in agricultural departments had fallen (also to two—Ariège and Aude). The rest of the leading socialist federations were in areas of mixed activity, though it may be significant that membership per head of the population was highest in departments with an unusually large number of small or artisan establishments (eleven of the twelve leading federations were so located).[17]

It would appear, then, that socialists were not notably more successful at recruiting in agricultural rather than industrial areas, although they were certainly failing to recruit in large numbers in the major industrial departments, always excepting the region around Lille. If we take a different measure, however, a clearer picture emerges.

In 1913, seven of the twelve leading socialist federations (again and always this is in size relative to population) were in departments where the urban population exceeded the national average. By Tours this had changed and seven of the top twelve were now in areas of above average *rural* population (using the French official definition of 'urban'

---

[17] For sources concerning the employment and occupation of the working population, presented nationally, by economic sector and by department, see sources listed in note 6.

meaning a community in which 2,000 or more persons resided within the commune). This figure remained unaltered in 1926, but had moved again a decade later, with just four of the leading federations now urban in character.

There is a further geographical yardstick one might apply. If one bisects France into 'north' and 'south', drawing an imaginary line from Le Havre to Geneva (and accepting the odd consequence of including the Côtes du Nord in 'southern' France!), it emerges that in 1913 the SFIO already was stronger to the south of that line: seven of the top twelve federations fell to that side. At Tours there had been a slight rectification, with six strong federations in each sector. By 1926, however, with the loss of the Seine region and industrial Lorraine the SFIO was much more solidly meridional in character—nine of the twelve leading federations conforming to that definition. This situation then remained stable for the inter-war period.

So far as geographical analysis may offer an indication of the sorts of person attracted to join the SFIO (and it is of course a very broad and imprecise approach to the question), the following points emerge. The membership base of the party was never particularly industrial, even before the war, but the split at Tours helped to accelerate the move away from the most heavily industrialized regions of France. Part of that move, of course, simply reflects the loss of Paris and the Seine region to the Communists at just the moment when the industrial belt around the city, heavily developed during and on account of the war, was expanding most rapidly.

This partial de-industrialization of the SFIO was accompanied by a discernible increase in the influence of the southern federations. Here, too, the scission served to accelerate rather than create a pattern. Indeed, there really never was a time when socialism in France was anything other than disproportionately southern in character; the unique and contrasting examples of the strongholds by the Belgian border underscore the point.

Finally, it seems very likely that an unusually large percentage of French socialists were small-town people (a point reinforced by the electoral figures, as we shall see). They may not have been concentrated in the big industrial cities, and they may have lived south of the Loire, but they were mostly *not* rural-dwellers, and so far as *membership* at least is concerned, they were not peasants. Moreover, despite the traumatic consequences of the split with the Communists at the time and amongst the leadership, the ideological divide seems to have had little immediate effect upon the sociology of the rump party. The SFIO may not have been, by 1936, the party of 1913, but it was clearly the party, give or take the odd Parisian hiccup, that the 1913 party was on its way to becoming.

How far do large-scale correlations of the above sort conceal and obscure small-scale details? It is hard to know because the SFIO kept very inadequate data on its membership, and little has survived. It is, however, possible to confirm the plausibility of some of our conclusions from scattered local data. The example of Marseilles is helpful, not just because it was a major socialist stronghold, but because the Bouches du Rhône department itself was an unusual mix of the rural and the urban, of industry, commerce, and agriculture.[18]

Of the 1,365 members in the city in 1930, an estimated 45 per cent were under thirty-five years of age. Compared with the national leadership, the average age of which did not fall below fifty from 1925 to the war, this confirms the impressions of contemporaries, that the problem of an ageing membership (which characterized the years immediately after the split) had been replaced in the early 1930s by a growing rift between middle-aged leaders and younger, more radical members.

Of the Marseilles members, only 19 per cent were *ouvriers*. Moreover, the higher up the local party echelons one looks, the smaller the number of ex- or present working men and women. Even more indicative of a sea-change in the nature of French socialism, if typical, was the fact that 20 per cent of the members were *employés*, and a further 30 per cent more loosely categorized as *classes moyennes*—small shopkeepers, artisans, government employees of various kinds. If these findings *are* representative, they suggest a national pattern: the SFIO was moving, slowly, away from its pre-war connections with the urban working population and a substantial peasant electorate, towards a close, if not exactly elective, affinity with the *employé/fonctionnaire* sector. There is no doubt that the party was aware of this—witness urgent efforts in the 1930s to form factory and shop-based groups, the *Amicales Socialistes*, to replace the traditional groups based on geography of residence (efforts marked by a conspicuous lack of success). However, since the tertiary sector was growing faster than any other in inter-war France, these developments were not necessarily to

---

[18] For Marseilles, see Michel d'Agostino, 'L'Implantation socialiste à Marseille sous le Front populaire', Mémoire de Maîtrise, Université de Provence UER d'Histoire, 1972. I am grateful to Dr David Levy for this reference.

the disadvantage of the socialists—witness their emergence in 1936 as the largest party in the country—but they hardly conformed to their preferred self-image.

There is a further feature of the Marseilles section which confirms an aspect of the SFIO's composition. Of the 1365 militants on which our figures are based, only 62 were women. This was actually rather above the national average—in 1929 the party's female membership was estimated at 3,500, constituting just 2.9 per cent of the total for that year. Furthermore, female membership was as geographically specific as that of the party in general: most women socialists lived in the Paris region, where the Groupe des Femmes Socialistes was based and where there was a longer tradition than elsewhere of welcoming women into political movements. The only other city with a large number of active women socialists was Strasbourg, possibly an inheritance from the strong and long-established women's socialist organization of the SPD in Imperial Germany.

Elsewhere, women were active in the Nord and the Isère, which together with the Drôme and the Haute-Garonne sent women as part of the delegation to national congresses on frequent occasions between the wars. That these particular federations should have given women a greater role in their leadership may reflect the fact that these were areas where the pre-war rate of female unionization had been high, and where women continued to be overwhelmingly present in the labour force. Elsewhere, even strong and lively socialist federations would often boast only a tiny complement of female members—in the Gard there were just 50 in the early 1930s, for a membership approaching 2000.[19]

A male party, then (though no more so than other French political

[19] The inter-war female membership of the SFIO seems never to have exceeded 4,000. This is in marked contrast to the female membership of the SDP, 220,000 in 1930. In the Czech Socialist Party, women represented 33 per cent of the membership. Sources for the history of women in French socialism are few: see Charles Sowerwine, *Les Femmes et le socialisme* (Paris, 1978); there were a number of important debates regarding the recruitment of women into the SFIO in the years 1928–35—see congress reports for these years. Some idea of the role played by women in the syndicalist movement can be gleaned from the reports of certain unions: *inter alia*, CGT, *Congrès Confédéral, séptembre 1929, Compte-Rendu Sténographique* and CGT, *Congrès Confédéral, séptembre 1935, Compte-Rendu Sténographique*, where female delegates are listed and where, in 1935, there was a debate over the 'condition féminine'. As a rule, women played a more prominent part in the CGTU—see for example the reports of the Paris meetings of the *Fédération Nationale des industries textiles-vêtement* (décembre 1924, novembre 1926).

organizations at a time when women were still denied the suffrage), increasingly replacing its older working-class membership with a rather younger, lower-middle-class one drawn from the trades, commerce, and government employment. Before going on to compare this picture of party membership with the Socialist electorate, it may be helpful to cast a glance at the men who represented the SFIO in the Chambre, serving as they did as a bridge between the party as movement and the party as electoral organization.

Elected representatives

From 1924 to the Popular Front, the SFIO was well represented in the Chambre—consistently stronger than the PCF and in 1936 finally outdistancing the Radicals. In 1924 the party elected 101 *députés* in the Cartel des Gauches; in the elections of 1928 and 1932 it had a representation in parliament of 100 and 131 respectively. In the elections of 1936, of course, the numbers reached an unprecedented 146. Who were these Socialist representatives?[20]

To begin with, they were not young men. OF those elected in 1924, all but twenty-two of them, that is 78 per cent, were over 45. This was considerably older than the average of all French parliamentary *élus* in the period 1898–1940 (of whom only 45 per cent were aged 45 or over) and markedly different from the age structure of Communist *députés* from 1920 to 1940, 71 per cent of whom were under 45. The 1936 election brought an influx of younger Socialist representatives, but as a rule grey-bearded men predominated, to the disadvantage of their image in the eyes of younger party members.

The occupations of Socialist *députés* changed subtly over the period. Of the Socialists elected in 1919, a clear majority had been working-class, although it is interesting to note that workers and artisans constituted only 20 per cent of Socialist *candidates* at that election—a disproportion explained by the predominance of successful proletarian candidates in certain districts where Socialists monopolized the seats (e.g. in the Nord department and the Calaisis). By 1924, only 36 of the 101 Socialists elected were *ouvriers*, eight of these being miners, four of them railway workers. The working-class quotient in the total had

---

[20] Information on the parliamentary representation of the SFIO is available in the following places: Jean Jolly (ed.), *Dictionnaire des parlementaires français* (Paris 1960–77); Alfred Wahl, 'Les Députés SFIO de 1924 à 1940: essai de sociologie', in *Mouvement social*, no. 106 (1977), pp. 25–44; Mattei Dogan, 'Les Filières de la carrière politique en France', in *Revue française de sociologie*, vol. 8, no. iv (1967), pp. 468–93; Judt, *La Reconstruction*, Appendix V.

been reduced to a large and homogeneous bloc, but no longer a majority. Most of the rest were from the tertiary sector, including ten from the teaching profession (four *professeurs*, six *instituteurs*). There were also nine journalists and thirteen lawyers.

The 1928 election accentuated this trend. Of the newly-elected *députés* (as distinct from those whose mandate was renewed), only nine of the Socialists were workers of one kind or another, eight were in the teaching profession, while twenty-nine were in the liberal professions. In that year the percentage of doctors and lawyers among the Socialists closely matched the average for the Chambre as a whole (8.2 per cent of the SFIO *élus* were doctors, 19 per cent lawyers, compared to overall averages of 10 per cent and 23.7 per cent respectively).

This pattern remained substantially unaltered in 1932, the only difference being that the sharpest increase came no longer among the higher professions, but rather from employees and government workers, notably in the postal and clerical sector, who together made up 18 per cent of the *newly*-elected Socialists of that year.

The Popular Front elections saw the apotheosis of this process of *glissage*. The largest single professional group in the parliamentary Socialist Party was the teachers, with 19 *professeurs* and 17 *instituteurs* (a taste of the overwhelming role to be played by these people in the revived Parti Socialiste of the 1970s). Second place fell to the professions, with a total of 50 representatives, including 20 lawyers and 10 doctors. The majority of the remainder were employees or civil servants (23 in all), with a mere sixteen *députés* from the working class. In 1936, as throughout the inter-war years, there were less than 5 per cent of representatives from agriculture, most of these from wine-growing districts and themselves often engaged in viticulture.

This portrait of a party increasingly represented in parliament by the *moyenne bourgeoisie* can be modified somewhat if one asks of these *députés* not what they did for a living, but from what social milieu they had come. Whereas the first criterion suggests that, but for the aggressive 'workerism' of the mining areas, there would have been almost no workers in the Socialist parliamentary group by 1936, the second illustrates a different theme: that of the upwardly mobile nature of Socialist leaders. In 1924, 34 per cent of the Socialists in the Chambre were from a working-class milieu; by 1936 that figure had fallen off relatively little, to 28 per cent. On the other hand, only eight of the 1924 *députés* were from professional backgrounds, and a further four had parents in the teaching profession (all four the sons of *instituteurs*). Conversely, and in sharp contrast to their actual occupations, 20 per cent of the SFIO *députés* in 1924 were from agricultural backgrounds, and the proportion was unchanged in 1936.

Thus at the time of the Popular Front, nearly half the Socialists in parliament came from agricultural or working-class families. To this observation may be added another. In 1924, when compared to the national population, Socialist parliamentarians were disproportionately likely to have been born in a major industrial city or town. By 1936, however, while the population at large was becoming more urban, the socialists were in one sense going the other way: they were now disproportionately prone to have their origin in a rural district. The SFIO may still have had its roots in a working population, but it was increasingly likely to be the working population, whether industrial or agricultural, of a small town or village rather than a major urban centre.

One might fairly conclude, then, that for all they were losing their overtly proletarian base to the Communists, the Socialist parliamentarians retained at least one significant advantage. They reflected, in the pattern of inter-generational upward mobility, in the origins and in the occupations of their number, *La France moyenne* (even their rural origin in 1936 was to their benefit, in a country where rural roots were still the norm and much valued). They reproduced, in miniature, not the experience, much less the ideal, of the members of their party, but rather those of the population as a whole. Better than any other party, the SFIO reflected the demographic and occupational trends in the country. It was thus doomed to succeed at the polls, in spite of itself as it were.

This picture of a political party whose elected representatives mirrored the experience and aspirations of the electorate even extends to the particular channels by which they achieved recognition: active participation in an economic organization was uncommon in France at the time, and so it was in the SFIO. Whereas in Germany, or (especially) Britain, experience in the union movement was often a safe path to a successful parliamentary career, in France there was no such relationship. Very few of the SFIO *élus* were active in *syndicats*, and none of them came into the Chambre directly through the support of a labour organization. This, and the frequent mutual suspicion of party militants and elected *députés*, meant that the SFIO's parliamentary successes were a direct result of its appeal to and relationship with the political nation.

The Socialist electorate

Beyond the simple business of ascertaining numbers,[21] any attempt to identify the inter-war electorate of the SFIO involves the acceptance of certain technical limitations. There were no opinion polls, and there is thus no possibility of understanding voters' contemporary perception of a party, nor of enquiring as to how a group of persons voted and then classing that information by age, occupation, etc. Secondly, women were denied the vote, and thirdly there were always electors who abstained. As a result, we are actually estimating the appeal of the party to, and the behaviour of a limited number of adult male voters. Yet in order to relate electoral data to social structure, the techniques of electoral geography to which we must resort require that we compare the votes of a limited group of men with the social character of a region, including in that character men and women, voters and non-voters alike. The heuristic benefits of such a method are limited. Nevertheless, they are the best we have: even an inconceivably tedious study of each and every one of the 36,000+ communes for five inter-war elections would still offer the same barriers to certainty, given the secret ballot.[22]

In what follows, then, I can do no more than indicate the likely character of the Socialist electorate, with much scope for error and misinterpretation. I hope to reduce the latter a little by confining myself to studying the Socialist vote as a percentage of all registered electors, rather than as a percentage of those who actually voted in any given election. This minimizes the confusion introduced by the varying rates of abstention, and it also enables us to concentrate on the strength of socialist support among the voting community as a whole, including those indifferent to politics, rather than focusing just on

[21] The SFIO's national performance at elections in this period was as follows:

1914: 1,398,000 votes at the first round
1919: 1,700,000 votes on a single-round list system
1924: impossible to estimate: the SFIO obtained 749,000 in those departments where it presented its own list, but in most

areas it presented itself jointly with the Radicals and the distinctively socialist support can thus not be identified.
1928: 1,676,000 voted at the first round
1932: 1,980,000 votes at the first round
1936: 1,942,000 votes at the first round.

[22] The best recent synoptic study of French electoral geography is that of Claude Leleu, *Géographie des élections françaises depuis 1936* (Paris, 1971). It is possible to compare voting behaviour with electoral lists, rather than departmental populations, but this too can only be done at a very local level. In any event, like all such undertakings which seek to relate essence and action, 'explaining' a particular vote never really becomes possible—even when we can identify an elector by name! Fortunately, this is a problem for psychologists rather than historical sociologists.

those who bothered to vote. Finally, all figures concern Socialist votes at the *first* round of a two-round electoral system. Throughout the inter-war years the SFIO made a point of putting up its own candidates at the first round. If they did badly, they usually withdrew at the second round for a better-placed candidate of another left party. If they did well, they frequently acquired at the second round the votes of other, less successful first-round candidates. In either event, the second-round vote is no indicator of socialist sentiment.

We have already noted that the Socialist electorate in 1914 was strongest in three distinct areas: the north, the north-western Massif Central and the Mediterranean basin. If we apply to the 1914 elections the same grid employed when discussing membership, the following points emerge: the SFIO was distinctly a southern party, sustaining a high vote north of the Loire only in the Pas de Calais/Nord/Ardennes corner and the Paris region. Eight of the twelve areas of highest Socialist voting were in the south or centre. On the other hand, this strength in the north, geographically confined as it was, meant that five of the twelve top areas were in the most industrialized parts of the country (the fifth department was the Isère, where textiles, silk manufacture and clothing production dominated the Grenoble region). Not one of the electoral strongholds of the SFIO was in a department of *unusual* agricultural predominance,[23] and the spread between rural and urban regions was remarkably even.

The comparison with 1928 is made all the more instructive in the light of these points (the elections of 1919 and 1924, based on a departmental suffrage and a different voting system, are non-comparable). In that year, a series of southern, and more properly rural departments, came into predominance as Socialist electoral strongholds: the Saône-et-Loire in Burgundy and the Haute-Garonne, Tarn, Hérault, Drôme, and Basses-Alpes, in a line running from Toulouse to the Italian border. As a result, the northern Socialist electorate continued to dominate only in the Nord and Calais regions,

---

[23] Note, however, that such generalized descriptions of departmental characteristics can be misleading. The Var, for example, does not register as a notably agricultural region, but this is a result of the distorting presence of Toulon and the coastal littoral from there east to St Raphael. Where the Socialists did well was in the *inner* Var, which *was* primarily agricultural in character. See Judt, *Socialism in Provence*, (Cambridge, 1979). Such observations need not invalidate necessarily general assessments, but they serve to warn against constructing too baroque an interpretive structure on rather shaky foundations.

and two-thirds of the leading departments on the Socialist list had become unusually rural in character.

Finally, in 1936, this process was accentuated by the emergence for the first time of the Communists as an electoral force. In that year, the Nord department alone remained of the SFIO bastions north of the Loire. It was also the *only* one of the leading socialist regions in which the majority of the population was urban. Moreover, excluding the Nord and also the Isère, all the leading regions were areas in which the population engaged in industry was lower than the national average. The Socialist electorate ran in a seemingly impregnable band across central France, from the Haute-Vienne, the Creuse, and the Corrèze to the Saône-et-Loire, via the Allier and the Nièvre. The other area of growing strength was again the far south, with Socialists taking large minorities of the electorate in the Pyrenean departments of the Ariège and the Haute-Garonne, as well as the Rhône-Alpine region encompassing the Isère and the Drôme.

The electoral history of the inter-war SFIO thus carves out a distinctly sharper curve than that offered by the pattern of membership. From a party reasonably spread across the country, sociologically no less than in geographical terms, the SFIO had become, at the moment of its greatest electoral success, the party of rural, agricultural, southern France, with a single and unique exception. This fact does not necessarily make it a 'peasant party'—many of the electors in departments like the Aude and the Allier were urban, and in the latter case miners or artisans. But the propensity of the SFIO to do well in rural departments a great distance from Paris cannot be ignored in any assessment of its political appeal—a lot of peasants must have been supporting the party with their votes. This in itself is an interesting point when contrasted with the non-agricultural occupations of the men they were electing, but the more common peasant *origins* of the candidates may have helped.

The electoral strongholds of 1936, more so even than those of 1914, correspond with older maps of French political behaviour—they reflect rather well, for example, the 1849 implantation of the *Démocrates-Socialistes*, the left in the Second Republic. They also correlate inversely with the geography of (Catholic) religious practice—indeed, they perform better in this respect than does a map of Socialist *membership*. This suggests a number of observations: we have seen that in its membership the SFIO recruitment was rather heterogeneous, displaying continuing social and geographical trends rather than sharp patterns; the electorate, on the other hand, had a distinct and different identity. It was, it seems, more likely to be found in rural, small-town, non-industrial France, with a marked penchant for anti- (or at least non-) clericalism and a meridional flavour. In other words, it was what political sociologists in France thought of as the 'Left' electorate, something which had not yet been true of the SFIO in 1914. From 1936 until the end of the Fourth Republic, the party was to become, *malgré lui*, the solid centre of traditional *radicalisant* politics in France.

That is a somewhat unsubtle view, emphasizing perhaps to excess the gap between the doctrinally committed militants and the more loosely identified voters. It is supported, however, by the evidence of Socialist electoral success at the *local* level. In 1919 the pre-Tours SFIO controlled 686 municipalities in France (which is to say that a Socialist was mayor in these communes—there were others where Socialists were part of a coalition municipal government). Of these a quarter were in the two departments of the Nord and the Pas de Calais, where the SFIO's formidable local organization gave it control not just of the cities (Lille, Roubaix, Lens) but also of many tiny mining villages and the textile-manufacturing suburban communes of the major conurbations. On the other hand, the vast majority of the remaining 518 Socialist communes were in very rural regions indeed, and normally did *not* include the departmental capital. Thus there were fourteen Socialist communes in the Hérault, but they included neither Béziers nor Montpellier, the dominant local towns. Clermont-Ferrand was not among the twenty-three town halls held by the Socialists in the Puy de Dôme; in the Saône-et-Loire the party controlled Chagny, Montceau, and twelve other communes, but not Châlons or Mâcon. All twenty-two Socialist mayors in the Nièvre were in tiny communes (and did not include Nevers), and the Socialists' victories in Grenoble, Limoges, and Narbonne were unusual. The general contrast with the geography of membership is accentuated by the fact that the SFIO held a majority in only twenty-four of the communes in the Seine region (mostly to the north-east of the city), despite having its largest concentration of membership in that department.

Ten years later, the contrast is more marked yet. The Socialist municipal implantation had spread, comprising 840 communes in 1929. Nord and Pas de Calais remained solid, with 99 and 59 mairies respectively, but more noticeable was the continued rise of Socialist municipal power in non-industrial departments. There were 98 Socialist-run town halls in the Haute-Vienne, 70 in the Hérault, 61 in the Gard, and 47 in the Saône-et-Loire. These were all areas in which Socialist membership was above the party average, but only the Haute-Vienne stood among the leading dozen federations in the party. Moreover, 532, or 64 per cent of the Socialist communes, were south of the Loire; some of them, such as the Basses-Alpes communes (13 in 1929) or those in the Aude (10) and the Creuse (11) were in the most rural and agricultural areas of the country.

Moreover, the Socialists' capacity to win municipal elections in areas where they had a strong membership was notably limited. In the Aisne, second in order of Socialist membership in 1936 as a percentage of the local population, the inter-war SFIO never succeeded in gaining control of more than a handful of town halls, eight at its peak. In the Bouches-du-Rhône around Marseilles, a growing force in the party and fourth largest federation in 1936, the party consistently failed to benefit from its active base in the port city, controlling only nine municipalities in 1929. The most notable failure, of course, was in Paris, although here for once the electoral and membership data tell the same story. Most of the 1919 *mairies* had fallen to the Communists, as had the bulk of the Seine area membership. At the beginning of the 1930s the SFIO controlled just seventeen town halls in the Seine department, none of them in the important industrial and working-class suburbs of the 'red belt'. This is not surprising in the light of the party's performance in Paris at national elections: in 1936 the SFIO returned just three *députés* for the Seine, the same number as it had in the small, rural and mountainous department of the Corrèze. Meanwhile the SFIO lost eight previously-held Parisian seats to the PCF, whose vote in the region was more than two and one-half times that of the Socialists.[24]

Given the unambiguous character of its electoral base, then, and the progressive shift of the SFIO away from the capital and into the heart of provincial France, it might have been supposed that the Socialist Party between the wars would make a virtue of necessity and come to replace the Radical Party as the natural representative of a reformist, centre-left, traditional republicanism in French political life. Its electorate, after all, vastly outnumbered its membership, and electorate and elected representatives alike pointed in such a direction. Indeed,

---

[24] For details of municipalities held by the SFIO, see Jean Charles *et al.*, *Le Congrès de Tours*, pp. 692–795; SFIO, *XXVIe Congrès National, 1929, rapports*.

by ontological inference from such data, many observers have assumed that just such a transformation *did* take place. They are wrong—the SFIO held out against the apparent logic of its own history and continued to emphasize its revolutionary and ideologically determined identity. Why this was so is a question to which we must now turn.

Ideology

I have argued elsewhere that marxism in France had stronger roots than is sometimes supposed.[25] Even avowedly non-doctrinal socialists such as Jaurès (indeed, especially Jaurès) were well versed in the marxist dogma of the time, and not even the reformist or right wing of the SFIO, represented by men such as Blum or Marcel Sembat, broke faith with the fundamentals of the marxist analysis of capitalism and the marxian theory of history. Pre-war differences surged not around the doctrinal basics, but over essentially secondary matters. One of the few genuinely unifying elements in the old SFIO was the shared commitment to what contemporaries understood by the theoretical premisses for revolutionary socialism. Opposition to Jules Guesde, and the traditions he had brought into the party from his POF, centred less on his theory than on the rigid organizational practice and unyielding formulae he (and especially his supporters) continued to espouse.

The Tours scission might have been expected to loosen this historical allegiance to doctrine, but it was quite otherwise in practice. There are various reasons for this, and it is important to identify them, since ideological rigidity and continuity account for much of the characteristic strength and weakness of the movement between the wars.

In the first place, the split with the Communists took place well to the left of the natural 'middle' of the party. Many, indeed most, of those who remained in 1921 were men and women who had supported the wartime opposition in the party. Some were even former members of the wartime neo-Leninists—Louise Saumoneau, for example, an ardent supporter of the Third International before 1920, a stalwart of the SFIO leadership thereafter. These 'ex-reconstructers' formed the core of the party, yet they differed in no significant way from those other 'ex-reconstructers' who led the PCF in its early years; with this exception: lacking the revolutionary mantle of their newly-Communist ex-comrades, they were under much pressure to assert their marxist

[25] See chapters one and two.

credentials in some other way. This they did, primarily, through keeping a firm hold on the ideological tiller throughout our period. What the SFIO had always been, that must it remain. In this way their choice at Tours could be justified.

The other element in the post-Tours SFIO was the remnant of the wartime majority, now pejoratively entitled 'reformists' and associated with Blum and many of his parliamentary colleagues. The 'reformists' were small in number—their mandates represented some 9 per cent of those present at Tours—but their real weakness was not numerical. The first problem for the 'reformists' was that their platform consisted of two rather unsteady planks (beyond, that is, their opposition to joining the Third International, a position they shared of course with the 'ex-reconstructers'). They advocated a return to membership of the Second International, and they favoured a more whole-hearted and necessarily non-revolutionary commitment to the parliamentary system of government, with all the responsibilities thereby entailed.

Return to the Second International, in 1920, meant not merely a rejection of Moscow and an unquestioning picking up of the discredited threads of the 1914 movement; it also supposed alliance with certain European Socialist Parties of doubtful credentials. The German party had split, and only its conservative majority, now notorious for its role in crushing the 1919 German revolution, had rejoined the Second International. Elsewhere it was the same story: only the most conservative wings of the official labour movements and Socialist Parties had failed to detach themselves from the old movement. An alliance with Noske's SPD and Henderson's Labour Party hardly recommended itself to the majority of the remaining Socialist militants.

Instead, the SFIO from 1921–3 attached itself to what Karl Radek dismissed as the '2½' International, a movement led by the Austrian Social Democrats and the Independent German Socialists (USPD), and whose objective was to construct a truly revolutionary Socialist International that would yet avoid the dictatorial centralism of the Third International of Lenin. Despite numerous international gatherings and much goodwill in the constituent parties (which included the Italian PSI and the British ILP, as well as the Swiss, French, Germans, Austrians, and various lesser groups), it was clear by 1923 that a reunification of all three international movements was not on the agenda. When the two German movements, under the threat of an emergent radical right in the economic crisis of 1923, reunited after six years of separation, the SFIO, which had tied its international commitments rather closely to the line pursued by the USPD, could no longer pursue an independent path, and with most of the rest of the '2½' International it rejoined the (Second) Socialist International, where it has remained. Notwithstanding this reunification, there remained much mutual suspicion and difference of policy between constituent parties in the international socialist movement, and the excessive enthusiasm with which the right wing of the SFIO greeted the renewal of relations with the Labour Party and the majority of the German Social Democrats was not reflected in the party as a whole. On the contrary—it was not until the rise of Nazism and the long years of bad feeling between Socialists and Communists that the mainstream of SFIO members came to accept the inevitability of their re-integration in a reform-minded international movement. Until then, the 'reformists" enthusiasm for a return to the old forms was a decided handicap, at least so far as intra-party influence was concerned.[26]

As for a more committed approach to participation in the political system, this posed even sharper dilemmas. We have seen that the pre-war unity of the SFIO hinged on a delicate balance established in 1905 between advocates of participation and those who opposed bitterly such disregard for the logic of socialist doctrine. To enter the post-war era with a firm tilt towards the former approach would be to provide a host of hostages to PCF propaganda. In the pages of *L'Humanité* and at public debates, the Communists during the 1920s and early 1930s ceaselessly propagated the view that the SFIO ('social democrats'—later 'social fascists') was misleading the workers and peasants, presenting a socialist façade while emulating the Radicals and enjoying the fruits of parliamentary success.

The experience of 1924, when the SFIO entered the elections in alliance with the Radicals in order to avoid another defeat along the lines of 1919, was salutary in this respect. The Communists dined out on it for a decade, while the SFIO, nervously refusing actually to provide ministers for the newly-formed Radical government of Herriot, was forced to support from the outside a government whose policies it did not much like and could do little to influence. From

---

[26] For the '2½' International (sometimes known as the Vienna International, from the location of its headquarters) see, essentially, André Donneur, *Histoire de l'union des partis socialistes pour l'action internationale, 1920–1923* (Sudbury, Ontario, 1967); also Julius Braunthal, *History of the International*, vol. 2 (London, 1967), and Milorad M. Drachkovitch, *De Karl Marx à Léon Blum: la crise de la social-démocratie* (Geneva, 1954).

1926, when the arrangement finally collapsed and the SFIO withdrew into opposition with a sigh of relief, the reformist case for participation in left-leaning governments could expect bitter international opposition. Sometimes the division of opinion was close—at a national council meeting of November 1925 Paul Faure overcame a Renaudel motion in favour of supporting the budget statement of the Radical government by just 1433 votes to 1228—and in 1933 the advocates of participation in government finally exploded in frustration and left the party, causing a minor but significant scission that pushed the SFIO still further to the left. None the less, the line was held. The SFIO, in 1935 as in 1905, was committed to the following joint position: it would not provide ministers for a government of which it was not the dominant partner, and it would not consider forming a government alone or in partnership with others, except in exceptional circumstances and only then with the clear expectation that it would be in power not to 'run' capitalism but to dig its grave.[27]

This motivated refusal of socialists before 1936 to soil their hands in government was seen by many at the time as myopic and destructive. This was not an empty charge: the refusal of socialists to join left-oriented governments explains the failure of the Left to capitalize on election victories in 1924 and 1932; it pushed the Radicals to the right in their search for allies; it severely limited the possibilities for peaceful change in post-war France. It encouraged the SFIO to persist in its failure to think through a coherent and detailed programme of its own, by emphasizing instead the extent to which a Socialist government would be 'more' than just another reformist attempt to tinker with social injustice. Perhaps most ominously it encouraged many on the French Right to think of government as somehow exclusively the territory of non-socialist parties. From here to the vicious attacks on Blum and the socialists after 1936 and the subsequent longing for a right-wing 'house-cleaning' there was little distance to travel. Finally, the success of the party left and centre in keeping the SFIO clear of the risks and opportunities of office helps explain the trauma occasioned in the socialist movement by the new experience of disappointment with a Socialist government in 1936, and the subsequent disputes that split the party in the months before the outbreak of the Second World War.

All of that, however, is directly germane to the reformists' other

[27] On the Cartel des Gauches, see the essay by Jean-Noel Jeanneney, *Leçon d'histoire pour une gauche au pouvoir: la faillite du Cartel (1924–1926)* (Paris, 1977).

major problem. Most of their leaders (and it is possible to speak of the reformists as a coherent group, with their own newspaper and spokesmen pressing a consistent line in party debates) were Paris-based and many of them were in the parliamentary group. This made them a natural object of suspicion to party militants, but it also meant they relied for their impact on party policy almost exclusively, especially after 1928, on the person and ideas of Léon Blum.[28]

This might be thought to have been to the advantage of the SFIO right. Blum had been distinctly moderate in pre-Tours party debates, a close admirer of Jaurès and an enemy of extremism, in action as in doctrine. But, and it is a vital caveat, Blum was also deeply committed to the concept of a united and democratic Socialist Party, in the image of the Jaurèsian pre-war synthesis as he understood it. No major thinker himself, he had followed closely Jaurès's own understanding of marxism and its claims upon the French socialist and republican tradition, and he seems to have understood better and sooner than most others the role ideology played not so much in informing socialist policies as in cementing the party together. He also, it should be said, deeply believed in the role a Socialist Party could play in France in advancing the cause of justice and democracy, and saw its commitment to the overthrow of capitalism as a necessary means to this end. It was this, rather than the more emotional and chauvinist sentiments of some of his reformist colleagues like Renaudel, which explains Blum's famous 'vieille maison' speech at Tours, in which he appealed to French socialists to reject the siren calls of an alien revolutionary tradition (that of nineteenth-century Russia), and preserve the structure and ideals of an autonomous but revolutionary *French* socialist movement.

It followed, then, that for Blum preserving the old party and its ideological apparatus was necessary *both* in order to continue and advance the cause of a truly democratic and revolutionary socialism in France, *and* to keep in one piece the preferred instrument to that end.

[28] The most important works on Léon Blum are Gilbert Ziebura, *Léon Blum et le Parti socialiste* (Paris, 1967); Colette Audry, *Léon Blum ou la politique du juste* (Paris, 1955); Jules Moch, *Rencontres avec . . . Léon Blum* (Paris, 1970); Joel Colton, *Léon Blum, a Humanist in politics* (New York, 1966); Jean Lacouture, *Léon Blum* (Paris, 1980). Of Blum's own writings, the most immediately relevant, in chronological order, are *Commentaires sur le programme d'action du Parti Socialiste* (Paris, 1919); *Pour être socialiste* (Paris, 1919); *Pour la vieille maison* (his speech at Tours) (Paris, 1921); 'L'Idéal Socialiste', in *La Revue de Paris* (mai 1924); *Bolchévisme et socialisme* (3rd edn., Paris, 1927); *Radicalisme et socialisme* (4th edn., Paris, 1936); *L'œuvre de Léon Blum 1940–1945* (Paris, 1955).

Participation in Government, and more generally a commitment to the daily tasks of a party in a parliamentary system, was not something that Blum found doctrinally repugnant, but nor did he see it as virtuous or an advantage *per se*. Sharing with the militants around Paul Faure a belief in the desirable and inevitable collapse of a system founded upon unjust exploitation, he could understand their desire to avoid contamination by excessive contact with the superstructure of such a system. He also grasped clearly that any socialist share in government, at least until 1934, would have divided the party badly, perhaps irrevocably. For Blum almost as much as for the party left, elections were a means to spread the socialist word, and only secondarily did they serve to elect men to a parliament, or even a local council. On the other hand, he saw no reason *not* to take advantage of the historical victories of earlier generations of republicans and democrats, and accordingly threw himself energetically into the battles over social and economic legislation in particular.

As leader of the SFIO group in parliament (and by the 1930s the most prominent public personality in the party), Blum thus walked a tight-rope. He even went so far as to present his dilemma in conceptual form, espousing in 1926 a doctrine that would later serve to justify the party's actions in 1936. Until the moment of capitalism's imminent demise, Blum held, socialists could hope to do no more, at best, than 'exercise' power in a parliamentary system, taking office to advance the course of history where possible, but with no misplaced revolutionary intentions or expectations. The 'conquest' of power, on the other hand, was an option that would present itself to a socialist movement at the proper time, and then (and only then) would a revolution, violent if necessary, be on the agenda. Exercising power meant governing from a position of authority (and it was not until the results of the second round of the 1936 elections that the SFIO would be in a position to fulfil such a prospectus). As to 'conquering' power, here Blum's account tends rather to meet the neo-determinist perspectives of Guesde and his early German socialist mentors. For him as for them, it justified the present stance of a powerless party, and allowed it too to retain its appeal to younger and more militant potential members.

Blum, then, created in his own person a synthesis of the aspirations of a frustrated parliamentary group (many of whose members ached for a ministerial portfolio) and the suspicions and ideas of a still-militant membership. His success went beyond simply holding together an unlikely coalition for the best part of two decades. He also managed to make plausible the socialists' claim to a place in French politics on the 'hard' Left, while continuing to emphasize the gap separating socialists from the PCF, particularly during the years of incipient Stalinization after 1924. All of this was much more difficult than the problems faced by Jaurès, for example, and it is worth emphasizing that Blum's achievement in many ways outdistanced that of his famous mentor. Jaurès lived in an era when the revolutionary claims of Second International marxism remained untested and thus plausible, when the SFIO *was* the only option for militant socialists in France and before, above all, the devastation and industrial changes wrought by a major war had created pressures for a new approach to politics.

This final point is worth emphasis. The increased role of the state in the economy, and the greater expectations of a governmental role in social welfare, both results of wartime interventions from above, meant that the simple socialist model of a capitalist government, rather accurately reflected in the behaviour of the governments of the early Third Republic, no longer made much sense. New problems—and new possibilities—required new solutions. In the late 1920s and early 1930s there sprang up a multitude of clubs, groups, circles, and other formations within the umbrella of socialist and syndicalist movements in France, favouring various forms of planning, interventionism, and other nostrums for the worsening ills of the French economy. Many of the younger and more academic socialists, together with those syndicalist leaders who had played a role in organizing wartime labour, no longer accepted that society was a war between economically opposed classes in which the government was the 'board of directors' for the ruling class. Keynesians before the hour in some cases, future neo-corporatists (and even neo-fascists) in others, they advocated the abandonment of the whole baggage of marxist analysis and its replacement by a socialist commitment to the organizing and running of a mixed economy.[29]

---

[29] See Martin Fine, 'Toward corporatism: the movement for capital–labor collaboration in France 1914–1936' (Univ. of Wisconsin Ph.D. thesis 1971). Also Lefranc, *Le Mouvement socialiste sous la troisième république*, vol. 2 (Paris, 1977). On Henri de Man, the Belgian socialist whose revisionist ideas exercised some hold over the younger socialist intellectuals of these years, see Peter Dodge, 'Voluntaristic Socialism, an Examination of the Implication of Henri de Man's Ideology', in *International Review of Social History* (1958); Peter Dodge (ed.), *A Documentary Study of Hendrik de Man* (Princeton, 1979) and H. de Man, *Au delà du marxisme* (Paris, 1929).

These were the ways of the future, and some of France's future leaders were active in such groups (notably the young Mendès-France). But their ideas made little sense to the average parliamentarian of the SFIO, whose formative experience was often in the Chambre of 1914 or earlier. They also had no appeal to party militants or leaders, to whom it all sounded suspiciously like the solidarism of the 1890s, or the various 'municipal' socialisms that had divided French socialism in the 1880s. Very little about the rhetoric of the *right* in these years suggested an end to the class war, moreover. And thus the *planisme* of the young socialists in the universities made no allowance for the sensibilities of either the Socialists' members or an equally traditionally minded Socialist electorate. Grown older, these *planeurs* now charge that Blum, Faure, and the others squandered the opportunity to renew the ideas and ideals of a socialist movement that consequently stagnated for two decades in nostalgic recapitulation of earlier days. As a result, young men and women left the party in search of other openings, and the SFIO takes the blame for much of the sorry state of the Third Republic when Hitler put it out of its misery.

This is partly true, mostly unfair. Blum himself acknowledged after the defeat of 1940 that the party had become bogged down in the repetition of empty phrases and a strategy of inanition. Yet at the time any alternative approach would probably have spelt disaster; it was the emphasis on a rigid ideological continuity, coupled incongruously with active electoral participation and success, that ensured the very survival of a distinctive French socialism. Too sharp a swing in either direction and the precarious alliance which had survived Tours would have fallen apart. It *did* come asunder, in 1938, under the impact of office, of the crisis of the Spanish Civil War and especially over Munich and the agonizing need to accept another conflict with Germany. Without the unjustly castigated efforts of Blum, and his sense of the need to be faithful to a doctrine that had acquired almost mythical status, the SFIO would have self-destructed a lot sooner.[30]

*

[30] For examples of the almost religious awe in which received doctrinal credo was held, see any of the pronouncements of Paul Faure in these years—thus, a representative quote: 'La doctrine, notre seule raison d'être, notre "ange gardien" qui nous protège contre nos propres erreurs et nos défaillances possibles, la pure déesse dont la robe d'or n'est jamais ternie par les abandons et les trahisons et par qui s'éclairent nos actes, nos pensées, se bercent nos espoirs, et sans qui, pour nous, le présent ne saurait s'expliquer ni l'avenir se comprendre.'

The practical consequences of the conscious and consistent emphasis upon doctrinal continuity can best be seen in two areas of socialist activity: in the party's relations with the Communists, and in its attitude to the syndicalist movement.

The SFIO's approach to the PCF was largely conditioned by the internal history of the Communists themselves.[31] The official position of the Socialists was that Tours had been a misunderstanding, an error, encouraged and orchestrated by the leadership of the Third International. Nothing of importance separated the two movements in theory (give the SFIO's insistence on the continuing marxist premisses for its actions), and the Communists' commitment to revolution in practice was a dead letter in the altered circumstances after 1921. On the other hand, since it was precisely the Communists' affiliation with the Third International that had brought about the split, there could be no question of a reunification so long as that affiliation remained in force.

As the years passed, however, attitudes hardened. Individual Communists left the PCF in disgust or disappointment and rejoined their old party, but the consistent and aggressively anti-socialist line of the PCF in the 1920s, and especially during the 'Third Period' after 1928, meant that 'anti-Communism' became endemic in the socialist movement. This applied as much at the local level, where speakers and stewards at meetings would engage in violent fights, as it did in Paris, where Faure, on behalf of the SFIO, wrote a series of bitter pamphlets detailing the chicanery and double-dealing of the PCF and its Muscovite masters. This anti-Communism was not incompatible with the view that there was no significant difference in doctrine between the two movements—on the contrary, it reinforced it by claiming that Communists were obliged to be aggressive, violent and dishonest in order to give themselves a 'revolutionary' identity they otherwise lacked.[32]

Mutual suspicion did not prevent occasional overlapping interests,

---

[31] Among the hundreds of works devoted to the history of the PCF, the following remain the most helpful, for all their weaknesses and *parti pris:* Annie Kriegal *Les Communistes français* (Paris, 1970); Ronald Tiersky, *Le Mouvement communiste en France 1920–1972* (Paris, 1973); Jacques Fauvet, *Histoire du PCF*, vol. 1 (Paris, 1964); J.-P. Brunet, *l'Enfance du Parti Communiste* (Paris, 1972); Louis Bodin and Nicole Racine, *Le Parti Communiste français pendant l'entre-deux-guerres* (Paris, 1972).

[32] Among the more venomous (and effective) anti-Communist pamphleteers was Paul Faure. See in particular his *Le Bolchevisme en France* (Paris, 1921).

however. As the self-proclaimed heir to the best traditions of the French Left, the SFIO made it a point not to oppose other candidates of the Left at the second round of elections if they were better placed to win. Honouring this claim, Socialists usually withdrew for both Radicals and Communists, depending on the circumstances, in the elections between 1924 and 1936. The PCF had no such scruples and frequently maintained a hopeless candidate into the second round. The results were usually disastrous for the PCF, but could equally divert some vital left votes away from a Socialist candidate, thus letting in the right. Such practices infuriated the Socialists, inclining them ever more towards sympathy for the Radicals instead, and on rare but important occasions even produced a Socialist response in kind. One such instance involved Blum, who refused to stand down in the second round of a 1928 election in Paris against the better-placed Communist candidate, Jacques Duclos. The Socialist Party hierarchy was much displeased and embarrassed, but the Seine Federation which had sponsored Blum's candidature stood firm; if the Communists would not respect the political traditions of the Left in France, then they disqualified themselves as members of that community and merited no respect in their turn.

Accordingly, the 1934 about-turn in Communist tactics and the prelude to the Popular Front created an ambivalent situation. The Socialists could not but accept the PCF's offers of alliance against fascism and the right, but they had no illusions as to the value of the Communists' protestations of solidarity and friendship. So far as the Popular Front programme was concerned, the alliance, now including the Radicals, illustrated an interesting paradox. The PCF wanted the mildest of platforms, in the tradition of left-wing alliances in France, designed to appeal to the radical bourgeoisie and thus create the widest possible coalition for a strong anti-fascist, pro-Soviet and decidedly unrevolutionary government. For the SFIO, a programme of government only made doctrinal sense in the terms spelt out by Blum's conception of the 'exercise' of power, and the SFIO thus entered the alliance with altogether more far-reaching ideas for post-election action. The Communists' visible unwillingness to support such a programme, and their refusal to join the government iself, in June 1936, placed the SFIO in an invidious and embarrassing position of just the kind it had sought to avoid for fifteen years. Having succeeded in maintaining its claim to match the anti-capitalist commitment of the PCF, it had now won an election only to find itself trapped in government while the Communists reaped all the fruits of a unique role on the extra-governmental left.

The logic of the Socialists' position thus became clear in 1936 (and accounts for the misgivings of many on the left of the party about the whole Popular Front experiment). It also explains why the experience of government had the effect not of cementing relations between the parties of the Left in France, but on the contrary of serving to reinforce and make permanent their distance from and suspicion of one another. This was all the more so in the light of the fact that it was the Communists who were the major beneficiaries of the SFIO's decline in urban and and industrial districts. Not that the PCF lacked a rural and southern electorate of its own—seven of the ten departments where the PCF scored best in the 1936 elections were in the south. But for marxists of this period, a secure claim to revolutionary legitimacy rested in the evidence of a properly proletarian constituency, and if one existed in France it was mostly to be found in the areas of rapid Communist expansion, especially in the Paris region. This development, which did not pass unnoticed in the SFIO leadership, only served of course to increase socialist fears, fast becoming paranoia, about a Communist threat to their own survival.

The attitude of the SFIO towards the syndicalist movement between the wars was in many ways the logical obverse to its response to the emergence of a Communist movement in the same years. Here, too, it is best understood in the context of the internal history of the syndicalist organizations themselves.

We have already noted that the CGT had emerged from the war with a less radical approach to its role and to relations with government. At first this new direction was buried in the onrush of revolutionary support in the years 1918–20. Thereafter, the defeats in the strikes of those years, and the revenge wreaked on the CGT by the government (for having purportedly planned 'insurrectionary' strikes) rapidly reduced the capacity of the CGT to adopt any but the most conciliatory strategy. This tendency was then further reinforced by the 1921 scission within the CGT, with a minority departing to form the CGT-Unitaire (CGTU) and adhere to the Syndical International, formed by and affiliated to Moscow and decidedly dependent for organization and strategy upon the dictates of the Comintern.

Throughout the 1920s and early 1930s the CGT was thus faced not merely with a succession of hostile governments (1920–4, 1926–32, 1934–5), but also by competition from its left. In combating these threats it could no longer call on the huge membership of the immediate post-war years; it lacked even the numbers attained in the heyday of pre-war revolutionary syndicalism. At 488,777 in the aftermath of the 1921 scission, it had reached only 577,280 in 1930, its best figure until the inflow of new members in 1936. The fact that the CGTU was doing even worse (349,000 in 1921, 258,000 in 1932) hardly altered the picture. Furthermore, whereas the CGTU, although tiny, was concentrated in industrial regions and in major growth sectors such as metallurgy, the CGT between the wars, until its 1936 reunification with the *Unitaires*, was much better represented in *towns* than it was in industry. Old towns with traditionally high union membership in the small workshops continued to dominate the geography of the movement, while major industrial regions such as Lorraine or the Loire-Rhône were grossly under-represented. Nor was new membership forthcoming, until the legislation of 1936 made it less of a risk for workers in industry openly to join a union affiliated to the CGT.[33]

The CGT, then, compensated for its organizational limitations and limited ability to mobilize the work-force by increasing its interest in legislation and sharpening its arguments for a wider social role for trade unions. This in turn led it, with the onset of depression, to favour central economic planning and investment and to urge the SFIO, with whom it was associated in the anti-fascist movement after 1934, to adopt its ideas and press for their implementation.

The socialists, however, were much less sanguine about plans and 'planism'—Blum in 1934 asserting that 'l'opinion populaire commence à se sentir désorientée par l'abondance des plans . . .'.[34] In general, ever since 1920, the SFIO preferred to keep its distance from the syndicalist movement, and on the whole was as much embarrassed as anything else by the tendencies towards 'governmentalism' in the CGT leadership. This was because the Communists' claim to hegemony over the trade unions, on sound Leninist principles, had opened for the SFIO the possibility of claiming that in this matter at least no one could dispute that it was the socialists and not the Communists who inherited the traditions of the pre-war movement (notwithstanding that many ex-Guesdists had never been very pleased with this particular tradition . . .). By pointing to their own respect for

[33] For information on the CGT in the 1930s, see the extremely useful work by Prost, *La CGT à l'époque du Front Populaire*, and sources listed in note 9.

[34] Lefranc, *Le Mouvement socialiste*, vol. 2, p. 313.

the autonomy of syndicalist organizations and contrasting this with Communist control of the CGTU, the socialists made a valid point—but not one that was necessarily to their advantage.

In theory, the 'hands off' policy of the SFIO was complemented by political neutrality on the part of the CGT. In practice, the old syndicalist movement was about equally hostile to Communists and the right alike, and was 'neutral' only as between the Radicals and the SFIO. It frequently found to its gratification that 'left' Radicals such as Daladier were sympathetic to its social policies on insurance, pensions, and the like, while the official SFIO line was to vote for such proposals in the Chambre, but on doctrinal grounds to avoid adopting them for its own. On the other hand the CGT was much more likely to have dealings with the socialists at joint public events such as May Day celebrations or political demonstrations.

Such contacts were limited, though, by syndicalist leaders' suspicions of the rhetoric and 'leftism' of the SFIO; it was characteristic of the European labour movements to find their socialist bedfellows embarrassingly oriented towards revolution, or simply 'ideas', but in France (uniquely in northern Europe) the union leaders had no direct way of putting pressure on the socialists to modify their stance. Thus the CGT, for example, placed much faith in the League of Nations and especially its International Labour Office (ILO), sending representatives to the latter and seeking closer contacts with other likeminded union movements. The SFIO, by contrast, although in principle a strong supporter of the League throughout our period, was doubtful and even cynical as to its effectiveness after a while. About the ILO it had even graver doubts, and when Albert Thomas (the Socialists' wartime minister of Armaments) became director of the Office the party leadership forced him to choose between that function and his parliamentary seat as socialist *député* from the Tarn.[35]

It should be noted, however, that while these official differences remained at the top of the syndicalist and socialist movements, a considerably greater degree of integration existed at the local level. The CGT, for example, although itself officially neutral in politics, did

---

[35] Thomas's federation supported him in his initial reply that there was nothing incompatible between being a socialist *député* and holding office in the ILO. However the CAP stood firm, and in November 1921 Thomas resigned his seat in the Chambre to avoid an open conflict between party secretariat and local federation. The latter was decidedly upset, and understandably—the affair had been the first open disagreement within the party since Tours and had resulted in a decisive victory for central authority over local autonomy.

not require of its member federations that they adopt a similar line outside of the activities of the Confederation, and some of the affiliated industrial unions, as well as certain inter-industrial departmental unions such as that of the Nord, were openly and actively socialist. Indeed in the Nord, party and syndicalist leadership overlapped to a point where the distinction lost its meaning. Socialist-controlled municipalities there would frequently lease labour exchanges and workers' centres (*Bourses du Travail*) to the union movement for a nominal sum, and in return the unions would exclude from the use of such facilities any of the Socialists' opponents, beginning with the CGTU and the Communists! And it should not be forgotten, too, that the SFIO remained firm in *its* conviction that all socialists should belong to the union of their trade or profession. How far this injunction was observed we cannot know, but it was faithfully preserved as a requirement of membership throughout these years.

What finally brought unions and socialists into closer and more formal relations was not any change of principle on either side (the organizational separation and the potential for mutual mistrust and recrimination remain to the present) but the experience of the Popular Front. In the years 1935–7 the CGT once again became a major force in the land. Reunited in early 1936 with the CGTU, courtesy of the change in Communist strategy, it grew from some 755,000 at the point of reunification to 3,958,000 in 1937. Even more important, it was now having daily dealings with a Socialist government which fully acknowledged and endorsed the unions' claim to represent the interests of the work-force, and which was implementing many of the policies advocated long since by syndicalist policy-makers. In this sense the SFIO in 1936 caught up with the changes that the CGT had undergone since 1918—it accepted the requirement to work within the constraints of the existing political system and abandoned the contrast between 'mere reform' and 'genuine revolution' in favour of a developing but still unformed conception of a welfare state in a mixed economy, along lines that would be articulated more fully after the Liberation.

An important distinction remained, however. For the CGT, revolutionary syndicalism was clearly defunct. To have resurrected it in the context of inter-war French politics would have been to court disaster, from below no less than from above. For the socialists, on the other hand, there was almost something gratifyingly ironic about this transformation of the syndicalist movement, confirming as it did the old Guesdist contention that the union movement could not *of itself* be the vehicle for significant social (and therefore political) change. If anything, the new face of the CGT was all the *more* acceptable in that it confirmed the socialists in their own ideological rectitude—even if for circumstantial reasons it remained unwise to assert superiority or even influence over the unions. And so, at least until 1936, the SFIO continued to proclaim the virtues of continuity, achieving the same goal as the syndicalists—survival in a hostile environment—by the opposite means.

Conclusion

By 1936 the SFIO was in no sense the party of any particular class. Nor did its political behaviour or its relations with other political forces in French society reflect or arise from the sociological configuration of either its membership or its voters. On the other hand, there was a fairly strong relationship between the SFIO's sense of the class whose claims it *ought* to represent and the political strategy it espoused in these years. This is the meaning of the continuing importance of marxism as the organizing concept at the heart of French socialism (independent of the inadequacy of the theoretical understanding of marxism by French socialists themselves). It is also the means by which some coherence can be fashioned out of the contradiction between the persistent reassertions of ideological purity in the SFIO after 1920, and the actual possibilities for political practice in this period.

It might be argued that the unwillingness of the SFIO to adapt to its new situation along lines indicated by the experience of other European socialist movements (such as those of Scandinavia) was a direct result of the more general refusal of French politicians and industrialists to recognize the need for change after the war: as the rest of France sought desperately to rediscover the security and stability of the pre-war years, it was not so naïve for the SFIO to pursue a similar strategy. The plausibility of such an interpretation is weakened, though, by the fact that the aftermath of the *Second* World War saw fundamental transformations in French society, but the SFIO still failed to grasp the ideological nettle, pursuing an incongruous and increasingly unsuccessful combination of doctrinal intransigence and political compromise until 1969.

The history of French socialism, then, does not relate very happily to the conditions in which it contingently found itself, at least not for those in search of causally plausible links. It seems, instead, to have responded to an essentially *internal* dynamic. On the other hand, there seem few grounds for treating the Congress of Tours as the central generator in this process. We have already seen the extent to which the electoral and militant bases of the party, although different, followed trajectories that trace back beyond Tours to the socialism of earlier years. The peculiarly French disjuncture between the socialist movement and its wider national constituency, itself fashioned by the conditions of radical politics in nineteenth-century France, continued essentially undisturbed into the 1920s.

The point is perhaps better understood when we grasp that it is substantially valid for the history of the Communists as well; with the exceptions we have noted, the PCF shared with the SFIO its character as a self-consciously 'proletarian' party dependent on a largely non-proletarian electorate. Both parties operated in a system where the real opportunities for fulfilling their declared maximum ends were nil, but could not be acknowledged to be so. Both came over time to the understanding that anything short of a full commitment in practice to electoral politics, in a country where universal manhood suffrage was almost a century old, was political suicide. The distinctive foreign and tactical concerns of the Communists should not blind us to this common condition.

One might go further. It was the Communists, not the SFIO, who came closest to disappearing in the period which concerns us, and just as the Popular Front marked the end of the socialists' delicate act on the tactical trapeze, so the experience proved to be a spring-board for a revived Communist movement. Nothing in the ideological under-standing of the participants or the sociological observations of outsiders can offer an independent account of this process. But the common and frequently parallel experiences of SFIO and PCF, taken over the longer period—say 1905–69 for the one, 1920–81 for the other—suggest a last reflection. Neither the strengths of the Com-munists in their halcyon years (1936–72), nor the endemic weaknesses of the socialists can be traced to the scission that divided them. It follows that neither the history of inter-war socialism nor that of the Communist movement in France offers fertile soil for reflections on the historical 'necessity' or the social 'logic' of that moment. The achievements of the organized movements of the Left in implanting themselves so successfully in French political culture, and their common failure to capitalize upon that success in order to further the ends for which they claimed to exist, may be traced in part to established features of the French historical landscape. But more soberingly to the protagonists, they seem to owe a lot to the enduring appeal but also the intrinsic limitations of the ideological assertions common to socialists and Communists alike.

Map 1. Active Population in 1906

Map 2. Active Population in 1931

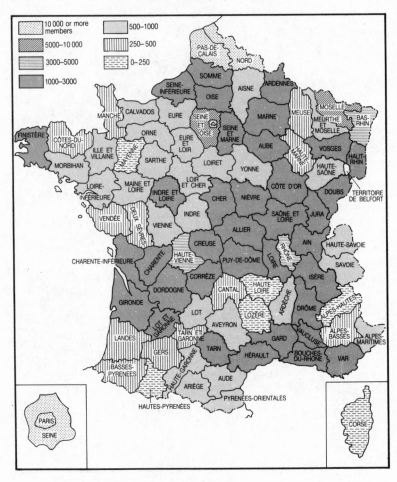

Map 3. SFIO Membership (absolute) 1920

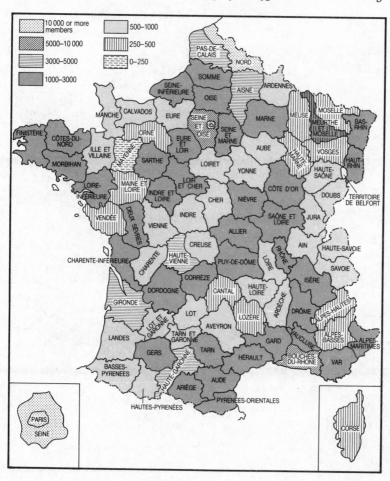

Map 4. SFIO Membership (absolute) 1936

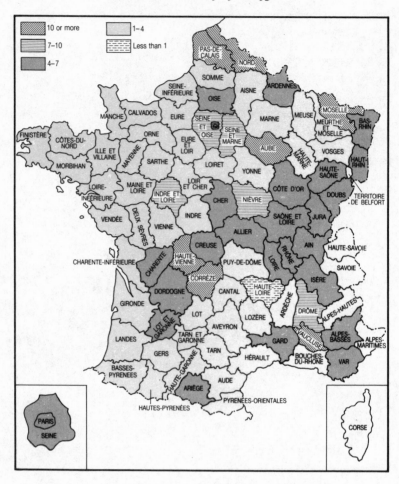

Map 5. SFIO Membership (as percentage of population) 1920

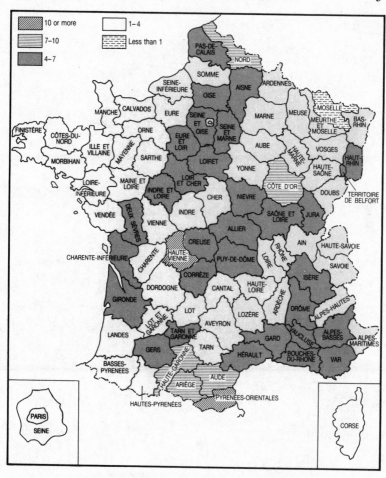

Map 6. SFIO Membership (as percentage of population) 1936

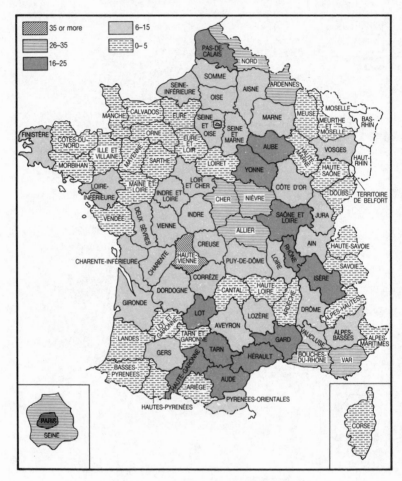

Map 7. SFIO Electorate (as percentage of all electors) 1914

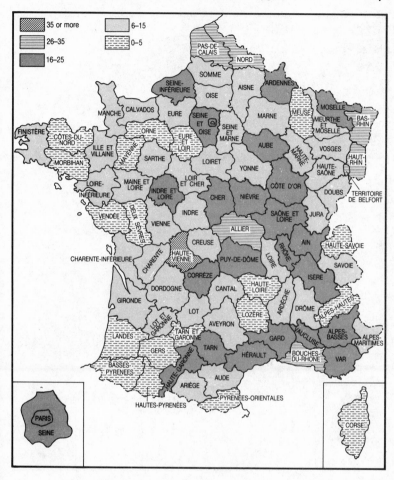

Map 8. SFIO Electorate (as percentage of all electors) 1919

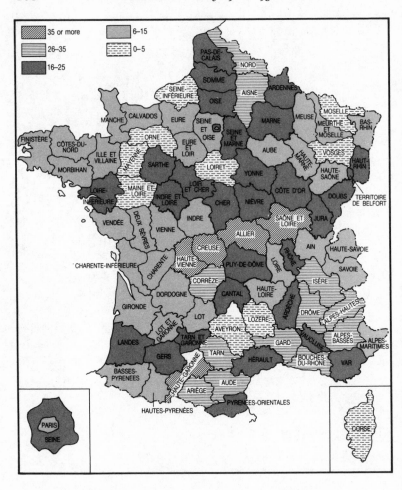

Map 9. SFIO Electorate (as percentage of all electors) 1936

4
French Marxism 1945–1975

Notre époque exigeait de tous les hommes de lettres qu'ils firent une
dissertation de politique française.

Jean-Paul Sartre

La lutte des classes dans la théorie n'est pas un mot. C'est une réalité, une
terrible réalité.

Louis Althusser

'C'est quoi, la dialectique?'
'C'est l'art et la manière de toujours retomber sur ses pattes, mon vieux'

Jorge Semprun, *Quel Beau Dimanche*, pp. 99–100

FOR a generation following the Second World War, the fashions in
left-wing thought in general and high marxist theory in particular were
set by the writings of a succession of French intellectuals, whose
names became synonymous with styles of marxist discourse. From
Maurice Merleau-Ponty to Louis Althusser, what was being argued in
Paris became the context for more isolated enterprises upon similar
lines from Yale to Canberra. The passage to Britain, the USA, and
beyond usually entailed some dessication of the original; what was
political in Paris became theoretical in London, before being reduced
to the merely academic in its final resting place further afield. This
only served to intensify the interest of foreigners, however: unable to
grasp the rather particular circumstances of intellectual production in
France, scholars and acolytes abroad could only attribute the intensity
of feeling aroused by the works of Parisian *maitres à penser* to an
originality and power of pure thought, to the identifying of which they
have since devoted many thousands of pages.[1]

There is nothing very wrong with this. If Perry Anderson feels the
need to publish a book defending the credibility of Louis Althusser
against crude empiricist criticism, if literary critics make of Jacques

---

[1] Notorious examples are *New Left Review* (*passim*) and the Yale English department.
Even Susan James in her very thoughtful work on holism treats the work of Althusser as
something timeless—he just has 'positions'. See Susan James, 'Holism in Social Theory:
the Case of Marxism' (Univ. of Cambridge Ph. D. thesis 1979).

Derrida more than he has ever, even at his most playful, felt constrained to make of himself, little harm ensues. But it is all a trifle peculiar, because at its heart there lies a fascination with an ideological production line once thought incapable of delivering the goods. That it should be *French* marxism and its offshoots which have aroused such latter-day interest is distinctly at odds with an earlier insistence by many upon the inadequacy of theoretical work in France when it purported to be 'marxist'. And yet, since 1945, there is no doubt that it is in France that theoretical discussion around problems in and of marxism has been liveliest.[2]

Until recently, however, it has not been possible to discuss this unusual moment in French intellectual history from any critical distance. The phenomenon was still unfolding. Studies of French marxism published in the years 1956–75 risked appearing just as the latest 'twist in the dialectic' curled obliquely off the presses.[3] Moreover, some kinds of critical distance were their own nemesis: accounts of disembodied entities called 'French Marxism' or 'Existential Marxism' packaged their subject-matter so as to remove it entirely from the political realm. Political chronology served at best as a distant backdrop for a detached account of the Life of the French Mind. This approach (for obvious reasons infrequently encountered in France itself) suggested a sort of timeless unarmed conflict between brachyce-phalic dyspeptics, with the elderly or conceptually crippled retiring on occasion, to be replaced by New (or newer) Left combattants.

Since the mid–1970s, however, circumstances have altered. At some point between 1973 and 1978 marxism, and the study of its theoretical implications and resonances, lost its stranglehold upon the intellectual imagination in France, a grip it had exercised unbroken for a generation. In the space of less than a decade it became fashionable to be not just non-marxist, but anti-marxist. The French discovered Popper, Hayek, and, with embarrassment at the oversight, their own Raymond Aron. Men and women who had once hawked *La Cause du Peuple* began writing tracts on the evils of totalitarianism and the crimes of Mao. Nor were they replaced in their turn by a rising generation—modern Parisian students are not so much opposed to marxism as simply indifferent.

[2] See for Perry Anderson's views, *Arguments within English Marxism* (London, 1980), p. 2.
[3] The phrase is borrowed from George Lichtheim. See Lichtheim, *From Marx to Hegel* (London, 1971).

The message travels slowly. On average it takes British radical intellectuals five years to grasp a change of mood on the Continent, and the transatlantic voyage adds a further three. Accordingly the English-speaking world is still much diverted by the residue of late French marxist thinking, and even more by the verbal gymnastics of the post-structuralists. But it remains the case that marxism in France is now history, albeit recent history, and the time has come to treat it as such.

*

The aims of this chapter are these. In the first place, to establish the identity of the marxist moment in France, and in particular to set in relief the homogeneity of marxist thought in France, in contrast with the usual emphasis upon opposition, differences, and contrasts. I shall try to illustrate the remarkable extent to which even the most apparently diverse and divergent thinkers were in fact negotiating their path through the same political and intellectual thickets.

My second objective is to emphasize the importance of the historical context for our understanding of modern marxist thought in France. By this I mean that it is not sufficient to note the general setting of French or Parisian intellectual and political history, but that the very debates and arguments themselves, so apparently abstracted from quotidien concerns, simply cannot be made to reveal their meaning except as a part of that history. It no more makes sense to lift Sartre or Althusser out of the France of their day and into a limbo of 'marxist discourse' than it does to ask of John Locke, for example, that he take part in a debate with latter-day liberals on the subject of property rights. It does not follow from this that Sartre and the rest would agree with such an approach; like Locke, they must, if they are consistent, suppose themselves to be writing for eternity. But for us they are users of a certain sort of political language at a certain moment in a very particular society, and our concern must be to learn just what that language meant at the moment of its appearance, for user and hearer alike. My contention in this essay will be that the theory and practices of marxism in France were unusually bound up with the political struggles and allegiances of the protagonists, and more generally with the terms of political argument in modern France.

A third goal to which this chapter is directed is the drawing up of a criticial balance sheet of the achievements of marxism in France as part of a wider account of the part marxist thought has played in the history of the French Left. The incorporation of these intentions into a single chapter inevitably entails selection, in subject-matter and perspective. I have chosen to focus upon those areas of marxist thought in post-war France which had the greatest impact either upon left-wing debate within the country, or else upon the history of marxist ideas in their wider international constituency. This involves neglecting some distinctions which others might find important. For example, I shall be discussing marxist thinkers both in the French Communist Party and outside it. Moreover, I shall make frequent reference to the common 'staging points' of recent French intellectual history—existentialism, humanism, structuralism, post-structuralism, etc. But I make no claim to treat each or any of these in any depth, with the result that some readers may feel that some of their favourite French thinkers get very short shrift in these pages. Even Maurice Merleau-Ponty figures largely in his capacity as founder-editor of *Les Temps Modernes* and author of books and essays on marxism and morality, rather than as a seminal figure in the history of phenomenology. Conversely, certain persons, notably Sartre, Althusser, Castoriadis, Lefebvre, Goldmann, and Gorz play a role that some may find out of all proportion to their contribution to the history of thought, *sub specie aeternitatis*. This I do not deny. It is, however, my contention that the only way to make reasonable sense out of the recent history of marxism is *sub specie temporis*, and in *that* context the selection needs no apology. Those in search of more general or synoptic accounts of the material alluded to in what follows are referred to the bibliography.[4]

The chapter begins with some notes on the intellectual and political context of left-wing thought in modern France. Following these I have set out a summarized account of the course of marxist thought in France since the 1930s. The purpose of this is to provide a frame of reference for the final, analytical section, where chronology takes second place in thematic presentation. The summary also serves as a preliminary guide to the relationship between context and discourse which is set out more fully in the final section.

*

'Pendant trente années les modes idéologiques parisiennes s'accom-

---

[4] Representative of what is available in English are Mark Poster, *Existential Marxism in post-war France* (Princeton, 1975); Michael Kelly, *Modern French Marxism* (Oxford, 1982); Arthur Hirsch, *The French New Left* (Boston, 1981) and Perry Anderson, *Considerations on Western Marxism* (London, 1976). In a class of its own, but very out of date, is George Lichtheim, *Marxism in Modern France* (New York, 1966).

pagnèrent à chaque fois d'une réinterprétation du marxisme.'[5] *Mutatis mutandis*, the various styles of marxism can only be grasped in the context of the peculiarities of intellectual life in France. The general standing of official intellectuals in continental Europe, from Moscow to Madrid, has always been prominent, if not high. In France this is especially the case. It derives in part from the circumstance of a rather small capital city containing within its boundaries, for the past eight centuries, the seat of national government and one of the world's top universities. The combination (to which one should add the locus of financial power as well) is peculiar to France and its significance was enhanced by the creation, in the Revolutionary years, of a series of élite academies whose graduates both know one another intimately and also form a very small, peculiarly self-reproducing, and distinctly self-aware (and self-regarding) intellectual and academic élite. Ever since AD 1300, the history of Parisian politics and left-bank argument and taste has been intertwined beyond distinction.

Accordingly, the politics of opposition have always been a daily concern of Parisian thinkers and their acolytes, and they have come to expect that the thoughts *they* espouse should be no less at the centre of the concerns of politicians and princes. This does not, of course, mean that French intellectuals have always been *engagés* (there is, not accidentally, no direct English equivalent). But even at their most determinedly anti-political or counter-cultural (as in the early 1890s or the 1920s) they have always considered themselves to be making a very political statement. Julien Benda did not endear himself to his peers in 1927 when he suggested that political commitment might of itself be a form of broken faith for scholars; nor was even he able, over time, to deny the pressures toward such commitment.[6] The worst thing that can happen to the Parisian community of writers and thinkers is to be, or be thought to be, irrelevant in the eyes of the political community. Hence the post–1981 embarrassments of the radical intelligentsia, faced with a Socialist government they could neither influence nor unstintingly support. And hence, too, the special appeal of Louis Althusser when he informed young supporters that by engaging in 'theoretical practice' they could participate to the full in the class struggle, *as* intellectuals. One may imagine their pleasure, too, upon

---

[5] Raymond Aron, *Mémoires* (Paris, 1983) p. 579.
[6] See Julien Benda, *La Trahison des Clercs* (Paris, 1927). By the end of the 1940s, Benda was an enthusiastic fellow-traveller.

learning in 1970 that *the* dominant ideological state apparatus was the university![7]

One very special characteristic of the French style of thought has been the emphasis upon 'totality', or the absolute. There has never been much room in French social theory for partial responses, nor even for the study of parts of a problem. With this has come a distaste for intellectual doubt, uncertainty, or scepticism, for all approaches which entail the admission that pure enquiry may prove ultimately inadequate. There is an interesting genealogy to this neglect of lesser or intermediate concerns, the ignoring of the part in the search for the whole. It is not absurd to see it emerging in the distinctively different concerns of a Descartes and a Bacon (one is tempted to add, Aquinas and Occam . . .). In the modern era it has taken the form of a clear preference for metaphysics over moral philosophy, and more specifically an energetic desire to exorcize from the thing-to-be-explained all random, or contingent, or causally under-determined phenomena. Because marxism offered a way of recovering the 'illusion of total knowledge' (Czeslow Milosz), a way of returning to Kantian certainties via the public sphere, modern French intellectuals were always likely to be susceptible to its appeal, appropriately packaged.[8] Indeed, the taste for paradox in Marx (his desire, for example, to show that the very production relations of capitalism which were most iniquitous would also prove its downfall) made his particular way of arguing especially well adapted to educated French tastes. Marx is not usually thought of as the author of moral tales, but he is in fact readily assimilable into a culture which incorporates La Fontaine and Eric Rohmer within its canon.

The holistic strain in French styles of thought is of course at ease with the intellectual and existential preferences of continental Catholicism. Quite consciously so, in fact; many intellectuals have remained in a state of unconcluded negotiation with the Catholic faith even while moving into and out of a committed marxism. For Lucien Goldmann, who noted the point, marxism amounted to an updated Pascalian bet upon an uncertain future, while ex-marxists like Edgar Morin attributed both the content and especially the *form* of their political affiliation to the Catholic predilection for ritual over belief. French intellectuals, it is true, had a marked preference for being

---

[7] See Jacques Rancière, *La Leçon d'Althusser* (Paris, 1974), pp. 89, 142.

[8] Czeslow Milosz, quoted in J. Verdès-Leroux, *Au service du Parti. Le parti communiste, les intellectuels et la culture, 1944–1956.* (Paris, 1983), p. 16.

known by their deeds, albeit the literary deed may not have been what the Apostle had in mind.[9]

Closely related to this way of thinking was the French emphasis upon essence. Again and again, from Rousseau and Helvetius and before, we find the essential privileged over the (merely) contingent. The object was always to construct systems of thought whose innermost fundamentals would be invulnerable to criticism, the latter always deflected onto secondary or accidental features which were dispensable. Hence the proliferation of *categories* in French discourse, with the object, à la Ptolemy, of preserving the core of a theory by rendering almost indefinitely flexible the periphery of the argument. Originally employed for distinguishing between nature and society (or, earlier still, between forms of godly creation), these distinctions served stoutly in the years after 1945 to preserve a notionally 'essential' marxism from its (contingent) errors and sins.[10]

The device was not peculiar to France—echoes of it rebound still in marxist and neo-marxist debate everywhere. The difference was that in France it was sustained by generations of mainstream philosophical argument, whereas elsewhere it not only *was* a rather specious exercise in special pleading, but actually sounded that way. But, as anyone who has ever engaged in serious argument with a French-educated person will know, secondary points in a dispute rarely attract serious attention. The accidental just doesn't really matter. Such interest as it arouses concern not its properties but its status (as accident or essence). The implications of this way of reasoning for the exorcizing of Stalinism in France will be considered later.[11]

What must already be clear is the disproportionate amount of intellectual time in France devoted to the Word. For two generations after Marx's death this would inhibit the French from engaging seriously with his opinions, as then understood. But with the decline of the Second International and the victory of Leninism in the East, the

[9] For Lucien Goldmann, see his work, particularly *Le Dieu caché: Etudes sur la vision tragique dans les pensées de Pascal et dans le théâtre de Racine* (Paris, 1955); *Recherches dialectiques* (Paris, 1959); *Marxisme et sciences humaines* (Paris, 1970). Note, too, the opinions of Henri Lefebvre (*La Somme et le reste* (Paris, 1959), p. 223) and Edgar Morin (*Autocritique* (Paris, 1958), p. 98).

[10] The irreductible (and uninvestigated) hypotheses of the theory of surplus value and the labour theory of value did valiant duty as essences in these years.

[11] For a good discussion of the distinction between the 'accidental'—'recul provisoire du mouvement ouvrier' and the essential—decline of capitalism, etc.—see Claude Lefort, *Sur une colonne absente* (Paris, 1978), p. 59. The text in question was published in *Lettres nouvelles* in 1963.

emphasis within western marxism switched from material causality to consciousness. As a result, the French inhibitions no longer applied and the route lay open to some truly remarkable semantic exercises. In its modern form the intoxication with the power of the spoken and written word (notably the abstract noun) took off into the stratosphere with the discovery by Saussure (discovered anew in the 1960s) that language itself can be an infinitely renewed subject of investigation for those who live by deploying it. The connection with marxism in the West after 1917 is clear: once the thought of Marx had ceased to be measured (or measurable) by its predictive or transformative capacities in its continent of origin, its appeal and its truth status became almost wholly narcissistic. Marxism became the subject-matter of marxists, where once that role had been filled by the real world of social relations. And at that point marxism became the perfectly-adapted focus for French intellectual effort.

As a result of this happy congruence, French intellectuals from Merleau-Ponty to Deleuze have been able to operate in a free state. For the former, marxism was superior to other Machiavellian politics because it knew itself to be dishonest, which self-knowledge implied a higher level of 'honesty'; for the latter, in his professional concern to deny that there really *is* anything, everything is a 'copy'. What distinguishes between them is that some copies of knowledge (or whatever it may be) know that they are copies, whereas others mistakenly take themselves for the real thing, or else believe the original to be 'original'. The former are to be preferred.[12] This sounds quite unrelated to marxism, and it certainly has nothing to offer by way of a political project, but the work of Deleuze and others is closely coupled both with Althusser's emphasis on Marx's 'silences' (a true silence being preferable to an erroneous utterance), and with the post-1968 obsession with the need to free ourselves from the *language* that oppresses. In the longer run this solipsistic strain in French intellectual life has rather run into the sand, declaring as its project the necessarily projectless and unattainable understanding of non-meaning, and it is perhaps symptomatic of its terminal trauma that it has been accorded the accolade of incorporation into official Communist discourse: when she wishes to say that Marx inverted Hegel's dialectic, Solange Mercier-Josa feels obliged to write of 'la substitution d'un signifiant à un autre', post-structuralist cant for a pre-1968 cliché.[13]

[12] For Gilles Deleuze, see his *Différence et répétion* (Paris, 1968).
[13] Solange Mercier-Josa, *Pour lire Marx et Hegel* (Paris, 1980), p. 71.

In this magma of language, French intellectuals have none the less incorporated one very powerful political experience, which colours both the form and the content of their work and explains not just the possibility of the incorporation of marxism sooner or later, but perhaps the inevitability of the process. Because the internal emphases of French intellectual output rather inhibit properly *political* theory (it is difficult to think of a single French thinker who has devoted any effort to the construction of such a thing—hence the fascination with the recently-translated works of the empirical and liberal schools), the latter has been substituted with French Revolutionary history. The symbolic moments of the Revolutionary experience of 1789–1794, and to a lesser extent 1848 and 1871, have entered the vocabulary of all academic thinkers as intellectual reference points. Consequently, the men who built the interpretative penumbra that François Furet calls the 'revolutionary catechism', Mathiez, Georges Lefebvre, Albert Soboul, as well as Jaurès and Lucien Herr, have acquired a status which is well deserved (if unique among historians): not only do most French writers over thirty owe their understanding of their political environment to the diffused work of these scholars, but it is to Mathiez *et al.* that French intellectuals are perforce obliged to look when seeking an empirical skeleton on which to graft their fleshy metaphysical corpus of thought. It is the French Revolution, understood as a process with meaning, which explains in the last instance all the unresolved contingents in French political reality, and provides the foundations for an account of how (marxist) essence may ultimately be incorporated into fact. In other words, the Revolution (and a certain reading of it) offers a safety net to even the most ambitious of intellectual high-wire acts (or did, until a recent generation of historians began to unravel the very premises of the traditional reading, with as yet uncharted results).[14]

For these purposes, French radical intellectuals since the 1840s, like Monsieur Jourdain, have been writing (marxist) prose all their lives. Until 1945, however, only a small minority of them had actually attempted to connect their unstated assumptions about the meaning of 1789 with their contemporary ideological affiliations. And the difference between reading Guizot on the French Revolution, and reading Marx, comes in the end to just such a connection, plus an appended teleology. Hence the ease of transition.

[14] See François Furet, *Interpreting the French Revolution* (Cambridge, 1981), *passim;* also Daniel Lindenberg, *Le Marxisme introuvable* (Paris, 1975), pp.157–9.

But the French Revolution was (is) more than interpreted content, it was also experienced form. The twin motifs of *Terreur* and *Rupture,* so prominent in the writings of the period covered in this chapter, derive directly from the fascination exercised by the style of the Revolution upon ensuing generations of men and women (usually very far removed from the experience of either motif in their own lives). There is a strange dialectic of esoteric thought and the taste for violent action in French life and letters, reaching its apogee in Sartre.[15] Aspects of this genre surface in earlier writers (for example Céline and Péguy) and are sometimes treated as representative of the generation which acquired its moral and aesthetic preferences at the time of and through participation in the First World War. But the continuing French fascination with *rupture, le grand soir, journée,* and so forth suggests a deeper indigenous tradition. Only in France was the Manichean emphasis in Zhdanovism ('two camps', 'two sciences', etc.) so well received and for so long, and no other community of students and intellectuals so took to its bosom the Chinese Cultural Revolution as did the French (in Italy this strain of chiliastic extremism was driven underground after 1969, and it is significant that the Italian authorities have felt able to pin the intellectual leadership and legitimation for terror and violence upon just one professor—in France a similar theory of intellectual responsibility would inculpate a whole generation of university teachers!).

This eschatalogical focus in French radical thought explains the warm reception accorded those who have played upon it in their own work. Althusser's theory of the 'epistemological break' in Marx's writings is the more comfortably digested for settling easily into a view of the world which registers the national experience as just such a series of 'breaks' (and if in practice, then of course in theory). The recondite vocabulary of the PCF, full of suggestions of rot, decay, and renewal, of Manichean oppositions and irreconcilable differences, appeals subliminally to this concern even when the actual discourse is repulsive to the conscious mind, and Sartre for one was always utterly frank about his preference for the *act* of revolution over the (presumably ensuing) establishment of Communism. He also expressed a nostalgia for the days when class struggle really *was* struggle and

---

[15] The classic text, of course, is Maurice Merleau-Ponty, *Humanisme et terreur. Essai sur le problème communiste* (Paris, 1947).

conflicting consciousnesses truly clashed: 'avant la Première Guerre Mondiale, la lutte des classes avait du je ne sais quoi'.[16]

In an intellectual community where the leading liberal light before 1945 was the essayist Alain, this nostalgic indulgence in a disembodied revolutionary spirit substituted as the politics of radical opposition for an intelligentsia which was always faced with the choice of being committed or entering nothingness. Indeed, as one man put it, the engagement of post-war intellectuals amounted to a commitment to being committed.[17] But until 1945, there had been no very obvious way in which these general characteristics of the French community of thinkers and writers could be channelled into one very restrictive ideological framework without experiencing undue constriction. What was hitherto lacking was a holistic account of the human condition which would respect the French metaphysical tradition while simultaneously engaging the actual experience of radical political action in all its annoying contingency. And such an account would moreover need to conform to the demanding requirements of the Parisian concern with the properties of the Higher Thinking.

The vehicle of this transformation was of course the introduction of Hegel into mainstream French thought, and the circumstances surrounding this introduction help to illuminate the context of later developments. During the 1930s a number of young philosophy graduates, among them Sartre and Henri Lefebvre, acquired an awareness of both the writings of Hegel himself and the hitherto unavailable works of the younger, more Hegelian Marx. As Sartre himself wrote, becoming aware of such things meant breaking clear of the dominant strand in French thought, the republican positivism which controlled the University from 1860 to 1930, and literally going to Germany to learn to think differently. Hegel himself was unavailable in French (the *Phenomenology of Mind* appeared only in 1947), and the early marxian texts appeared sporadically in French during the course of the later inter-war years. For those unable to read German or study abroad, access to Hegelian ways of thought came via lecture courses delivered in Paris by Alexandre Kojève and Alexandre Koyré, which served simultaneously to domesticate Hegel for French students, *and*

---

[16] See Jean-Paul Sartre, 'Les Communistes et la paix', in *Situations VI* (Paris, 1964), p. 329.

[17] Morin, *Autocritique*, p. 82.

to present for the first time a thoroughly Hegelianized Marx, an altogether original experience for the French.[18]

Within the ensuing decades a series of publications by the rising generation of scholars offered to a still wider audience the essentials of a phenomenological reading of Hegel and a philosophical reading of Marx. Henri Lefebvre, who had joined the PCF in 1927, published his *Matérialisme Dialectique* in 1939, shortly after the appearance of *Morceaux Choisis* from Hegel, edited by Lefebvre and Norbert Guterman. Lefebvre had also begun work on his *Marxisme*, the first outright presentation in France of Marx as a theorist of alienation, and a pure product of the 1930s, for all it did not appear until 1948. Also published post-war but conceived in the mood of the previous decade was Jean Hyppolite's *Genèse et Structure de la Phénomenologie de l'Esprit de Hegel* (1946), followed a year later by the appearance between covers of Kojève's lectures on an *Introduction à la lecture de Hegel*. Thus, by 1948, there had been laid the foundations for the construction in French thought of a new kind of marxism.

The appeal of this new departure appears to have been overwhelming. Lefebvre himself has written of the powerful impact upon him of the works of the young Marx, while both Merleau-Ponty before the war and the young Emmanuel le Roy Ladurie in the 1940s were fascinated by the implications of the master–slave relationship.[19] The experience of the Occupation and the Resistance, even if only at second hand, undoubtedly strengthened the sentiment in favour of political engagement, and the centrality of the theme of alienation both struck a chord in recent French experience and simultaneously proposed a moral basis for marxist politics which had been lacking in earlier years (or, more precisely, had been incorporated into radical politics only at the cost of obscuring the distinctions between marxist socialism and progressive nineteenth-century republicanism). The autonomous individual having been at least temporarily expunged from the moral universe by the joint efforts of Hitler and Pétain, it was replaced by a

---

[18] Sartre was writing in October 1961, upon the death of Merleau-Ponty. See *Situations IV* (Paris, 1964) p. 192. For the period of the 1930s, see Lindenberg, op. cit., p. 198; Vincent Descombes, *Modern French Philosophy* (Cambridge, 1980), p. 11; Verdès-Leroux, op. cit., p. 80.

[19] Henri Lefebvre, *La Somme et le reste*, p. 109; for Merleau-Ponty, see especially Sonia Kruks, *The Political Philosophy of Merleau-Ponty* (Brighton, 1981) *passim*. Le Roy Ladurie's comments are in Natasha Dioujeva and François George (eds.), *Staline à Paris* (Paris, 1982), p. 173.

more complex subject, in a determinate but constantly changing relation with other individuals and the social whole.

The results of this sea-change were paradoxical. On the one hand, everything became overwhelmingly simple, for the vast majority of radical or would-be radical intellectuals. If it would be too much to say that it boiled down to whether you were 'for' Hegel or 'against' him, Michel Foucault was certainly right to note in retrospect that 'our entire epoch struggles to disengage itself from Hegel'.[20] More precisely, all hitherto plausible intellectual systems were discredited in the face of the greater holism: 'le vieux rationalisme, le vieux libéralisme, le vieux individualisme' were disqualified, leaving only Catholicism or marxism (in this very particular form).[21]

On the other hand, the rise to hegemonic status of Hegelian categories, inside of marxism and out, did not so much resolve the problem of the place of Marx in French thought as bypass it. In effect, philosophers who knew that what passed for official (i.e. Communist) marxism was inadequate and banal, but who wished to be able to believe in a fully-formed political ideology of the active left, were now able to call themselves marxist—subject to scrutiny of the Hegelian small print. But it remained uncomfortably the case that 'real' marxism was still alive, and living an active existence inside the largest political party in France. If anything, then, matters became rather more complicated than hitherto; varieties of marxism had entered the scene, and would compete for intellectuals' attention at different levels. What was worse, the injection of a metaphysical Marx on to the French scene tended to aggravate pre-existing difficulties among would-be intellectual marxists, pointing up sharply (though not necessarily to the person concerned) the wider problems posed by the urgent desire to assimilate marxism into French thought.

I have discussed in chapter two the risk of overstating the case for seeing marxism as foreign to indigenous French socialism in the nineteenth century. The same is true for commentaries on more recent French marxism. It is an exaggeration, for example, for Lichtheim to characterize it as 'at best an approximation and at worst a caricature'.[22] If this is true, it is only because much the same applied to marxism in its adapted political form everywhere it found itself so adapted. Indeed, there had been times when *academic* interest in marxism in France

---

[20] Foucault is quoted in Descombes, op. cit., p. 12.

[21] The quotation is from Henri Lefebvre, *Le Marxisme* (Paris, 1961), p. 14.

[22] George Lichtheim, *Marxism in Modern France*, p. 9.

actually exceeded that shown even in Germany.[23] But there was one glaring gap in the understanding of marxism in France which can hardly be overstated. This concerns marxist economics.

French intellectuals in general had little interest in the study of economics—as an independent discipline it had no recognised existence before the early 1950s. The very emphasis upon economic determinism and simple economic 'laws' was the feature of the marxism of the Second International which much of the idealist intelligentsia found so repugnant, not because it was in error (on this they had no opinion) but because it was crude and lacked conceptual subtlety. This distaste was reinforced both by their own education and by the inter-war emergence of the PCF, with the accompanying Stalinist reduction of marxist economic theory to a short series of undisputed theorems.

With the renewed interest in Marx the philosopher, it was no longer possible to dismiss Marx's economics; if marxism was 'true', or even merely capable of pointing towards truth, then it could hardly carry at its heart a faulted (or worse, foolish) economic theory. However, the essence of marxism was now its theory of human alienation, the conditions of that alienation and the necessity of overcoming this condition. All else, being secondary, could therefore be taken on trust.

And this is precisely what happened. Placing the emphasis upon more readily assimilable categories such as waste, moral exploitation, commodity-fetishism, inequality, and the like, all the major marxist intellectuals of France simply took as given the central economic tenets of the theory. Sartre, for example, assumed that the argument of *Capital* was 'obviously true' and thus needed no commentary. He simply took it that the labour theory of value must be correct, if only because it had the disarming virtue of simultaneously describing a system and predicting its demise (no intellectual system so dramatically 'total' in its claims was likely to be abandoned without a struggle by French thinkers of this era). Althusser also took Marx's economics (in this case the theory of surplus value) as an instance of Marx's genius, preferring to assert its necessary scientificity by ontological ratiocination. Even Henri Lefebvre found it reassuring to think of Marx's work as more *objective* than that of the classical economists, arguing that the theory of fetishism enabled it to surpass its competition by being both a science and a critique of economics, announcing the historicity of the

[23] See Eric Hobsbawm, 'La diffusione del Marxismo (1890–1905)', in *Studi Storici*, vol. 15, no. 2 (1974), pp. 241–70.

latter. Here again, what appealed in Marx's economics was the sheer intellectual audacity of its conclusions, rather than the credibility of the technical devices employed to obtain them.

It comes as no surprise, then, to find that some of the most powerful minds in France saw no reason to take issue with the traditional claims of left-wing popularizers that Lassalle's iron law of wages was the work of Marx, nor to dissent from Thorez's claim in 1955 that the French working-class was undergoing absolute pauperization, nor to pay any attention to Mendès-France, in 1946 or again in 1954, when he strove to set left-wing economic policy on a better footing. They did not so much make a virtue of economic ignorance as suppose it to be irrelevant, since secondary to the sorts of truths whose standing they were equipped to establish and defend.[24]

The marxism of French intellectuals asserted a monopoly on radical thought by restricting the categories worthy of consideration. This device was not peculiar to French thinkers, and over time it has been the first line of defence of western marxism as a whole when faced with intractable external circumstances. But in the context of post-war France, the most immediate result of this regulation of intellectual trade was that the marxism of *non*-intellectuals was accorded undue respect—if only because it was all too happy to take up where the thinkers left off. This would not have mattered fifteen years earlier, when the PCF was an insignificant disturbance on the political landscape. But by 1945, when Sartre and Merleau-Ponty brought to press the first issue of *Les Temps Modernes*, the Parti Communiste Français was supported by five million voters and was the most important political organization in the country.

From the Liberation until 1981, the PCF exercised a serpentine fascination over the radical intelligentsia of France. Together with the peculiarities of Parisian intellectual life, this above all provides the indispensable context for an understanding of the marxist writings of these years. Without an appreciation of the extent to which the work of French marxists constituted a permanent debate with the organization of 'official' political marxism, any account of theoretical production in this generation amounts to a digital recording of the sound of one hand clapping.

The fascination that the Communists could exercise over

---

[24] This is true even of some of the work of Castoriadis. See, for example, his essay 'Recommencer la Révolution', written in 1963, in *L'Expérience du mouvement ouvrier:* vol. 2, *Prolétariat et organisation* (Paris, 1974), esp. pp. 357–9.

intellectuals had its origins, quite simply, in the inconvenient fact that marxism in France (in contrast with experience elsewhere) may have been ideologically etiolated, but it had been, from the outset, the doctrine of a workers' movement. Herein lay its legitimacy, and its claim to attention, massively reinforced by the evidence, after 1945, that real workers, and not just their spokesmen, confirmed with their votes the claims made on their behalf by their self-appointed leaders. With the decline of the SFIO, and until the much later emergence of the new Parti Socialiste, there simply was no alternative plausible representative of the tradition of mass revolutionary mobilization in France. Stalinism made it difficult to be 'with' the PCF, but history made it impossible to be against it. Above everything, intellectuals in these years strove to define themselves with reference to the Communists, to share their myths and move on their terrain. The Communists knew this and capitalized on it (preferring, as a rule, to keep such intellectuals at arm's length, as non-members, where their guilt at being outside the workers' own movement rendered them far more docile and sympathetic to PCF practice than they might have been from within).[25] By the later 1970s the moral blackmail thus entailed had been reduced to its simplest and purest form, shorn of dialectic and subtlety. Thus spoke Georges Marchais in November 1979, responding to intellectuals' criticisms of the USSR and PCF support for it: 'Il aurait mieux valu que l'Union Soviétique reste la vieille Russie, et que son peuple soit maintenu dans l'arriération par le féodalisme et le joug tsariste?'[26]

This was the crux of the matter. French intellectuals were inducted despite themselves into a condition of permanent bad faith. As Merleau-Ponty noted in retrospect, 'Dire, comme nous l'avions fait, que le marxisme reste vrai à titre de critique ou de négation, sans l'être comme action ou positivement, c'était nous placer hors de l'histoire et en particulier hors du marxisme, le justifier pour des raisons qui ne sont pas les siennes, finalement organiser l'équivoque. Dans l'histoire, la critique et l'action marxistes sont un seul mouvement.'[27] More

---

[25] See Verdès-Leroux, *Au Service du Parti*, passim.

[26] See Georges Marchais, in *Les Intellectuels, la culture et la révolution* (Paris, 1980), p. 23.

[27] Maurice Merleau-Ponty, *Les Aventures de la dialectique* (Paris, 1955), p. 338. Merleau-Ponty is also quoted on this subject by Aron (*Mémoires*, pp. 314–15): 'Il est donc bien impossible de couper en deux le communisme, de lui donner raison dans ce qu'il nie et tort dans ce qu'il affirme car concrètement, dans sa manière de nier, sa manière d'affirmer est déjà présent.'

inclined than his erstwhile colleague to make of equivocation an intellectual virtue, Sartre put it thus: 'Le Parti, c'était notre seul pole; l'opposition du dehors notre seule attitude envers lui.'[28]

This condition of bifocal historical vision inevitably led to a confusion as to the identity of marxism itself. It was all very well to acquire a fresh understanding of Marx the young Hegelian, but the heirs of Marx the politician retained the high ground of daily practice. We are thus presented with a confusion which went to the heart of the intellectual self-doubt of this generation.

In his major work of the 1950s Henri Lefebvre, at the very moment of his departure from the Party, wrote at one point of 'marxism' as a thing-in-itself, the mode of thought of reasoning philosophical radicals. But earlier in the same work he referred to 'marxism' in France in a way which clearly suggests that for him the term still stood for the theory and practices of the French Communist Party.[29] Even Cornelius Castoriadis, a consistent left critic of the Party, could write as late as 1963 of 'the ruin of classical marxism', yet on the very same page make the distinction between 'vulgar marxism' (i.e. the crude dialectics of Communist hacks) and 'le meilleur de l'œuvre de Marx'.[30]

What was at issue here was not some confusion in the minds of French intellectuals as to what distinguished marxism from 'marxism'. It was a preference, openly acknowledged, for according some credibility to the form marxism had actually taken in French political life (the PCF) while retaining the self-respect to admit that if *this* was marxism, then no one could embrace it as a system of thought. Until or unless the PCF would somehow just go away (an eventuality never seriously envisaged before 1973) intellectual engagement required a daily exercise in triple-talk. Marxism was a whole, it could not be rendered into distinct packages labelled 'theory' and 'practice'. *But* the PCF itself was not a whole. What it *said* (against the USA, capitalism, etc.) was good; what it *did* (or what was done in the Soviet Union and approved by the Party in France) could not be borne so comfortably. *Therefore*, the marxist totality was retained by dividing it *sotto voce* into present and future. The former could be explained (and exculpated) by constant reference to the latter, and both were contained in a higher theoretical singularity of purpose. The whole process was well suited

---

[28] Sartre, *Situations IV*, p. 228.
[29] See Henri Lefebvre, *La Somme et le reste*, pp. 320, 318.
[30] Cornelius Castoriadis, *L'Expérience du mouvement ouvrier*, vol. 2, p. 308.

to the French variant of Hegelian argument, but remained a constant source of niggling discomfort all the same.

At this point I should again emphasize that many French marxists of the kind I shall be discussing were never members of the Communist Party. Henri Lefebvre and Louis Althusser rank among the more prominent exceptions. The contrast with the British experience, for example, is illuminating. It was not for want of wishing that they could be members. It was primarily because the repulsive character of Thorez's party, when taken together with the peculiar form in which marxism as an intellectual commodity entered France, ensured that for most intellectuals theirs would be a fascination from without—and all the more enduring for that.

Part of the strength of this attraction-repulsion relationship came from the concern with national identity which surfaced in the aftermath of the Vichy humiliation. Both before and after the onset of the Cold War, the PCF evinced an obsessive solicitude for the integrity of the French nation. Until 1948, by reference and by metaphor, Communist discourse set the Party firmly in the Jacobin-nationalist tradition of revolutionary patriotism, adopting as its own the whole republican pantheon (with the addition of Stalin).[31] In the high years of Stalinism, from 1948 to the mid–1950s, this emphasis shifted subtly into an anti-Americanism which was parasitic upon deeper traditions of anti-German sentiment; French independence was being 'alienated' for the benefit of US imperialism acting through its 'agents' in West Germany.[32]

While this patriotic (and frequently xenophobic) vocabulary helped root the PCF in what it identified as its local ancestry, it provoked confused feelings among the intelligentsia. No one would want to claim for the intellectual élite of France a multinational (much less multilingual) cosmopolitanism, but while anti-Americanism (in 1950 as in 1980) always aroused an echo, the philo-Russian sentiments which inevitably accompanied PCF pronouncements were less easily digested. If there is a slavophil leaning in France, it has historically inclined towards a sympathy for Poles (usually locked in struggle with

[31] See François George in *Staline à Paris*, pp. 248–9.

[32] Duclos in 1952 spoke of 'la lutte actuelle pour la libération de notre patrie'—see Jacques Duclos, 'Être Stalinien', in *Cahiers du Communisme*, no. 6, 1952, (from a speech to the Ecole Centrale of the PCF, 10 May 1952). But note how little things changed in the next quarter-century: in 1977 Althusser could still speak of the Federal Republic of Germany as 'the local representative of American imperialism' (in 'On the 22nd Congress of the French Communist Party', in *New Left Review* no. 104 (1977)).

Russians), and the requirement that marxists both look sympathetically upon Moscow and take their lessons from it has never really been integrated into older French habits of revolutionary fraternity. Yet this leaning towards Russia (which from 1945 until the late 1960s reached hysterical levels of uncritical adulation in Communist circles in France) was part of the bedrock doctrine of the PCF, hard to dislodge even today. Faced with this, even the guiltiest of sympathetic intellectuals had occasionally to keep their distance (it was, after all, this issue more than any other which distinguished the convoluted and uneasy apologetics of a Merleau-Ponty from the hatchet-work of a Dominique Desanti).[33]

With these considerations in mind we can now move to an account, albeit in outline only, of the development of French marxist thought in these years. If modern marxism in France has a starting-point it might as well be the programmatic declaration of intent by Maurice Merleau-Ponty in the first number of *Les Temps Modernes:* 'En somme, nous avons appris l'Histoire et nous prétendons qu'il ne faut pas l'oublier.'[34] Moving with history meant commitment to marxism, even if at one and the same time 'cela ne pouvait suffire et . . . nous n'avions rien d'autres'.[35] Although Merleau-Ponty and others eventually became disenchanted by the impossibility of answering adequately for the course of events in the Stalinist bloc, Sartre, his collaborator, never wavered. What to outsiders appeared as a particularly self-absorbed existentialism was to its founders and their colleagues an endless search for the philosopher's stone of a phenomenological marxism that could also *act*. Even when the Communist publication *Nouvelle Critique* lumped Sartre with Malraux and Mauriac as an American tool he did not abandon his efforts.[36] Indeed, the intensity of the search was accelerated after 1949, culminating in 1952–3, when confrontations between Communists and government were at their peak, with Sartre's major essay *Les Communistes et la paix*, in which he presented in its fullest form the Sartrian doctrine of commitment in general and the legitimate claims of the PCF in particular.[37]

As for Merleau-Ponty, his own progression was facilitated by a growing disenchantment with efforts to provide a philosphical basis for

[33] For Desanti at her worst see, *inter alia, Masques et visages de Tito et des siens* (Paris, 1949). For her distinctly self-serving and misleading 'autocritique', see Dominique Desanti, *Les Staliniens* (Paris, 1974).

[34] *Les Temps modernes,* Oct. 1945.   [35] Sartre, *Situations IV,* p. 243.

[36] Quoted in Verdès-Leroux, *Au service du Parti,* pp. 179–80.

[37] The essay is reprinted in full in *Situations VI.*

progressive politics, but the process was considerably accelerated by the death of Stalin. Until that point, and especially in the high years of French Stalinism, from 1948 to 1953, the obsession with choosing sides had paralysed radical thought in the country, inside the Communist Party and outside it alike. Yet within two years there came the recognition that non-Communist marxism in this short period had acquired a distinct identity of its own. This point of view was first offered by Merleau-Ponty in his *Aventures de la Dialectique* (published in 1955) which was both a critical disengagement from his own earlier opinions and a commentary upon his own thought and that of his contemporaries which he saw as a humanist marxism, in contrast to the official 'materialist' variety. The post-war French experience could now be assimilated, so he claimed, to earlier German writings as well as Lukacs, part of a genre he dubbed 'western marxism'. For Merleau-Ponty this was less a requiem than a programme: unlike Sartre he was all too pleased to abandon the less successful efforts of the western marxists to distance themselves from 'mere' materialist marxists and to propose instead a new agenda for the future. Indeed, the next few years saw him writing at the boundaries of marxism, psychoanalysis, linguistics and ethnology, proposing by example the very programme of concerns which would fascinate his successors of a later decade.[38]

However, it was more than just a shift in the interests of the editors of *Les Temps Modernes* which accounts for the important switch in direction which marxist discussion in France underwent from the mid–1950s. Four political developments of the period conspired to alter the terms of debate, moving the focus away from the need to explain away events in the East. These were Khrushchev's secret speech, the invasion of Hungary, the war in Algeria, and the coming of the Gaullist Republic. Collectively they served to disillusion Communists and their supporters, to focus attention on domestic problems, and to transfer radical concerns away from the industrial proletariat and towards foreign nationalist movements as the objects of revolutionary expectation. At the theoretical level the shift in direction was felt almost immediately. Whereas Sartre (not a Party member) had been seeking in the early 1950s to justify Stalinism, Henri Lefebvre (who until 1957 remained in the PCF as one of its most prominent intellectuals) was by 1958 making it his project to 'reprendre' marxism

---

[38] On Merleau-Ponty's contribution to other disciplines, see Claude Lefort, *Sur une colonne absente*, esp. pp. 4 ff.

from Stalinism.[39] In the same years (from 1955 to 1961) a group clustered around the review *Arguments*, notably Edgar Morin, François Fejto, Roland Barthes, Kostas Axelos, and Pierre Fougeyrollas, strove enthusiastically to construct a decontaminated marxist politics capable of dealing directly with contemporary moral issues, of which torture in Algeria was by 1961 the most pressing. It was not that anyone sought directly to reject the rather nebulous humanist Marx of previous years, nor had the Communist Party ceased to pose an obstacle for marxists in search of a revolutionary politics. The difference now was that the revelations about Stalin (revelations, that is, in the sense that things which many had known were now acknowledged) and events in Hungary and Poland released progressives from the need to 'cover' for official marxism. The latter was left more and more to fend for itself, the more so in the light of evidence from the 1958 elections that the hitherto impregnable mass base of the PCF might be beginning to crumble.

All these developments gave added credibility to the views of a little-known group of critical left-wing writers based in the periodical *Socialisme ou Barbarie*. Founded in 1947 and dominated by the formidable Cornelius Castoriadis, *Socialisme ou Barbarie* had from its inception attacked the domineering tendencies and bureaucratic pretensions of the Leninists, whether in the Third or Fourth International. The group drew on traditions of syndicalist discourse from the turn of the century, as well as on more recent work by such ex-Communists as Boris Souvarine. Its chief targets were the 'vanguardism' of the Communists and the Trotskyist 'microbureaucratie'. Among its achievements were some of the most penetrating contemporary analyses of the Soviet government and economy. As for its own preferences, these were for a radical and autonomous proletarian movement, the only legitimate source of genuine revolutionary change—'La grève reste notre mot d'ordre central. L'élargissement et la généralisation de la grève, couronnée du mot d'ordre de la grève générale, forment toujours la base de notre orientation.'[40] All attempts to lead the workers from above or from the outside were a *tromperie*,

[39] See Henri Lefebvre, *La Somme et le reste*, p. 366. Lefebvre's other important work in this period includes *La Pensée de Lenine* (Paris, 1957); *Problèmes actuels du Marxisme* (Paris, 1958); *Sociologie du Marx* (Paris, 1966), and *Au delà du structuralisme* (Paris, 1971). But he is perhaps best known for the multi-volume *Critique de la vie quotidienne*, which first appeared in 1947.

[40] Cornelius Castoriadis, *La Société française* (Paris, 1979), p. 45. The quotation comes from a piece first published in 1947.

and all other marxist schools a 'travesty'. This angle of vision, combined with Castoriadis's biting sarcasm and the almost complete absence of any proletarian audience for its ideas made few friends for *Socialisme et Barbarie* and secured it little influence in its early years. Yet it is in its pages more than anywhere that the ancestral roots of the 1960s critiques are to be found.

Part of their importance lies in the fact that even as they were laying the groundwork for a different sort of marxism, Castoriadis and his companions were actually drawing away from marxism itself. Their preference for radical criticism as a way of life (and the absence of restraining institutional attachments) led them, by the end of the 1950s, progressively to detach themselves from the mainstream of marxist thought. Or rather, as Castoriadis put it in 1963, 'Le mouvement ouvrier, en tant que mouvement organisé de classe contestant de façon explicite et permanente la domination capitaliste, a disparu.' And with it had gone the central premiss of classical marxism, the primacy of production relations. The newly-dominant structure was the 'bureaucratic-hierarchic' organization of society. This confirmed an earlier proposition from the same source, that both the basic postulates and the logical structure of Marx's economic theory were 'essentially bourgeois ideas', with no distinctively revolutionary identity.[41]

All this was not quite so iconoclastic as it sounded. For one thing, Castoriadis continued to see Marx's interest in the proletariat as a matter of real *political* importance. Moreover, jettisoning economics, even Marx's economics, as a secondary affair of little note was nothing new in France, as we have seen. But the blunt presentation of such truisms was unusual (it was sufficiently contentious to split the *Socialisme et Barbarie* group), and Castoriadis had struck one significantly new note in left-wing argument: the prospect, visible as early as 1963, that it might be necessary to abandon Marx in order to save the revolution.

The implications of this lay in the future, however. At that time the decisive shift in the post-war history of French thought was only just taking place. At some point between 1958 and 1963 (Alain Touraine dates it to the Evian agreements which resolved the Algerian war) a vital transition occurred. Despite his publication of a philosophical magnum opus designed to absorb and re-cast the thinking of the

---

[41] See Castoriadis, *L'Expérience du mouvement ouvrier*, vol. 2, pp. 307, 310, 317 (and note 7).

previous fifteen years, Sartre somehow ceased to matter very much any more.[42] The humanist reading of Marx retained its credibility and study of the early Marxist texts continued apace, but the debate between Sartre and the PCF (to put the matter in shorthand) had lost its urgency. By 1963 there had grown up a new generation for whom marxism was part of the intellectual furniture. They did not need to be convinced of its importance, or its claims upon their attention. But at the same time they increasingly saw the Communists not as the heroes of Stalingrad or the martyrs of the Mont Valérien, but as the ageing Thorez and his colleagues, quashing all attempts to reform the Communist student movement, first denying Khrushchev's speech, then minimizing the Stalinist 'deviation', finally suppressing all attempts to reform or 'Italianize' the Party from within. For this first post-war generation of marxist students, humanist marxism was going nowhere in particular, while 'official' marxism had been places they would rather not visit.

Worst of all, the current of history was moving away from them. Not only could revolution in Europe no longer be justified (or even identified) retrospectively; it could not plausibly be inferred in anticipation from the contemporary capitalist boom and a quiescent proletariat. While events in Algeria or Cuba pointed to alternative grounds for optimism, they hardly encouraged expectation of profitable domestic political engagement. And so, just as the 1950s had perhaps corresponded in their optimism to the marxism of the 1840s, so the 1960s at first saw a concern with the unchanging *structures* of the system much as they had occupied Marx's own attention in his work on capitalism in the corresponding years of the previous century. And it was in just such a mood that the generation which passed through the *grandes écoles* in the years 1962–6 was thus captivated by the appeal of linguistic and anthropoligical structuralism, and passed the more readily into a new era of thought dominated by the work of Louis Althusser.

It may seem a trifle cavalier to pass from the era of Sartre to that of Althusser with no reference to the emerging influence of Foucault or Jacques Lacan, or to treat of a concern with structures without a diversion by way of Lévi-Strauss. But in one sense it is not so improper. Those who, after 1961, pursued an interest in Nietszche, Freud, or their contemporary commentators, or who evolved a concern

---

[42] J.-P. Sartre, *Critique de la raison dialectique*, vol. 1, *Théorie des ensembles pratiques* (Paris, 1960).

with structuralism *per se*, were already distinguishable from radical intellectuals for whom these new departures in the history of ideas were only ever a starting point for the renewal of debates within marxism. In retrospect this distinction is blurred by the merging of these strands in 1968, but the lines did not cross for long. To take only the most obvious example, Louis Althusser's contribution was to rework Marx in the new intellectual vocabulary of the 1960s, but it was this reworking, rather than the identity of that vocabulary for its own sake, which placed him at the centre of marxist debates for the next half-generation.

Althusser was the product of so many 'overdetermined conjunctures' (not least his own intellectual biography) that it is difficult to situate him satisfactorily. He was the last Party intellectual to capture the imagination of the non-Party intelligentsia, and he did this precisely because of the difficult nature of his work, which distanced him sufficiently from daily political concerns to give him an air of intellectual autonomy which could yet point to an unwavering political commitment. His intellectual project will be discussed in the next section. Here I shall confine my comments to the variegated appeal of his claim to undertake an epistemological renovation of marxism by grounding it in structural and scientific criteria derived from its own methodology.

In the first place, the Althusserian approach rejected all interest in the 'humanist' Marx at about the time when humanism had run its course as an intellectual fashion in Paris. By focusing on structures, both in society and in the argument itself, Althusser diverted attention from human acts (and thus human errors) and thereby swept away ten years of guilt over the 'mistakes' and 'deviations' of Stalin. By urging a renewal of interest in Marx the materialist, Althusser offered added credibility to the traditions of 'official' (Party) marxism, which had been overshadowed by the efforts of its critical 'humanist' opponents since the late 1940s. At the same time he helped to legitimize the role of the Party in France: the absence of revolution need no longer be attributed to Communist volition (or lack of it), while the assertion that it is structures and not people who make history cut the ground from under those who sought to return the initiative from a vanguard party to a self-conscious proletariat. And as a bonus, Althusser attributed to intellectuals a central role in the class struggle as participants in a 'theoretical practice' which asked of them only that they practice theory! In the circumstances of the time, this amounted to inviting his colleagues and students to make a virtue of necessity, and also offered to resolve the Sartrian dilemma of engagement by abolishing it. Praxis became Practice.

Althusser's social achievement was considerable, then (of his intellectual claims I shall speak later), and from 1966 to 1968 Althusserism reigned unchallenged. At a meeting of Communist Party intellectuals at Argenteuil in 1966 Roger Garaudy, unofficial guardian of the Party line since the late 1940s, attempted to have Althusser condemned for the sectarian implications of his thought (at a time when the Party was promoting a strategy of united action with the non-Communist Left). Garaudy and his supporters argued that a suitably modified marxist humanism was the only theoretical position consistent with the departure from Stalinist practices and an 'open' political engagement, including an appeal to the new classes of white-collar and technical workers. But notwithstanding the reasonable and politically directed nature of Garaudy's criticisms it was Althusser who emerged victorious from the debates. This was not because Garaudy was deemed by the Party hierarchy to have been in error, but precisely because he was all too correct. The point was that Althusser, in his rebarbative sectarianism, was an excellent guarantee of marxist rigour, a convenient marker for future use even if temporarily out of line. And indeed, being out of line in a harmlessly abstruse sort of way he was also proof of that very openness that Garaudy was advocating, a Party intellectual whom the Party allowed to say and write as he wished![43]

Hardly had Althusser's influence reached its apogee, however, than the circumstances which had facilitated its rise were radically altered by the events of 1968. Here, again, a historical account of that year would require an emphasis upon the strike movement of May and June, together with some extended discussion of the state of the universities. But for the internal history of French marxism, 1968 has a strange, counterpointed significance. The student leadership was composed for the most part of Trotskyists on the one hand, and non-ideological radicals on the other. The latter, while they had thoroughly absorbed the earlier critiques of bureaucratic Communism, and indeed of bureaucratic capitalism, were much more directly influenced by linguistic theory—back to the Word. They were openly interested in

---

[43] For the debate among Communist intellectuals at Argenteuil in 1966, see Robert Geerlandt, *Garaudy et Althusser. Le débat sur l'humanisme dans le parti communiste français et son enjeu* (Paris, 1978). See also Verdès-Leroux, op. cit., p. 141.

form rather than content, language over action (except in so far as language *was* a form of action—*épater les bourgeois*—or action a variant of language, the position of the situationists). My own impression at the time was that a clear majority of the student participants in the events of 1968 was disengaged from official marxism and only occasionally interested in the unofficial varieties, regarding the contemporary proliferation of which they were entertainingly cynical ('Je suis marxiste, tendance Groucho,' etc.).

On the other hand, the experience of 1968 raised afresh a number of problems in marxism that had long been neglected, or else supposed resolved. The mass strike, so obviously beyond the control of government and (Communist) labour organization alike, not only offered strong evidence for critics of vanguardism, but also posed a simple empirical threat to the Althusserian theorem which had supposedly abolished such acts of conscious mass volition in De Gaulle's France. There were many strikers and students from the new (and old) middle class, too, and this gave sustenance to those critics who had been emphasizing the emergence of new social classes since the 1950s. The temporary vacuum of power at the heart of Europe's most centralized and authoritarian democracy aroused renewed interest in the vulnerability of capitalism. Finally, the inability of the Communists to take advantage of the situation, and the degree to which they had lost the allegiance of a whole cohort of student activists since 1962, renewed speculation concerning the PCF's plausibility as a (as *the*) party of revolution in contemporary France.

As if all this were not enough, the spring of 1968 was followed in short order by the Czechoslovak tragedy of August. In many ways this mattered more—the Prague spring had been the last best hope for many older Communist intellectuals clinging to the wreckage of the apologetics of the 1950s. But if Stalinism had been only a deviation, why had Brezhnev begun to deviate too? The Party did its best to condemn and approve simultaneously (though the condemnation annoyed Jeannette Vermeersch and the hardliners, while the 'understanding' extended to Russian policy infuriated others), but the accumulated embarrassments at home and abroad took their toll. Althusser struggled heroically to limit the damage, assuring his admirers that the 1968 students were petty bourgeois opportunists who claimed absurdly to lead the workers (a few years later he further modified the facts, describing the student events as having 'accompanied' the workers' strike).[44] But his influence was on the wane, with some of his most prominent erstwhile collaborators preparing devastating critiques of his thought.[45]

As for those marxists who were not, or had ceased to be, Althusserians, the aftermath of 1968 suggested at least one alternative outlet: Maoism. The fact that the same year saw the Vietnam War at its peak and the Chinese Cultural Revolution in full flood gave added credibility to the view that marxism in the West had broken down and could only be restored with parts imported from the Orient. Facile analogies between May 1968 and the Red Guards gained a passing popularity, and there was a fashion for 'going to the people' (in France this meant abandoning university for factory work). This in turn was seen as a process which would lead to the overthrowing of class and occupational barriers and would thus, by analogy with events in China, give the idea of revolution a new momentum in Europe. Even the Althusserians were not immune to the appeal of Maoism: in its adapted form it offered a sure source of revolutionary authority without the need to bend the knee to the discredited domestic model. And as for the theoretical dimension, there was surely no history so utterly 'subjectless' as that of the anonymous Chinese masses (the more so in that Althusser, as we shall see, never denied that the 'masses make history'—he merely insisted that this did not entail recognizing the role of any particular persons in the process, a categorical distinction then thought to be of prime significance) . . .[46]

Maoism also appealed to Sartre, for whom it had attractions rather similar to those of Stalinism (violent action changing other people's worlds at a comfortable distance in time or space), and the added bonus of offering him a renewed part in active politics at minimal personal risk. Hawkers of the Maoist press in the repressive atmosphere of post–1968 France had been subject to harassment and arrest, and thus Sartre was wheeled out of political retirement to sell

---

[44] In a letter to Maria Macciocchi dated 15 Mar. 1969, in M.-A. Macciocchi, *Letters from inside the Italian Communist Party to Louis Althusser* (London, 1973).

[45] See Jacques Rancière, *La Leçon d'Althusser*, pp. 115, 130, where he describes Althusser as having established a '"philosophie de parti" concue comme police des concepts'. Confirmation from an unlikely quarter of Lacan's theory about La Mort du Père. The punning qualities of Lacan's work are regrettably confined to French, a weakness of significant proportions when revealed in attempts to transpose his 'theories' into less malleable languages.

[46] Louis Althusser, *Réponse à John Lewis* (Paris, 1973), p. 42.

newspapers on the street in an effort to taunt the regime. Uncharacteristically, however, the regime failed to swallow the bait and left him in peace, the engaged philospher incarnate. For a couple of years there was a frenetic revival of neo-Sartrian subjectivism, taking its vocabulary from 1968 and its underlying theses from the remembered humanism of the late 1950s (shorn of its obsession with Communism). In its more respectable guise it saw Lucien Goldmann, for example, reviving Lukacs and a faith in the proletarian consciousness (a further interpretation of the 1968 experience) while incorporating that other novelty of the period, the active participation of an alienated middle class. The struggle for socialism was to be conceived as 'une lutte pour les consciences fondées sur les possibilités ouvertes par le développement des nouvelles couches moyennes salariées'.[47]

But the very admission, by Goldmann and others, that the socialist struggle might centre upon the subjective consciousness of middle-class wage-earners showed just how far marxist intellectuals had moved, and how the certainties of an earlier decade had dissipated. 1968 was not a beginning but an end. It pointed not to new possibilities but to all the old difficulties. If the workers were no longer Communist, well enough. If a large minority of them voted for the Gaullists, this too could be explained. If the Communist Party was discredited, for many this was old news. If students, technicians, or women were more likely to be mobilized for radical social change, this in itself was no bad thing. If Sartre was selling Maoist sheets and Althusser preparing an *Autocritique* of his 'theoreticist' errors, while Garaudy was being expelled from the PCF for taking humanism in general and himself in particular altogether too seriously, there would be others. If French capitalism looked stronger than ever and the only action was happening 10,000 miles away, this was a problem but not conceptually insuperable. But taken together, and with the sheer disappointment engendered by the aftermath of the 1960s effervescence, what did all of this do to marxism?

From about 1971–3 it left it in limbo. The only new writing came from an increasingly dogmatic and rigid Althusser, and, more significantly, from Castoriadis, now working alone. No longer was he pointing valiantly to problems within the marxist tradition but rather writing of marxism as *the* problem. Not merely did many of the marxist

[47] Lucien Goldmann, *Marxisme et sciences humaines* (Paris, 1970), p. 8.

ideas no longer correspond to reality or to the exigencies of socialist revolutionary activity—they had *never* done so. And casting his net retrospectively he concluded, in 1973, that 'le marxisme reste pour nous une source inégalée d'inspiration théorique, mais il a cessé d'être une théorie vivante depuis quarante ans.' This was a significant advance on Goldmann who three years earlier had written that 'nos propres positions aboutissent à nous éloigner des perspectives politiques de Marx mais à conserver presque intégralement ses positions théoriques en général'—a point of view which made nonsense of the efforts of the previous twenty-five years and bore little relation to the thought of Marx himself, but which is perhaps best seen as a way of easing the reluctant intellectual into the cold shower of disillusion.[48]

The dike, according to Edgar Morin,[49] broke in 1974, though the really important breakthrough was the publication in French of the *Gulag Archipelago*. Circumstances then came together to precipitate the flow of disabuse. Solzhenitsyn's work offered no particularly new evidence of Stalin's crimes, but it renewed awareness of their scale at a time when the PCF was trying hard to restore its domestic credibility, threatened anew by the revival of a Socialist Party, and it aroused the interest of a new generation for whom Stalinism was history. The steady decline in the Communist vote, and the diminished numerical and sociological significance of the industrial proletariat contributed to a further dilution of the central mobilizing myth of the political Left. Developments in China and Cambodia suggested that the faith placed in their example had been at best naïve, while the overthrow of Allende warned ageing student radicals and their mentors alike of the danger of not taking seriously threats to bourgeois democracy (which at about this time ceased to be 'bourgeois democracy').[50]

Within the purely intellectual circuit the mid–1970s saw the appearance of a series of works, many begun in the critical atmosphere of the mid–1960s, that engaged directly the inadequacies of what Marchais continued to call 'real socialism'. Together with a rash of more-or-less revelatory memoirs from ex-Communists these books and theses contributed to the creation of a new experience for France: the realization that anti-Communism was not a sin, and that one could be both a committed radical *and* critical of marxism. In its extreme

---

[48] See Castoriadis, *Expérience du mouvement ouvrier*, vol. 2, pp. 376, 383.
[49] Edgar Morin in *Staline à Paris*, p. 291.
[50] For further discussion of the political and social background, see chapter five.

form this new mood saw a return of the perennial French intellectual self-obsession, with André Glucksmann, B.-H. Lévy, Régis Debray, and others packaging Marx, Sartre, Hegel, Nietzsche, Althusser, Stalin, and a ragtag list of obscure French pedagogues into a single commodity labelled 'totalitarianism', the self-generating source of three generations of crimes and mystifications. For the most part this served to reproduce some of the less endearing characteristics of the thing under attack (and make a lot of money for authors and publishers alike in the years 1977–80), but it did have one enduring outcome. By the time the air had cleared in 1980 or thereabouts, and all the ex-Maoists were writing foreign policy analyses for the conservative press, anti-marxism had entered the French intellectual bloodstream. The only significant marxist literature in France today is produced either by marxisant historians or official party theorists, which leaves matters about where they were when Henri Lefebvre began to collect his notes on Hegel in 1939.

*

The concerns of marxist intellectuals in France since 1945, while varying in emphasis, have been concentrated steadily upon five discrete areas of ideological and political interest. These are the theory of a proletariat, the role of a revolutionary party, the interpretation of Stalinism, the status of the individual in marxist thought, and marxism itself as an object of study. The shifts in emphasis within and between these themes have never amounted to an unconcern with any one of them, but the varying degrees of interest have undoubtedly reflected changing circumstances. The order in which I have listed these themes, then, is consonant with the chronology just presented, and it therefore does little violence to the material, and reflects a certain historical symmetry, to take them in turn.

For French students of Marx, recognizing the status of the proletariat in his thought entailed acknowledging one indisputable element in that thought, and one unresolved problem arising from it. The theory of a proletariat lay at the very heart of Marx's philosophy. It both accounted for the historical unfolding of which its own present and future actions were the centre-piece, and it licensed the moral philosophy which gave marxism its peculiar magnetic attraction. Because it derived not from empirical observation but from a *petitio principii* (the 'proletariat' having the capacity to differ from any particular community of workers as observed), the term had from the outset a highly abstract connotation for this generation of marxists. Nor was it even just one form of the abstract phenomenon 'class'—it differed from other collective historical actors precisely in *knowing* (or having the capacity to come to know) its nature and the meaning of its acts. Released from the grip of the cunning of Reason, it bore the sign of Reason itself.[51]

Because the proletariat could only fulfil its potential for universality in the act of ceasing to be a proletariat, however, it remained in the mean time a category of ascription: that was 'proletarian' which worked towards the goal of the negation of the proletariat. This rather open-ended capacity, incorporating the ability to deny legitimacy to any particular act by or for present-day workers in the name of a higher knowledge, provided philosophical marxists with their most valuable semantic weapon, but it also raised a real problem. Marx may have begun with a metahistorical abstraction, but he very clearly intended it to bear some determinate relation to the real experience of an empirical movement of industrial workers.

This need not have been an insuperable challenge. When the actual workers' movements of the turn of the century went astray (and responded to the appeals of reformers or social democratic trade-unionists) they did not by their actions dislodge the theory of proletarian destiny. But it follows that when they followed the 'correct' path it was not their actions which made it correct—the correctness was established a priori. Thus nothing very much need be learnt about the standing of marxist thought from observation of workers' behaviour. But sooner or later some sort of identity of a consistent kind would have to be detectable between the two, if Marx was not to stand accused of something embarrassingly akin to idealist utopian specula-tion. Lenin's claim to have achieved such an identification depended upon two propositions. Firstly that the proletariat could not be expected to come spontaneously to an awareness of its tasks (and thus that workers' movements might continue to fall short of expectation for a very long time if this point was not fully grasped); and secondly that it was reasonable to infer from Marx the need for the logic of history to be introduced into actual history via the services of a political organization incorporating that awareness.

The difficulty was that the more time passed, the more scepticism as

---

[51] For some interesting comments on the implications of Hegelian concepts of Reason for modern political movements, see Charles Taylor, *Hegel and Modern Society* (Cambridge, 1979), pp. 98, 122.

to the proletariat's potential tended to rise, with the absence of evidence in support of Marx's projections. But the *same* negative evidence could be invoked in defence of the Leninist proposition (in the absence, that is, of a recognized vanguard leadership). In France, matters were more complicated still. Most of what Marx had to say about the political practices of workers derived from his observations of mass protest in France in the years 1792–1871, thus placing uncomfortable pressure on French theorists, who could hardly invoke national peculiarities to justify exclusion clauses covering the inadequacies of the local working class. Furthermore, the speed of social change in France in the years 1950–70 put acute pressure on radical sociologists to admit that the proletariat in France was not only not developing a revolutionary class consciousness, but was actually being replaced, at an accelerating rate, by 'new' social classes. Hence the dilemma of someone like Nicos Poulantzas, who strove to 'save' the marxist definition of a 'real' working class by limiting it severely to productive manual workers, but could only do so by conceding (via a 'silence' . . .) that the universal revolutionary class was slipping out of sociological vision altogether.[52]

This is the conundrum which engaged the attention of post-war marxists in France. From the very beginning they were more inclined than most to invoke openly the theory of the proletariat in defence of the practice of revolutionary politics. Much of Merleau-Ponty's early attention was taken up with defending the Moscow trials by reference to the historicity of a body of actors whose deeds *only* made sense if seen through the prism of proletarian history. Merleau-Ponty was not selecting his target arbitrarily: if the proletariat could be successfully invoked to justify the most immoral and senseless of actions, then marxists would have little trouble grasping lesser nettles. And since it had to follow that history made *some* sense, one might very well conclude that some recent history only *could* make sense via the telos of proletarian logic (what less ambitious empiricists might see as a theory of justificatory ends).[53]

Merleau-Ponty and his successors were doing more than merely restating Vyshinsky or Thorez in Hegelian terms. It was important for them that the proletarian fulcrum of marxist theory also provide the support for an account of Communist practice. It mattered less that

[52] See, in particular, Nicos Poulantzas, *Les Classes sociales dans le capitalisme d'aujourd'hui* (Paris, 1974), but also *Pouvoir politique et classes sociales* (Paris, 1968).
[53] This is the skeleton of the argument put forward in *Humanisme et terreur*.

what was taking place in Moscow or Prague or Budapest be right (on this they simply refused to pronounce) than that it be theoretically consistent. This was the essence of the matter, the moral discomfort a secondary concern.[54]

Merleau-Ponty was in this but a preface to Sartre. For the latter the theory of the proletariat was a sequence of catechisms. Recognizing the yawning gap between 'proletariat' and actual workers, he converted it into a virtue. The worker, he asserted, is different from 'us'. His estate, his condition, is pure negativity. He can only become a proletarian 'dans la mesure même ou il refuse son état'. Failing that, he is a mere unit in a series, incapable of conscious existence.' How might he overcome this condition, refuse his state? By 'daily action': 'il n'est qu'en acte, il est acte; s'il cesse d'agir, il se décompose.'

But the only form of collective action open to the French workers in the early 1950s, according to Sartre, was the Parti Communiste. Why this came to be, Sartre suggested, was an open question, but it having become the case, the working class should now be supposed to have chosen the PCF for its leadership. And in that light, to suggest that the PCF was a deeply mischievous or even merely inadequate institution of no benefit to workers carried direct implications for one's view of the latter: 'il faut donc que le prolétariat tout entier soit criminel, menteur et hystérique. Sinon comment expliquer qu'il demeure communiste.' What is more, should the French working class by some misfortune cease to support the PCF, this could only be by ceasing, quite simply, to be a proletariat: 'Si la classe ouvrière veut se détacher du Parti, elle ne dispose que d'un moyen: tomber en poussière.'[55]

Sartre never ascribed an active subject to this odd process—'une classe, ça s'organise', 'les dirigeants qu'elle (the working class) s'étaient choisis'. The true subject, then, is the selfsame proletariat that the actual working class only becomes *after* the choice is made. The Cunning of History thus selects out not the working class but the PCF as the vehicle of history. And thus, although he lost interest in the

[54] Merleau-Ponty quotes Marx (from *The Holy Family*) in support of this position: 'Il ne s'agit pas ici de ce que tel ou tel prolétaire ou même le prolétariat tout entier peut quelquefois se proposer comme but, il s'agit de ce qu'il *est*, de ce qu'il sera historiquement contraint de faire conformément à cet être.' Quoted in *Les Aventures de la dialectique*, p. 72.

[55] All quotations come from 'Les Communistes et la paix', in *Situations VI*, especially pp. 86–252. Sartre offers a sombre warning of the dangers of proletarian disaffection from the PCF: 's'ils perdent confiance dans le PC, ils se défieront de tout la politique, ils se défieront de leur classe; l'univers sera bourgeois' (p. 252).

problem in later years and found a range of alternative vehicles in which to ride the historical road, Sartre can be credited with identifying the style of argument employed by his successors to similar ends. Writing in 1978, Althusser asserted baldly the need for a party as the indispensable basis 'pour aider la classe ouvrière à s'organiser en classe'.[56] And in this Sartre and Althusser are joined by Ernest Mandel, speaking for the Trotskyist position: 'A denial of the community of interests of the world working class means a rejection of the principal premises of marxist theory that the socialist emancipation of humanity is indeed possible.'[57] Which is an alternative way of insisting on the *necessity* (and not merely the convenience) of incorporating real proletarians into the theory of the 'proletariat', with ony the vehicle of incorporation differing according to taste.

Castoriadis approached the same question from the opposite angle, acknowledging that there was some deep-rooted difficulty surrounding the marxist account of the proletariat. His solution was to find the contradictions and divisions in capitalism *within* the proletariat rather than outside it, and even in the 1950s he was drawn to the conclusion that the marxist faith in the collective self-realization of the working class was an error, if left at that. The proletariat was not a 'positivité pleine', containing within itself the solutions to the questions of history. It was the bearer of its own contradictions (a polite way of noting that most French workers were manifestly unconcerned with radical political or syndicalist action), and these could only be overcome by its own actions. Incorporating the workers into a bureaucratic hierarchy (the Party) merely exported the contradictions onto the political realm, and moreover destroyed the working class as an autonomous actor, capable of that self-management which had to be the basis for its struggle. Like Sartre, Castoriadis conceded that the proletariat was not, a priori, socialist (though he did not insist that without socialism it was therefore nothing)—'il le devient, ou plus exactement il se fait socialiste'. The difference was that for Castoriadis the actual French worker was the unambiguous subject of the process.[58]

From the 1960s this topic slipped into the background, with writers such as Gorz or Mallet conceding from the outset that the real

---

[56] Louis Althusser, *Ce qui ne peut plus durer dans le parti communiste* (Paris, 1978), p. 111.
[57] Ernest Mandel, *From Stalinism to Eurocommunism* (London, 1978), p. 36.
[58] Castoriadis, *Expérience du mouvement ouvrier*, vol. 2, pp. 50, 73, 77.

proletariat in France was no longer the centre of attention (and thus its relations with the PCF, again, a matter of secondary significance). By the end of the next decade only the Communists maintained a consistently high level of interest in the real and hypothetical deeds of the industrial worker-as-revolutionary. In this they are now in lonely and ironic dialogue with the Trotskyists. For the former, it is still asserted (and by some of their most 'modern' and 'liberal' intellectuals) that 'la classe ouvrière s'est donné un parti qui fait s'interpréter connaissance intellectuelle et expérience des luttes populaires', a formula remarkably akin to that of Sartre in 1953.[59] As to the Trotskyists, they 'stand 100% on the side of the workers, whatever their ideological level may be (and if it is low and confused, this is the fault of the bureaucratic dictatorship)'—which treats in one sentence of all possible conditions of actual proletarian inadequacy![60]

It is perhaps worth adding that even those writers who have been the most disabused of the prospects of proletarian revolution remain subliminally attached to the theory which purported to sustain those prospects. In a work published in 1980, André Gorz confirms the passing of the 'ouvrier professional polyvalent' and the consequent end of a 'classe capable de prendre à son compte le projet socialiste et de le faire passer dans les choses. La dégenérescence de la théorie et de la pratique socialistes *viennent* fondamentalement de là'. [my emphasis].[61] Yet it is the very assumption of such an inseparability which cast into the limelight for so long the effort to confirm the standing of at least one half of the equation.

For those who had grasped the Sartrian idea that truth and knowledge lay in the act of remaking reality, and for the rather wider community of persons who could agree that altering reality was the task of an alliance of philosophy with the proletariat, consideration of the epistemological status of the latter led inexorably on to the problem of the Party, as we have seen. The search for an assimilation of workers and party was not peculiar to France, of course. What was peculiar was that only in France and Italy did the revolutionary class and its putative vehicle actually come together. Elsewhere the former had become firmly attached to social democratic or labour parties, or else was relieved of the obligation to make political attachments of any kind at

---

[59] Guy Hermier, speaking at a meeting of the Conseil National of the PCF, 9–10 Feb. 1980. See *Les Intellectuels, la culture et la révolution*, p. 69.

[60] Mandel, op. cit., p. 51.

[61] André Gorz, *Adieux au prolétariat* (Paris, 1980), p. 101.

all. And in Italy the fascist experience had deprived local intellectuals of that unbroken dialogue with a domestic Communist Party which was thus unique to France.

The position of the Communists themselves on the relationship between class and party has been very consistent. The role of the PCF, said Duclos in 1952, 'Comme nous l'a indiqués Maurice Thorez [est] . . . d'arracher les travailleurs à l'idéologie de la capitulation devant la bourgeoisie, à l'idéologie du renoncement à la lutte pour la révolution prolétarienne.'[62] This 'arrachement' implied two premisses. Firstly, that there was an identifiable and unaltering line which distinguished the proletariat and divided it from its enemies. This was openly asserted in the Zhdanovite period of the 'two camps', when not just politics but all areas of human endeavour from music to biology were divided into a Manichean universe of 'proletarian' and other. But even in later years it has of necessity remained the premiss of Communist argument, albeit in the diluted form of generically 'revolutionary' and 'bourgeois' behaviours which are not always attached to any particular work of art, science, or imagination. And when political exigencies have tempted the Party to practice a blurred vision of class conflict, there has never lacked a spokesman for intellectual rigour to remind it of the structural requirement of two camps. Thus Althusser in his 'critique' of the Party in 1978: 'Quand un parti ouvrier tend à abandonner les principes de l'indépendance de classe de sa pratique politique, il tend à reproduire . . . dans son propre sein, la pratique politique bourgeoise.'[63]

The second premiss was that knowledge of the precise whereabouts of the line separating proletariat from bourgeoisie was an *exclusive* property of the Communist Party. This is the more interesting claim, because asserting it in practice means denying such knowledge to mere workers when left to themselves. Adopting unacknowledged the Gramscian idea of a collective organic intellectual, the PCF has asserted (more or less aggressively according to context) the intellectual authority of its theory because of *who it is*. This is simple Leninism, of course: to have the authority of practice which goes with the claim to represent a universal class one must of necessity claim a theoretical hegemony on parallel grounds. And it explains the nervous distaste of the Communist leadership for even the most sympathetic of theoretical writings by Sartre, Lefebvre *et al.* Because even when they were

[62] Jacques Duclos, 'Etre Stalinien', loc. cit., p. 591.
[63] Althusser, *Ce qui ne peut plus durer dans le parti communiste*, p. 109.

correct, as when they accorded the Party full authority in its domain, they could not be *fully* correct in their understanding, since *that* was something one could only be *with* the Party, never outside it.

Similarly, marxist theorists who were not party members and who could never privately digest the idea that Stalin or Maurice Thorez was the 'best dialectician' or 'leading intellectual' of his times were still drawn by their own reasoning to agree with Sartre or Lefebvre that knowledge could only come through the Party, rather than one coming to the Party via the onset of knowledge.[64] Faced with this situation, you just thought as hard as you could and then gave the Party the nod. Or, as Sartre put it in a reply to Camus, 'Il ne s'agit pas de savoir si l'Histoire a un sens et si nous daignons y participer, mais, du moment que nous sommes dedans jusqu'aux cheveux d'essayer de lui donner le sens qui nous paraît le meilleur, en ne refusant notre concours, si faible-soit-il, à aucune des actions concrètes qui le requierent.'[65]

The point was that the mobilizing organism of the working class, the entity which gave the latter its *groupness*, 'ne peut se concevoir que comme une autorité'.[66] And it was *it* which did the conceiving. There was no other source of information as to the rightness or wrongness of an action or a political choice except that emanating from the party of the proletariat (which affirmation did not inhibit Sartre from sounding remarkably secure about the truth status of the proposition in his own mouth!). In the early years even Castoriadis and the Socialisme ou Barbarie group had accepted the idea of a party, rejecting only the peculiarly Leninist insistence on external authority as the *only* source of historical certainty. But even this was too much for Sartre, who rounded on Claude Lefort (at that time a close collaborator of Socialisme ou Barbarie) and informed him that 'quand un communiste fait connaître les intérêts ou les sentiments du prolétariat, à tort ou à raison, c'est au nom du prolétariat qu'il parle'. It is difficult to see the force of 'à tort ou à raison', given Sartre's views on the epistemological standing of the proletariat, but the wider point is unambiguous.[67]

When the troubles of the 1950s had passed over, and the Communist Party had ceased to be in daily confrontation with the rest of civil society, the urgency with which its claims were defended was

---

[64] See Henri Lefebvre, *La Somme et le reste*, p. 346.

[65] Sartre, 'Réponse à Albert Camus', in *Situations VI*, p. 125.

[66] Sartre, *Situations VI*, p. 247.

[67] For Castoriadis, see *Expérience du mouvement ouvrier*, vol. 1, p. 129; for Sartre's reply to Lefort see *Situations VI*; Sartre is also quoted in Merleau-Ponty, *Aventures de la dialectique*, p. 219.

relaxed. During the later 1960s, however, precisely because the PCF could no longer expect the convoluted adherence of extra-party intellectuals, and was faced instead with a new generation who ignored dialectics and pointed instead to social evidence to refute the Party's claims, a new direction was opened up. Instead of insisting that the Party acts consciously and in the name of a correctly comprehended History, Althusser, Rancière, Balibar, and others argued that the older, humanist distinctions between party, class, and workers were misleading. History was not made by actors but was a subjectless process. To suggest that actual proletarians could contrive to alter their world was to serve the class interests of the enemy, and thus all debate about who chose whom and on what sort of subjective basis was irrelevant. The flavour of this line of reasoning, in the confused aftermath of 1968, emerges in Althusser's *Reply to John Lewis*, and must be quoted in full for maximum appreciation:

Quand on dit aux prolétaires 'ce sont les hommes qui font l'histoire', il n'est pas besoin d'être grand clerc pour comprendre qu'à plus ou moins longue echéance on contribue à les désorienter et les désarmer. On leur fait croire qu'ils sont tous puissants comme 'hommes', alors qu'ils sont désarmés comme prolétaires en face de la véritable toute puissance, celle de la bourgeoisie qui détient les conditions matérielles (les moyens de production) et politiques (l'Etat) qui commandent l'histoire. Quand on leur chante la chanson humaniste, on les détourne de la lutte des classes, on les empêche de se donner et d'exercer la seule puissance dont ils disposent: celle de *l'organisation en classe*, et de *l'organisation de classe*, les syndicats et le Parti, pour conduire leur lutte de classe à eux.[68]

Althusser is here asserting, on behalf of the PCF, the *only* non-negotiable element within a modern Communist Party, the kernel of class authority that comes with the title, but he is asserting it as a consequence of theoretical investigation rather than as the starting point for argument. This is where he differs from earlier French marxists, whose humanist concerns prevented them from discovering a structural basis for party authority, but who could find nothing else on which to ground the legitimacy of Communism except Communism itself.

It is the deep misfortune of the French Communists that they were vouchsafed this unimpeachable (if oddly unmarxist) authority for their status and claims about twenty years too late. A comparably confident account of why the Party could impose its authority on the French

---

[68] Althusser, *Réponse à John Lewis*, pp. 48–9.

working people, coming from inside the PCF and yet consistent with the concerns of non-party intellectuals, would have been a distinct bonus for the Communists in their earlier years. At that time they lacked not political sympathy but intellectual credibility. As it is, the era of Althusser coincided with a generation during which the PCF has had to spend much of its intellectual capital in negotiating the conditions of its release from a Stalinist past, an observation which moves us forward from the arguments surrounding the theory of marxist agencies to the discussion of the actions of those agents in real life.

The cult of Stalin, Thorez, and the Soviet Union, and the style of political behaviour and argument practised by the cultists, collectively dubbed 'Stalinism', flourished in France from 1948 to 1953, although its origins trace back at least to 1934 and the veneration for the Soviet Union endured until the late 1970s.[69] As a way of being and behaving, especially towards opponents and dissenters, Stalinism has of course never died; on the other hand, it might as well be said to have its origins in political and intellectual developments long before Stalin himself. Rather than engage these matters, I shall confine my attention here to the high years of the Stalinism of the Stalinists, from the late 1940s to the early 1960s.

Communists and their sympathizers everywhere were Stalinist in these years, but the phenomenon in France was in certain ways distinct. In the first place, and at the risk of repetition, it should be noted that the Stalinized institution, the PCF, just was more prominent in France than its homologues elsewhere (saving the special Italian case). Secondly, Stalinism was very particularly a characteristic of the *intellectual* Left at this time. As J. Verdès-Leroux has noted, French thinkers 'supportaient mal les sottises, mais ils avalaient les crimes'.[70] Thirdly, Stalinism in France was in some measure the pursuit of the Resistance by other means—the psychology of war, of a continuing struggle against the forces of evil to be pursued by all available avenues, appealed to many young men and women who had received their political radicalization through the armed resistance of 1943–4. The Communists very deliberately emphasized this theme, and deployed to considerable effect the militarized vocabulary of Leninism. Fourthly, the cult of personality was domesticated in France by the sanctification of the absurd Maurice Thorez, a surrogate local

---

[69] See, for example, *L'Humanité* for 23 Jan. 1934.
[70] Verdès-Leroux, op. cit., p. 57.

Stalin in a way which was never the case for other western Communist leaders, however venerated.

The cumulative result of these circumstances, taken together with the appeal of Stalin's own all-embracing intellectual claims to an intelligentsia guiltily embarrassed by its own privileged expertise, and attracted to such a disingenuously holistic doctrine, was that the experience of being a Stalinist was profound and widespread. First there came an uncritical adulation of the USSR and things Russian. Academics and writers travelled to Russia (as in the years 1919–21 and 1932–6) and returned enchanted. A double standard quickly emerged: what was good about the Soviet Union was genuinely good, while what was bad was actually good, either because it had the potential for a greater Goodness than the mere bourgeois goodness of the West, or else would be good when contingencies (and American obstacles) had been finally removed from history's path.

This way of thinking moved easily to the 'dialectical' proposition, in the hands of Merleau-Ponty and Sartre, that the USSR was *already* freer than the USA and other liberal regimes because it alone bore the possibility of true freedom within its (contingently unfree) self. Sartre proposed his own double standard for such comparisons: pre-revolutionary bourgeois regimes had to demonstrate that they were superior in the face of overwhelming presumptive evidence to the contrary; the post-revolutionary Soviet state was presumed virtuous unless there was overwhelming (and in the nature of things unavailable) proof to the contrary.[71] Neither they nor most other French marxist intellectuals (with the honourable exceptions of Castoriadis and his group) thus batted a public eyelid when confronted with socio-economic data, reports of concentration camps, news of show trials, and so forth. Anything that happened over there was at worst evidence of the difficulties entailed in constructing Communism under conditions of permanent social mobilization.

The personality cults were not inherent in these positions, but given the blank cheque on offer to Communist parties, there could be no overt questioning of their decision to elevate a leader or leaders to god-like status. The stance of most non-affiliated marxists was a guilty silence, an uncritical audience for the pronouncements of the faithful. No one was likely to object to Duclos's characterization of Thorez as 'le meilleur stalinien français' (nothing Duclos said was ever free of a

---

[71] For a belated criticism of Sartre's inability to see the scale of Stalin's crimes, see Merleau-Ponty, *Aventures de la dialectique*, p. 246.

sibylline series of *arrières pensées*, but this at least he probably meant), but some people will have swallowed hard at Garaudy's 1946 account of how Stalin taught the correct reading of Marx.[72] Yet there was no apparent limit to the willingness of non-Communist marxists to retreat in the face of the most outrageous verbal and ideological aggression, prefaced by an association with Stalin or Thorez, whether it concerned 'proletarian physics' or the manifestly hilarious claim that Thorez was an authentic war hero. Edgar Morin's explanation has the charm of simplicity: his generation simply took the standard marxist account of bourgeois society—that the velvet glove of democratic rights hides the iron fist of bourgeois power—and inverted it; the unpalatable excesses of Stalinism, in word and deed, merely hid the fact of a good and true 'démocratie ouvrière'.[73]

This is perhaps a little too simple, but it identifies an important element in 'radical chic' Stalinism. People believed it for as long as they were able to do so, which was just as long as they really wished to. Sartre never ceased to wish as much, which is why even in 1961 he could write that 'Un anticommuniste est un chien, je ne sors pas de là, je n'en sortirai plus jamais.'[74] Of Althusser, more later. But for most others, the desire to disassociate from Stalinism, then to be seen to disassociate from it (a very different affair), finally to make sense of it, grew steadily in the years after 1954, increased sharply in 1956–8, 1964–6 (the death of Thorez and the emergence of the New Left), 1968–9 (Czechoslovakia), and of course since 1974. What is of interest here is the ways in which sense was made of Stalinism, and how personal commitments and collective actions were retrospectively explained.

I am not writing here of people such as Annie Kriegel or Auguste Lecœur, who went from full-blooded party dogma to conservative anti-Communism, but of that larger number for whom the real difficulty lay in retrieving some sort of respectability for their marxist beliefs from the wreckage of Stalin's actions and their own support for them. This group was divided between ex-Communists such as Henri Lefebvre, Claude Roy, Morin, and (later) Pierre Daix and Jean Elleinstein, and non-party marxists such as Sartre, Merleau-Ponty,

[72] For Duclos, see 'Etre Stalinien', loc. cit., p. 585. For Garaudy, see Roger Garaudy, 'Les Sources françaises du marxisme–leninisme', in *Cahiers du Communisme*, no. 12 (1946).

[73] Edgar Morin, *Autocritique*, p. 137.

[74] Sartre, *Situations IV*, pp. 248–9.

J.-P. Vernant, and a host of other major French intellectuals. As a rule the ex-Communist thinkers were more interested in explaining the Stalinist phenomenon, while those who had never actually joined the Party showed a greater interest in preserving the credibility of marxism by limiting the scope and the significance of the Stalinist moment.

Saving marxism from Stalin was a particularly painful exercise because it involved the need to acknowledge distinctions among elements of what one had once striven to demonstrate was an indivisible whole. But this was incommensurately easier than the task facing those who stayed *in* the Party, who had to save the PCF itself from the stain of Stalinism by radical historical surgery. Not that the removal of embarrassing limbs was a new undertaking for the Party doctors—the about-turns of the past thirty years had given them ample practice at rewriting the official history. But that was the past—de-Stalinization meant surgery on a living organism.

These exercises in self-amputation did not occur simultaneously. The major French marxists began to rearrange their intellectual furniture from the time of Hungary and the Khrushchev speech (Merleau-Ponty was an early exception to this rule), and by 1964 most of them had gone as far as they would go, at least in public. But the *Party* did not even acknowledge the existence of a problem, much less a need to engage it, until the early 1960s, and until Thorez's death in 1964 there could be no question of engaging directly the problem of the personality cult. By this time Khrushchev had been overthrown (as Thorez had anticipated) and the drive to reform had passed. As a result, de-Stalinization *within* the PCF, in so far as it entailed facing the problem of what the Stalin era was and what it had meant for Communist Parties, had to wait until the later 1970s, when the crisis of the PCF was so acute that confronting its past and disclaiming any link with it might even work to its advantage.

Broadly speaking, the French marxist community adjusted its debts to Stalinism in six different ways, according to the nature of the previous relationship and the desired outcome. The first approach, quite simply, was to historicize the whole problem. Sartre undertook this in his *Critique of Dialectical Reason* with the theory of the 'pratico-inert', that condition of the human experience which requires violent engaged action for its overcoming.[75] The Russian Revolution had to be what it was (in particular it had to be violent) in order to realize a

---

[75] Sartre, *Critique de la raison dialectique, passim.*

proletarian victory. Sartre does not actually say that violence in revolution is thus subject to a sort of cost–benefit analysis, but this is what he implies. And it is also why he turned to Maoism when it occurred to him that the long-term result of Stalinism was a return to the pratico-inert. Lucien Goldmann laboured similarly to construct a complex architectonic device whose object is to show that the defects of the Soviet Union are the direct result of the conditions of production in the Russian state, combined with the absence of democratic traditions. This, he wrote, may 'en partie rend compte du décalage entre la vision marxienne de la société socialiste future et la réalité effective de celle-ci dans la première période de son existence'. This unsatisfactory effort to pretend that he had missed the point was published in 1970![76]

Significantly, neither Sartre nor Goldmann thought there was any need to engage the entailed problem of Stalinism in *France*. No doubt this derived from their awareness that distancing the problem was self-evidently something that would work better the further away the thing to be explained. And Sartre in particular had long shown a taste for *post-facto* justifications of the sort which require maximum geographical mileage between the event and the speaker. The harsh judgement of Castoriadis upon the French writer who, above all others, still commands foreign admiration, is worth quoting:

Sartre maoisant [this was written in 1973] reste fidèle à Sartre stalinisant: l'adoration du fait accompli . . . la justification anticipée de tous les crimes possibles d'une dictature bureaucratique (auxquels, 'bien entendu', la belle âme s'oppose une fois qu'ils ont eu lieu et que l'on n'y peut rien).[77]

A more demanding exercise was to attempt to erect a dike between Marxism–Leninism and the theory and practice of Stalin. This had always been the Trotøskyist position, of course, and gave them the freedom to label the PCF from the start as a mere Stalinist excrescence upon the healthy body of the labour movement (just as they have more recently announced that the only begetter of Eurocommunism was none other than Stalin himself).[78] But for others the work was not easy. Lefebvre in 1958 characterized Stalinism as the incomplete attempt to suppress all intermediaries between the political and the economic, the state and the productive forces, authority and the individual. The result was the abandoning of all social analyses of

[76] Lucien Goldmann, *Marxisme et sciences humaines*, pp. 309–10.
[77] Castoriadis, *Expérience du mouvement ouvrier*, vol. 1, p. 248.
[78] See, e.g., Mandel, op. cit.

any value, he writes, there being no 'relations' left to analyse. This was an interesting attempt to account for the intellectual nullity of Stalinism, and its political brutality, as part of a single process, and it laid an unmistakable emphasis upon the point that this process *could* only have begun once power had been acquired. It need not, therefore, reflect pejoratively upon the *fact* of that acquisition of power, and Lenin (and before him, Marx) was thus relieved of responsibility.[79]

Predictably it was Louis Althusser who took this line of reasoning to its highest levels of dialectical subtlety. For him, Stalinism was a 'deviation', a crust of dogmatism on a political practice whose inherent health it in no way damaged. Since for obvious reasons Althusser had no desire to investigate the defects of the Leninist party-type, and treats as axiomatic the 'enormous world role' of the Soviet Revolution, his attention is perforce confined to the 'horrors' of the Stalinist regime itself, guilty above all of having perverted the achievements of Marxism–Leninism. It is for this, rather than for its mundane crimes against humanity, morality and so forth, that Stalinism must do penance. How did things reach such a pass? Not because of error, but because of the failure to recognize error, and thus correct it. For Althusser as for Lenin, the failure to analyse a mistake is far worse than the mistake itself. This may sound liberal enough, and it lends itself to a nauseous series of Communist self-criticisms, but it is in truth a brilliantly conceived exculpatory device. Stalinism becomes a metaphenomenon, not the things done but the failure to see that they should not have been done. And once again, the things that actually were done thus become secondary, of little importance. With these set aside, the task of the would-be de-Stalinizer is much simplified.[80]

As a codicil to this approach there was the Theory of the Two Stalins, the Good Stalin of Soviet industrialization and the Great Patriotic War, and the Bad Stalin of the purges and Lyssenkian biology. In a sense everyone acceded to this way of seeing things, and for good reason. It was, after all, Stalingrad which more than anything else accounted for the popularity and credibility of the USSR and the PCF in the immediate post-war years, and all could agree, too, that industrialization was a necessary condition of any sort of move away

---

[79] Lefebvre, *La Somme et le reste*, p. 118. See also *La Pensée de Lenine, passim.*

[80] See Althusser, *Ce qui . . .*, *passim;* also *Réponse à John Lewis*, p. 93, and Althusser's contribution to *Power and Opposition in post-revolutionary societies* (London, 1979), p. 226. See also the remarks of Valentino Gerratana in 'Althusser and Stalinism', in *New Left Review*, nos. 101–2 (1977).

from feudalism and towards socialism. And there was also a silent or secret clause to this sort of critique of Stalin. If there was a Good and a Bad Stalin, it must follow that there were analagous divisions within the domestic Communist movement—the Good PCF which organized the Popular Front, fought in the Resistance, opposed the Korean War, and the like, and the Bad PCF which promoted the cult of Thorez, expelled and excoriated dissidents, accused Sartre of working for the US, etc. No one could be blamed for having supported the one in good faith only to be tarred with the brush of the other.

One still hears this argument on occasion, normally in the form of an intellectual autobiography. It may strike the listener as less than resolutely marxist in its style of reasoning, but it has the ring of psychological truth (the fact that intuitive psychological plausibility and marxist argument tend to mutual exclusivity has been the source of much misgivings among French marxists since the mid–1960s). But it is hardly a position that could be adopted very comfortably by anyone who has chosen to remain *in* the Communist movement. It is one thing to make the whole Stalinist experience a parenthetical error in the history of Marxism–Leninism, but to bifurcate Stalin himself smacks of an excessive concern with the individual (and pays an inadvertent compliment to the cult of the personality, moreover). As for the domestic analogy, this is even more troubling.

That is because it simply is not easy to decide exactly which bits of the French Communist experience shall be rejected and which incorporated. To speak of 'le Parti autrefois . . .' is only to criticize the present (or to praise it, depending on context). It does not adequately address the question, why then and not now? Until the 1970s French Communists were not given to criticizing the Party's past behaviour, preferring to deny embarrassing episodes. More recently they have taken to speaking of errors, including Thorez's own failure to de-Stalinize the Party with sufficient speed. All this is terrible bad faith, of course, since it wishes to imply that some de-Stalinization has taken place, and the result is once again to agree that yes, Stalinism was bad, but never to take the time to say in what precise ways. Because the Party now concedes that errors were made, it is able to locate its earlier deviation—but as with Althusser's Stalin, it turns out that the gravest error was the failure to admit error (the only sin of which Thorez has ever been openly accused). Error having now been admitted, the problem of Stalinism is resolved and no particular moment in the PCF history needs to be expunged (other, that is, than those already long since painted out of the Party's account of its development).

All this is for public consumption. For the favoured few, Althusser offers a more rarified version of such efforts, incorporated into his general theory.[81] He presents a twofold solution to the problem. In his early writings he placed great emphasis on the scientificity of Marx's economic discoveries, in particular the theory of surplus value and the seminal status of *property relations* in marxist thought. What therefore must distinguish at a structural level pre-revolutionary from post-revolutionary societies was above all else the forms of property relations. The relations of production in post–1917 Russia are thus unmistakably distinct from those of bourgeois societies in precisely the way they need to be for Lenin's revolution to have been what it claims to have been (private property having been abolished). The achievement of 1917 is thus secure, however much contemporary Soviet industrialization may seem to emulate and compete with capitalist industry.

Secondly, the theory of overdetermination (see below) enables Althusser to establish that while there are no laws that could predict revolution (and which could thus be adduced, by their failure, in evidence against marxist claims), nothing is ever an accident. Lenin's revolution was thus what it claimed to be in a further sense (note, though, that 1917 is the *only* example Althusser ever troubles to offer in support of his theory). The Russian Revolution is 'evidence' of the contradictions of history—structures of determination (causes) must not be supposed to work in tidy conjunction with one another, and simply being overdetermined doesn't make 1917 a product of multiple structures at work in synchrony. In other words, it can be what it says it was, and *still* bring forth the error of Stalinism, the latter a product of the contradictions of the moment of revolution.[82]

This is Althusser's first solution, which makes Stalinism something neither random nor accidental, but still quite distinct from the Leninism which precedes (and succeeds) it. His second string, so to speak (presented in his later, more directly political writings), is to argue that Stalinism is not just a problem *in* theory (as we have seen), but one *of* theory. Stalin's crime was to transform marxism into a justificatory dogma of the state, to fix its thinking into formulae and thereby to freeze the efforts of marxists and their proletarian followers

---

[81] See Althusser, *Pour Marx* (Paris, 1965), especially the preface and the essay entitled 'Contradiction et surdétermination'; also *Réponse à John Lewis, passim*.

[82] Susan James, *Holism in Social Theory*, p. 194.

for a generation. By effecting a 'closure' in marxism Stalin did violence to both the practice of theory and also to the theory of revolutionary practice. Overcoming Stalinism means, above all else, thinking very hard about marxism and going back to the Marxist–Leninist texts. And a further fruit of this exercise will be the (as yet incomplete) construction of the categories and concepts necessary for a truly complete understanding of just how the Stalinist deviation could have happened.[83]

No one not already convinced is likely to have been converted by this entertaining account of Stalin as the man whose major crime was to pervert the self-understanding of marxism (which is rather like suggesting that Hitler's sin was to give physical anthropology a bad name). And one should note in passing that it is this style of reasoning and the expectations it has of its audience which give some credibility to the charge that Althusser is a true Stalinist himself. But one should not underestimate what is at issue here. In a more sympathetic political environment, the intelligentsia's desire to see real political acts transformed into theoretical problematics and thus become truly important objects of concern might have afforded Althusser's account of Stalinism a very wide audience indeed.

But even in such an environment, there would have been limits to Althusser's achievement. In effect, de-Stalinization in France was always an illusion. No one was willing to undertake any critique of the Soviet Union which involved a direct denial that it was the home of 'real socialism'. Sartre, as usual, explained why: 'Etions-nous si sûrs qu'on pouvait rejeter le régime stalinien sans condamner le marxisme?'[84] The answer, of course, is 'no'. Since the humanist or Hegelian generation could not consistently deny the role of consciousness or action, they confined their attention to the social and circumstantial terms of the Stalinist experience, and simply never raised the question of how much and in what ways Stalin was heir to marxism at a theoretical level. Even Goldmann, who had no reason (given his admiration for the early Lukacs) to mince his words on the subject of

---

[83] Thus Castoriadis on Althusser's account of Stalinism: 'Et que dit-il maintenant [1978]? A peu près ceci: Nous ne disposions pas d'une théorie vraiment satisfaisante de l'origine des espèces; aussi, avons-nous tout fait pour vous persuader que les loups étaient des moutons. Aujourd'hui, nous ne pouvons plus nier que la question de savoir quelle espèce d'animaux sont les "moutons réels" se pose: mais ce qui est vraiment urgent, c'est de parler des lacunes et des difficultés critiques du néo-darwinisme.' See *La Société francaise*, p. 306.

[84] Satre, *Situations IV*, p. 229 (this was written in 1961).

vanguard parties, confined *his* attack on Stalinism to a condemnation of the 'caractère extrêmement contestable des mœurs de l'époque stalinienne'. *Mœurs* being subject to change, the *essence* of marxism was unaffected by such a disapproving slap.[85]

Structuralist marxism, then, resolved the old humanist dilemma of the distinction between the abstract 'proletariat' (perfect cause) and the actual experience of workers and Communists (imperfect contingency) by denying its postulates. Actual experience never being the work of free agents, of historical subjects, it could not reasonably be subjected to any criticism at all. But this left people like Althusser in an odd position, since they had to say *something* negative about Stalin. But in the name of what? If there are no subjects, how can there be errors? The problem was resolved by invoking the idealist category of 'error in theory', which left Althusser, not for the first time, in a condition of epistemological self-contradiction (see below).

But it was not just epistemology which restricted Althusser's vision. Like Sartre, or, later, Gorz, he knew that no serious analysis of Stalin dare pass on to a discussion of Lenin, because this risked drawing attention to the idea that the Leninist party-type was itself a contributory factor in the emergence of Stalinism. This would link Stalin to the PCF, whereas part of Althusser's project was to sever all such links. The smokescreen he used was the claim that Thorez (!) was the model for serious de-Stalinizers, because of his 'efforts théoriques méritoires' in the Party's formative years.[86] This shows Althusser at his best—admitting the offence and then so misdescribing the offender and the offended alike that the jury cannot in all conscience return anything but an open verdict. If it does not work on this occasion, that is because Thorez was *too* successful precisely at inculcating the PCF in its *mœurs contestables*. Althusser can save marxism by incriminating Stalin and the PCF, or he can save the PCF by bracketing marxism and Stalin. What he cannot do is save marxism *and* the PCF by pointing the finger at Stalin alone.

The obvious response to the story of de-Stalinization in France is that it failed because French marxism just was Stalinist. But this is slightly misleading. It may be true that Stalinism and marxism in general can no longer be separated and the latter purged of the association. But so far as the *French* marxists were concerned, the experience of Stalinism was simply sloughed off, because no alternative

[85] Goldmann, op. cit. p. 151.
[86] Althusser, *Ce qui . . .*, p. 91; see also p. 30.

compatible with local political imperatives was available. Survivors from the first post-war generation remain fascinated by their trajectory, just as the generation of 1968 cannot stop writing about itself, but until marxism fell from fashion the best way to deal with the encumbrance of Stalinist Communism was to deny it that very legitimacy which had been accorded it with such conceptual facility a few years before. Habits of mind undoubtedly remained, but styles of argument shifted, and the unencumbered allegiance of marxist thought *outside* the Party in the post-Stalin years shifted to new ground.

The interlude from the discrediting of Stalin to the final victory of the structuralists constitutes the idyll of humanist marxism in France. Outsiders are occasionally surprised at how brief this moment really was: just ten years separate the secret speech from Garaudy's defeat at Argenteuil. The enduring impact of the period owes much to the personalities associated with it (Sartre, Lefebvre, Lefort, Goldmann, Gorz, and, in a different key, Mallet), and the pleasing contrast with what went before (and came after). There was also a rather less contorted relationship than hitherto between the writings of these years and the political concerns of the wider intellectual community— notably the Algerian war and opposition to the institutions of the new Fifth Republic.

Marxist humanism may be said to have come into its own with Sartre's announcement (in September 1957) that existentialism was nothing other than an ideology *within* marxism (and parasitic upon it).[87] This important reversal of status, a preface to Sartre's later attempt to ground the whole marxist enterprise in a post-existentialist metaphysics, placed man, the author of the text of experience, at the epicentre of philosophy, the source of meaning. Not that the hypostasized proletariat ceased to matter, but its striving to negate its own existence was reduced to a chapter in a more Nietszchean account of *all* human experience as the struggle to 'self-overcome'. At one stroke this endorsed the legitimate struggle of the workers, while de-emphasizing its radical primacy (a not insignificant move at a time when the French working class had not only endorsed capitalism with its votes but was being steadily overtaken by other social categories in the organization of capitalist production).

This unashamedly idealist account of human history (consciousness as the source of its own history) provided the backdrop for a renewed interest in the interior experience of workers. Castoriadis of course had been plugging away at this theme for a decade or more, but his writings of 1958 and thereafter for the first time coincided with a general sympathy for such concerns. The claim that the autonomous organizations of the workers *were* the workers' struggle, that 'la gestion ouvrière de la production' (= *autogestion*) could be generalized into a total project which was socialism, was echoed not only by André Gorz in 1964, but by a new generation of syndicalist militants.[88] These began to look back to the pre-Communist independent unions of the *fin-de-siècle* as a model of practical socialism, and the men and women who would form the future leadership of the CFDT acquired their activist enthusiasm in this light. Moreover, and unlike the earlier syndicalists, they had access to the works of the young Marx which offered the hope of reintegrating proletarian autonomy and initiative into the marxist schema from which it had long been expunged.

This interest in the early Marx because of what he offered to the proletariat, rather than for what he could do for philosophers, distinguished the marxist humanism of 1963 from the Hegelian Marx who so fascinated the previous generation. Entailed in this change was a move away from the powerful strain of positivism in French thought, which had informed the apologetics of Sartre and Merleau-Ponty even as they denied it in principle. Marx seen through the eyes of Lukacs (or, rather, through the writings of Goldmann, Lukacs' principle French apostle) did not demand an acceptance of the primacy of a dialectic of material life; the dialectical negotiations would take place between conscious subjects. There was still a problem surrounding the *productivist* emphasis in marxism, however. So long as this remained undiminished, the Engelsian requirement of a final (material) cause could not be abandoned. Some (like Castoriadis) already appreciated this and were beginning to treat the marxist emphasis upon *work* as the most bourgeois of Marx's own inheritances from the thought of his time. Others, like Gorz, incorporated the older way of thinking into a consideration of new evidence: automation and technical development would end unqualified work and leave as a residual work-force the sort

---

[88] See André Gorz, *Stratégie ouvrière et néo-capitalisme* (Paris, 1964). Other important work from this period was by Serge Mallet (*La Nouvelle Classe ouvrière*, Paris, 1963), Pierre Fougeyrollas (*Le Marxisme en question*, Paris, 1959, and *La conscience politique dans la France contemporaine*, Paris, 1963) and Kostas Axelos (*Marx, penseur de la technique: de l'aliénation de l'homme à la conquête du monde*, Paris, 1961).

of highly-skilled men and women capable of self-regulation.[89] This drew a welcome analogy with the syndicalist élite of 1900, but entailed a persistent faith both in the 'natural' unfolding of capitalist production forms and in the beneficial consequences that must accrue thence for the proponents of socialism.

In the meantime, a renewed faith in the active human subject, taken together with a reading of Marx's texts on alienation and the nature of ideology, cast an uncomfortable light on the distinctly *un*aroused consciousnesses of contemporaries. If historical self-awareness must come from within, and was not to be imparted by Communist bureaucrats and their militant activists ('parfois . . . déformés par un "marxisme" étriqué'[90]), some explanation was still required for the failure of man in general and the proletariat in particular to emerge as a *conscious* participant in human history. Since it would hardly do to attribute blame exclusively to a Stalinist leadership (which would pay the latter the compliment of taking seriously its own claims), the solution was the newly-fashionable belief in ideological hegemony, the power of illusion.[91] The attraction of this sort of marxist apologetic was less the publication of the relevant Gramscian texts (still largely unknown in France) than the fact that Marx in *these* terms sounded fascinatingly like Freud, whose own star was in the ascendant at the hands of Jacques Lacan.

Ideological hegemony, however, as Aron noted, is presumptively contagious. Why is it just workers who are unable to 'see through' the veil of bourgeois mystification—or else, how is *anyone* able to do so, and in that case how do we know of its existence? How can we *know* that it hides a deeper reality? On what epistemological grounds? It all began to sound as though the solution offered by Sartre many years before was still the only one open to a consistent marxist: knowledge of *this* sort comes only via action, and the only action on offer comes from organized official marxism.

It was questions of this nature which began to sow self-doubt among the younger would-be humanist marxists. 'Total man' and his infinitely recessive false consciousness looked less heuristically promising than the fresh approach offered by the theory of structures.

[89] For Castoriadis, see works cited. For Gorz, see *Stratégie ouvrière et néo-capitalisme*, but also Gorz's own criticisms of it in *Adieux au prolétariat*, p. 46.

[90] Castoriadis, *Expérience du mouvement ouvrier*, vol. 2, p. 74.

[91] On some difficulties with the theory of ideological hegemony and its pre-suppositions, see Jon Elster, 'Belief, Bias and Ideology', in Martin Hollis and Steven Lukes (eds.), *Rationality and Relativism* (Oxford, 1982), pp. 123–48.

From 1964, and reaching a crescendo in 1966–7, the attacks on humanism began to appear. Communist theorists had always been deeply averse to the emphasis on alienation, of course. This was not only because, having manifestly failed to end alienation in practice, they could hardly assert it as their goal in theory.[92] They also found the faith in a final 'overcoming' of the human condition distinctly undialectical and utopian, as well as likely to distract attention from the more mundane daily tasks of a political movement. But worst of all was the claim advanced by the younger humanists that 'everyone' was alienated under technological, bureaucratic capitalism (and its Communist *alter ego*). As Michel Simon, for example, warned: if everyone is alienated under capitalism, then everyone has a revolutionary vocation. In that case why should the working class preserve a privileged status and an avant-garde role? Why indeed, replied his opponents, who thereby laid themselves open to the charge of having forgotten the most elementary ABC of marxism.[93]

It was at this juncture that Althusser and his troup of *normaliens* took up the argument. Conceding to his opponents that social structures are opaque to their agents, he insisted that if true at all this must be true always. Disalienation was thus out of the question. This was logically impeccable, but it risked making of marxism a theory of society *in general*, rather than of capitalist society alone. Marxist definitions for class societies would remain valid for post-revolutionary societies too. The optimistic eschatology of the early Marx would be replaced by Marx the scientific exponent of social statics. This removed from vision the marxist concern with revolution, but it also placed a high premium on official knowledge in place of the unofficial variety which Althusser and others felt had been circulating for too long, raising false hopes of change at a time when the Communists' own strategy entailed a long slow march through the institutions.

The rapidity of the shift in mood was remarkable. By 1966 mention of 'man the subject' or the 'alienated human condition' in certain Parisian circles was likely to provoke at best a scornful derision. The protagonists of workers' self-control retreated to the newly constituted CFDT, or to work in the Michel Rocard's PSU, a tiny breakaway socialist organization born in the turmoil of the Algerian crisis. Those students who would not so readily abandon the theories and theorists of the immediate past moved away from marxism towards the

[92] See George Lichtheim, *Marxism in Modern France*, p. 170.
[93] Michel Simon is quoted in Geerlandt, *Garaudy et Althusser*, p. 62.

ideologically heterogeneous and sociologically self-regarding *groupuscules* which surfaced in 1968. The 'humanists' within the PCF were put firmly in their place, and the humanism of Marx himself resolutely denied in Paris in the very years that saw its emergence as the best hope for peaceful transformation in Eastern Europe. 'Man' was everywhere expelled from the hearts and minds of French academic marxism. The 'class struggle in theory' had been won.[94]

*

The concern with marxism itself as an object of study is quite properly associated above all with Althusser and his group, but it was not entirely confined to such narrow quarters. In a sense all marxists have a continuing interest in the foundations of their system of thought, partly because it just is that sort of theory, partly too because since 1921 marxists have had an unwelcome amount of time to spend upon theoretical investigation of the narcissistic kind. In France the habit was further encouraged by the generically Parisian elevation of theory as a whole. Marxism's claim to rest on a peculiarly scientific foundation made it uniquely well-adapted to this pursuit, since it further rooted it in the world of positivist social science which the French could claim, with some justice, as their own.

Thus Sartre in 1950, Merleau-Ponty a few years later, and Henri Lefebvre throughout his intellectual career all asserted the privileged status of marxism as an object of introspection, though Lefebvre in later years came to recognize the risk that the real achievement of such efforts was nearly always to 'correct' the work of Marx or Engels with a view to removing contradictions one had found there. This could involve one of a number of exercises: criticizing Marx with his own words (Castoriadis), distinguishing between an ideal and a 'degraded' marxism (Sartre), following the *mouvement interne* of Marx's research in preference to the formalized (published) statements (Lefebvre), discovering in marxism the 'philosophy of our time' which thus rendered *all* criticism pure bad faith (Sartre again), graciously providing Marx with that theory of consciousness which he had hitherto mysteriously lacked (Merleau-Ponty), distinguishing between an early and a later Marx (Goldmann and many, many others).[95]

---

[94] For an informed, if splenetic, account of these years, see Rancière, *La Leçon d'Althusser*, esp. p. 158.

[95] For Castoriadis see in particular *L'Expérience du mouvement ouvrier*, vol. 2, *passim*; for Sartre, *Situations VI*, pp. 26 ff., and Lefort, *Sur une colonne absente*, p. 66; for Henri

But none of these pursued this *sort* of exercise so single-mindedly and with such impact as Louis Althusser. He did this in two stages, which are distinct in emphasis but not in project. Until the end of the 1960s, Althusser and his students devoted their efforts to 'correcting' Marx by drawing out and identifying the sense in which his work was to be understood as scientific. This they did by a series of 'symptomatic' readings designed to elucidate the reasoning which lay behind Marx's 'silences' and which had been obscured by the misplaced emphasis upon his earlier, 'humanist' work. After 1969 the Althusserian project purported to take a more overtly political turn, concerning itself with politics directly and claiming for philosophy not the status of the 'science of sciences' but that of an act of political intervention in itself. Over time Althusser allowed a less rigorously exclusive reading of Marx in theory (for example by according a limited role to experience, even if only in the theoretical realm), but he balanced this with an even narrower account of just what marxism was. The 'epistemological break' (before which all Marx's writing was non-marxist) had originally been placed by Althusser in the mid–1840s. By an essay of 1973 he had shifted it forward to 1857, thus excluding vast tracts of Marx's own major writings as essentially outside the canon.[96] And with the same taste for balance, Althusser's last political intervention, in 1978, saw him criticizing the PCF for its rigid inflexibility—and then concluding that the true source of the problem lay in an *insufficiently* rigorous attention to theory in general and the theoretical demands of Marxism–Leninism at its most dogmatic in particular![97]

Thus it is not prima facie absurd to offer some comments on the Althusserian enterprise taken as a whole, and in acknowledgement of the fact that it is probably the last of the all-embracing exercises in marxist argument that France will see for a long while. Althusser's project (and this, too, it shares with the more ambitious work of other French marxists) can be described in two ways. Technically, the aim was to establish a scientific standing for historical materialism via a regrounding of the materialist dialectic in Marx's method of argument. The aim was to confirm the arguments propounded by Engels, for

Lefebvre see *La Somme et le reste*, p. 237. Merleau-Ponty discusses Marx's failings in *Aventures de la dialectique*, p. 64 (where he also claims that Lukacs was engaged in similar rectificatory work). See also Lucien Goldmann, *Marxisme et sciences humaines*, p. 164.

[96] See *Pour Marx* (1965) and *Réponse à John Lewis* (1973) *passim*.
[97] *Ce qui . . .*, *passim*.

example, in his work on Feuerbach (where he emphasizes the *final* or ultimate causality of economic relations), while rescuing them from a crude and vulnerable natural materialism. This would cut the ground from under the hitherto ascendant humanists, by re-establishing the autonomy of History via something better than the discredited 'reflection' theory of Lenin. This was the least a marxist could do if he wished to render marxism respectable once again in the intellectual community.

This is where the second account of Althusser's project can be illuminating. For Althusser was also, as we have seen, engaged in an urgent effort to liquidate the Stalinist problem while preserving the claims of the Communist Party of which he was a member. The only serious way to set about this was to renew the terms in which marxism was discussed, to restore Marx's *own* thought to a scientific impregnability which would refute all charges of eclecticism or opportunism in the de-Stalinization process. And the only way to renew Marx in *this* sense was to have him saying something epistemologically different from what had hitherto passed as marxist philosophy, a desire readily abetted by the contemporary enthusiasm for Lévi-Strauss and structuralism, which urgently invited an account of Marx's project with people and events removed.

The Althusserian method was to retain the previously discredited term 'dialectical materialism', but to make of it a 'theory of theories'. Historical materialism then becomes one of those theories (the theory of the science of history). Theory itself is unified with the rest of human knowledge and activity in a package of four distinct 'practices': economic, ideological, political, and theoretical. These remain distinct even though the precise content of each varies a little with different Althusserian pronouncements. No one of these practices has permanent priority over the others, and it is thus not a simple matter of giving the 'economic practice' control over the 'theoretical practice' (as Engels and Lenin, in their way, had done). On the other hand, the course of history *is* determined, so at any given moment one of these practices is dominant over the rest and is controlling matters. But determined does not mean predetermined: the dominant structure (e.g. economic practice) will not always and inevitably have this causal hegemony, and determining *which* practice is dominant at a given moment is the task of that scientific understanding of the whole process which dialectical materialism provides. At all events, reductionism pure and simple is ruled out because each of the practices is autonomous relative to the others, related to them but not consistently dependent on any one of them.[98]

This autonomous status of the various practices is limited, however, by Althusser's desire to retain the requirement that there must *be*, at all times, a final cause, Engels's 'last instance'. But the admission of a hypothetical last instance which is economic practice (the structure of production relations) does not preclude an infinite number of mediations deriving from all the other practices and thus obscuring, delaying, perverting the determined event. This resolves the old problems of the role of the individual, the 'accident' in history, and so forth, by eliminating the conceptual possibility of their occurrence. Everything is causally related, but in ways which while scientifically ascertainable in principle, are always in fact invisible to the naked eye. The verb 'to dominate' is important here. It covers a territory ranging from the unambiguous 'to determine' down to the inoffensive 'to influence', and allows Althusser to make claims for his structures which are not so much contentious as unassailable and never subject to proof.[99]

This heavy dependence upon fixed structures in indeterminate relationship to one another altogether abstracts the role of the human agent. On this Althusser never wavered. Marx's principal debt to Hegel, he wrote, was the concept of the 'procès sans sujet. Il soutient le Capital tout entier. Marx en avait parfaitement conscience.'[100] This is the core of the Althusserian innovation, for he is claiming (in a piece published in February 1968) that Marx himself was aware of the structural, dialectic, scientific method which it is claimed he was employing in his major work. In earlier Althusserian writing on the other hand there had been a tendency to concede that Marx had carried over into his scientific work (after 1845) the optimistic Hegelian idealism of his youth, and had as a result failed to make clear his method of procedure, leaving it to later generations to dig it out by close inspection of his silences. The following is a fine example of the line of reasoning thus deployed: 'Si Marx n'a pas jugé nécessaire d'établir des différences terminologiques, c'est qu'il n'a jamais pensé

---

[98] See Alex Callinicos, *Althusser's Marxism* (London, 1976), esp. p. 43.

[99] See Raymond Aron, *D'une sainte famille à l'autre. Essais sur les marxismes imaginaires* (Paris, 1969), esp. pp. 290–1.

[100] Althusser, 'Sur le rapport de Marx à Hegel' in *Lénine et la philosophie* (Paris, 1972), p. 70.

rigoureusement la différence de son discours avec le discours anthropologique du jeune Marx.'[101]

The most obvious difference between the young and the mature Marx is that the latter was interested in understanding the capitalist world, while the former had sought more urgently to change it. Rather than deny this, Althusser incorporates it into his method. By labelling 'scientific' the premises upon which Marx supposedly constructed his theory of economic processes and contradiction within capitalism, Althusser recognized that these served only to explain the workings and self-reproduction of the system itself, and threw no light on the *means* by which one socio-economic system might give way to another. The marxist science was synchronic, and any diachronic capacity within it would need somehow to be extrapolated. The appeal of this distinction is that it excuses marxism from any obligation to offer an account of revolution, and similarly precludes it from being employed as a tool of analysis for *post*-revolutionary societies—so no marxist critiques of the USSR! This requires of course that a society's genuinely 'post-revolutionary' status be confirmed by reference back to the Althussero-marxist definition of pre-revolutionary capitalism as a system dominated by economic processes based on the extraction of surplus value.[102]

The Althusserian method amounts to little more than that. Its complex and lengthy exposition in the literature derives in part from the fashionable impenetrable style, but chiefly from the need to work through Marx's huge output in some detail, cataloguing those contradictions which reveal the scientific Marx at war with his conscious (or younger) self, and extruding (and justifying the extrusion of) Marx's many references to the human agent. In their place there is posited an interplay of impersonal structures and practices, determining history according to their relation to one another, with humans engaged secondarily as agents within the various practices.

Just as the Althusserian *project* can be presented as the harmonious matching of two sorts of concerns, so the conclusions deriving from his method can be described in two ways. The theoretical outcome is the less interesting because it can never be other than a restatement, in programmatic form, of the method of investigation itself. The

---

[101] Jacques Rancière in Louis Althusser *et al.*, *Lire 'Le Capital'* (Paris, 1965) vol. 1, p. 198.

[102] In *Lire 'Le Capital'*, vol. 2, p. 183, Althusser explicitly recognizes that Marx failed to provide a theory of transition from one mode of production to another.

distinction between 'natural' laws and the laws of human history, a distinction which had occupied the attentions of Engels and Lenin and led to the more embarrassing of Stalin's excursions into doctrine, was abolished. There was now but one theory, no longer engaged in the search for the workings of reality but merely a tool of investigation subject to rules of its own devising. The problem of causality disappeared. In its place there came the interplay of instances whence emerges (in the never-to-be-attained 'last instance') the evidence as to which structure is in dominance. All talk of man making his own history is declared senseless—'le sujet n'est que le support des rapports de production constitutifs de l'objectivité économique.'[103] The activity of theoretical production (i.e. what Althusser was engaged upon) is a practice like any other and thus activity within it as subject to class struggle as activity in any other sphere. This not only resolves the ancient theory/practice dilemma but provides that justification for the role of intellectuals in the class struggle which had long been sought by Althusser's spiritual precursors.

The practical implications of the Althusserian contribution to marxism were felt almost immediately.[104] Given the scientific requirement that individual acting agents be the creations of existing practices, and given that the latter are in turn coloured by context (so to speak), the behaviour of persons with whom Althusser was out of sympathy become subject to aggressive reductionist criticism. The most notorious instance of this came in March 1969 in his letter to Macciocchi[105] in which he ridicules the students of May 1968. The manipulated *subjects* of social democratic *practice*, they could only be purveyors of 'petty bourgeois ideology' (an almost verbatim repetition of Georges Marchais's own dismissal of the events). More interesting, perhaps, was Althusser's gentle criticism of the PCF a decade later for precipitately abandoning its revolutionary vocabulary in the search for votes. The 'dictatorship of the proletariat', wrote Althusser, points to a real and *inevitable* problem, the fact of the dictatorship of the bourgeoisie through its class state. Classes are the products of structural instances, and it is theoretically incoherent for a class party to neglect this reality in its (laudable) desire to form a mass movement.

---

[103] Rancière in *Lire 'Le Capital'*, quoted by Geerlandt, op. cit., p. 69.

[104] One of them is well described by Daniel Lindenberg. Louis Althusser offered a Cartesian marxism 'qui nous rendait la fièrté d'être communistes, au lieu de culpabiliser jour et nuit pour des crimes du stalinisme'. Lindenberg, *Le Marxisme introuvable*, p. 26.

[105] In Macciocchi, *Letters from inside the Italian Communist Party*.

Given what the bourgeois state *must* be, there are certain things its class opponent *must* be, too.[106]

One of these requirements is loyalty to the ideas of Marx and Lenin. Whereas until 1969 Althusser contented himself with making claims on behalf of Marx's writings alone, the work of later years never failed to bracket Marx with Lenin. While in part attributable to some criticism voiced of Althusser's neglect of Leninism in his earlier exclusive concern with theory, the shift also represents a practical redressing of a political imbalance in his thought. If, after all, the laws governing the dissolution of a structure are, as we have seen, different from those governing its function, then the neo-positivist evolutionism which the PCF had inherited from Lenin, with its emphasis upon a smoothly functioning economic causality and the eventual (peaceful) transition to socialism, must be dismissed as profoundly unscientific. But any such departure from party loyalty would have been unthinkable. Althusser's practical achievement, after all, was to renew the credibility of large areas of the old *langue de bois*: proletarian dictatorship, state power, class conflict, monopoly state capitalism, the relation of theory to practice, all could again be spoken of in respectable circles. Rather than prejudice his party standing and destroy his achievement, Althusser pursued the easier alternative of reading Lenin into his account of marxist thought. Reading Lenin symptomatically, after all, posed no more of a problem than doing likewise for Marx, and the hitherto difficult issue of Lenin's political actions and their consequences could now be redefined as the *locus classicus* of over-determination (the Russian Revolution itself) and secondary contradictions (the context of Russian history before and since). Lenin the thinker became a supreme exponent of theoretical practice, while Lenin the revolutionary ceased to be a subject, in the sense of bearing, or indeed being able to bear, any responsibility for events.[107]

The approach to the study of marxism associated with Althusser and dominant in France during the latter part of our period poses a

---

[106] Althusser, 'On the 22nd Congress', in *New Left Review*, vol. 104 (1977) (esp. pp. 12–13).

[107] See Rancière, *La Leçon d'Althusser*, p. 95. On the Althusserian view of the subject see Susan James, op. cit., p. 217. On Althusser's role in making marxism academically respectable here is François Châtelet, writing in 1979: 'Aujourd'hui, l'althussérisme est devenu une partie constituante de l'idéologie universitaire en France; il est la manière d'être du marxisme académiquement respectable.' (*Questions–Objections*, Paris, 1979, p.246).

number of problems and raises doubts which reflect back on the whole experience of French marxist philosophy in this era.

Some of these can be noted in passing. Rather than engage in the problem of contradictions between Marx and history (or within Marx himself), Althusser merely abolishes them, or incorporates them within his theory. In earlier times this was called 'dialectics', but it was precisely part of Althusser's claim to have gone beyond the sort of word-play which had given official marxist philosophy such a bad name. Yet he reaffirms the absence of any contradiction between Marx's political predictions and the actual course of events by redescribing the former as peripheral to the true science of marxism and the latter as secondary contradictions (and thus not themselves objects of investigation). This cavalier approach has in turn licensed a new generation of Communist philosophers to abandon *any* attempt at explaining the inexplicable.[108]

Althusser has also reconfirmed the uncritical approach in dealings with the marxist pantheon. He never actually corrects or criticizes Marx, preferring to treat the unacceptable passages as anthropological hangovers for which Marx the scientist cannot be held responsible. The same attitude informs his dealings with Lenin and all his successors. Marxism thus becomes the success story of an idea, where the failures are just written out as part of another (untold) story, whose empirical chapter headings (the social democratic proclivities of workers, the establishment of dictatorships in the wake of Communist revolutions, the survival of capitalism, the dismal history of western Communism) render it of little interest to the philosopher of structures.

Thirdly, and this at least has been noted by some of Althusser's French contemporaries, marxists among them, Althusser's own method and conclusion are profoundly unmarxist (this involves denying his claim to have discovered a more basic marxism lurking hitherto unseen in the texts, of course). Most obviously, Althusser's way of discussing marxism as a body of thought requires evaluating it in isolation from its own history. But if *any* marxist propositions are true, then this at least must follow, that marxism may not stand apart from its historical fate. There is also something oddly out of character

---

[108] See e.g. Solange Mercier-Josa, *Pour lire Marx et Hegel*, p. 131. She acknowledges that the connection between ideology and 'mode of production' is 'complexe'. It is, she says, *neither* subjective *nor* a mechanical law. 'Nous ne traiterons pas vraiment de la question de cette connexion'!

about a marxism which makes a *virtue* of its inability to explain the occurrence of change (or, more precisely, to describe it *as* change). And finally, the reduction of marxism to a galaxy of concepts orbiting around the fixed point of the theory of surplus value may make things clear, but it hardly renders them appealing to large masses of people. Yet in history marxism has always been attached, for good or ill, to the experience of a combative labour movement. And as Henri Lefebvre has noted, 'personne ne s'est jamais battu et n'a risqué sa vie pour ou contre le concept de plus-value, si clarifiant qu'il apparaisse.'[109]

The two major difficulties, however, lie in the realm of the higher methodology. The first concerns Althusser's idealism. On first glance this seems contradictory—the Althusserian project is nothing if not resolutely opposed to *all* idealism. It establishes a profound division between materialist and idealist thought, classing the latter as firmly bourgeois (and liable to try to infiltrate and dominate the materialism of the marxists if the latter are not ever vigilant). It is not ideas, 'not even marxist ideas', which make history.[110]

And yet when Althusser in 1978 published his first direct criticism of the Communist Party, of what did he accuse it? Of having resorted to an obsession with ideas. 'La conscience, c'est des idées, et les idées c'est ce qu'il faut connaître, c'est à dire répandre et diffuser. Conscience, idées, diffusion d'idées. Parfaite conception idéaliste de la pratique politique.'[111] Two problems thus arise. How did it come to be that a concern with ideas could so distort the *practice* of the PCF? Why was that practice so vulnerable to distortion from that source? And why, in the rest of his critique of PCF behaviour, does Althusser confine himself to the theoretical errors of the leadership, never once engaging an account of the material conditions of the Party's intellectual production? There are some ready cynical answers of course, but the fact remains that Althusser's own criticism of his party is confined to the realm of ideas.

This is not as surprising as it appears. Althusser's own work is passionately Hegelian in spirit; it is a search for a 'higher' unity that will join the products of the mind with the conditions of real existence so absolutely that the very distinctions must disappear. And since this unity can *only* be a product of pure ratiocination, the outcome is classical idealist speculation. What sounds at first reading like a return

---

[109] Henri Lefebvre, *Une pensée devenue monde . . . faut-il abandonner Marx?* (Paris, 1983), p. 63.
[110] Althusser in *Power and Opposition*, pp. 227–8.   [111] *Ce qui . . .* p. 21.

to the mechanistic styles of the eighteenth century ends up reproducing the difficulties of the original: since there has to be agency in history, a dualism emerges. There are those (persons and things) which are products of structure, and those (persons and relations) which alter the conditions of existence. The process whereby this leads to an élitist idealism is well described by Lucien Goldmann:

Comme tout matérialisme mécanique, le groupe althussérien arrivera finalement à se contredire puisqu'après avoir nié tout caractère significatif à la vie humaine il accordera une signifiance outrancière, dépourvue de tout élément idéologique et de toute erreur, à un petit groupe privilégié, à ceux qui élaborent une 'partie théorique' radicalement dépourvue de toute idéologie (le corollaire de ce privilège accordé par Althusser aux théoriciens étant par la suite, chez certains théoriciens se rattachant plus ou moins à ce meme courant, le privilège d'une petite élite révolutionnaire sur le plan d'action).[112]

This sort of camouflaged super-idealism has serious implications for the new marxist account of the history of marxist labour movements. The whole of the history of the latter becomes a mere footnote in the history of theoretical practice, which thus both describes and explains the errors and 'contradictions' without which every problem, from reformism to Stalin, need never have been. Here is Althusser's own version of labour history as a by-product of a mistake in marxist theory:

You can in fact seriously wonder whether this misunderstanding, concerning the arithmetical presentation of surplus value being taken for a complete theory of exploitation, has not in the end constituted a theoretical and practical obstacle in the history of the Marxist labour movement to a correct understanding of the conditions and forms of exploitation, and whether this restrictive conception of exploitation (as a purely calculable quantity) has not contributed in part to a classical division of tasks in the class struggle between the economic struggle and the political struggle, and hence to a restrictive conception of each form of struggle, which began to hinder, and is today still hindering the broadening of the forms of the whole working class and struggle of the masses.[113]

One might choose to believe this, but one could not do so while continuing to denounce the heresy of idealism.

It would be wrong to lay the blame for the 'idealist deviation' exclusively at Althusser's door. His assertion in 1968 that the whole of the class struggle can sometimes be summed up in the struggle for one word against another could as well have been made by Sartre in an

---

[112] Goldmann, *Marxisme et sciences humaines*, p. 167.
[113] Althusser in *Power and Opposition*, pp. 233–4.

earlier period.[114] But the difference was that the idealism of a Sartre or a Merleau-Ponty was the self-conscious product of the difficult encounter between two antagonistic intellectual traditions. With Althusser we are seeing the belated revenge of the French idealist heritage, asserting its primacy in the very act of justifying the most materialist of marxisms.

The second difficulty in Althusser concerns his epistemology. The whole post-war marxist enterprise in France was focused upon the quest for a theory of knowledge which would be unique to marxism. Althusser's rejection of the testimony of consciousness as a source for knowledge is what pointed him towards the need for an alternative grounding for marxist accounts of the human condition. The answer he offers is that science produces knowledge. We truly know the world when we bring to it a scientifically correct method for acquiring that knowledge. The next question ought then to be, what are the scientific criteria which guarantee the validity of our perception? But this, according to Althusser, is to misread the matter. The very idea that the object of our knowledge, and some supposed object-in-itself might be in a problematic relation, that perception might play havoc with truth, implies the existence of a *permanent* difficulty in epistemology. And such an implication can only arise out of an ideologically-determined position, that of relativism. This Althusser dismisses on the a priori grounds that it is evidence, quite simply, that the holder of such an opinion is *already* in a condition of ignorance.[115]

Distinguishing between knowledge and belief, then, is a problem which *cannot* arise once one has grasped the scientific understanding which from the outset will guarantee the former and identify the ideological standing of the latter. Attention thus focuses on that scientific understanding. But Althusser never actually names it. He works, of course, within the tradition associated with Bachelard, whereby scientific understanding is said to proceed via profound 'breaks', after each of which there comes a wholly novel way of understanding hitherto familiar phenomena. It is just such a break that Althusser identifies in Marx. The problem is that Marx is said by Althusser to have continued to employ the Hegelian language which

---

[114] See Althusser in *La Pensée*, Apr. 1968.
[115] See the comments by Norman Geras in 'Louis Althusser: an assessment' in *New Left Review*, no. 71 (1972). Merleau-Ponty had already identified and criticized the Althusserian position *avant l'heure* in a comment on some early work of Lefebvre and Jean-Toussaint Desanti in *Aventures de la dialectique*, p. 92 n. 1.

predominated before the break, leaving commentators to *infer* the new method of understanding. But how is this inference to be confirmed? By the argument that a new method *must* be present for the conclusions of Marx (as described by Althusser) to be valid. In other words, we are told everything about the post-*rupture* marxist science except what it actually *is*. The temptation to believe in it is strong, thanks to the possibilities it opens up; but the external grounds for such a belief are quite absent (and it really is not very convincing to be told that this is necessarily the case, and that such empirical tests of theoretical presence could *only* be demanded by those predisposed on ideological grounds to disbelief).[116]

What we are left with is an old-fashioned tautology. Althusser would have us 'read' Marx (in particular *Capital*) in order to discover within his work the scientific logic of his method. But on Althusser's own reasoning, we could only choose to do this if we were already predisposed to believe that *Capital* is a work of science. Yet this is something we could not conceivably know, since only a reading of the work will provide us with a grasp of the criteria for establishing what it is to *be* scientific.

This sort of reasoning would not have been totally unfamiliar to an earlier generation of marxists, raised on Engels's account of dialectical philosophy, in which everything is relative except the revolutionary character of the dialectical knowledge-source itself, which is unassailably absolute.[117] And it is a testimony to the universality of Althusser's concerns that his own epistemological inadequacy reflects a wider difficulty in marxist thought as a whole. Marxism seeks to historicize all knowledge save that which it itself offers as truth. Even when marxism emphasizes its own historicized status it is vulnerable to the usual charge against relativism that it lacks on its own reasoning any basis from which to be so sure of the absence of certainty. Peculiar to marxism, though, is the teleological option of grounding present knowledge on future events: the radically altered conditions of a post-revolutionary world will obviate our present inadequate striving for knowledge and will confirm retrospectively the validity of marxism in

[116] On all of this, see George Lichtheim, *From Marx to Hegel*, p. 156; John Dunn, *Western Political Theory in the face of the future* (Cambridge, 1979), p. 100. Also Edith Kurzweil, 'Louis Althusser: between philosophy and politics', in *Marxist Perspectives*, vol. 2, no. ii (1979), pp. 8–24.

[117] See Friedrich Engels, 'Ludwig Feuerbach and the End of Classical German Philosophy' (e.g. in Robert Tucker (ed.), *The Marx-Engels Reader* (New York, 1972), esp. p. 363).

its account of that inadequacy. But to believe this we must accept that marxism cannot also be the ideology of the transition to socialism, because the very forms of that transition will fundamentally alter the conditions of knowledge, and one of the products of our *present* condition of knowledge is marxism itself. All marxism can thus offer is a theory of the present. It cannot give reasons for believing anything very particular about the revolutionary future— and the grounds on which it could not possibly do that are entailed within marxism *as* a theory of the present.

The study by marxists of the entity 'marxism' is thus riddled with conundrums and contradictions. Althusser's effort to reduce the thing under study to manageable proportions and then to locate it in an unimpeachable certainty does not resolve these difficulties, but it certainly magnifies them. He seems to have appreciated this himself in his later writings, when he moved from negotiating his path *within* marxism to behaving as though he had already resolved the difficulties and could now apply the results to political practice. Thus in his *Autocritique* he plays down the distinction between science and ideology, but only to conclude by treating *both* as products of the class struggle (in theory). In any case, he has no hesitation in invoking the conclusions derived from earlier work when they can function to serve a political end, as we have seen.

The abandoning of the attempt to rebuild the marxist edifice on structural foundations coincided with the end of the Parisian engagement with marxism in general. It would be an exaggeration to suggest that the two were causally related, but the solipsistic character of French intellectual life adds plausibility to the idea that Althusser's failure to solve the marxist riddle did contribute to a wider loss of enthusiasm for marxist discourse (and it is a line of argument which would appeal, ironically, to Althusser himself). In any event, Althusser's lengthening silences reflected a wider disillusion, and allow us to treat the mid–1970s as the end of the marxist epoch in the history of French thought.

*

I have tried to bring out the extent to which the history of marxist theory in France in inextricably intertwined with the wider history of the Left in France. From Thorez's theory of 'absolute pauperization' or Jeannette Vermeersch's attack on the 'bourgeois Malthusianism' of birth control, through Sartre's anti-anti-Communism and on to

Althusser's dominant structures, the silent partners in the history of marxist thought in France have been the Resistance, the colonial struggles in Indo-China, Madagascar, and Algeria, the miners' strikers of 1948 and 1963, Korea, Stalin, student 'adventurism', and the falling Communist vote. This is so not just in the obvious sense that these matters form the backdrop for political argument in modern France, but because these *were* the argument. They could not, however, be debated or negotiated in so crude a form, but were recast so as to suit that other, parallel, context, the communal concerns of an élite circle of writers.

This said, the peculiar currents of marxist philosophy in France were not randomly adopted according to circumstance. The years 1945–75 do seem to confirm Karl Korsch's insight, to the effect that Marx the philosopher surfaces in moments of revolutionary optimism, but that in what Merleau-Ponty was to call 'des périodes d'affaissement' subject and object disassociate and flexible relations become, for marxist observers, immutable structures. It was a peculiarity of postwar France, however, that 'revolutionary optimism' corresponded not to some empirical observation of social possibilities, but to the condition and the credibility of the revolutionary party. A strong PCF produced Sartre, a declining Party brought forth Althusser.

It will by now be clear just how intimately related are the recent history of the PCF and the unfolding ideas of its best-known intellectual. Nowhere was this more clearly seen than when Althusser focused his attentions upon the Party itself. The Althusserian philosophy of order, of discipline, was applied conscientiously to its source and much of the philosopher's attention became devoted in his later years to presenting the PCF in the best available (marxist) light. At the end of the 1970s some foreign commentators sought to interpret Althusser's muted criticism of the Party as a sign of a longstanding disengagement between the marxism of the intellectuals and the unacceptable face of official Communism. Perry Anderson, for example, excused Althusser's silence before 1978 as a 'long-term choice to remain within the Communist movement. This option involved paying the price of silence in order to maintain activity in the major party of the French working class.'[118]

This, the *locus classicus* of anglophone apologetics for French marxist discourse, succeeds in misreading almost every point at issue. 1978

---

[118] Perry Anderson, *Arguments within English Marxism*, p. 113.

saw no break with silence. What Althusser actually wrote at the time was a statement indicating a preference for a theoretically self-confident return to the old discipline of Marxism-Leninism, shorn of the ambivalence and contradictions of the tactics of the 1970s. If he was critical of his party, it was for having moved too far from the Leninist high ground, not for having failed to move far or fast enough.[119] Nor had there ever been a 'silence'—Althusser in the years 1964–77, like Sartre in the 1950s, was unsparing in his public aggression towards any and all critics of the PCF.[120] Far from paying a price for this (what price? to whom?), it was precisely his faithful engagement with Communism which gave his marxism a value in the intellectual market-place. And since 'maintaining activity', for a practitioner of theoretical practice, means nothing more than continuing to think on to paper, it is hard to see how this activity could ever have been denied to him, in France at least.

The point which eludes Anderson and others is that French marxists could *never* have imagined their situation as similar to that of their Anglo-American admirers. *Their* problem was not that they were condemned to marxist phrase-making in a political vacuum. For them the need was to find a way of saying what the official marxists were saying, but to say it in a more plausible and engaging manner. When a Guy Besse or a Françette Lazard dilates upon the incomparable claims of marxism in its Communist fortress, the political and intellectual world reacts predictably, and has done so since 1956. When Louis Althusser, Henri Lefebvre, Jacques Rancière (in his early years) or, *e*

---

[119] See, for example, this comment by Althusser on inner-party democracy: 'If recognised and organised tendencies are rejected, it is not so as to fall *behind* that political practice towards less freedom or the crushing of all freedom in the Party (as under "Stalinism" or its variants), it is to go *beyond* it, towards more freedom. Not for the pleasure of "freedom for freedom's sake", but the better to respond to the demands of the political practice of the vanguard of the working class, to ensure a closer and deeper relationship with the aspirations of the masses of the people, the better to prepare itself for the hard struggles ahead.' 'On the 22nd Congress', in *New Left Review* (1977). This, then, is Althusser the subterranean critic of French Stalinism? This piece, in content and language alike, could have been written in 1949. It is the pure product of the Stalinist theoretical mind, which has forgotten nothing and learned nothing from the last forty years of history.

[120] Here, as an antidote to Anderson and Althusser's many other Anglo-Saxon admirers, is Castoriadis on the subject of Althusser's 'critical' relationship with the PCF: 'On remarquera en passant que si, "pendant les années soixante", Althusser "se rendait à l'évidence", c'était en quelque sorte un plaisir solitaire. En public, étaient anathématisés et foudroyés ceux qui ne voyait pas la totalité unifiée et achevée de la théorie marxiste, la science de l'histoire, le continent du matérialisme historique, etc.' *La Société française*, p. 308 (written in 1978).

fortiori, Sartre said essentially similar things, the intellectual world—their world—listened. That was the positive achievement of marxism in post-war France.[121]

The negative achievement was of even greater significance. The enormous faith placed in marxism as a theory of the proletariat, resting in turn upon a longer tradition of guilty *ouvriérisme* among French progressives, always risked generating an era of disillusion when the revolutionary proletarian epicentre of marxism dissolved in a morass of sociological and theoretical doubt. It was not so much that marxism's conceptual incoherence itself let down its adherents, rather that the particular form of that incoherence—the false expectations placed in the telos of the proletariat—had the unfortunate capacity to transform itself into a justification for *utter* disillusion, and not simply intellectual disappointment. From an absurdly blind faith, marxists were drawn towards an empty nihilism. If no proletarian basis for the intelligibility of a utopia of *homo faber* could be secured, then it was not just marxism which had failed, but truth itself. The post-structuralist rejection of certainty in *any* form has its roots in this loss of political faith.

The intellectual price was matched by a moral one. The thirty-year-long dialogue of French marxist philosophy with its Communist *alter ego* gave to the latter hostages it could otherwise never have secured. As a theory of radical politics, after all, marxism died with Stalin. As a sociology it retained enormous potential, but no *marxist* intellectual could ever concede this distinction. And thus they failed to grasp that their own disquisitions on marxism, entertainingly analogous to the work of the young Hegelians a century before, differed in one important respect. From 1948, marxism was the *raison d'état* of a large area of Europe. In some of these lands, what was said and done in France served directly to bolster and justify the practices of the

---

[121] For speeches by Guy Besse, Françette Lazard, and Lucien Sève see *Les Intellectuels, la culture et la révolution*, pp. 47, 103–5, 132. According to Besse (speaking in February 1980), 'Le parti communiste français, en respect des obligations qui sont les siennes, et fort d'une irremplaçable expérience, ne se décharge sur personne des responsabilités qui lui incombent dans le développement présent et futur du marxisme.' Or Sève, informing his audience that all theoretical errors were definitively overcome: 'Au cours des vingt dernières années, il nous a fallu effectuer, de façon souvent têtonnante et contradictoire, un vaste et au total fécond travail pour détruire de façon critique, comme dit Gramsci, la conception dogmatisée du marxisme. C'est chose faite.'! It is instructive to compare the recent work of Sève, the Party's foremost 'official' philosopher, with his publications of an earlier period, to see how little of importance has changed. See Lucien Sève, *Une introduction à la philosophie marxiste* (Paris, 1980) and *La Philosophie française contemporaine et sa genèse de 1789 à nos jours* (Paris, 1962).

regimes newly in place.[122] In the name of the proletariat and the class struggle, Sartre and his contemporaries (in and out of the Party) made a daily contribution to the legitimation of the enslavement of the satellite states. From 1945 until the end of the 1960s, French marxists were granted their dearest wish: to contribute to the construction of real socialism, however indirectly.

This may seem a harsh judgement. It might be offered in their defence that during and after their efforts to justify show trials and prison camps, French marxist thinkers also contributed massively to the defence and furtherance of the claims of national movements for freedom in many other parts of the world. But this, too, has its unflattering aspect. The French intellectuals' preference for concerning themselves with the interests of Africans, Arabs, Asians, and Latin-Americans was not wholly disinterested. It was the product of a search for the historical subject that would succeed where the French workers' movement had ostensibly failed (it is to Althusser's credit in this respect that, denying such a failure, and not interested in historical subjects, he never lifted a finger by way of theoretical practice on behalf of any oppressed person outside the Fifth Arrondissement).

The results of this onset of hyperopia may occasionally have been beneficial for Algerians, for Chilean refugees, or for Guinean peasants. But in France itself it served only to accentuate still further an unconcern with daily local politics and to widen the distance between marxist discourse and the real needs and concerns of workers (or socialists, come to that). No one troubled to think very hard about what a socialist practice *in France* might ever be, in the event of a left-wing victory at the polls. The Common Programme of 1972, the joint effort of socialists, Communists, and independent left-wing experts, was in truth a platform for social democracy à la Austria or Norway, with some local touches. But right and left alike preferred, needed to speak of it in apocalyptic terms, by analogy with the hopes and fears aroused at the mention of Chile, Cuba, even Yugoslavia. This ridiculous gap between language and reality led directly to the problems of the 1980s, where a victory of the united Left provoked only massive intellectual disaffection with the boring reality of socialist power *at home*.

Everyone in France knew that the worst thing that could happen to the Left was to come to power under almost any conceivable

---

[122] See, for example, Arthur London, *L'Aveu* (Paris, 1968) on the role played by prominent French Communists at the time of the Slansky trials in Prague.

circumstances, but the special contribution of French marxist thought had been to ensure not only that this would be true for economic and political affairs, but also that it would apply to that realm of intelligentsia-power relations which so peculiarly inform French public life. Having poured scorn on the inadequacies and compromises of 'social democracy' for thirty years, the heroes of French intellectual discourse had nothing to offer those of their heirs who, in their turn, were now seeking political engagement. Appropriately enough, the reaction of the ex-Maoist generation to the excesses of their own youth (as well as the moral indulgence of their spiritual fathers) has been to denounce *all* holistic thought as the work of the devil. From this premiss one could draw three conclusions. The first would be a move towards the politics of liberal empiricism, but nothing in French thought today suggests an environment any more favourable than it has been since 1750. A second option would be to disengage from politics altogether, while a third line of reasoning leads from the equation marxism = totalitarianism on to a growing sympathy for political conservatism. In Mitterrand's France there have been worrying signs of growing enthusiasm for both these latter tendencies. Both are inimical to the confidence (and the electoral prospects) of socialism, and thus to the interests of the working population and the underprivileged. This, to date, is the major medium-term achievement of thirty years of marxist conversation in Paris. Marx, and the French labour movement, deserved better.

5

The Elections of 1981 in Historical Perspective

Les conditions d'une véritable alternance démocratique seront crées. Au lieu de conquérir le pouvoir une ou deux foix par demi-siècle, portée par de brefs mouvements d'humeur, la gauche apparaîtra comme la garantie permanente d'un bon gouvernement de pays.

François Mitterrand, interviewed in *Libération* 10 May 1984

IN 1981 French socialism won a famous victory at the polls. In the presidential elections of April/May, François Mitterrand first trounced the Communist candidate, Georges Marchais, then went on to defeat Giscard d'Estaing, the incumbent, and become the first popularly elected Socialist president of France. A month later, with parliament dissolved, Mitterrand's Parti Socialiste won handsomely at the general elections, securing an absolute majority of the seats in the Assembly. This unprecedented sequence of electoral successes for the Left aroused tremendous enthusiasm and a great wave of optimism and expectation.[1]

The degree of exhilaration shown by the Left's political constituency reflected the unexpected nature of the events of that spring. The Left had not won a national election since the founding of the Fifth

---

[1] Presidential elections:

	1st Round % of the vote	2nd Round (%)
Giscard	28.31	48.24
Mitterrand	25.84	51.75
Chirac	17.99	
Marchais	15.34	

Legislative elections:

	1st Round (%)	No. of seats after 2nd Round
UDF	19.2	61
RPR	20.8	83
PS (+MRG)	37.5	269 (PS alone)
PCF	16.2	44

Republic in 1958; moreover, the non-Communist Left had not since 1936 so clearly surpassed the PCF in national political preferences. And in none of the Left's previous victories (1924, 1936, 1946, and 1956) had power been so utterly available for the taking. The very centripetal structures of the Fifth Republic could now be made to work for the forces of progress as they had for so long functioned to protect and strengthen the parties of the *Ancienne Majorité*. 'La France', as a magazine headline put it on 1 June 1981, 'a basculé'.

Nor was this mere journalistic hyperbole—there seems to have been a widespread belief that the events of 1981 were an utter surprise (divine or otherwise). In a public opinion poll taken in May 1981, 53 per cent expressed themselves 'surpised' at Mitterrand's election.[2] Allowing for some *schadenfreude* from the losers, this still suggests that a substantial minority of left-wing voters no more expected to win in 1981 than in the previous elections of the Gaullist Republic. Little wonder, then, that there was such dancing in the streets—and such high hopes for an imminent social and political revolution, albeit peaceful. Small wonder, too, that the inevitable sequence of minor successes and frequent set-backs which followed were to result in declining support for Mitterrand and his governments, and in a heightened sense of disappointment and frustration. For in 1981 there was no 'mur d'argent', and such conservative bastions as the Senate and the Constitutional Council had strictly limited powers. What did not happen after 1981 would be attributed to Mitterrand's failure to make it happen. The implications of this for the future of French socialism are considerable.

Although most voters are of necessity not assiduous students of political trends, it *is* a little odd that the surprise of 1981 should have been as sharp as it appeared (with consequent disillusion to match). For the course of events leading to the Socialists' victory was far from obscure even well before the event. This can be seen in three interrelated features of the Socialists' advance: the Mitterrand factor, the relative decline of the Communists, and the problem of the Right.

So far as Mitterrand is concerned, it might almost be possible to summarize his trajectory by saying that he won in 1981 because he stood in the presidential elections of 1965. Although beaten by De Gaulle in that year, he established himself early in the Fifth Republic as the *presidential* candidate of the Left, whatever the parties did at

[2] *Nouvel Observateur*, 1 June 1981.

legislative elections. And one of the first effects of this was that the parties of the Left began to invoke Mitterrand in their *own* campaigns. Two years after his respectable showing in the 1965 elections, Mitterrand was to see his campaign slogan, 'France libre, fraternelle et heureuse' employed by parliamentary candidates of the SFIO and its allies. In the campaign of 1967 there were even Mitterrand pins and photos on sale![3] But more significantly, Mitterrand in 1965 already culled more votes in the old conservative bastions of the east and west of France than candidates of the parliamentary Left (Socialists and Communists combined) had managed in 1962. His 1981 achievement in exceeding, at the second round of the presidential election, the Left's combined vote at the first round was thus already foreshadowed in his personal successes of an earlier decade.

I shall discuss the decline of the Communists later in this chapter, and at this stage it is pertinent to make just two observations. The first is that although it was not until 1978 that the Socialists actually replaced the Communists as the majority party of the Left, the balance was swinging in that direction from 1962, sharply so after 1967. This is true both on the national scale (see for example Figure 1) and even in the PCF's Parisian strongholds. In 1967 the Communists led the rest of the Left at the first round of parliamentary elections in 22 out of the 31 seats in the Paris metropolitan region; in 1973 that lead was maintained in only 18 seats, by 1978 it was down to just nine. There are various ways of interpreting this course of events, depending upon the emphasis one places upon different elections (the Socialists began to dominate the rest of the Left at the *municipal* level from 1971). It is also possible to argue that while the Socialist rise and the Communist decline were symbiotic, they were not causally related to the exclusion of other factors—the Socialists had risen to a position of potential victory by 1978, but it was not until 1981 that the Communists had fallen low enough for the PS to benefit from the change of attitude which the PCF's decline prompted among Communist and centrist electors alike.

---

[3] See *L'Election présidentielle de décembre 1965* (Paris, 1970), and *Les Elections législatives de mars 1967* (Paris, 1970), especially pp. 221–3. Since then the Mitterrand coat-tails effect has grown considerably—witness the campaign literature of 1981. The whole emphasis of many candidates was upon the qualities of the Socialist President 'qui tient ses promesses'. Gérard Collomb, in Lyon 2ᵉ, was one of many who prided himself upon his *personal* relationship with the fountainheads of power. See *France: Assemblée Nationale, Programmes et Engagements Electoraux. Elections généraux des 14 et 21 juin, 1981*, 3 vols. (Paris, 1982).

What is not in doubt, however, is the second observation concerning the Communist decline, which is that it benefited the rest of the Left in important indirect ways from the beginning of the 1970s. The weaker the PCF was perceived to have become, the less likely it was to dominate a hypothetical left-wing government, the more acceptable a Socialist candidate became, locally and nationally, to non-Communist voters. Moreover, beyond a certain point, the PCF's own electors began to think about 'voting usefully', and in 1981 many of them voted for Mitterrand at the first ballot. This suggested that a Communist vote was now seen as wasted (and perhaps damaging to the Left's changes), and also that the Communist presidential candidate (Marchais) was recognized as a 'spoiler'. And even this final collapse of the Communist electoral monolith did not date from 1981: in 1978 more than 60 per cent of the PCF's lost votes came from the Paris region, the epicentre of the Party's once impregnable power base.[4]

As to the Right, its problems were twofold. De Gaulle's capacity to build electoral bridges to left-wing voters died with him, and Mitterrand, as we have seen, showed in 1965 (and again in 1974) an ability to attract voters in traditionally conservative areas, something which would ultimately translate into similar success for local Socialist candidates. Indeed, the decline of the Right in Alsace, for example, was just as important in explaining the PS's victory as was the collapse of the Communist vote. And this fundamental shift in French electoral geography was also no sudden break, but can be traced to the elections of the mid- and late 1960s.[5]

The second difficulty of the Right was of course more circumstantial. Since 1976 personal and policy differences between Chirac's RPR and Giscard's coalition of parties in the UDF had grown ever sharper, and by 1981 many of Chirac's supporters were not unhappy at the prospect of a Mitterrand victory (either to spite Giscard or else as the strategic prelude to a successful Chirac candidacy in 1988). It is estimated that some 16 per cent of Chirac's votes at the first round of the 1981 presidential election switched to Mitterrand at the second round. There is no doubt that departments where Chirac had done well (for example in south-central and south-western France) were especially

[4] See David Goldey and R. W. Johnson, 'The French General Election of March 1978', in *Parliamentary Affairs*, vol. 31, no. iii (1978), esp. p. 304.
[5] See F. Platone and J. Ranger, 'L'Echec du Parti communiste français aux élections de printemps 1981', in *Revue française de science politique*, vol. 31, nos. v–vi (1981), pp. 1033–4.

hostile to the official candidate of the Right at the second round and played a vital part in Mitterrand's victory.[6]

Many hitherto conservative voters were also persuaded to switch their preferences by a change in their understanding of the implications of a socialist victory, a change itself much influenced by the decline of the Communists as partners in the Left alliance. Whereas in April 1974 some 60 per cent of voters thought a Mitterrand victory in that year would 'profoundly transform' French society, only 40 per cent held this view in 1981.[7] In other words, and in contrast to Mitterrand's own supporters within the socialist community, many non- or anti-socialist voters had ceased, during the 1970s, to think of a victory of the Left in the traditional millenarian terms.[8]

Thus the election of Francois Mitterrand was neither as intrinsically surprising nor as radically significant as it initially seemed. Even the rather more sweeping parliamentary success of the following month had more to do with the coat-tails effect (and the workings of the electoral system) that with any nation-wide philo-socialist sentiment. And it, too, can be seen as part of a series of electoral and social mutations long since in progress. Why, then, the very high expectations, the eschatalogical vocabulary, of 1981? And what will emerge from the frustrations and disappointments of the ensuing experience of Socialist government? Has something fundamental been altered, are the changes of enduring significance, and what effects will they have?

Part of the answer to these questions lies in the pall of stagnant corruption which lay over the political system of France after twenty-three years of a political monopoly. Any change would have been welcome, and much of Mitterrand's programme was morally uplifting and socially urgent. Nor is the decline of the PCF a very complicated matter in itself. In this chapter, however, I want to confine myself to a consideration of the events of 1981 primarily in terms of the experience of the Left in France as a candidate for office. To see why this already poses some fascinating problems it is first necessary to grasp the ambiguity for Socialists and Communists in France of the very act of standing for election. And this, in turn, requires the telling of a certain history.

---

[6] See poll in *Nouvel Observateur*, 1 June 1981, and David Goldey and Andrew Knapp, 'Time for a change: the French elections of 1981', in *Electoral Studies*, vol. 1, no. i (1982).

[7] Sofres poll, published in *Nouvel Observateur*, 16 Mar. 1981.

[8] Of Chirac's voters, 62 per cent thought one 'could' vote safely for Mitterrand in 1981. See Ibid.

Republicanism in France meant representative democracy, and representative democracy in turn meant parliamentary elections based upon manhood suffrage (universal from 1944). Because none of the major strands in French socialism before 1914 chose to stand outside the republican tradition, participation at elections was never seriously questioned by the Left in its formative years. This changed briefly with the emergence in 1920 of a revolutionary Communist Party, but even the PCF soon recognized the impossibility of functioning as a political unit in France without serious participation in elections.

The difficulty for doctrinally consistent left-wing politicians (and doctrinal consistency was always a paramount consideration) was that the implicit purpose of taking part in an election is to win it, and victory implied the assumption of political power. But for the Socialists until 1936 and for the Communists until very recently (excepting the special circumstances of 1944–7) assuming political power was only consistent with their principles in the event that it led directly to the replacement (by whatever means) of the capitalist system by one which was Socialist or Communist in identity. Anything short of this was ideologically inconsistent and politically dishonest.

A second difficulty for the Left lay in the electoral system of France. Since 1870, the preferred means of selecting parliamentary representatives has been by two-round single constituency elections. There were exceptions in 1885, 1919, 1924, and during the Fourth Republic, when various unsatisfactory systems of proportional representation were introduced, but these have failed to displace the dominant arrangement. Single-member constituencies are a problem for centralized and doctrinally rigid organizations, because they place a premium on the individual candidate, on the candidate's person and personality, making the imposition of party discipline a risk-laden affair. As for the two-round system, it imposes the necessity for alliances, for withdrawal in favour of someone else at the second ballot, without which a split vote may favour an opponent.

From its earliest days, then, the political Left in France faced frequent decisions of a difficult nature: whether to put up candidates for election, while at the same time assuring would-be voters that the capitalist system would not and could not be altered fundamentally by vote; what to say at election meetings without arousing false hopes on the one hand or ensuring a negligible degree of support on the other; what tactics to pursue for the first and second rounds, and so forth.

So far as the latter was concerned, the SFIO in the decade before the First World War took the position, inherited in various forms from its constituent founding organizations, that participation in elections was acceptable (and, it was recognized, inevitable, in France) if what was said to the electorate was rigorously monitored for doctrinal consistency. There was never to be any pretence that a socialist victory would, in itself, constitute the overthrow of capitalism. It was to be made very clear that Socialist candidates, if successful, would never take part in a non-Socialist government (this was not just a reference to the Millerand Affair of 1899, but a proposition which ante-dated the latter episode). This particular stance could the more readily be adopted in that there was virtually no chance of a Socialist Party forming a government of its own, or even one in which it was predominant.[9]

Within these limits, Socialist candidates were free to put forward the Party's own proposals for political reforms respecting pensions, anti-militarism, anti-clericalism, taxes, constitutional revision, and the like. The point of electing a man was to enable him to advocate these reforms, both in his campaign and in the parliament, but only in the context of his advocacy of the socialist principles which underlay them. And the significance of the parliamentary forum as a place from which to present a political argument was considerable—far more than would be true today.

The question of electoral tactics was less easily absorbed into an acceptable *socialist* strategy. It came up at SFIO congresses in 1908 and 1909, and again throughout the 1920s. In simple terms, it was a question of deciding whether or not to put up Socialist candidates in every constituency. If not, should voters be encouraged to support a Radical candidate on prudential grounds, or should Socialist militants in that constituency wash their hands of the matter? If yes, what should such (Socialist) candidates recommend to their supporters in the (likely) event of their being outdistanced by a Radical at the first round? Should they switch their support, or was neutrality to be preferred? The case in favour of switching arose from the need to be consistent in advocating short-term reforms: Radicals in parliament

[9] On the Millerand affair, see Leslie Derfler, *Alexandre Millerand: the socialist years* (Paris, 1977); Harvey Goldberg, *The Life of Jean Jaurès* (Madison Wis., 1962); Georges Lefranc, *Le Mouvement socialiste sous la Troisième République* (Paris, 1963). From its very inception the POF, in Lille, insisted in organizing its members by electoral district rather than *quartier*, while entering elections with intransigent and uncompromising programmes designed, *inter alia*, to demonstrate the futility of taking elections too seriously . . .

were better than conservatives. The case against was that the desire to elect someone left-leaning at any cost was an admission of the importance of elections in capitalist society.

These matters were resolved in favour of doctrinal rigidity at the first round and political flexibility at the second, a combination of discipline, dogma, and realism very characteristic of the old SFIO. What rendered it all just about acceptable to socialist militants was the continuing belief that what elections were *really* about was education: educating militants in mass propaganda and recruitment, educating the electorate in the nature and appeal of socialism and in the hopelessness of reforms under capitalism. Legislative elections were thus both an opportunity for 'agitprop' and an education, sentimentally speaking, in their own right.[10]

After the First World War and with the birth of the PCF there was a sharpening of these distinctions. The Communists quickly appreciated the *functional* serviceability of elections (especially since many Communist militants had been SFIO stalwarts before 1914), and they turned the four-yearly election campaign into a permanent recruiting exercise. The PCF in the 1920s did what the Guesdists of 1906 had advocated—they blanketed France with candidates at every election. This produced three consequences: it routinized the business of organization, propaganda, and mass mobilization, thus honing the PCF's members and electorate alike into an experienced and disciplined political weapon; it politicized the Communists' mass base, training it to see every aspect of private and public life as political (and conflictual), through the medium of contests for public office; finally, by emphasizing that *this* was what they were engaged in, rather than the sordid struggle for capitalist office, the Communists undermined those on the far Left (in and out of the Party) who feared the integration and assimilation of the PCF as an electoral machine (by simultaneously winning elections and being excluded from office after 1947, they were well served by their opponents in this respect).

---

[10] The exception was local, especially municipal elections, where the SFIO gained control of a number of major towns before 1914 and attempted to govern them as examples of socialist probity and humanity, much as the PCI has presented Bologna and other cities as show-pieces for Italian Communism. But this inevitably produced contradictions, as when Gustave Delory, mayor of Lille but also leader of the Socialist Federation of the Nord, received President Alexandre Millerand, in his capacity as municipal representative, while the socialist movement was bitterly opposed to all dealings with Millerand's conservative regime at the national level. This produced much discontent in militant ranks during 1921, most party members taking seriously and literally the injunction to have nothing to do with the representatives of capitalist power.

Ironically, the Communists' success in adapting and refining the theory and practice of pre–1914 socialism in its approach to elections gave the SFIO no choice but to follow suit—anything else would have suggested that the Socialists now *believed* in elections, and this would have been gleefully seized upon by the PCF. Hence the concern of Paul Faure, the general secretary of the SFIO from 1920 to 1940, to emphasize more forcefully than ever the tactical discipline and doctrinal reserve surrounding Socialist participation in elections.

On the face of it, all this came to an end in 1936, with the Socialists' assumption of power. Certainly, winning office rather cut the ground from under the official doubts about electoral participation, and the Communists' refusal, until 1934, to countenance tactical agreements had forced the SFIO into many embarrassing 'arrangements' with Radicals at the local level. And yet, the post-war years saw very little change. Following Guy Mollet's defeat of Blum and his assumption of power in the SFIO in 1946, the Socialists the following year came very close to abandoning office after the departure of the Communists, the party militants arguing that a non-marxist majority in the government rendered Socialist participation therein unacceptable. It is true that the new combination of multi-member seats, cross-list voting, anti-Communism and the Cold War obliged the SFIO to abandon its tactical purity in ensuing elections, but the vocabulary of electoral proclamations in the 1950s reveals a high degree of embarrassment and confusion as to the nature and purpose of elections. In fact, until the retirement of Guy Mollet in 1969, the dominant tone of official SFIO election literature remained one of 'distance'—broadly speaking, it was no longer possible to avoid dirty hands, but there remained the insistence that this was, indeed, dirt. The return after 1958 to a two-ballot single-member system, and the Socialists' distaste for a Gaullist constitution, rather reinforced this way of thinking.

As for the Communists, whatever the variations in their formal position, their *use* of elections remained unaltered. In 1956 they were the only party to put up candidates in every department, and in 1981 they again put up 472 people in the legislative elections (against the Socialists' 444). Like the new PS of the 1970s, the Communists use elections at the local, cantonal, departmental, and regional level to strengthen their organizations, provide their militants with administrative experience (and occasionally cream public money off the top . . .), and as a spring-board for national elections. But there are still relatively few Communists who will readily admit that the point of elections is accession to office.

If the Left in France has always seemed disproportionately obsessed with the fact and function of elections, this must be understood in the context of a country where elections, as a device for the expression and control of national opinion, play a very important role—and have done so for longer than is the case in most comparable nations. And for all the frequency of various kinds of local elections, it is national elections which capture public interest—'la grande politique est d'abord nationale et elle se déroule à Paris'.[11] That the Left, whose political legitimacy rides on the support of large numbers of people, should have paid the greatest attention to electoral activities (notwithstanding ideological misgivings) is thus not surprising.

A less immediately obvious reason for the interest of the Left in mobilizing and enthusing its support lies in the geographical disposition of the latter. I discussed in an earlier essay the heavy support for the Left south of the Loire. This also happens to be the region of France least disposed to turn out and vote. From the 1890s to the present, the line from La Rochelle to Geneva denotes a permanent, and quite acute, distinction between departments where the turn-out is often around 90 per cent of registered electors, and those where it no less frequently falls well below 80 per cent. In general, the extremes are attained by the north on the one hand (the Nord, Pas de Calais, and Somme departments in particular) and the south-west on the other (with the interesting exception of the Tarn). Nor is the link fortuitous: a 1978 study showed that in the elections of that year people declaring themselves 'Left' were most likely to abstain. To some extent this historical disadvantage for the Left is compensated by the propensity of rural and village constituencies to vote in large numbers, participation in elections being something of a social event in regions of dispersed habitat. But the gain among left-wing peasants is in its turn compensated by a loss among the small and medium-sized towns of provincial France, where abstention is at its highest and has been so for many decades.[12]

The Left's traditional difficulties are compounded by a further

[11] See Pierre Barral, 'La Sociologie électorale et l'histoire', in *Revue historique* (juillet–septembre 1967), p. 129.
[12] See Alain Lancelot, *L'Abstentionnisme électoral en France* (Paris, 1968), esp. pp. 74–87, 202; also J. Capdevielle *et al.*, *France de gauche, vote à droite* (Paris, 1981), pp. 22, 261.

observation, which is that the working class has a higher rate of electoral abstention than any other socio-economic group, a problem for both major parties of the Left, but the Communists in particular. In the 1983 municipal elections the national figure for abstentions was 16 per cent, but for the workers it was 23 per cent. It is not certain that this has actually had a crippling effect on the strength of the modern Left (see below), but it has most certainly been *perceived* as a handicap, and one which there has been much effort to combat.[13]

Of more recent significance for the position of the Left in national politics has been the 'presidentialization' of elections, consequent upon De Gaulle's use of referenda and the post–1962 direct election of the Head of State. Until the mid–1960s, both the SFIO and the PCF were primarily parliamentary organizations, even if despite themselves, and their understanding of electoral competition in a democracy was concentrated exclusively upon the cumulative election of local representatives to a national assembly. They thus adapted slowly and badly to the constitutional alterations—which is one of the reasons they failed for so long to gain access to power. It was, after all, no accident that the joint Left candidate at the 1965 presidential elections was Mitterrand, who was associated only with the tiny, Paris-based club movement of the dissident non-Communist Left.

The introduction of direct presidential elections made national electoral politics even more central to the French public experience, if that were possible. By 1971 a disgruntled local politician could accurately observe that 'France lives only in anticipation of the next presidential election'.[14] Abstention at presidential elections was lower than at parliamentary elections, and over time even municipal elections became suffused with concern for the implications for parties and their presidential candidates. The historical distaste of the Left for the direct election of executives (dating back to the disastrous consequences of the 1848 election of Louis Napoléon, and the attempted coup of the over-powerful President MacMahon in 1877) was not easily overcome— indeed the PCF has never really overcome it, putting forward as its personalized image the unlikely and unlikable jowls of the egregious Georges Marchais. But it has had little option but to recognize the changes wrought by the new system.

[13] See Sofres poll taken in April 1983, in *Nouvel Observateur*, 29 Apr. 1983.
[14] Michel Durafour, mayor of St Etienne, quoted in Jack Hayward and Vincent Wright, 'The 37,708 Microcosms of an Indivisible Republic: the French local elections of March 1971', in *Parliamentary Affairs* (Autumn 1971), p. 285.

The first of these has been the decline in local influence at elections, something readily measured by the steady fall in the number of parliamentary seats won at the first round over the course of the Fifth Republic. Party identity and the issues of party dispute have become ever more 'nationalized'. Patronage has ceased to be parliamentary and has switched its source to the executive, with the result that a failure to identify with the 'president's party' is an even more serious handicap than was the analagous lack of 'ministrability' in the Third Republic. Gone, too, is the old multi-party contest which both justified and confused the Left's historical obsession with electoral tactics. At the second round in 1978, there was just one tripartite contest. All the rest were straight fights between representatives of right or left (or, very unusually, between constituent parts of right or left in areas monopolized by one side). All candidates were thus identified very clearly with a party and a presidential candidate (UDF—Giscard, RPR—Chirac, PS—Mitterand; the exception was the PCF, with no former presidential candidate at that time). In 1973 there had been more than sixty three-way contests, while in the Third Republic three-, four- and five-way battles at the second round were the norm.[15]

Despite its misgivings, the Left has in fact benefited from this change in the system. It has not suffered net losses of support under it, and in some old conservative areas it actually gained. In the first place, pockets of left-wing voters in Brittany, Lorraine, and the southern Massif have been present since elections began, but they have always been buried in an overwhelming local right-wing majority. In a national presidential election they count, and in counting, multiply. Secondly, while the PCF would always put up a candidate in the most forlorn of implausible places, the Socialists (SFIO and PS alike) frequently did not bother, counting the effort wasted. In such constituencies, especially during the 1930s and 1940s, left-leaning voters would abstain rather than choose between a Communist and a clerical candidate. Beginning in 1965 they could (and increasingly did) vote for a non-Communist Left candidate for president. By the mid-1970s the PS had woken up to this fact and was beginning to 'work' such areas—with rewards in 1978 and, especially, 1981.

Thirdly, the personal emphasis inherent in a presidential election was probably an error from the point of view of the Right. Competing with De Gaulle on equal terms, Mitterrand might become his equal.

---

[15] See Goldey and Johnson, 'The French General Election of March 1978', in *Parliamentary Affairs*, vol. 31, no. iii (1978).

Certainly, by 1974 the candidate of the Left (Mitterrand again) had a legitimacy and national status every bit as plausible as that of his opponent(s). Even Marchais in 1981 (like the Communist Duclos in 1969) benefited from the media exposure to present his party and his claims as the equal of any. The aura of unreality attaching to the idea of a Socialist government and an elected Socialist president was dissipated.[16]

This question of the legitimacy of a left government prompts two final considerations concerning the Left's attitude towards elections. Until 1945 there had been just one Socialist head of government, and Leon Blum's tenure of office was retrospectively clouded by an aura of failure and impropriety for Left and Right alike. And although Vincent Auriol became president during the early Fourth Republic, and presided over a number of Socialist-led governments, neither he nor they exercised anything remotely approaching unrestricted power. Nor were the electoral conditions of 1945 and 1946 representative of the real balance of opinion in post-war France, as later elections showed. As for Guy Mollet, the only other Socialist prime minister between Paul Ramadier and Pierre Mauroy, his major historical achievement was simultaneously to split his own party while paving the way, via the Algerian crisis, for the return of De Gaulle.

Accordingly, that current within the Left, in PCF and Socialist Party alike, which maintained an all-or-nothing approach to office could point to much evidence in its support (the same is true, of course, for the far-left groups which flourished again after 1963). The track record of Left governments was, all in all, disastrous, *especially* in the eyes of their most fervent supporters. Taken with the post-Commune assumption of a monopoly of political legitimacy by the republican centre and right, the real difficulty for the Left in France was not winning elections. Nor was it, over time, whether or not to take part in them. It was the question of whether or not the Left *ought* to govern in France. In treating this as an unresolved dilemma, Socialists, Communists, and their opponents remained uneasily united, from 1899 to 1981.

For the Socialists, however, there has been a further problem. Throughout its existence the socialist movement in France has been, *inter alia*, a vehicle for the upward social mobility of the educated working and lower middle classes, rural and urban alike. Inevitably, it

---

[16] On the seminal presidential election of 1965, see *L'Election présidentielle de décembre 1965* (Paris, 1970).

has therefore been seen by some as the road to office and power, much as British trade-unionists once saw the Labour Party. The same is true, *mutatis mutandis*, for the Communist Party, with this difference that the controlling ideology (and the controllers themselves) have exercised a greater historical restraint. But in 1900, 1921, 1933, 1947, and throughout the 1950s, the SFIO was divided between those for whom the party was in some sense the means to overthrow capitalism, and those for whom it was an avenue to public office. The latter were always a minority until the 1970s, when the reconstituted Parti Socialiste began with increasing success to appeal to what Philip Williams in 1951 called the 'managerial element' and Paul Faure in 1922 the 'parlementaristes'.

For the latter, now dominant in the upper strata of the PS, access to power requires no teleological justification, and most of them no longer respond guiltily to the charge of providing hostages to Communist propaganda. The homage they pay to the ideological traditions of their movement is largely instrumental—it secures them a base within a major national political organization. But they have still to negotiate such matters with the militants and voters for whom socialism just does have to be more than an improvement on the alternative. How both sides, not to mention the Communists, have resolved the historical legitimation crisis opened up by the Left's victory in 1981 is something I shall consider in the conclusion to this chapter. At this stage it is sufficient to note that the successful electoral vehicle which is the modern Socialist Party has broken with its past in ways beyond what was intended, and with uncertain consequences. Before coming to these, however, it is necessary to indicate with a little more precision the sort of changes which have taken place, beginning with some observations on the course of events since the years of the Popular Front.

*

From the point of view of the modern Left, the recent political history of France falls into three periods. The first, running from the elections of 1936 to the end of the Fourth Republic, saw the rise of the PCF as a political force in the nation, and the accompanying decline of the SFIO. The second period, from 1958 to approximately 1973, opened up a time of flux, with an altered balance of intra-Left relations and the rebirth of French socialism. Finally, from 1973 to the 1981 elections,

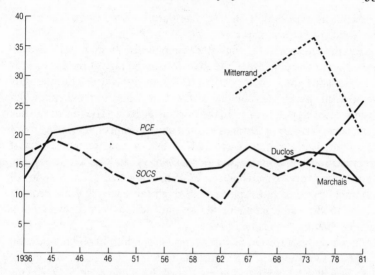

Figure 1. Socialist and Communist % of the electorate, 1936–1981

came the years of Communist decline and the emergence of Mitterrand's PS.

The graph of left-wing electoral fortunes (Fig. 1) shows clearly enough the course of the first twenty years.[17] Although the SFIO improved in 1945 on its Popular Front vote, the increase was insignificant in the peculiar circumstances of the time, and it was the Communists who emerged straightaway as *the* party of the Left, a status they maintained throughout the Fourth Republic. But what the figures also show, and what is less commonly recalled, is that the PCF 'peaked' as early as 1946. By 1951 it had ceased to make inroads into the electorate, and the increased share of seats won in 1956 (50 more than 1951, while the SFIO actually lost two seats in the act of winning office) reflected very little shift in voting. The fact is that from 1946 to 1956 the PCF stagnated, albeit in a position of electoral strength, its vote in many areas hardly changing from one election to the next (in that decade it varied by no more than 0.81 per cent in the Nord, 0.74

[17] For concise summaries of election results since 1936 see Claude Willard, *Socialisme et Communisme français* (Paris, 1967), Annexe 1; R. W. Johnson, *The Long March of the French Left* (London, 1981), Table 8:i, p. 137; David Bell and Byron Criddle, *The French Socialist Party* (Oxford, 1984), p. 267. Excellent maps of electoral behaviour can be found in Claude Leleu, *Géographie des élections françaises depuis 1936* (Paris, 1971).

per cent in the Pas de Calais[18]). The Party's period of expansion and consolidation was remarkably brief.

By the elections of 1958 the Communist bastion was already crumbling. The collapse of the PCF vote in the face of De Gaulle was *never* made good. The SFIO, although its steady decline was temporarily accelerated by the Algerian and constitutional crises, did begin slowly to pull back from the brink after 1962. The reason for this long-term contrast in fortunes was not any weakness in the structure of the PCF, nor any hidden strength in the by-now decrepit Socialist organization. The latter was losing voters and members by the thousands every year, while the PCF had survived intact a series of internal struggles and expulsions through the 1950s.[19] What brought about the transformation in the second period was an extraneous, almost technical consideration.

Precisely because De Gaulle was so successful, between 1958 and 1962, at sweeping into his camp the various conservative and centre groups which had emerged in the Fourth Republic, the SFIO, already weakened by defections over Algeria and by electoral defeat in 1958, found itself without the option of forming the electoral and parliamentary alliances known as the 'Third Force' and through which it had played a central role in politics from 1947–51 and again since 1956. With the reintroduction of single-member two-ballot constituencies[20] the Socialists under Mollet could look only to the Communists to save them from electoral oblivion.

For a variety of reasons, the Communists were receptive to such an arrangement. The ending of the Stalinist freeze, their own calamitous defeat in 1958 and the fact that the Socialists in their reduced circumstances posed no competitive threat all meant that the PCF had everything to gain from electoral agreements. Communist voters would ensure the survival in the second round of a respectable number of SFIO *députés*, and in return the PCF would re-enter the national political fold—as well as themselves benefiting, in turn, from at least some of the Socialist votes.

[18] See *Atlas Electoral Nord—Pas de Calais 1945–1972* (Lille, 1972), p. 50.

[19] Even the major (and well-publicized) divisions within the PCF, such as the expulsions of Auguste Lecœur and André Marty, had no discernible impact upon the Party's fortunes at the 1956 elections, which followed closely upon them. See *Les Elections du 2 janvier 1956.* (Paris, 1957), p. 441 n. 16.

[20] For details on the workings and the technicalities of French electoral systems, see Peter Campbell, *French Electoral Systems and Elections since 1789* (London, 1966, 2nd edn.); Frédéric Bon, *Les Elections en France* (Paris, 1978); Jacques Godechot (ed.), *Les Constitutions de la France depuis 1789* (Paris, 1970).

These tactical considerations gained in addition from the Gaullist insistence upon presenting the Left as nothing but Communists and their allied stooges. This sort of aggressive Manicheism pushed the SFIO towards the Communists as their only available partners, a process further encouraged by the electoral reforms of 1964. The latter altered the rules for municipal elections in towns with over thirty thousand inhabitants, requiring that slates of candidates be 'blocked' —that is, there could be no shifting of alliances and altering of lists to accommodate to the needs of the second round. For the Socialists in particular to retain any hope of local control in larger towns they had to draw up lists of candidates who could benefit from maximum support at the first round—and this, too, meant pre-emptive alliances with whoever was available, increasingly the Communists.

This 'rapprochement' of the major parties of the Left was not easily achieved. Anyone who has studied the acrimonious intra-Left arguments of the years 1921–34, or 1947–61 (or, for that matter, 1977–80) will appreciate the point. Sentiment ran especially high at local level, where militants had been literally fighting each other for two generations. As to any residual camaraderie dating from the Resistance (there had never been much) this disappeared in the peculiarly bitter struggles of the Cold War years. In 1956 an observer could still speak of the 'perpetual socialist-communist duel',[21] and most Socialists in that year preferred to lose seats rather than contemplate any sort of joint arrangement with Communist candidates, a sentiment both reciprocated and widely shared among the respective electorates. It was certainly no surprise that there were still many Socialists in 1967 who would not vote for a Communist under any circumstances, and even in 1978 the anti-Communist sentiment among *older* PS voters was far from dead.

And yet these years were characterized by a rapprochement all the same. In November 1962 Guy Mollet formally announced that Socialists and Communists would withdraw for the better placed among them at the second round of that year's legislative elections, in order to 'barrer la route à l'UNR'. The volte-face did Mollet's reputation little good, and many of his own electors quoted him against himself in meetings, reminding him of his visceral anti-Communism in the 1950s. What he was proposing, after all, was not an occasional tactical manœuvre; there had been joint PCF/SFIO lists in earlier

[21] Philip Williams, *French Politicians and Elections 1951–1969* (Cambridge, 1970), p. 51.

elections, in places such as the Vosges where both parties were weak.[22] What Mollet and his Communist partners were setting out was an electoral strategy for future encounters with the voters for the duration of the Gaullist regime.

It is remarkable how well the strategy worked, albeit with a long initial period of overlap, during which many local elections and some national ones were fought on a mixture of Third Force and Left Alliance tickets. Predictably, the Communists proved the more adaptable—part of the SFIO's problem was that the smaller and weaker it became, the less effective it was at mobilizing, instructing, and disciplining its members (and its electors). By the 1967 legislative elections the PCF was campaigning under the slogan 'Voter communiste, c'est voter pour l'union de la gauche'. The SFIO, on the other hand, was arguing for left union at the national level, but maintained its alliance with Radicals, Christian Democrats, and various Independents in its efforts to hold on to municipal power in cities like Marseille, Lille, Toulouse, and Limoges. This just made voters cynical, and hastened the party's demise. It was also an impossible policy. With a formal agreement to withdraw for the better-placed candidates after 1966, and with promises in 1967 of a common programme of government if the Left won, the Socialist attempt to have it both ways collapsed, and by 1971 even Guy Mollet had to ally with local Communists in order to retain his municipal office. By that year the Communists, the Socialists, and their various tiny allies were presenting a united front in 124 out of the local contests in France's 193 largest towns.[23]

In the short run the strategy was a limited success. Both parties improved their vote in 1967, and the alliances at the second round converted the votes into seats with reasonable efficiency. The Communist embrace helped to restore Socialist fortunes in France and thereby turned the non-Communist Left away from the temptation to seek alliances with dissident Gaullists and their centrist friends. The Communists, needing to restore the plausibility of their ally, actually gave up their first place in thirteen constituencies in 1967 in order that a Socialist candidate might win the seat.[24] Even if this was not always a

---

[22] See F.-G. Dreyfus, 'Jalons pour une sociologie politique de la France de l'Est', in *Revue française de science politique*, vol. 10, no. iii (1960).

[23] Hayward and Wright, loc. cit., pp. 301–4.

[24] David Goldey and R. W. Johnson, 'The French General Election of March 1973', in *Political Studies*, vol. 21 (1973), p. 337.

disinterested act (many such seats could not be won by a Communist, and the PCF thus had little to lose) it undoubtedly benefited a socialist movement which, in the 1967 election, had been unable to elect more than one candidate at the first round—that candidate being, symptomatically, François Mitterrand in the Nièvre.

In the long run, of course, the whole design backfired—for both partners. So long as the Communists remained the dominant partner there was little hope of the Left breaking through the 44 per cent barrier at the first round, and this thus guaranteed defeat at the second. So long as the SFIO continued to wheeze its way through French political life, the Communists would stay dominant. But thanks to the events of 1968, the retirement of De Gaulle and the manœuvrings of Mitterrand and his associates, the SFIO finally laid itself to rest in a series of congresses between 1969 and 1971 and was replaced by a new Parti Socialiste in which the old SFIO militants were but one of a number of constituent components. This new Socialist Party then proceded to wreak havoc upon the balance of forces on the Left.[25]

Electorally speaking, this process was visible from as early as 1973, with the Communist vote climbing much less slowly than that of the new PS. And whereas the Socialists lost some ground in the old SFIO strongholds of north and centre, they more than compensated by beginning the process of 'nationalization', whereby Socialist candidates did rather better than hitherto in almost every kind of area. But the Communists started to slip in their major voting centres, while maintaining or even increasing their strength in departments like the Corrèze, with a shrinking electorate and a declining economy, a course of events precipitated still further by the cantonal elections of 1976, the municipal elections of 1977 and, disastrously, the legislative voting in 1978. The PS, meanwhile, went from strength to strength, given added buoyancy by Mitterrand's very strong challenge to Giscard in the 1974 presidential contest.

The steady attrition of Communist support can be measured in other ways. In 1962, the PCF ran ahead of the Socialists in 281 seats at the first round of the legislative elections. In 1967 it was ahead in 251, and in 1973 in just 203. In the Paris region, the PCF centre of

---

[25] On the circumstances surrounding the emergence of the Parti Socialiste, see Bell and Criddle, *The French Socialist Party;* C. Hurtig, *De la SFIO au Nouveau Parti Socialiste* (Paris, 1970); J. Mossuz, *Les Clubs et la politique en France* (Paris, 1970); T. Pfister, *Les Socialistes* (Paris, 1977); P. Alexandre, *Le Roman de la gauche* (Paris, 1977).

gravity, the PCF led the Left in 22 of the constituencies in 1967; in 1973 it led in just 18 of them, and by 1978 in only 9.[26] Nationally, then, the Communists' most significant losses came in 1973, but were only reflected in Paris five years later. In either event, the Communist vote in France by 1978 was already concentrating and contracting, whereas that of the Socialists was expanding to take in most of the country. The remarkable turnabout of 1981, with the PS sweeping the country and the Communists reduced to a rump presence in departments they had once controlled, was by way of emerging nearly a decade before.

This is not to discount more immediate reasons for the Communists' final fall. The manner in which the PCF leadership panicked in the mid–1970s in the face of the electoral Frankenstein it had created was not calculated to charm that significant minority of Communist voters who really believed their Party's proclaimed desire for unity to defeat the Right. Some 69 per cent of those questioned in a 1981 post-election poll assumed that Mitterrand's smashing defeat of Marchais was the result of the electorate's desire to defeat the Right at all costs. Moreover, there was (in 1981) a steady 22 per cent of the PCF electorate that found Marchais himself unsympathetic, perhaps unelectable. There is little doubt that the PCF contributed hand-somely to its own losses in 1981.[27] But the roots of that contribution lay in the decisions of the 1960s, at a time when the configurations of the 1980s were hard indeed to foresee.

At this point one should insert a comment on the electorate's response to these tactical manœuvrings. It might be supposed that it was one thing for a candidate at an election to withdraw after the first round and recommend that his or her supporters cast their votes for an opponent consistently maligned during the campaign, quite another for the voters to play along with the charade. Because of the implausibility of the exercise, observers have readily assumed that it was only the Communists, with their well-trained and disciplined cohorts of committed voters, who could 'deliver the goods' at the second round, withdrawing in favour of a lifelong Socialist opponent and swinging the Communist electorate 100 per cent behind him. Socialist electors, thought to be both less malleable and in any case

[26] See Goldey and Johnson, 'The French General Election of March 1978', in *Parliamentary Affairs*, vol. 31, no. iii (1978).

[27] See opinion polls published in *Nouvel Observateur* for 1 June 1981 and 23 Jan. 1982. For a close analysis of the nature and extent of Communist losses and gains between April and June 1981, see Platone and Ranger, 'L'Echec du Parti communiste français', in *Revue française de science politique*, vol. 31, nos v–vi (1981).

strongly anti-Communist, would not shift so readily; hence the Communists' inability to benefit to the full from such an electoral tactic.

In fact, the history of this sort of manœuvre was always rather more complex and interesting. In 1914, for example, there were 24 constituencies in 14 departments where a Socialist (SFIO) candidate outdistanced a Radical at the first round of the legislative elections. The official Radical candidates withdrew, most of them recommending to their voters that they cast a vote for the SFIO candidate at the second round. The average switch, allowing for changes in the number of voters at the second round, was 91 per cent, with a low of 69 per cent in one seat in the Nord. By any count, this shows remarkable loyalty and discipline from the *Radical* electorate. Not surprisingly, the figure for Socialist voting discipline in 1914 was close to 100 per cent, when it came to supporting a Radical at the second round.

Such figures were not unusual for the time, and speak well for the rather underestimated power of the ideal of republican unity. What changed, of course, was the relationship between the competing parties after the birth of the PCF. Whereas Socialist voters continued to be instructed in the idea of 'no enemies on the Left', the PCF educated a whole electorate into the discipline of tactical and ideological versatility. Since this included total opposition to Socialist candidates *in particular* at elections in 1924, 1928, 1932, 1951, and 1956, as well as at hundreds of local and regional elections in between, Socialist electors in their turn came to exclude Communist candidates from the leftist electoral pantheon. This sentiment of outright opposition was reciprocated until the early 1960s, whereupon the PCF started to ask that its electors favour the SFIO under a variety of circumstances. But although the SFIO (and, later, the PS) has adopted the same formal position, *neither* party has succeeded in reconstructing the spirit of left loyalty as it existed before 1914. And the higher the percentage of local party militants to voters in any district, the less efficient the vote transfer,[28] which suggests that party squabbles on the ground, conducted by enthusiastic and numerous local members, accentuate the differences which then show up in voting behaviour.

Two studies, for 1967 and 1978, bear out these observations. In the second round of the 1967 elections, about 40 per cent of Socialist voters preferred the Right to the PCF, when they had to choose. There

---

[28] See Goldey and Knapp, loc. cit., p. 39.

was much regional variation: in the northern half of France, about 67 per cent of Socialist voters could be relied on to transfer their votes to a Communist candidate if called upon to do so, but in southern France the figure was only 52 per cent. This is not so very remarkable. What is interesting is that the figures for Communist voters facing analogous choices were 85 per cent and 67 per cent respectively. Moreover, in central and south-eastern France in particular, only 45 per cent of Communist voters would switch to a Socialist at the second round, with 27 per cent preferring a Gaullist candidate, and 28 per cent choosing to abstain. In Mediterranean France, where loyalty was rather higher, 49 per cent of non-Communist voters of the Left would switch to the PCF at the second round.

In other words, in 1967 there were many instances where the Communist electorate in one part of the country was considerably less reliable than the Socialist voter in another region. Communist discipline and the 'culture unitaire' could not be relied upon, and were frequently even less malleable than the traditionally fickle Socialist voter.[29]

In 1978 the situation was not very different, with some 39 per cent of Socialist voters preferring not to adopt a united front with the Communist candidate at the decisive round. In the south, but also in the Limousin and in parts even of far northern France, the Communist voters similarly failed to transfer their allegiances, especially in cases where the successful Socialist candidate would also be dependent upon right-wing transferees.[30] But then in 1978 the Communists were, it is true, conveying a double message to their electors: 'Vote Left', but also 'Don't vote Left with such efficiency that it results in a Socialist victory'. It is thus not possible to measure with confidence the motives of the Communist electorate on that occasion.

In 1981 Mitterrand's sweeping presidential victory naturally coloured the actions of voters in the ensuing legislative elections, but even then there were many minor instances of disloyalty, with Communists abstaining and thus narrowing the victory margin of a successful Socialist (e.g. in the Saône-et-Loire 1st district), or Socialists voting against a prominent PCF candidate at the second round (the experience of André Lajoinie at Gannat in the Allier). But with little danger of a Communist majority, or even a Communist-influenced

---

[29] See *Les Elections législatives de mars 1967*, pp. 373–8.
[30] See source cited in note 26, and J. Capdevielle *et al.*, *France de gauche, vote à droite*, p. 86.

Socialist majority, Socialist electors could usually indulge in the spirit of unity on the rare occasion in 1981 when a Communist made it to the second round. If anything, it was the Communist electors who broke ranks and defected in greater numbers. In any event, 1981 seems finally to have laid to rest another of the myths surrounding the preferences and moral disposition of the Left electorate in France.

*

In the light of that observation, we can now look more carefully at some of the other distinguishing features of the Left's constituency in France, in order to see what remains of traditional patterns following the recent upheavals. There are four major categories within the terms of which French observers have traditionally assigned political preferences, and against which they have measured the performance of parties: geographical distribution; the relation between religious practice and political choice; the differences in electoral behaviour between men and women, and the correlations between voting preference and social class. Each of these has lent itself to the establishment of enduring assumptions about the Left constituency in France, and the elections of 1981 provide an excellent occasion for investigating these.

The peculiarly French interest in electoral geography, the close concern with *where* different parties do well and badly, is a direct consequence of the administrative fiat of the early nineteenth century, which established the electoral districts, together with the characteristically French continuity in political families over time. The latter provides the rationale for a focus upon the geography of electoral behaviour (which, being relatively stable, became a significant variable in the measurement of other changes). The former meant that the spatial distribution of votes was one of the easiest and most reliable pieces of information available concerning the public preferences of private citizens.[31]

---

[31] The classic students of electoral geography in France are of course the works of André Siegfried, *Tableau politique de la France de l'ouest sous la Troisième République* (Paris, 1913) and *Géographie électorale de l'Ardèche sous la Troisième République* (Paris, 1949), the compilations of François Goguel, notably *Géographie des élections françaises* (Paris, 1951), and, more recently, the works of Alain Lancelot and Claude Leleu already cited. See, too, the provocative commentaries in H. Le Bras and E. Todd, *L'Invention de la France* (Paris, 1981). The low esteem in which electoral geography is currently held in certain Anglo-American historical circles points to a disturbing distance from and ignorance of one of the more interesting (and enduring) characteristics of French political culture.

A further justification for this mode of enquiry has been that it *works*—it does indeed reveal quite a lot. One reason for this seems to be that the French, especially the rural French, tended to a high level of communal conformity. It was frequently the case, for example, that where a minority preference existed (as in the left-wing vote in predominantly conservative areas like early twentieth-century Brittany) it afflicted whole villages, rather than isolated persons within otherwise conservative communities. Deviation, like conformity, was a collective practice, normally for obscure historical reasons which ante-dated elections by many generations. Thus the relatively crude calibrations of geographical measurement sufficed to pick out the significant variations.

In 1974, for example, a map is the best tool for grasping the appeal of Jean Royer, the conservative mayor of Tours who stood as an independent candidate in the presidential election. He did best in his own city of Tours, and in the Indre et Loire, the department of which it is the capital. He then scored 7.5 per cent of the vote in the three neighbouring departments, 5 per cent in a rather wider concentric area taking in parts of western France and the north-western fringe of the Massif Central, but only 3.2 per cent in the country as a whole. A similar study of the support for Chirac in central south-western France in 1981 would be equally revealing.[32]

The electoral geography of the PCF during the early Fourth Republic, when the Party was at its peak, consisted of three clearly-defined regions within which the Communists exercised a form of electoral hegemony. These were the Seine region (especially the inner suburbs); the south-western fringe of the Massif, and the Mediterranean littoral from Perpignan to Fréjus. In 1951, when nine departments gave the PCF the support of more than 26 per cent of their registered electors, five were in the Massif, three on the south coast, and the other was the Seine (where four constituencies returned Communists with overwhelming majorities).

In adjacent areas (north from Paris to Lille, in central Gascony and in the lower Rhône valley), the Communists did well though not spectacularly. Elsewhere, in south-central France, throughout the east and west and in parts of the Seine valley, the PCF vote varied from poor to infinitesimal.

---

[32] On Royer, see the article 'Defense and illustration of electoral geography', in H. R. Penniman (ed.), *France at the Polls. The Presidential Election of 1974* (Washington, 1975), p. 150.

This map of Communist support, already visible in 1936, remained valid throughout the Fourth Republic and into the Fifth. It is a closely accurate description of the support for Jacques Duclos in the presidential elections of 1969, and only occasionally misleading for the general elections of 1973. For nearly forty years the PCF neither expanded its base nor lost any of its important strongholds. But in 1981 there was a dramatic change. Although the proportional relations between strong and weak areas remained broadly the same, the figures were quite altered. There was the same relative strength in the centre-west (three departments in the Party's best twelve) and in the Midi méditerranean (four departments), but the northern vote had dissipated and been reduced to the national average. Marchais scored 12 per cent of the electorate in the country as a whole, yet in his strongholds he did little better: departments such as the Corrèze, where the PCF scored 33 per cent in 1951, gave him just 19 per cent in 1981. The Communists' average in their best four northern departments (Nord, Somme, Ardennes, Pas de Calais) was only 18 per cent of the electorate.

The real change of course came in Paris, where the department of Seine-St Denis (once the PCF national showplace) saw the Party obtaining just 21 per cent of the electorate, with other 'red belt' districts faring worse still. In 1951, with a rigged system designed to reduce Communist representation to a minimum, the PCF elected 19 *députés* in the Seine alone. In June 1981 they elected just 12 (only four of whom secured their seats without a run-off) and none in Paris itself.

This process has continued since the PCF took up its place in Mauroy's governments. In the municipal elections of March 1983 the PCF vote fell nation-wide to its lowest level in more than a generation, and the Party lost control of municipalities such as Nîmes, Sète, Arles, and Levallois, all in former Communist redoubts. In four more of its Paris-region bases, and in three others elsewhere, it was deemed to have falsified the election returns and was thrown out of office.

More recently still, in the European elections of June 1984, the PCF fell to ignominious levels, defeated in 52 departments by the list of the National Front, and obtaining 20 per cent of the *vote* in only five departments. Significantly, these were the Seine-St Denis, the Party's only remaining respectable showing in the Paris region; the Gard, in Mediterranean France, and the Allier, the Corrèze, and the Haute-Vienne, the last remaining strongholds of the south-western region and the centre.

The decline of the PCF has received copious commentary elsewhere. My point here is to underline the *qualitative* change wrought in very recent times. There is now no longer a powerful Communist presence in key strategic districts and constituencies of France; there are just some (a few) departments in which the PCF does a little better than elsewhere. The fact that there were many areas in 1951, for example, in which the PCF did badly was of no great significance—they were very adequately compensated by its huge support elsewhere. Today, the fact that there just is not a Communist electorate in much of France is very much to the point. In the 1984 European elections, there were 45 departments, half of France, in which less than 10 per cent of the vote went to the Communists, with their share of the electorate hovering between 3 per cent and 7 per cent. And even where there *are* still some solid Communist districts, their rather implausible distribution begins to merit comment. For it is more than ever the case that the PCF, outside its last remaining Seine districts, does best in areas of rural depopulation and economic decline, such as Tulle in the Corrèze, La Soutteraine in the Creuse, or in the most decayed and desperate towns of the north and Lorraine. The PCF is reduced to the status of a party of forlorn protest against change and crisis. Not surprisingly, it is much less impressive and plausible in this role, at a time of socialist governmental monopoly, than the far right, currently its closest competitor.[33]

The SFO in the 1940s and 1950s was as closely identified as the Communist with a particular geography, although its was a story of decline and shrinkage from as early as 1946. The map of Socialist support was not so tidy as that of the Communists: the twelve strongest departments in 1946 covered parts of the north (Pas de Calais, Nord, Ardennes), the Mediterranean region, some of the Pyrenean departments and distinctly *not* the Paris basin. There was also one department of the south-western Massif, the Haute-Vienne, which divided its affections between SFO and PCF equally.

In essence, the Socialists like the Communists had their strong and their weak areas, except that the SFIO was neither so well established in its fiefs, nor so absent in regions such as Brittany or Alsace. Taken together, however, the two maps comprise the electoral geography of

---

[33] On the link between Communist support and economic decline, see, among many, François Goguel, *Modernisation économique et comportement politique* (Paris, 1969), esp. p. 20. On the municipal elections of 1983 see Jérôme Jaffré, 'Les Elections municipales de mars 1983', in *Pouvoirs*, no. 27 (1983).

the Left, a geography which corresponded well enough with the experience of the two parties in inter-war France and of the SFIO alone before 1914.

It was the Socialists, however, who broke the mould. Even as they continued to decline in absolute numbers through the 1950s, their roots began to spread (because this was accompanied by further falls in their traditional areas of support the change was not seen, at the time, as an advance). As early as 1956 the SFIO was improving its showing in a few regions once thought securely conservative (the Doubs in eastern France, and even parts of the Vendée). By 1965, when Mitterrand led at the first round of the presidential elections in twenty traditionally left-leaning departments, he *also* was securing Socialist support, for the first time in forty years, in the Parisian suburbs, and doing better than De Gaulle in many rural and small town districts of conservative departments (such as the Drome). This success was, again, rather overshadowed at the time by De Gaulle's unique ability to attract urban and working-class voters, especially in Catholic areas of northern France, but it was the beginning of an important change in the geography of French socialism.[34]

By 1973, when support for the new PS was still markedly greater in the traditional areas of centre and south-west, the 'spreading out' process had been pursued none the less. In even the most recalcitrant arrondissements of Alsace and the West, Socialist candidates normally secured the support of between 10 and 20 per cent of the electorate. Mitterrand's 1974 campaign extended the claim of the non-Communist Left to speak to an ever-expanding constituency, and by 1978 the geography of PS support no longer bore any very clear relation to that of the SFIO in 1936 or even 1956.

By 1981 the transformation was complete. Of the twelve departments where Mitterrand did best in that year, only two (Landes, Haute-Garronne) had been in a similar list for 1951. The rest were scattered from the south-west (Gironde, Gers) to the east (Haute-Saône, Belfort), with strong support everywhere in between. More significant still, the variation between the average and the maximum in Socialist votes was sharply diminished. In 1951 the SFIO had drawn 11 per cent of the electorate as a whole, but in the Pas de Calais, Landes, and Haute-Vienne it had secured 22 per cent, 24 per cent, and 28 per cent respectively, a very extensive variation. In 1981 Mitterrand's national

[34] See *L'Election présidentielle de décembre 1965*, esp. p. 437.

score was 21 per cent at the first round; with the special exception of
the overwhelming support in his home base in the Nièvre (32 per
cent), his best showing, in the Gers or Landes, for example, was 28 per
cent, just seven points over the average, compared to a gap of
seventeen points thirty years earlier. As a result of these changes, it no
longer makes much sense to speak of *the* electoral geography of the
Left, especially as Mitterrand's victory was both foreshadowed in the
municipal results of 1977 and confirmed in June 1981. Even when the
Socialist vote has fallen in the years since then, as in various cantonal
and municipal elections, it has not fallen back into the traditional map
of opinion. The PS did not do well, for example, in the 1984 European
elections, securing just 21 per cent of the vote. But that 21 per cent
was remarkably evenly spread, with the party getting less than 17 per
cent of the vote in only seven departments (two of them in Corsica . . .).
Mitterrand's advances in, especially, the second round of the 1981
election, when he did spectacularly well in Brittany, Normandy, and
the west, appear to be no fluke or personal success but a reflection,
albeit exaggerated, of an enduring shift in the geography of French
political preferences.[35]

With religion as with geography, certain truisms have been long
present in any discussion of French politics. So far as could be
affirmed from maps, polls, political programmes, school attendance,
and so forth, men and women who attended church on a regular basis
were unlikely to vote for the Left (except in those minority instances
where the church they attended was other than Catholic). This was
long held to be absolutely the case regarding antipathy to Communism, of
varying accuracy when it came to Socialist electors, but in either case
more likely to survive detailed investigation than any other observation
regarding French political behaviour. Is it still the case?

We must first remind ourselves of the rather particular sense in
which it *was* once the case. There is no doubt that as late as 1970,
religion was still the most reliable guide to voting behaviour. In the
1965 election, 86 per cent of practising Catholics voted for De Gaulle
or Lecanuet, while 72 per cent of those 'without religion' voted for
Mitterrand.[36] Church attendance and priestly influence were what
united such different and distant department as Lozère and Maine-et-

[35] For commentaries on the 1981 elections, see *Nouvel Observateur*, 28 Apr. 1981; for
the 1984 European election results in France, see *Le Monde*, 19 June 1984.

[36] See Christel Peyrefitte, 'Réligion et politique', in *SOFRES, l'opinion française en 1977*
(Paris 1977), p. 118, and note 2.

Loire in their hostility to all things Left. Even when religious practice declined it remained, in its very absence, the best predictor of a citizen's vote. And there are a number of places were Catholic practice was once high but has lately diminished; yet it has left behind it those political traits associated with church-going communities: hence the occasional 'de-Christianized' canton with solidly right-wing electoral proclivities.

None of this in itself points to the *nature* of the link between religion and politics in France; it merely illustrates its existence, for which there is ample evidence. Even though as many as 31 per cent of PCF electors in 1978 declared themselves 'in favour' of retaining the catechism, the same survey found that 57 per cent of the Communist electorate was 'irreligious' (compared to 38 per cent for the PS), and that this was especially the case among younger men.[37] In Lyons in 1956 a district-by-district survey showed that the Communist bastions in the city (in the south-east and between Vaise and Fourvière in the western fringe) were also those where church attendance was lowest—below 15 per cent. Catholics in general were nine times less likely to vote Communist even in the mid-1970s than non-Catholics, and we have already seen that the 'pagan' peasants of west-central France were among the PCF's staunchest supporters.[38]

All of this may be seen in Fig. 2, showing the relationship between Communist voting and Catholic practice in 1969. The general tendency is clear—the greater the level of religious practice, the lower the PCF vote, with only a few exceptions. The inverse correlation would be even more marked were the data on religious practice not confined to rural cantons. Fig. 3 shows the same information for 1981. The religious factor is now less significant, but only because the Communist vote is generally so low that it allows for little graphic variation. But in 1981 it is still clear that *if* Communists do well, which is not often, it is not in regions of active Catholic practice—the original proposition but reduced in significance.[39]

For the Socialists the picture is quite different. Although the official

[37] Capdevielle, op. cit., pp. 61–2.
[38] The Lyons study can be found in *Les Elections du 2 janvier 1956* (Paris, 1957), esp. p. 317.
[39] In the Aveyron, for example, in the canton of Aubin in the second electoral district, the PCF has always done strikingly well, in contrast with its generally poor showing in the region. The canton is remarkable for its low level of church attendance—the lowest in the department. The PS, in the same canton, does no better than average. An invaluable source-book on religious practice in France is F.-A. Isambert and J.-P. Terrenoire, *Atlas de la pratique réligieuse des catholiques en France* (Paris, 1980).

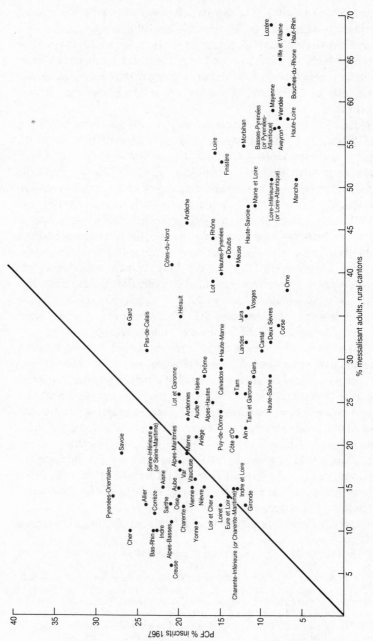

Figure 2. PCF % electorate in 1969 / % of adults attending Mass (rural)

Church position may have been that the SFIO was beyond the pale (as late as 1956 *La Croix du Nord* specifically instructed its Catholic readers not to vote for any Socialist), the party did in fact secure a respectable minority of religious voters.[40] The Lyons study already quoted showed that the SFIO did well in districts where the percentage of attendance at Mass was 15–20 per cent, and from the late 1960s it was possible to detect the growing 'availability' of a Catholic working class in the industrial towns of eastern and north-eastern France, released from the politics of obedience and turning to the Socialist movement in these areas.[41]

This, too, can be roughly illustrated in graphic form (see Figs. 4 and 5). In 1967 the SFIO and its allies definitely did better in non-practising departments, but not with that secular efficiency shown by the PCF (and far left minority parties too). This is not because the SFIO did well in very religious areas (it did not), but because areas where it *did* well, although none of them departments of high church practice, shared no common propensity to shun the Church altogether. It seems that the Socialists did best in departments where religious fervour was about average for the country—which is to say that even in the 1960s the SFIO did not conform to 'type'.

By 1981 there can no longer be any doubt—there is *no* relation between church attendance and voting preference as expressed in the presidential election, so far as support for Mitterrand was concerned. In religion as in geography, Mitterrand's appeal (and that of his party) crossed the old lines and evened out ancient distinctions. One of the few reliable definitions of 'Left' in French politics may be on the road to oblivion.

At first glance, this conclusion would appear somewhat cavalier in the light of more recent controversies over the role of the Church in private education. But this re-emergence in 1984 of an old dispute is seriously misleading. Only 12 per cent of the French population is actively Catholic in 1984, and many of them voted Socialist in 1981. The Socialists' error was to make of the schools issue a major legislative event. The perfectly reasonable expectation that the state should have some measure of quality control over schools in the private sector which it helps maintain was transformed by the anti-

[40] On the attitude adopted by the northern Catholic hierarchy, see the commentaries in *Atlas électoral Nord-Pas de Calais 1945–1972*, p. 47.

[41] See M. Dogan and J. Narbonne, *Les Françaises face à la politique. Comportement politique et condition sociale* (Paris, 1955), p. 78.

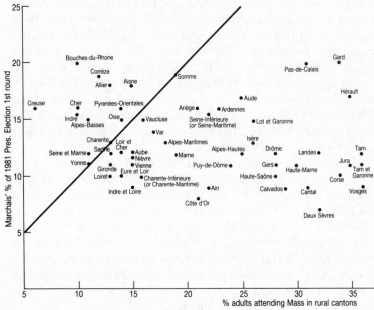

Figure 3. Marchais % electorate in 1981 /% of adults attending Mass (rural)

clerical pressure groups and the militant school teachers in the PS ranks into the final stage of a century-long struggle against religious influence in primary and secondary education. The Catholic hierarchy had no interest in this—many of the private schools are secular, and it is only in a very few areas that church-school attendance remains significant (e.g. in Brittany, where 40 per cent of children attended parochial school in January 1984). But the Right took full advantage of the opening and transformed the genuine debate about the reform of French education into an imagined effort by the 'socialo-communist' state to monopolize instruction. The result was a very real mobilization of millions of people around an almost wholly artificial and manu- factured dispute, for which the Socialists are at least partly to blame.

Yet in spite of the high emotional levels reached in the summer of 1984, both elections and opinion polls of that time suggest that wider issues remained predominant and religion in itself had not re-emerged as a significant variable in political choice. It is certainly true that the PS lost votes as a result of its handling of the education issue, but many

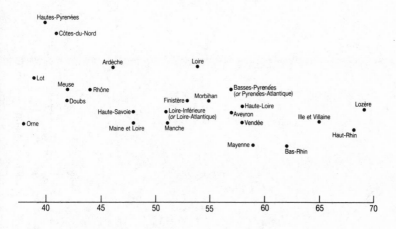

of the disillusioned ex-Socialist voters were retreating in disappointed sorrow rather than righteous anger. The highest levels of doctrinal fury were reached on the Left, where traditionally-minded militants resented Mitterrand's refusal to conduct an anti-clerical crusade. What the whole episode suggests is that the church/state motif in French political emotions is still available for mobilization, but can no longer be relied upon to fall tidily into place upon demand. If the Left can show even a modest level of tactical competence in dealing with such sensitive issues, it can continue to rely on social changes in France to paper over the historical sentiments. Of course, should it persist in providing its enemies with attractive opportunities for demagogic nostalgia, then it may yet succeed in disavowing its own achievements. But this need not come about.

If religion and the voting public are departing company, what of the almost equally ancient assumptions regarding the conservatism of the female voter? This issue is especially complicated for a number of reasons. Women in France have only had the vote since 1944, and thus

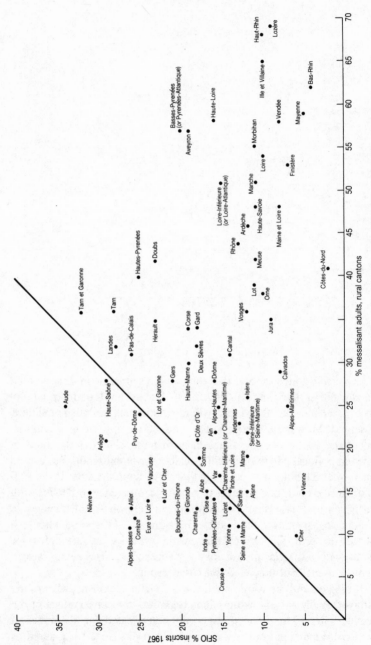

Figure 4. Socialist % electorate in 1967 / % of adults attending Mass (rural)

the history of the relationship between women and politics is for the most part composed of myths, prejudices, and guesswork. Moreover, the assumption that women were under the thumb of the Church, a belief firmly held by republicans, Radicals, and Socialists since the 1840s, has coloured the attitude of the Left towards women as members or voters, and this in turn has probably acted as a disincentive for women who might otherwise have been attracted to the Left on any of the usual sociological or ideological grounds.

A third difficulty concerns, as usual, the nature of the evidence to hand. A few studies were undertaken in the 1950s to determine how men and women voted (by the use of separate voting booths), and these are of some interest. But there were few of them, and they are not at all representative. Much of the later evidence derives from polls and questionnaires, and this is a field in which their reliability is more than usually suspect. And finally, no one knows to what extent the response of the female electorate in France may have been influenced by the sex of the candidate(s) for election, which thus renders difficult all national comparisons over time.

Given these observations, all conclusions about the relationship between sex and political choice in France are uniquely tentative. But within these limits it is possible to offer some comments on the plausibility of the standard beliefs. Historically, the SFIO was always divided over the likely impact of a truly universal suffrage. The majority favoured it on general principles,, the minority preferred to postpone it for fear of the benefits that would accrue to the clericalist Right. As late as 1934 this was a contentious issue at national Party Congresses. Earlier still, it had been part of a wider debate on issues of women's rights and emancipation. Here too the party, like socialists in general, had been divided. On the one side stood those (like Guesde) who supported women's claims as an end in themselves; on the other, with Jaurès, those who preferred to see them as peripheral, secondary to the more 'important' issues facing contemporaries. The former group was in its turn split between the marxists, who saw the emancipation of women as a desirable *consequence* of a socialist revolution, and the 'socialist feminists', who wished to see women's emancipation presented as a necessary *corollary* of the emancipation of the proletariat.

Thus divided, the SFIO presented a far-from-sympathetic face to women of any class, and after the First World War, with the

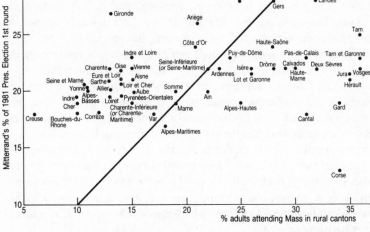

Figure 5. Mitterrand % electorate in 1981 / % of adults attending Mass (rural)

emergence of the Communist Party, it effectively relegated the whole matter to some unspecified future date.

The Communists on the other hand, more tactically flexible, more opportunist, but also in one sense more consistent, had no fears of a clerical backlash in the event of women getting the suffrage. Until 1934 they were only interested in the support of women from a certain social class, and such women were best won for the Left by being offered maximum access to political and economic opportunity. On the face of it, the Communists should thus have been far better placed, after the Liberation, to capitalize upon the creation of a female electorate.

That they distinctly failed to do so does suggest certain differences between men and women voters, and these are readily identified. To begin with, a sizeable minority of women voters (20 per cent in a 1945 survey) opposed women's suffrage! Secondly, there was a widespread belief that women should at best play a passive role in electoral politics—in 1953, 61 per cent of men interviewed and 67 per cent of women thought it 'inappropriate' for a woman to speak at an electoral meeting. Given that an electoral meeting where women spoke was

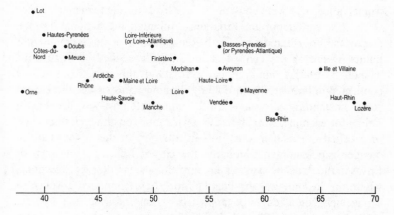

more likely to have been organized by the Left, this too represented an invisible handicap not easily overcome.[42]

There was also evidence to suggest, at least in the years immediately following the extension of the suffrage, that there was a difference in political awareness between men and women. If opinion polls are to be believed, women were much worse-informed than men (other things equal) in the years 1944–53 (though of course the men may have been claiming to know more than they did and the women, characteristically, less . . .). By the mid–1950s this 'information gap' had all but disappeared (which speaks to the educating process inherent in political participation), but had been replaced by a more selective distinction: women appear to have been better informed on domestic and economic matters such as housing or inflation, men on foreign policy. By the beginning of the 1970s, even these differences had waned; women were as likely as men to read a candidate's literature in a municipal election campaign, almost as likely to attend meetings. The only remaining distinction appears to have been the response to

[42] See M. Dogan and J. Narbonne, *Les Françaises face à la politique. Comportement politique et condition sociale* (Paris, 1955), p. 78.

political reporting in the press and on television, which men followed more closely than women.[43]

One of the ways in which these small differences became magnified in political terms was via levels of abstention. In general terms, French women after 1945 were consistently less likely to vote than men. There were, however, important variations. Although the national average during the Fourth and early Fifth Republics was a gap of about eight points (where 18 per cent of male electors abstained, the figure for women hovered around 26 per cent), and although this gap was confirmed in local studies in Dijon, Grenoble, and Lyons, there were some outstanding exceptions. In the immediate post-war elections in Dijon, for example, women in the town's four constituencies equalled or excelled the men in turn-out—it was only in the 1950s that the 'gender gap' emerged. Similarly, the city of Lille and the town of Privas in the Ardèche saw women outvoting men in the 1951 elections, where the hypothetical explanations for 1946 (continued absence of servicemen, etc.) did not apply. In Lyons, during the Algeria referendum of 1961, the relationship of male to female turn-out was distinctly class-dependent: in middle-class areas like Lyons 2^e, men and women voted in equal numbers, but the percentage of abstainers in general and women abstainers in particular rose sharply in the city's more popular districts.

Age, too, was an important factor. Younger women in Lille in 1951 consistently outvoted older women (and older men). The same point was made in a study in Billancourt in the Paris 'red belt' in 1965, where women voted in large numbers until their mid-thirties, but thereafter withdrew increasingly from electoral participation.

The conclusion, as one expert noted nearly a generation ago, is that 'l'influence du sexe n'est pas directe sur la participation', but is more influenced by age and social class. Younger, middle-class women (like men of their social class) voted more than older, poorer, and working-class persons of either sex. Nor was this pattern influenced by the fact of employment. Although actively employed women are (perhaps predictably) more left-inclined than the non-employed, both groups *vote* in equal proportions, and appear to have done so since the 1940s.[44]

[43] Ibid., pp. 74–7; Hayward and Wright, 'The 37,708 Microcosms of the Indivisible Republic', loc. cit., p. 305, citing an April 1971 poll.

[44] On abstentionism in general, see Lancelot, *L'Abstentionisme électoral*, esp. pp. 172–84; also Raymond Long, *Les Elections législatives en Côte d'Or depuis 1870. Essai d'interprétation sociologique* (Paris, 1958) (for Dijon material); Jean Stoetzel, 'Voting

The important remaining factor is, of course, religion. There is no doubt that the Church has played a greater role in the lives of women than in those of men in modern French history, even if only because it offered them a social forum during long periods when they were excluded from the public world of men. Throughout the late nineteenth-century years of controversy over church schools, girls were more likely than boys to have received a religious education, and in the more devout regions of upper Normandy, the west, and the inner (southern and south-eastern) Massif this is still the case. Not surprisingly, then, women leaned disproportionately towards church-linked parties when they secured the vote. The rapid rise of the MRP in the post-war years reflects a distinctly female bias in its electorate (in 1955 it was the only party which women recalled having supported in 1951 in greater numbers than was the case for men similarly questioned). Yet even here the distinctions were not so very acute: only one-third of women electors supported the MRP at its peak in 1946, only one-sixth in 1951. Considering that some 50 per cent of French women attended Mass in the post-war years, and the other three major parties in 1946 were all of the anti-clerical Left, this is a rather low correlation.[45]

The fact is that while the Church had a greater influence on women than on men, this influence can be exaggerated. The relationship between religion and voting, for women, was always imperfect. Women, after all, were *more* religious than men, distinctly so. Yet overall, and even in the frozen voting patterns of the 1950s, they voted much as did the men of their class, age, milieu, and region, albeit in a diminished electoral key, as it were. If anything, then, they were more likely to 'contradict' their religious persuasion than were men, who were in this respect more consistent.

How was the electoral sociology of the Left affected by these

---

behaviour in France', in *British Journal of Sociology*, vol. 6, no. ii (1955); for Lyons see also Madeleine Grawitz, 'Le Réferendum, la ville de Lyon et les femmes', in *Les Cahiers de la République*, no/6 (1961), esp. p. 81. In a very recent study it has been suggested that there may be a subtle difference in voting behaviour between formerly active women and those who have always been 'femmes au foyer'. The former, it would appear, are more likely to be Left than Right, and are proportionately more inclined to favour Communists over Socialists. In the 1978 elections, housewives favoured the PS over all other parties. See these and other interesting indications in Janine Mossuz-Lavau and Mariette Sineau, *Enquête sur les femmes et la politique en France* (Paris, 1983), p. 53 ff.

[45] See Stoetzel, loc. cit., Table 11, and Dogan and Narbonne, *Les Françaises face à la politique*, p. 59.

considerations? For the PCF, the female voter has proven steadily
elusive. In 1952 the PCF's electorate was 61 per cent male, and in
1962 the imbalance had actually increased, with men representing 65
per cent of the Communist vote. In 1981, when Marchais took 16 per
cent of the vote in the presidential election, he won only 14 per cent of
the female vote. When we recall just how compact and homogeneous
the Communist vote has always been, these discrepancies are
especially significant. Nor was the problem confined to Marchais's
peculiarly rebarbative personality; at the 1978 legislative elections the
PCF's electorate was 53 per cent male (men represented 48 per cent of
the electorate as a whole), after a decade of hard work and appeals
aimed deliberately to the female interest. From 1945 to the present the
Communists have unfailingly secured the lowest percentage of female
voters of any major French party.

The picture for the Socialists is predictably more complex. Always a
party with more men than women supporters (47 per cent of the SFIO
electorate was female in 1951, 47 per cent still in 1973 for the new PS,
49 per cent in 1978), the Socialists, SFIO, and PS alike, never
suffered the acute imbalance of Communist voting patterns. When one
recalls the absolute lack of Socialist interest (during the lifetime of the
SFIO) in questions concerning women's rights, their employment,
their representation in office, the party's relative success in securing
such a large number of women voters is actually striking, and tends to
confirm the limited significance of sex as a political variable. In this
context the achievement of the PS in June 1981 in securing a record
vote among women (38 per cent of women voted for the PS against 39
per cent of men) is less a remarkable breakthrough than the next step
in a regular progress.

The stages of this process are readily traced, and they point once
again to the importance of the presidential system in general and to
Mitterrand's exploitation of it in particular. In 1965 those who
considered the improvement in the situation of women to be 'very
important' were predominantly Mitterrandist in their sympathies (69
per cent of his supporters considered the issue very important, against
only 54 per cent of De Gaulle's electors). Together with 'laicity' and
'the defence of workers' interests', the 'woman question' emerged as
early as 1965 as an area in which the gap between Gaullists and the
Left was widest, and it was one which Mitterrand implicitly exploited.
The gap is all the more interesting for being widest among
middle-aged women (50–64) with only limited educational back-

ground, while the issue was of least interest to highly-educated young men, in 1965. This, interestingly, contrasts rather sharply with the image that was shortly to emerge of the new Socialist Party, as one of young, educated, and ambitious males![46]

A further element in the progressive alignment of Socialist politics and female voters in France has been the rise of the 'New' or unofficial Left, and its success at appealing to women voters, largely via the medium of political feminism. The schisms on the Left in France have usually been studied either for their splintering impact upon the far Left (with Trotskyist candidates at elections taking a salami slicer to the PCF vote), or else for their part in the rebirth of a major Socialist party. But feminist politics were as important a part of the realignments of the radical Left in France as they were in the USA, and in France, predictably, they took a more immediately electoral form. Not only did the feminist movement Choisir put up dozens of candidates in the 1970s, but both the PSU and one of the Trotskyist parties presented women as their candidates at the 1981 presidential elections (the Trotskyist, Arlette Laguiller, had also stood in 1974). Both women were feminists who thereby associated themselves and their ideas with the political Left. Between them Huguette Bouchardeau (for the PSU) and Laguiller (for Lutte Ouvrière) polled 989,000 votes, or about 3.4 per cent of the votes cast, with Laguiller getting twice as many as Bouchardeau. Both stood on programmes which specifically included feminist statements and positions. Moreover, when Laguiller stood in 1974, as an unknown representative of a Trotskyist splinter group, she won 2.33 per cent of the vote, more than six times that of the better-known 'official' Trotskyist, Alain Krivine.

It is not practicable to try to calculate the proportion of women in the electorates of Laguiller and Bouchardeau. But there can be no doubt as to its importance. In a major survey taken after the 1978 elections it emerged that the PSU electorate was 57 per cent female, and that taken as a whole, the left-wing electorate *excluding* the PCF and the PS was 51 per cent female, very close to the figure for the electorate as a whole. Moreover, the Ecology movement, taken separately, actually matched the national balance exactly (48 per cent male, 52 per cent

[46] See *L'Election présidentielle de décembre 1965*, pp. 464–81. Pre-election polls in 1981 showed that sixteen years later Mitterrand was still thought to be the candidate most sympathetic to issues of concern to women. For some examples of Mitterrand's occasional difficulties with the feminist movement—and theirs with him—see Gisele Halimi (préface), *Choisir (la cause des femmes): Quel président pour les femmes—réponses de François Mitterrand* (Paris, 1981).

female), a point of some importance for the major Left parties who usually stood to benefit from the votes of Ecologist electors at the second round.[47]

Some of the female support for the minor parties of the Left represents a reaction against the inhospitable character of the big organizations, and cannot be treated as part of the general increase in female support for the Left. It is simply evidence of a long-buried female vote which has hitherto had nowhere to go. It is certainly not, for example, a candidate for adoption by the PCF. The latter has been consistently hostile to and dismissive of the women's movement (witness its reaction to the abortion issue in 1979[48]), and the hostility is amply reciprocated. Only 15 per cent of the female supporters of the PSU and the Trotskyist parties in 1978 declared themselves willing to switch to Marchais in a presidential election, and only 27 per cent would transfer their votes at the second round of a general election if it meant electing a Communist. Some of this is part of the common far-left hostility to the PCF, but it is noteworthy that the men in the same study showed much less anti-Communist sentiment. Mitterrand and the PS, on the other hand, received an altogether more sympathetic hearing.[49]

The PCF might be forgiven for feeling a trifle hurt in the face of such hostility. Historically, it has always made a distinctly greater effort than any other party to appeal to women by including them in party office and, after 1945, by presenting them at elections. In the October 1945 elections 30 women were elected to the Assembly, 17 of them Communists. In November 1946 there were 34 women in the Assembly following the elections of that month, and 20 of them were in the Communist group. Of course, these figures were quite disproportionate to the number of women who *stood* for election: where one in four Communist candidates in November 1946 was a woman, there was only one woman in every seven *députés*, a result of judicious selection of men for the more 'winnable' constituencies.[50]

---

[47] See Capdevielle *et al.*, *France de gauche, vote à droite*, pp. 40 n. 26, 100–1, 241.

[48] Responding to the March for Abortion in Paris in March 1979, *L'Humanité* haughtily proclaimed that 'Seuls les Communistes mènent la bataille sur l'avortement' (!). See *l'Humanité*, 18 Oct. 1979. The following day Roland Leroy refused to meet a women's delegation that came to see him in Rouen, and his bodyguards dealt very roughly with those who persisted. For further details of the PCF's real attitude towards women, see *Question féministes*, no. 7 (fevrier 1980), esp. 111–17.

[49] See Capdevielle, op cit., pp. 69–70.

[50] For details see *Le Monde, Élections et Réferendums (octobre 1945 à décembre 1946)*, 2 vols. (Paris, 1946).

None the less, these figures were vastly better than those for the SFIO. In 1946 the Socialists put up 68 women in a total of 537 candidates (1 in 8), but only *3* of these women made it to the Assembly, out of 90 Socialists elected. By 1962 the novelty of trying to appeal to women by putting up female candidates had passed, and in the legislative elections of that year the SFIO put up just two women candidates (even the tiny PSU managed three). The PCF, on the other hand, presented 29 women candidates, but most of them in hopeless constituencies (such as Rodez or Pau, where Victoria Pascal and Marie Dufourcq respectively had no chance of obtaining 10 per cent of the vote). Only five were elected. Altogether in 1962 there were 53 women standing for election in France, just 2 per cent of the total!

The late 1970s thus saw a remarkable change. By 1978, 684 women stood for election, one in seven candidates. More than one in three of these was standing for a Trotskyist party, the Ecologists, Choisir or the PSU. Only 14 were elected, however, of whom just *1* was a Socialist (Marie Jacq, the mayor of Henvic, near Morlaix in the Finistère); 12 were Communists. In 1981 the PS finally caught up with the PCF: although the latter had 14 per cent women among its candidates and the Socialists had just 8 per cent, the two parties managed equal proportions of women among their *successful* candidates, with 18 women sitting with the PS, 3 for the Communists.

Until 1978, then, the PCF consistently put up more women as candidates than any other party (even in municipal elections—24 per cent of its candidates in major towns in 1971 were women[51]), elected more of them (though relegating most to hopeless seats)—and got less of the female vote than anyone else. This was particularly irksome given that the Communists' female *membership* was consistently higher than that of the Socialists. In 1951 only 12 per cent of the SFIO's members were women (the figure for the PS in 1973 was 13 per cent!), while for the PCF the percentage was 18.[52] And yet the PS, even as it remained an overwhelmingly male preserve through the 1970s (only 3.7 per cent of its *Comité Directeur* was female in 1973), has improved its showing among women, while the PCF, which has very deliberately included women in its higher (though not highest) echelons, has sunk ever lower.

[51] Hayward and Wright, loc. cit., p. 291 n. 17.

[52] For the PS, see the article by P. Hardouin, 'Les Caractéristiques sociologiques du Parti Socialiste', in *Revue française de science politique*, vol. 28, no. ii (1978). For the PCF see Dogan and Narbonne, op. cit., p. 138.

There are additional contributory factors, of course. The Parti Socialiste has done much better in Paris with respect to female membership (nearly one-third of its Parisian members were women in the mid–1970s), and it has benefited from the increase in the numbers of women at work during the years of its own rapid growth. And the Socialists after 1977 have established quotas to ensure the presence of women at all levels of the party. But the presence or absence of female members, or even female candidates, seem to have had very little direct bearing upon the fortunes of left-wing parties among the female *electorate.* And the latter, in its turn, has progressively moved away from the vestigial conservatism so readily imputed to it. So far as the PS and the minor parties of the non-Communist Left are concerned, women are as much a part of their national constituency as are most Catholics and many of the residents of Brittany or Alsace. The exception, in this as in other respects, remains the French Communist Party.

This increased isolation and peculiarity of the Communists in recent years does of course reflect, in a distorted form, the Party's own claims to uniqueness. In the light of what I have discussed so far, they might say that it is clear that the Communists are the *only* left-wing party in France. And the determining characteristic, the vital clue, would be precisely that aspect of the left-wing electorate which it now remains to discuss: its occupational and class identity. For here, at least the issue is unambiguous. Communists and their opponents alike have identified the PCF with the working class, and the working-class voter with the PCF. The SFIO and its successor party and subsidiaries long since ceased to be of the Left, it is asserted, by virtue of the increased heterogeneity and flux of their social base. It is not necessary to sympathize with the PCF in order to hold this view, for all that it is one which well serves the Party's own ends. It is an account of the history of the French Left which can be found everywhere. Is it well founded in the evidence?

One aspect of this question, as it concerns the earlier history of the Socialist movement, is discussed in chapter three. With its contracting base in the 1950s, the SFIO did not so much cease to be the popular movement of the inter-war years; more precisely, it came to rely upon certain of those popular features to the exclusion of others. It remained, by any measurement, a party with its roots firmly in the industrial working class, particularly the textile and mining communities of the northern departments. Twenty-four per cent of its members in these years were working-class, while a further 11 per cent were workers in the public sector and thus misleadingly classed as 'fonctionnaires'. Although this was less than the average for the active population as a whole, it represented a higher proletarian membership than was to be found in any other party save the Communists. The salient difference between Communists and Socialists, in fact, was that the latter's proletarian constituency lay in the workers of the smaller, skilled sectors, rather than in the giant worker fortresses.[53]

The second outstanding feature of SFIO membership in the 1950s was the over-representation of government employees and white-collar workers generally, contrasting with disproportionately few peasant members. But neither of these characteristics was surprising for a parliamentary organization inevitably centred on Paris, and both were equally as true for the SFIO in its formative years half a century earlier.[54]

A similar picture emerges from a study of Socialist representatives in the National Assembly in 1956. The 25 per cent of SFIO *députés* in 1963 who were workers, employees, artisans, or lower-level civil servants had fallen to 17 per cent, with the difference made up by the educational profession: 17 per cent of the Socialist *députés* were primary schoolteachers, 16 per cent lycée or university professors. But substantially absent, in 1956 as earlier, were the middle class, in private or public sector, excepting only those in the higher echelons of teaching. The vast bulk of the SFIO's members and representatives were wage-earners, and the SFIO of the Fourth Republic remained a popular party, speaking to the 'petit peuple', especially those employed in the public sector. This did not prevent it from asserting its putative proletarian identity,[55] but most of the genuine blue-collar workers in the party were old and growing older, with little renewal after 1958.

This picture of the SFIO helps to explain how it could merge so fluently into the Parti Socialiste, announced in 1969 and placed on a permanent footing two years later. Despite the loss of members and dynamism, the SFIO in its declining years was already preparing the ground for a shift from the old industrial and rural strongholds of

[53] Hardouin, loc. cit., pp. 223–5.

[54] In 1951 there were only 7.4 per cent of SFIO members actively employed in agriculture, compared to 26 per cent for France as a whole.

[55] In these years the SFIO still spoke of itself as embodying the class interests of the proletariat. Thus Daniel Mayer, writing to René Mayer upon the latter's formation of a government excluding socialist representation: 'Votre gouvernement constitué sans la classe ouvrière est peu à peu amené à gouverner contre elle.' See *Les Elections du 2 janvier 1956*, where Mayer is quoted on p. 18.

north and south to areas of diversified industrial activity and to the tertiary sector (often within these same regions). This transition, seen at the time as disconcerting evidence of a loss of the traditional foothold in the working-class cities, was in fact a first stage in the creation of a new Socialist electorate. And even the distorting presence of educationalists in the modern PS (31 per cent of its 1981 candidates were *professeurs*) can be seen emerging in the SFIO, including the progressive replacement of *instituteurs* by teachers in secondary and tertiary education as stalwarts of local party organizations.

It was thus not at all surprising that the PS should take on the traditional socialist function as a vehicle for inter-generational upward mobility. Like the SFIO of the 1930s and 1940s, it is a party whose members have improved upon the social condition of their parents: in 1973 only 4 per cent of the party's *cadres* were workers, whereas that had been the condition of 37 per cent of their fathers. Like the SFIO, too, the PS was not (and is not today) a 'catch all' party, but one which is strong in certain well-defined social areas. During the 1970s, it came to rely very heavily for members and activists upon those social groups categorized as 'employees' and *cadres moyens*, and on the young (one area of difference from the SFIO, always a party of the middle-aged). The PS was not well represented among women, outside Paris, and it had little enough base among farmers. The result of this clutch of social characteristics, taken together with the superabundance of public-sector workers and schoolteachers, helps explain much of the actions, and errors, of the Socialists in government.

In its *electorate*, on the other hand, the PS did come rapidly to reflect the balance of social forces in the nation, something that had ceased to be true of the SFIO after 1945. In 1979 a survey found that the Socialist electorate and the electorate as a whole were remarkably similar,[56] with only this difference, that the PS under-represented farmers and slightly over-represented urban dwellers. Its respectable

[56]	Socialist electorate %	French electorate %
Cadres moyens, employés	23	17
Cadres supérieurs et professions	9 ⎱	15
Artisans, commerçants	5 ⎰	
Ouvriers	35	32
Agriculteurs	5	12
Inactifs	23	24

showing among the well-educated and the comfortably-off probably helps to explain the multiplier effect in its vote in recent years—these are people who abstain less at elections, whereas the old SFIO had always depended most heavily on those who, because of class or region, were most likely to abstain.

The PS, then, borrowed much from the SFIO and then added features of its own. Like its predecessor it is an electoral, not a membership party—its sociological characteristics as measured by membership alone would never have secured it political success. Indeed, as already noted, its militant base includes an over-representation of virulently anti-clerical teachers, whose own concerns are likely to prove highly detrimental to the party's interests if allowed free rein.

But there is one very profound difference from the old Socialist movement, and it is a change which entails considerable risk. This concerns the altered image that political socialism in France now presents to the electorate. As recently as 1974, when people were asked why they were 'on the left', the most popular reply was that they belonged to a 'milieu social défavorisé'. In 1981, however, the chief reason people gave for being on the left was 'a belief in certain ideas and values'. This was the answer of 37 per cent, whereas only 22 per cent offered social disadvantage as a reason for voting Left (the corresponding figure in 1974 had been 32 per cent).[57] A lot hinges on this change. It shows what French socialism was, until very recently, and it suggests what it has become. It also points to a danger: although less and less people had come to think of themselves as members of a 'milieu social défavorisé', as long as they did so, a traditional party of the Left would still have a guaranteed role to play. But belief in 'certain ideas and values' is an altogether more volatile affair, liable to change in many ways, for all sorts of reasons and in a very short time. It is also not at all easy for the PS to remain identified with such subjective preferences, especially once in office. The most volatile and unfaithful social group, to judge from the results of the municipal elections of 1977 and 1983 in particular, is the 'cadre supérieur/professions libérales' category, French socialism's newest acquisition. This is also, of course, the group least likely to have turned to socialism through any sense of class identification or personal disadvantage.

This, at least, is not a problem with which the Communists have to

---

[57] See Sofres poll published in *Nouvel Observateur*, 30 Mar. 1981.

contend. During the 1920s the PCF established itself as the dominant electoral force among the industrial workers of the Paris region. From this long impregnable base it moved, slowly, to compete with the SFIO for the support of the working-class voter in northern, eastern, and southern France. In general it succeeded best where the old syndicalist movement had deepest roots (with the special exception of Alsace). Because the PCF established organic relations with the heavy industry unions, rather than the service and public-sector unions where socialist influence remained strong, it benefited commensurately from post-war growth in industries such as car and aircraft manufacturing. By the early 1950s the PCF could claim with some plausibility that it, if any, was *the* 'parti de la classe ouvrière'.

This claim was most obviously fulfilled at the level of party leadership and political representation, where the promotion and presentation of workers was carefully stage-managed (even if, like Thorez and Duclos, they had not worked at their trade in thirty years). Of the PCF' *députés* in 1956, 42 per cent were *ouvriers*, according to their stated occupation, and the party favoured such persons in the allocation of constituencies (in 1951 the PCF, a victim of electoral gerrymandering, lost 69 metropolitan seats, but only 13 of its working-class representatives). Many of the party's parliamentarians were also ex- or present union officials; indeed in some areas the selection of union secretaries for a seat was part of a long tradition of preferment.[58]

Concerning the proletarian element in the Communist *electorate*, the picture is more complex. As a proportion of the total Communist vote, the working-class quotient was always high, higher than that for any other party; in 1956 it was fully 75 per cent of the PCF vote in Paris (the comparable figure for the SFIO was 33 per cent). In 1962 it was estimated that 69 per cent of the Communist vote, nation-wide, came from workers.[59] But in its share of the working-class vote as a whole, the PCF has not done so well. In 1962 about 38 per cent of working-class voters supported the PCF, in 1973 about 33 per cent, in 1978 about 36 per cent. Only in Paris was the figure significantly higher than

[58] In the Moselle, for example, six of the eight SFIO candidates at the 1919 elections were union secretaries. In 1924 four of the eight PCF candidates were likewise secretaries of their syndicat. In 1928 three of the PCF candidates were similarly employed, and the tradition continued for many years. See E. L. Baudon, *Les Elections en Mosselle 1919–1956* (Metz, n.d.).

[59] See Joseph Klatzmann's observations in *Les Elections du 2 janvier 1956*, pp. 255–73, and Mattei Dogan, 'Le Vote ouvrier en France. Analyse écologique des élections de 1962', in *Revenue française de sociologie*, vol. 6, no. iv (1965), pp. 462–6.

this—in 1956 seven out of every ten workers who voted supported the Communists.[60]

In general, then, the PCF has been a working-class party, though not the party of the working class (a claim that could as plausibly have been made by De Gaulle himself, who did very well among urban workers in the elections and referenda of the 1960s). Moreover, the PCF's capacity to mobilize a working-class constituency depended upon the size and density of the community in question. Where the urban proletariat was the overwhelming majority, there the PCF would do handsomely. But where the proletariat was thinner on the ground, the correlation between workers and Communists was poor, further evidence for the importance of community, and thus geography, in French electoral behaviour. In most of France, as a result, the PCF actually did better in rural areas (especially in the south), and rather badly in working-class communities isolated among agricultural or mixed populations.

This helps to explain the pattern of Figs. 6 and 7. There is very little correspondence, in 1954 as in 1981, between the presence or absence of industrial workers in a department, and the size of the Communist vote. Taken in isolation, at least, the variables which determined the Communist vote were clearly not occupation and social class.

If the PCF has not always had so firm a grip upon the working-class voter (especially the *female* working-class voter) as it has striven to suggest,[61] it could at least claim, from 1936 until the late 1970s, that what it had, it held. This may no longer be the case. A growing minority of the French working population is now immigrant and thus frequently unenfranchised. The PCF has oscillated between exploiting

[60] Of course the term 'working class' is far too sociologically insensitive to illustrate all the varieties of the popular votes in France. In some parts of the Corrèze in the 1960s, for example, the PCF benefited from popular political traditions of Left allegiance in some areas, while simultaneously gaining support in certain areas, like Brive, precisely *because* of change and the breaking of traditional patterns—in this case the creation of a new working population in recently created light industry. See J. Lord, A. Petrie and L. Whitehead, 'Political Change in Rural France: the 1967 election in a Communist stronghold', in *Political Studies*, vol. 16, no. ii (1968).

[61] In 1979 Paul Laurent went to great lengths to demonstrate that the PCF was still a (the) working-class Party. But in order to show that the working class constituted an absolute majority of Party members in that year, he managed to include under the rubric 'classe ouvrière' not only skilled and semi-skilled blue-collar workers, but also all farm workers, most categories of technician, all lower *cadres*, and office and shop employees of every kind! This kind of ontological sleight of hand will be familiar to students of radical sociology in France. See Laurent's assertions, printed as an annex to *Les Intellectuels, la culture et la révolution* (Conseil National du PCF, 9–10 fevrier 1980, Paris, 1980).

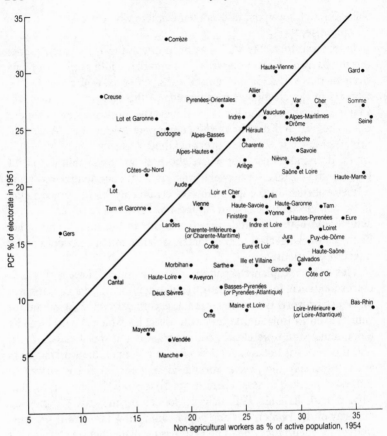

Figure 6. PCF % electorate 1951 / % of non-agricultural workers in active population

this fact through racist appeals to the white worker, and mobilizing the immigrant work-force through factory-based union activity. In neither case does it stand to benefit from the immigrant vote. Taken together with the shrinking role of the blue-collar work-force in the French economy, this has obliged the PCF to move quietly away from its emphatic identification with the proletariat (not without discontented grumblings from its working-class members, most of them distinctly older than the work-force as a whole). In the 1981 elections the PCF candidates included 29 per cent of men and women from the teaching profession and 17 per cent of *cadres moyens*. The *ouvrier* quotient was

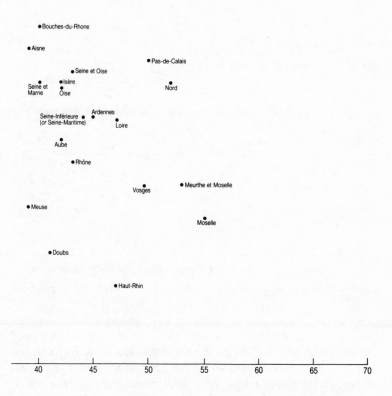

down to 27 per cent.[62] Whether the PCF can plausibly present itself as a party open to all and emulate the success of the Socialists is another matter. It is not even clear that its leaders wish to make the attempt, and the Communist departure from government in 1984 probably signals a temporary retreat to the role of spokesman for the oppressed. But the PCF's prospects for revival are slim indeed if it has to depend upon such a base for its political fortunes in coming years.

It is clear, then, that in respect of its sociology, as with religion,

[62] See A. Guede and S. A. Rozenblum, 'Les Candidats aux élections législatives de 1978 et 1981', in *Revue Française de science politique*, vol. 31. nos. v–vi (1981), p. 994.

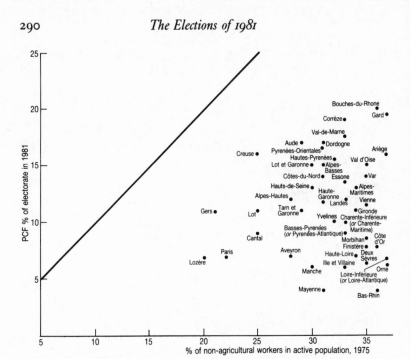

Figure 7. PCF % electorate 1981 / % of non-agricultural workers in active population

geography, and distinctions of sex, the Left in France has parted company with its past. The traditional distinctions between Right and Left have been blurred, and within the family of the Left itself the old distinguishing features have been obliterated. This process, which culminated in the elections of 1981, raises the question: was the electoral revolution of 1981 a major turning-point in French political history, of qualitatively greater significance than any hitherto?

*

The answer, I believe, is yes. This is not because of anything very dramatic about the details of the Left's victory in 1981—as we have seen, these represent the cumulative effect of changes under way for many years. Nor is it because the Left has won power, though in France this alone is always something worthy of comment. It is because the circumstances under which the Left was victorious utterly preclude a return to the status quo ante, and in this respect the events of 1981 are indeed unique. How this is so can be seen most clearly by

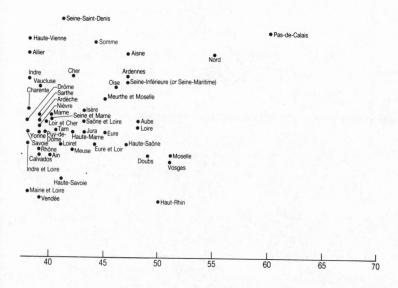

making a distinction between the effect of the 1981 elections upon each of the major partners in the victorious coalition.

For the Communists, there is a particularly ironic twist to these events. The formation of Mitterrand's successful political coalition coincided with years of crisis for the PCF, years in which the respectability of the USSR in the eyes of the Left fell sharply and the intellectual hegemony of marxism disappeared. The PCF re-entered the political fold in a state of acute internal division, with a series of policy changes between 1974 and 1980 which utterly disoriented and disturbed party militants and voters alike. The Party was thus grotesquely ill-equipped to face the problems posed by Mitterrand's success and that of his party, and 1981 served more than anything else to precipitate a further series of internal debates which were then reflected in yet more disasters at the polls.

On the face of it, the PCF ought even so to have some grounds for optimism. Having left a government in which it was audibly uncomfortable, it should be able, via its control of the CGT, to

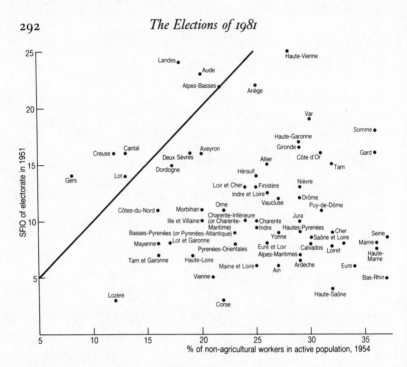

Figure 8. SFIO % electorate 1951 / % of non-agricultural workers in active population

capitalize on the Socialists' economic and political embarrassments, and it is still well placed to benefit from any electoral system which obliges most Socialist candidates to count on the Communist vote at a second round. But these are technical and, as it were, negative weapons. And, what is worse, they point to the Communists' greatest difficulty—that its strategy is now wholly dependent upon reacting to the actions and words of the Socialists, in or out of office. As a powerful and *autonomous* force in the land, French Communism is on the way out. It can only change by ridding itself of those very particular features which gave it its special character and position—and yet without them, it is nothing.

For the Communist Party has two enduring weaknesses which have been magnified by the events of the past few years and about which it can do very little. In the first place, it is historically attached to just those parts of France and French society which are most archaic and troubled, in urban and rural districts alike. Within any given department, the PCF strength in cantons of industrial decay and

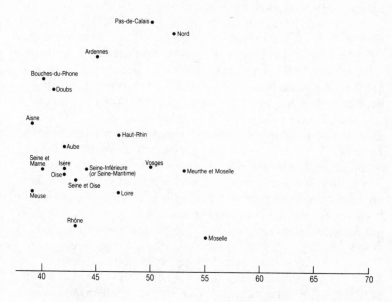

demographic decline is unmistakable. Little wonder that the Communists pressed the Socialist governments so hard for a policy of support for France's declining heavy industries (they are also a firm backer of price supports and agricultural subsidies). Because France was economically 'backward' for so long, the PCF was a net beneficiary of the country's peculiar economic history. But the correlation between 'Communist' and 'economically troubled' in French political ecology was a historical time bomb for the Party. As departments modernized, their work-force frequently turned to the Gaullists in the 1960s and early 1970s. More recently it has been the Socialists who have benefited. If there has been any consolation for the PCF it has been in isolated pockets of protest which have emerged in traditionally conservative areas, but these have been very insufficient.[63]

The PCF's second problem concerns its enduring Stalinism.[64] So

---

[63] See e.g. Goguel, *Modernisation économique et comportement politique*, pp. 13, 82–3.

[64] It ought no longer to be necessary to justify the claim that the PCF remains an essentially Stalinist organization, in its organization, its vocabulary, its mores. The rather

long as it remained doctrinally rigid and thus off-putting to the floating
left-centre voter, the Left had no access to power. Reforms (of the sort
hesitantly undertaken in the later 1960s and again in 1976) undercut
the fear of Communism (and upset many PCF stalwarts); but all this
meant was that voters trooped into the Socialist camp, no longer
fearing that the PS was a mere Communist stalking horse. Either way,
the PCF was blocked in its advance. It did not dare return to all-out
doctrinaire isolation, for all that this would have been to the taste of
some of its leaders and many of its militants; 38 per cent of its *own*
electors in 1982 thought it to be still insufficiently independent of
Moscow.[65] But it has no other role to play, a truth severely underlined
by its inability to influence Socialist policy from within the government.
In 1981 the PCF only succeeded in maintaining its vote between the
presidential and parliamentary elections in those constituencies where
it was strong enough to win a seat for the Left. Where it could not hold
out this promise, its vote collapsed. For its own voters, then, the PCF
in itself no longer offered a sufficient object of commitment.

It is this which renders its long-term prospects so gloomy. Two
major electoral disasters in a quarter of a century, followed by a series
of further set-backs in 1983 and 1984, place in question the historical
credibility, much less the necessity, of a Communist Party in France
(in June 1984 it was supported by just 6.2 per cent of the electorate).
They also raise the suggestion that the PCF may *never* have been as
significant as people once believed. Deprived of its formidable strength
in Paris and its environs, the PCF in recent years has not been much of
a force in the country. Its rapid rise to prominence was the result of a
fortunate combination of a major role in the Resistance and the good
fortune of an electoral stranglehold upon the capital city of the world's
most centripetal political culture.[66] There remains, of course, the

successful exercise in whitewash undertaken by the Party leadership in the years
1969–77 has been substantially negated by the PCF's own activities in the fields of race
relations, international politics, and in its dealings with those of its own members who
took altogether too seriously the promises of free speech and inner-party democracy.
Among many witnesses to this process, see the essay by Henri Fiszbin, *Les Bouches
s'ouvrent* (Paris, 1980).

[65] Sofres poll, in *Nouvel Observateur*, 23 Jan. 1982.

[66] 'Depuis les origines, la puissance du communisme parisien masquait les inégalités
d'implantation du Parti dans l'ensemble du territoire français. Dans la grande tradition
jacobine, il suffisait au P.C d'être fort dans la capitale pour être considéré comme un
grand parti national.' Le Bras and Todd, *L'Invention de la France*, p. 336. This is
something of an exaggeration, and benefits from hindsight and the particular
circumstances of the PCF's precipitate decline after 1977, but it points to a neglected
feature of the Party's history.

CGT, and also the hitherto steady stream of adhesions, albeit short-lived, from young people. But the mortgage on the future of the French Left which was for so long the Communist Party's greatest asset is just not credible any more, and this lesson will have been effective even if the PCF succeeds in increasing its vote in future elections. Hindsight is cheap and prediction unwise, but that 1981 posed for the French Communist Party its most intractable problem ever is not a conclusion which many in or out of the Party will care to dispute.

For the Socialists, 1981 was their finest hour. Not only did Mitterrand and his party transform national politics in France, but they have even succeeded in effecting a vital shift in French perceptions of the Left. For example, from the 1880s until the 1960s, the Left was associated with internationalism, and anti-militarism, and with a radically un-national stance in foreign affairs. Yet the one issue on which the PS has *not* fallen in public esteem since 1981 is Defence—in October 1983 a consistently high number of persons questioned agreed that a Socialist government was well able to 'assure French security in the world'. Even in 1984, at the height of popular discontent with government policy, 57 per cent approved Mitterrand's foreign policy, the unique case of majority support for governmental action.

What is more, the Socialists have been largely successful in aligning their movement with the nation at large—as we have seen, the Socialist electorate reflects with surprising accuracy the French electorate as a whole, in age, education, location, and occupation. And when 72 per cent of all Socialist supporters in 1983 expressed a desire to see the Socialists govern France 'without major changes', they too spoke for the country—74 per cent of all voters wished for the same thing. Only the 23 per cent who yearned for the 'mise en œuvre du socialisme' were out of line.[67]

This is where the difficulties begin. After a few months of heady enthusiasm and legislation, the Mauroy governments were faced by an economic crisis which prompted a return to old-fashioned 'rigour'. In 1984 this was then replaced, or rephrased, by an emphasis on modernization, the need to update France's economic institutions in line with the social and political changes of the first year of office. Shorn of apologetics and smokescreens, this meant that the

[67] See Capdevielle, op. cit., pp. 250–70; also Sofres poll, published in *Nouvel Observateur*, 21 Oct. 1983.

governments of Mauroy and, later, Fabius were to place steady economic growth, accompanied by social justice and political reforms, ahead of the 'transformation' of the system which had been the dominant motif in Socialist speeches until 1982. Inevitably, the result has been much discontent in the ranks of the party militants, who had expected something more.

All this sounds a lot like 1936, and many have feared that the Socialist 'experiment' would end similarly, with a divided party and a disillusioned electorate allowing the Right to inherit the failed dreams of the Left. But 1981 was not 1936; it is much more significant, and the problems were much more serious.

The government of Mauroy had some very real achievements, which will not readily be undone. These include an overhaul of the social security system, the establishment of workers' rights in enterprises, the beginnings of a very large-scale decentralization of power in France, reform of the judiciary, abolition of the death penalty, lowering of the retirement age, and so on. Mitterrand's prime ministers have also been the first in decades to face up to the problems of economic restructuring, albeit with limited success. But most of all, the Mitterrand era has resolved the problem of political legitimacy. Ever since 1944, with the adoption of a 'transitional' programme, the SFIO recognized the necessity of accepting office under capitalism. But so long as it cast the subject thus, it offered its opponents the weapon of excommunication—Socialists should not govern because they do not wish to do so, and their motives in doing so are suspect. The Right under Chirac continues to exploit this theme, but it lacks credibility. Under Mitterrand, the Left in France now speaks of government as an end in itself, and many of the younger leaders of the PS (Quilès, Fabius) are in the party for nothing less than the acquisition of office and power.

But it is not sufficient for a political party to be in office, it must also acquire the political culture of a party of government. Without this it always risks doubting its own claim to run the country, which was one of Blum's chief handicaps. But how could the Socialist movement in France acquire such a political culture, in the manner of the Swedish or Austrian Social Democratic parties? Its whole history was built upon the rejection of the struggle for office. More recently the alliance with the Communists required a reiterated lip service to the thesis of a final transformation of the capitalist system, the moment of change which alone would justify the pursuit of electoral success.

Some have suggested that the initial Socialist legislative surge, with nationalizations, wage increases, and the participation of the Communists in government, were mortagages upon the Left which had to be paid off before the path to social democracy in France could be opened up at last. This is true, in part, but it underestimates the extent to which the past weighs still upon the Socialist present. Every act of the Socialists, in or out of office, from 1899 to 1984, has been measured and described in terms of its relation to the theoretical propositions which alone can justify it. And the more the PS, or Mitterrand, has in practice moved away from any sort of residual marxist or socialist position, the more acutely has this need for doctrinal purity been felt. This was most in evidence at the 1981 Valence Congress of the PS, where delegates, supremely disdainful of the sociological facts of socialist life in France, announced the revolutionary millennium for tomorrow. Even in 1984, the left wing of the party has been issuing dire warnings of the dangers of a 'Bad Godesberg' in France (the 1959 venue of the German Socialist congress at which marxism was formally and finally abandoned). They need not worry. At the very moment of François Mitterrand's speech in April 1984, proclaiming the virtues of a mixed economy and the need for modernization 'à l'américaine', the PS leadership assured party militants and electors alike that the government was pursuing a 'coherent and continuous' policy, unaltered since 1981 and beyond.[68]

The emphasis upon continuity may be understandable, but it is unwise, to say the least. It reflects an instinctive return to a long-established pattern in marxist rhetoric, dating back to Kautsky and beyond, whereby the inevitable gap between theoretical preference and practical necessity is bridged by mirrors and magic. Unwilling to revise theory and unable to manipulate practice without restriction, Socialists from Blum to Chevènement have preferred to construct delicate pontoon-like structures quite incapable of bearing the demands placed upon them.

But why, the northern European socialist might ask, do the French not simply cut their losses, accept that what they are practising is social democracy, and make a virtue of necessity? Why do they persist in applying the symbols of their theory, such as nationalizations, while abandoning its essence—the break with capitalism? Would they not do better to begin afresh?

[68] Mitterrand's speech, a turning-point in the *formal* terms of socialist government in France, is reported in *Le Monde*, 11 Apr. 1984.

The question goes to the heart of the difficulty. At one level, the retention of old theoretical nostrums has certain tactical virtues. It enabled Mitterrand to forge an alliance against Michel Rocard, for example, from the old and new left groups within his party, and thus ensure his candidacy in 1981. Rocard may complain that Mitterrand then proceeded, after an initial delay, to apply his (Rocard's) own social democratic programme with vigour, but he cannot put it thus if he wishes to carry his Socialist colleagues with him. Similarly, too enthusiastic a grasping of the social democratic nettle by the Socialists might, it is feared, open up the ideological terrain for a Communist recovery.

But all this is secondary. The major difficultly is this. To be a socialist today is to find oneself in one of two positions. On the one hand, you can be in favour of a generalized moral project which asserts itself in conscious defiance of capitalist (interest-related) priorities. Or else you must argue from a series of premisses, stated or otherwise, which are still best characterized as 'marxism', and which entail a firm commitment to certain propositions about the life span and self-destructive properties of capitalism. These two avenues of advance are sometimes blurred in their distinctive differences in countries like Britain with no indigenous marxist traditions, or in non-European nations where the moral and the political opposition to authoritarian regimes are of necessity intertwined. But in France there can be no such confusion.

It is the unwillingness of most socialists in France to think of themselves as engaged in a project of an essentially indeterminate and partial kind which prevents them adopting the first of the two approaches. But so far as marxism is concerned, the only practically existing form of it is still that in force in Communist regimes. Since *some* sort of a project is a necessary condition for being a socialist, most of the non-Communist Left in France has been faced with a very difficult choice: take office with no very clear idea of what to do with it, or else retain clarity of perspective at the price of political impotence. Until 1981, the choice could be postponed, but not any more.

Indeed, it is not even a choice. Since the Socialist government and the Socialist presidency are absolutely secure until 1986 and 1988 respectively, they cannot, like Blum in 1936 or Mollet in 1956, simply enact a few bills and then quietly disappear. They are forced to live with the experience of office, and Mitterrand has already made clear that he sees this as a very proper task for Socialism in France. But what, then, will they do with it—and it with them?

Like the Communists, the Socialists are a trifle embarrassed by the fact of arriving in power at a moment of intellectual flux (see previous chapter). They have no ready-made political theory, nor even any significant theoreticians, and the old certainties have been pulled from under their feet by a combination of *realpolitik* and the discrediting of marxism. The more they continue to speak in the old ways, the more they alienate their marginal electors—yet they know no other way to speak. The importance of theory in the French Left has always lain in its manner of posing the questions (it is this which links the Jaurès–Guesde debates to the Blum–Mollet arguments of 1946, and thence to the present disagreements). But the sorts of questions best posed in such terms are not those most appropriate to the needs of a government facing a series of daily problems at home and abroad and seeking to resolve them compatibly with each other and its own programme. French Socialism is ill-adapted to such matters.

No one can tell how these problems will be resolved. François Mitterrand is presiding over huge changes in the political movement which he has brought into power—indeed, one of the difficulties he faces is that he brought the PS to power by playing hard upon the traditional socialist register, but is now constrained to govern in almost daily defiance of most of the terms upon which Socialist militants supported him. He has certainly disappointed his supporters. None the less, even if he fails to make social democrats of them, and if he or his party are defeated at future elections, as is almost certain to happen, he will have done something of immense historical significance, far surpassing any legislation or broken promises for which his governments may be remembered.

Communists and Socialists in France are the most important remaining constituent parts of the generic Left as the country has known it since 1793. The history of that Left's relationship to power has always been an ambivalent one—power (though not necessarily office) has been sought and secured at periodic intervals, only for it to be taken back forcibly by the Right. This process, dating from Thermidor to 1937, has generated (or, rather, ensured the survival of) a myth surrounding the nature of change in France. The Left, so goes the theory, will not be allowed to come to power peacefully—or, if it *is* able to secure power, it will not be able to be true to itself in the exercise of that power, without risking violent defeat. The limited truth of this account, so far as it describes the unbending opposition of the French bourgeoisie to all forms of change, reinforced its credibility.

The only occasion on which power in France was seen to have changed hands, with real historical effect, was during the great Revolution, in a series of *journées*. And thus, with Marx, the French Left (marxist and non-marxist alike) assimilated revolution in general to the model of the French Revolution in particular. It also thereby committed itself to the myth of the *grand soir*, the once and for all occasion when real shifts in social arrangements could be brought about. Because one of the teleological definitions of a *grand soir was* the successful ascent into power of the Left, the latter implies, *mutatis mutandis*, that a major change has indeed occurred. And thus 1981 *was* a *grand soir*, comparable to those of 1791 and 1871. But in the light of the controlled, limited, and somewhat undramatic changes wrought by Mitterrand and his governments, what price the myth?

It is not just the eschatalogical, all-or-nothing political vision which has suffered at the hands of the electorate. The very language of political debate in France, so changeless in six generations of conflict, no longer fits the mundane facts of political life. This is what, in part, lies behind the crisis of marxism in contemporary France, and it also of course accounts for the undertow of discontent in the Socialist movement since 1982. Party leaders have taken to complaining that the intellectuals are no longer on 'their side', that the powerful intellectual currents which once ran with the forces of the Left have forsaken them in their moment of triumph. And yet this is really no cause for surprise—one hundred and ten years after the Paris Commune, the moral imbalance which prompted and justified the academic *gauchisme* of most French intellectuals has been put to rights, at least for the time being. There thus no longer exists any very credible *language* in which to be 'Left' in modern France.

What this will mean for the forces of protest and the voices of resentment in France remains to be seen. In countries with strong social democratic traditions, where it has long been accepted that alternation in office is at worst inevitable, at best virtuous, and where the Left entered the political nation many years ago, the marginal workers and the unrepresented special interests have either abandoned politics or else sought their ends by alternative, occasionally extra-political means. In France this option has been invoked only on rare and short-lived occasions. It may yet emerge in the form of a radical

Right. It may also, though this is less likely, encourage the PCF to return to the ghetto as the party of the excluded (but the Communists have too many vested interests, institutional, financial, and personal, for this to be an appealing option).

In either event, however, the old Left, the Parti de Mouvement, the alliance of the dissatisfied and the traditionally radical, is beyond recall. De Gaulle, from beyond the grave, Giscard, in defeat, and Mitterrand, in victory, wrought greater changes than they knew. The elections of 1981 may only have been the *terminus ad quem* for a long social and electoral process, rather than the political revolution that some hoped and many proclaimed, but they will prove to have been the vehicle for a fundamental and profoundly disconcerting shift in the long history of national politics in France.

Select Bibliography

THE books and articles listed below are those which have been of particular help in preparing this book, or which may be of interest to anyone wishing to follow up themes raised in the text. The list, which includes some suggestions for background reading, is very far from inclusive, but further suggestions may be found in the notes, and in many of the books included in the bibliography. With only a very few exceptions the suggested reading is confined to secondary sources.

Adam, Gérard, 'Eléments d'analyse sur les liens entre le PCF et la CGT', in *Revue française de science politique*, vol. 18, no. iii (1968).

—— and Ranger, J., 'Les Liens entre le PCF et la CGT: éléments d'un débat', in *Revue française de science politique*, vol. 19, no. i (1969).

Agéron, C. R., 'Jaurès et les socialistes devant la question algérienne de 1895 à 1914', in *Mouvement social*, no. 42 (1969).

Agulhon, Maurice, *Une ville ouvrière au temps du socialisme utopique. Toulon de 1815 à 1851* (Paris, 1977).

—— 'Plaidoyer pour les Jacobins', in *Le Débat*, no. 13 (1981).

Alexandre, P., *Le Roman de la gauche* (Paris, 1977).

Allen, J. S., 'Towards a Social History of French Romanticism: authors, readers and the book trade in Paris, 1820–1840', in *Journal of Social History* (Fall 1979), pp. 253–77.

Althusser, Louis, *Pour Marx* (Paris, 1965).

—— *Lénine et la philosophie* (Paris, 1972).

—— *Réponse à John Lewis* (Paris, 1973).

—— *Eléments d'autocritique* (Paris, 1974).

—— *Ce qui'ne plus durer dans le parti communiste* (Paris, 1978).

and Balibar, Etienne, Establet, Roger, Macherey, Pierre, and Rancière, Jacques, *Lire 'Le Capital'*, 2 vols. (Paris, 1965), repr. 4 vols. (Paris, 1970).

Aminzade, Ronald, *Class, Politics and early Industrial Capitalism: a study of mid-nineteenth century Toulouse* (Albany, NY, 1981).

Anderson, Perry, *Arguments within English Marxism* (London, 1980).

Andreucci, Franco, 'Problemi di storia del marxismo contemporaneo', in *Studi Storici*, no. 16 (1975).

Ansart, Pierre, *Naissance de l'anarchisme. Esquisse d'une explication sociologique du proudhonnisme* (Paris, 1970).

Armengaud, André, *Les Populations de l'Est-Aquitain 1845–1871* (Paris, 1961).

—— *La Population française au XIXe siècle* (Paris, 1971).

Aron, Raymond, *D'une Sainte Famille à l'autre. Essais sur les marxismes imaginaires* (Paris, 1967).

Artisans, commerçants, petits industriels, il faut que ça change! (Speeches to PCF meeting, 12 Mar. 1951, Paris, n.d.).

Atlas electoral Nord—Pas de Calais, 1945–1972 (Lille, 1972).

Audiganne, Armand, *Les Populations ouvrières et les industries de la France dans le mouvement social du dix-neuvième siècle*, 2 vols. (Paris, 1854).

Audry, Collette, *Léon Blum ou la politique du juste* (Paris, 1955).

'Au Pays de Schneider' (Colloque, Le Creusot, 1976), in *Mouvement social*, no. 99 (1971).

Avec les communistes. Pour le bonheur et L'avenir de nos enfants (Paris, 1966).

Aviv, Isaac, 'Le PCF dans le système français des années '30 à la fin de la IVᵉ République', in *Mouvement social*, no. 104 (1978).

Axelos, Kostas, *Marx, penseur de la technique: De l'aliénation de l'homme à la conquête du monde* (Paris, 1961).

—— *Vers la pensée planétaire* (Paris, 1964).

Bacot, P., 'Le front de classe', in *Revue française de science politique*, vol. 28, no. ii (1978).

—— *Les Dirigeants du Parti Socialiste* (Lyons, 1979).

Badie, B., *Stratégie de la grève. Pour une approche fonctionnaliste du PCF* (Paris, 1976).

Baker, D. N., 'The Politics of Socialist Protest in France: the left-wing of the socialist party, 1921–1939', in *Journal of Modern History*, vol. 43, no. i (1971).

—— 'The Socialists and the Workers of Paris: the Amicales Socialistes 1936–1940', in *International Review of Social History*, vol. 24, no. i (1979).

Balibar, Etienne, *Cinq études de matérialisme historique* (Paris, 1974).

—— *Sur la dictature du prolétariat* (Paris, 1976).

Bancal, Jean, *Proudhon, pluralisme et autogestion* 2 vols. (Paris, 1970).

Barral, Pierre, 'La Sociologie électorale et l'histoire', in *Revue historique* (juillet–septembre 1967).

Bauchard, Philippe, *Léon Blum. Le pouvoir pour quoi faire?* (Paris, 1976).

Baud, Lucie, 'Les Tisseuses de soie de la région de Vizille', in *Mouvement socialiste* (1908).

Baudon, Eugène, *Les Elections en Moselle 1919–1956* (Metz, n.d.).

Baudouin, J., 'Les Phénomènes de contradiction au sein du Parti Communiste français, avril '78–mai '79', in *Revue française de science politique*, vol. 30, no. i (1980).

—— 'L'Echec communiste de juin 1981: recul électoral ou crise hégémonique', in *Pouvoirs*, no. 20 (1982).

Becker, J. J., and Kriegel, Annie, 'Les Inscrits du Carnet "B" ', in *Mouvement social*, no. 65 (1968).

Bell, D. S., and Criddle, B., *The French Socialist Party* (Oxford, 1984).

Berstein, Serge, *Histoire du parti radical*, vol. i: La Recherche de l'âge d'or (Paris, 1980).

Besançon, Alain, *Les Origines intéllectuelles du Leninisme* (Paris, 1971).

Besse, Guy, Milhau, Jacques, and Simon, Michel, *Lénine, la philosophie et la culture* (Paris, 1971).

Bezucha, Robert, *The Lyon Uprising of 1834* (Cambridge, Mass., 1974).

Blanc, Louis, *Organisation du travail* (Paris, 1848, English edn. repr. Oxford, 1913).

Blanqui, Adolphe, *Des classes ouvrières en France pendant l'année 1848* (Paris, 1848).

Blum, Léon, 'L'Idéal socialiste', in *La Revue de Paris* (mai 1924).

—— *Pour être socialiste* (Paris, 1931, 8th edn.).

—— *La Réforme gouvernementale* (Paris, 1936).

Léon Blum, chef de gouvernement (Paris, 1967).

Bodin, Louis, and Racine, Nicole, *Le Parti Communiste français pendant l'entre-deux-guerres* (Paris, 1972).

Bon, Frédéric, *et al.*, *Le Communisme en France* (Paris, 1969).

Bonnet, Serge, *L'Homme de fer: mineurs de fer et ouvriers sidérurgistes lorrains, 1889–1930* (Metz, 1975).

Bosi, Mariangela, and Portelli Hugues (eds.), *Les PC espagnol, français et italien face au pouvoir* (Paris, 1976).

Bourdé, Guy, *La Défaite du front populaire* (Paris, 1977).

Bourderon, Roger, *et al.*, *Le PCF: étapes et problemes* (Paris, 1981).

Bourguin, Maurice, *Les Systèmes socialistes et l'évolution économique* (Paris, 1913, 4th edn.).

Bouvier, Jean, 'Mouvement ouvrier et conjonctures économiques', in *Mouvement social*, no. 48 (1964).

Braque, René, 'Aux origines du syndicalisme dans les milieux ruraux du centre de la France' in *Mouvement social*, no. 42 (1963).

Braunthal, Julius, *History of the International*, 2 vols. (London, 1967).

Brécy, Robert, *Le Mouvement syndical en France, 1871–1921* (Paris, 1963).

Bruhat, Jean, 'Anti-cléricalisme et mouvement ouvrier en France avant 1914', in *Mouvement social* no. 57 (1966).

—— 'La Révolution française et la formation de la pensée de Marx', in *Annales historiques de la Révolution française* vol. 38, no. 184 (1966).

—— *et al.*, *La Pensée socialiste devant la Révolution française* (Paris, 1966).

Brunet, J.-P., 'Reflexions sur la scission de Doriot', in *Mouvement social*, no. 70 (1970).

—— *L'Enfance du Parti Communiste (1920–1938)* (Paris, 1972).

—— *St Denis la ville rouge, 1890–1939* (Paris, 1980).

Burguière, André, 'Qui avait ligoté la France?', in *Nouvel Observateur*, no. 871, 18–24 juillet 1981.

Burnier, Michel-Antoine, *Les Existentialistes et la Politique* (Paris, 1966).

Cachin, Marcel, *et al.*, *The People's Front in France*, speeches at 7th World Congress of Communist International (New York, 1935).

Callinicos, Alex, *Althusser's Marxism* (London, 1976).

Camus, A.-G., *Voyage dans les départements nouvellement réunis, et dans les départements du Bas-Rhin, du Nord, du Pas de Calais et de la Somme, à la fin de l'an X . . .*, 2 vols. (Paris, An XII).

Capdevielle, J., *et al.*, *France de gauche, vote à droite* (Paris, 1981).

Carron, M-A., 'Prélude à l'éxode rural en France: les migrations anciennes des travailleurs creusois', in *Revue d'histoire économique et sociale*, vol. 43, no. iii.

Casanova, Laurent, *Le Parti communiste, les intellectuels et la nation* (Paris, 1949).

Castoriadis, Cornelius, *L'Expérience du mouvement ouvrier*, 2 vols., (Paris, 1974).

—— *L'Institution imaginaire de la société* (Paris, 1975).

—— *La Société française* (Paris, 1979).

—— *Capitalisme moderne et révolution* (Paris, 1979).

Caute, David, *Communism and the French Intellectuals* (London, 1964).

Cayrol, R., 'L'Univers politique des militants socialistes: une enquête sur les orientations, courants et tendances du Parti Socialiste', in *Revue française de science politique*, vol. 25 (1975).

—— and Jaffré, J., 'Y-a-t-il plusieurs électorats socialistes?', in *Le Monde*, 22 Mar. 1977.

—— and Ignazzi, P., 'Cousins ou frères? Attitudes politiques et conceptions du Parti chez les militants socialistes français et italiens', in *Revue française de science politique*, vol. 33, no. iv (1983).

Cazals, Rémy, *Avec les ouvriers de Mazamet* (Paris, 1978).

Ce que veulent les communistes (Paris, n.d.).

Chabert, Alexandre, *Les Salaires dans l'industrie française: les charbonnages* (Paris, 1957).

—— *Les Salaires dans l'industrie française: les textiles* (Paris, 1960).

Chagnollaud, J.-P., 'La Fédération socialiste de Meurthe-et-Moselle' (1944–1977), in *Annales de l'Est*, no. 30 (1978).

Charles, Jean, 'Les Débuts de l'organisation ouvrière à Besançon, 1870–1904', in *Mouvement social*, no. 40 (1962).

—— *et al.*, *Le Congrès de Tours* (Paris, 1980).

Charlot, Jean, 'Le Double Enchaînement de la défaite et de la victoire', in *Revue politique et parlementaire* (mai–juin 1981).

Charlot, Monica, 'Women in Politics in France', in H. Penniman (ed.), *The French National Assembly Elections of 1978* (Washington, 1980).

Charnay, J.-P., *Le Suffrage politique en France* (Paris, 1965).

Châtelain, Abel, 'Les Migrants temporaires et la propagation des idées révolutionnaires en France au 19ᵉ siècle', in *Etudes de la Révolution de 1848*, (1951).

Chevalier, Louis, *La Formation de la population parisienne au dix-neuvième siècle* (Paris, 1950).

Choisir (La Cause des Femmes), *Quel Président pour les femmes?* (Paris, 1981).

Christianisme et monde ouvrier (Paris, 1975, Cahiers du mouvement social, no. 1).

Classe contre classe. La question française au IXe Executif et au VIe Congres de l'Internationale Communiste, 1928 (Paris, 1929).

Clément, P., and Xydias, N., *Vienne sur le Rhône* (Paris, 1955).

Codaccioni, F.-P., *De l'inégalite sociale dans une grande ville industrielle: Le drame de Lille de 1850 à 1914* (Lille, 1976).

Cogniot, Georges, 'Les Positions du parti dans le domaine idéologique à la lumière des travaux de Staline sur la linguistique', in *Cahiers du communisme* (juin 1951).

Collinet, Michel, *L'Ouvrier français* (Paris, 1952).

—— 'La Notion de prolétariat', in *Le Contrat social*, vol. 3, no. iv (1959).

Comment le parti communiste dirige la CGT (BEIPI, Paris, 1953).

Coornaert, E., 'La Pensée ouvrière et la conscience de classe en France de 1830 à 1848', in *Studi in onore di Gino Luzzato*, no. 3 (Milan, 1950).

—— *Les Compagnonnages en France du moyen age à nos jours* (Paris, 1975).

Corbin, Alain, *Archaisme et modernité en Limousin au dix-neuvième siècle (1845–1880)*, 2 vols. (Paris, 1974).

Cotten, J.-P., *La Pensée de Louis Althusser* (Paris, 1979).

Couderc, Pierre, *La Région urbaine de Montluçon-Commentry: origines, structures et activités* (Clermont-Ferrand, 1971).

Courtheoux, J.-P., 'Naissance d'une conscience de classe dans le prolétariat textile du Nord 1830–1880', in *Revue économique*, no. 1 (1957).

—— 'Privilèges et misère d'un métier sidérurgique au dix-neuvième siècle: le puddler', in *Revue d'histoire économique et sociale*, vol. 37, no. ii (1959).

Courtois, Stéphane, *Le PCF dans la guerre* (Paris, 1980).

Craipeau, Y., *Le Mouvement trotskyste en France. Des origines à 1968* (Paris, 1971).

Crossick, Geoff, and Haupt, Heinz-Gerhard (eds.), *Shopkeepers and Master Artisans in nineteenth-century Europe* (London, 1984).

Cuvillier, A., 'Une des premières coopératives de production: l'Association buchézienne des "bijoutiers en dore" (1834–1873)' in *Revue d'histoire des doctrines économiques et sociales* (1933).

—— *Un Journal d'ouvriers: 'l'Atelier' 1840–1850* (Paris, 1954).

—— *Hommes et idéologies de 1840* (Paris, 1956).

Dagnaud, Monique, and Mehl, Dominique, 'Profil de la nouvelle Gauche', in *Revue française de science politique*, vol. 31, no. ii (1981).

—— *L'Elite rose. Qui gouverne?* (Paris, 1982).

Daix, Pierre, *La Crise du PCF* (Paris, 1978).

Dale, L. A., *A Bibliography of French Labor* (New York, 1969).

Dalotel, Alain, Faure, Alain, and Freiermuth, Jean-Claude, *Aux origines de la Commune: le mouvement des réunions publiques à Paris 1868–1870* (Paris, 1980).

Daubie, Julie, *La Femme pauvre au dix-neuvième siècle* (Paris, 1866).

Daumard, Adeline, 'L'Evolution des structures sociales en France à l'époque de l'industrialisation', in *Revue historique*, no. 502 (1972).

Dauriac, Ferdinand, 'La Travail des femmes en France devant la statistique', in *Revue d'économie politique*, no. 47 (1933).

Delaye, Jules, *Rapport sur les sociétés de secours mutuels d'ouvriers* (Toulouse, 1862).

Delcourt, R., *De la condition des ouvriers dans les mines du Nord et du Pas de Calais* (Paris, 1906).

Deleuze, Gilles, *Différence et répétition* (Paris, 1968).

——*Anti-Oedipus: Capitalism and Schizophrenia* (New York, 1977).

Denier, François, 'Les Ouvriers de Rouen parlent à un économiste en juillet 1848', in *Mouvement social*, no. 119 (1982).

Denquin, J.-M., *Le Renversement de la majorité électorale dans le département de la Corrèze 1958–1973* (Paris, 1976).

Derfler, Leslie, *Socialism since Marx* (London, 1973).

Derivry, D., 'Analyse écologique du vote paysan', in Y. Tavernier (ed.), *L'Univers politique des paysans* (Paris, 1972).

Derville, Jacques, and Croiset, M., 'La Socialisation des militants communistes français', in *Revue française de science politique*, vol. 29 (1979).

——and Lecomte, P., 'Le Parti communiste français au miroir de ses partisans: une image contrastée', in *Revue française de science politique*, vol. 33, no. iv (1983).

Desanti, Dominique, *Les Socialistes de l'utopie* (Paris, 1970).

Descombes, Vincent, *Modern French Philosophy* (Cambridge, 1980).

Désert, Gabriel, 'Aperçu sur l'éxode rural en Basse Normandie à la fin du dix-neuvième siècle', in *Revue historique* (1973).

——*Une société rurale au dix-neuvième siècle: les paysans du Calvados, 1815–1875* (New York, repr. 1977).

Désiré-Vuillemin, G., 'Les grèves dans la région de Limoges de 1905 à 1914', in *Annales du Midi* (1973).

——'Une grève révolutionnaire: les porcellaniers de Limoges en avril 1905', in *Annales du Midi* (1972).

Desjardins, Thierry, *François Mitterrand: un socialiste gaullien* (Paris, 1978).

Destray, Jacques, *La Vie d'une famille ouvrière. Autobiographies* (Paris, 1971).

Dezamy, T., *Le Code de la communauté* (Paris, 1842).

Dioujeva, Natasha, and George, François, *Staline à Paris* (Paris, 1982).

Documentation sur la politique communiste, Supplément des informations politiques et sociales, no. 305 (Paris, 1958).

Dogan, Mattei, 'Le Vote ouvrier en France. Analyse écologique des élections de 1962', in *Revue française de sociologie*, vol. 6, no. iv (1965).

—— 'Les Clivages politiques de la classe ouvrière', in *Les Nouveaux Comportements politiques de la classe ouvrière* (Paris, 1962).

—— 'Les Filières de la carrière politique en France', in *Revue française de sociologie*, vol. 8, no. iv (1967).

—— and Narbonne, J., *Les Françaises face à la politique. Comportement politique et condition sociale* (Paris, 1955).

Dolléans, Edouard, *Histoire du mouvement ouvrier*, 3 vols. (Paris, 1939–53).

—— and Dehove, Gérard, *Histoire du travail en France*, 2 vols. (Paris, 1953–5).

Dommanget, Maurice, *L'Introduction du marxisme en France* (Paris, 1969).

—— *et al.*, *Babeuf et les problèmes du babouvisme* (Paris, 1963).

Donneur, André, and Padioleau, Jean, 'Local Clientelism in Post-industrial Society: the example of the French Communist Party', in *European Journal of Political Research*, no. 10 (1982).

Dreyfus, F.-G., *Histoire des gauches 1940–1974* (Paris, 1975).

Droz, Jacques, *Le Socialisme démocratique 1864–1960* (Paris, 1966).

—— *Socialisme et syndicalisme de 1914 à 1939* (Les Cours de la Sorbonne, Paris, 1972).

Duhamel, Alain, 'L'image du P.C.', in *Sondages*, no. 1 (1966).

Duhamel, O. and Parodi, J.-L., 'La Dégradation de l'image de l'Union Soviétique', in *Pouvoirs*, no. 21 (1982).

—— and Weber, H., *Changer le PCF?* (Paris, 1979).

Dumay, J.-B., *Mémoires d'un militant ouvrier du Creusot (1841–1905)* (Grenoble, 1976).

Dupeux, George, *Le Front Populaire et les élections de 1936* (Paris, 1959).

—— *Aspects de l'histoire sociale et politique du Loir-et-Cher 1848–1914* (Paris, 1962).

Dupuy, Fernand, *Etre maire communiste* (Paris, 1975).

Duveau, Georges, *La Vie ouvrière en France sous le Second Empire* (Paris, 1946).

Duverger, Maurice, *The Political Role of Women* (Paris, 1955).

—— *Les Orangers du Lac Balaton* (Paris, 1980).

L'Election présidentielle de décembre 1965 (Paris, 1970).

Les Elections du 2 janvier 1956 (Paris, 1957).

Les Elections législatives de mars 1967 (Paris, 1970).

Elleinstein, Jean, *Le P.C.* (Paris, 1976).

Elwitt, Sanford, 'Politics and Ideology in the French Labor Movement', in *Journal of Modern History*, vol. 49 (1977).

Evans, D. O., *Social Romanticism in France 1830–1848* (Oxford, 1951).

Fabre-Rosane, G., and Guede, A., 'Une sociologie des candidats de grandes formations', in *Le Monde*, 17 Mar. 1978.

Les Faiblesses actuelles du PCF, Supplément du BEIPI (Paris, 1953).

Fasel, George, 'Urban workers in provincial France, February–June 1848', in *International Review of Social History,* no. 17 (1972).

Faure, Alain, 'Mouvements populaires et mouvement ouvrier à Paris (1830–1834)', in *Mouvement social,* no. 88 (1974).

—— 'L'Epicerie parisienne au dix-neuvième siècle, ou la corporation éclatée', in *Mouvement social,* no. 108 (1979).

—— and Rancière, Jacques, *La Parole ouvrière 1830–1851* (Paris, 1976).

Fine, Martin, 'Towards Corporatism: the movement for capital-labor: cooperation in France, 1914–1936' (Univ. of Wisconsin Ph.D. thesis, 1971).

Fischler, Claude (ed.), *Marxisme, révisionnisme, meta-marxisme* (Paris, 1976).

Flonneau, J.-M., 'Crise de vie chère et mouvement syndical, 1910–1914', in *Mouvement social,* no. 72 (1970).

Fohlen, Claude, 'Crise textile et troubles sociaux', in *Revue du nord* (1953).

Fortin, A., 'Les Conflits sociaux dans les houillières du Pas de Calais sous le Second Empire', in *Revue du nord,* no. 43 (1961).

—— 'L'Evolution démographique du département du Pas de Calais durant le Second Empire', in *Revue du nord,* no. 49 (1967).

Fougeyrollas, Pierre, *Le Marxisme en question* (Paris, 1959).

—— *La Conscience politique dans la France contemporaine* (Paris, 1963).

—— *Contradiction et Totalité* (Paris, 1964).

—— *La Révolution prolétarienne et les Impasses petites-bourgeoises* (Paris, 1976).

Fournier, Pierre-Léon, *Le Second Empire et la législation ouvrière* (Paris, 1911).

Frader, Laura, 'Grapes of Wrath: vineyard workers, labor unions and strike activity in the Aude, 1860–1913', in Tilly *et al., Class Conflict and Collective Action* (Beverly Hills, 1981).

France, Min. de l'Intérieur, *Les Elections législatives du 17 juin 1951* (Paris, 1953).

—— *Liste des candidats aux élections législatives du 2 janvier 1956* (Paris, 1956).

—— *Les Elections législatives de 1962* (Paris, 1963).

—— *Les Elections législatives de 1973* (Paris, 1973).

Frears, J. R., *Political Parties and Elections in the French Fifth Republic* (London, 1977).

—— and Parodi, J.-L., *War will not take place: the French parliamentary elections, March 1978* (London, 1979).

Fruit, Elie, *Les Syndicats dans les chemins de fer en France (1890–1910)* (Paris, 1976).

Furet, François, *Interpreting the French Revolution* (Cambridge, 1981).

—— 'La révolution sans la terreur? Le débat des historiens du 19ᵉ siècle', in *Le Débat,* no. 13 (1981).

Gaillard, Jeanne, 'Les Usines Cail et les ouvriers métallurgistes de Grenelle de 1848 à 1851', in *Mouvement social,* nos. 33–4 (1960–1).

—— 'Les Associations de production et la pensée politique en France, 1852–1870', in *Mouvement social*, no. 52 (1965).

—— *Paris, la Ville (1852–1870)* (Univ. of Paris doctoral thesis 1976).

Gallico, Loris, *Storia del partito communista francese* (Milan, 1973).

Gallie, Duncan, 'The Agrarian roots of working-class radicalism: an assessment of the Mann/Giddens thesis' (unpub. MS).

Garaudy, Roger, *Pour un modèle français du socialisme* (Paris, 1969).

Garmy, R., 'Un mythe: "La Mine aux mineurs" de Rancié (Ariège) de 1815 à 1848', in *Mouvement social*, no. 43 (1963).

Garraud, P., 'Discours pratiques et idéologie dans l'évolution du parti socialiste', in *Revue française de science politique*, vol. 28, no. ii (1978).

Gaumont, Jean, *Histoire générale de la coopération en France*, 2 vols. (Paris, 1947).

Geerlandt, Robert, *Garaudy et Althusser. Le débat sur l'humanisme dans le parti communiste français et son enjeu* (Paris, 1978).

George, Pierre (ed.), *Etudes sur la banlieu de Paris* (Paris, 1950).

Georges, B., 'La CGT et le gouvernement de Léon Blum', in *Mouvement social*, no. 54 (1966).

Geras, Norman, 'Althusser's Marxism', in *New Left Review*, no. 71 (1972).

Gerstlé, Jacques, *Le Language des socialistes* (Paris, 1979).

Geslin, Claude, 'Les Syndicats nantais et le congrès coopératif de Nantes, 1894', in *Cahiers d'histoire*, no. 22 (1977).

Gille, B., *La Sidérurgie française au dix-neuvième siècle* (Geneva, 1968).

Gillet, Marcel, 'Aux origines de la première convention d'Arras: le bassin houillier du Nord et du Pas de Calais de 1880 à 1891', in *Revue de nord*, no. 154 (1957).

—— 'l'Affrontement des syndicalismes ouvrier et patronal dans le bassin houillier du Nord et du Pas de Calais de 1884 à 1891', in *Bulletin de la Société d'Histoire Moderne*, no. 1 (1957).

—— *Les Charbonnages du nord de la France au dix-neuvième siècle* (Paris, 1973).

—— and Hilaire, Y.-M., *De Blum à Daladier; le Nord-Pas de Calais, 1936–1939* (Lille, 1979).

Girault, Jacques, *et al.*, *Sur l'implantation du PCF dans l'entre-deux-guerres* (Paris, 1977).

Glucksmann, André, *Les Maîtres penseurs* (Paris, 1977).

Godechot, Jacques (ed.), *La Presse ouvrière 1819–1850* (Paris, 1966).

Goetz-Girey, R., *La Pensée syndicale en France. Militants et theoriciens* (Paris, 1848).

Goguel, François, *Modernisation économique et comportement politique* (Paris, 1969).

—— *Géographie des élections françaises sous la Troisième et Quatrième Républiques* (Paris, 1970).

—— *Chroniques électorales* (Paris, 1983).

—— and Barral, Pierre, Leleu, Claude 'Pour qui votent les femmes?', in F. Goguel (ed.), *Nouvelles Etudes de sociologie électorale* (Paris, 1954).

Goldey, David, and Johnson, R. W., 'The French General Election of March 1973', in *Political Studies*, no. 21 (1973).

—— 'The French General Election of March 1978: the redistribution of support within and between Right and Left', in *Parliamentary Affairs*, vol. 31, no. iii (1978).

—— and Knapp, Andrew, 'Time for a Change: the French elections of 1981', in *Electoral Studies*, vol. 1, no. i (1982).

Goldmann, Lucien, *Le Dieu caché, Etudes sur la vision tragique dans les pensées de Pascal et dans le théâtre de Racine* (Paris, 1955).

—— *Marxisme et sciences humaines* (Paris, 1970).

Gorz, André, *Stratégie ouvrière et néo-capitalisme* (Paris, 1964).

—— *Adieux au prolétariat* (Paris, 1980).

Gossez, Rémi, *Les Ouvriers de Paris*. 1: *l'Organisation, 1848–1851* (La Roche sur Yonne, 1967)..

Gratton, Philippe, *La Lutte des classes dans les compagnes* (Paris, 1971).

Grauwin, Charles, *Les institutions patronales des compagnies houillières du Pas de Calais* (Lille, 1909).

Grawitz, Madeleine, 'Le Référendum, la ville de Lyon et les femmes', in *Les Cahiers de la République*, no. 6 (1961).

Greene, Nathaniel, *Crisis and Decline. The French Socialist Party in the Popular Front Era* (Ithaca, NY, 1969).

Gruner, Shirley, 'Le Concept de classes dans la Révolution française: une mise à jour', in *Histoire sociale*, vol. 11, no. 18 (1976).

Guerry, Emile, 'Les syndicats libres féminins de l'Isère' (Grenoble, Thèse de Droit, 1921).

Guilbert, Madeleine, *Les Femmes et l'organisation syndicale avant 1914* (Paris, 1966).

—— 'La Présence des femmes dans les professions et ses incidences sur l'action syndicale avant 1914', in *Mouvement social*, no. 63 (1968).

Guillaume, P., 'Grèves et organisations ouvrières chez les mineurs de la Loire au milieu du dix-neuvième siècle', in *Mouvement social*, no. 43 (1963).

Guin, Yannick, *Le Mouvement ouvrier nantais* (Paris, 1976).

Guinot, J.-P., *Formation professionelle et travailleurs qualifiés depuis 1789* (Paris, 1946).

Guterman, Norbert, and Lefebvre, Henri, *Hegel: Morceaux choisis* (Paris, 1939).

Hainsworth, Raymond, 'Les Grèves du Front populaire de mai et juin 1936. Une nouvelle analyse fondée sur l'étude de ces grèves dans le bassin houillier du Nord et du Pas de Calais', in *Mouvement social*, no. 96 (1976).

Halbwachs, Maurice, 'Budgets de familles ouvrières et paysannes en France en 1907', in *Bulletin de la statistique générale de la France*, vol. 4 (1914–15).

Hardouin, P., 'Les Caractéristiques sociologiques du parti socialiste', in *Revue française de science politique*, vol. 28, no. ii (1978).

Harmel, C., 'La Composition sociale du parti communiste français et son évolution de 1959 à 1966', in *Est et Ouest*, no. 286 (1967).

Haupt, Georges, *La Deuxième Internationale 1889–1914. Essai bibliographique* (Paris, 1964).

Hayward, Jack, and Wright, Vincent, 'The 37,708 Microcosms of an Indivisible Republic: the French local elections of 1971', in *Parliamentary Affairs* (Autumn 1971).

Hilaire, Yves-Marie, 'Remarques sur la pratique réligieuse dans le bassin houillier du Pas de Calais dans le deuxième motié du dix-neuvième siècle', in *Charbon et sciences humaines* (Paris, 1966).

Hilaire, Y.-M., et al., *Atlas Electoral Nord-Pas de Calais, 1876–1936* (Lille, 1977).

Hincker, François, *Le Parti communiste au carrefour* (Paris, 1981).

Histoire du PCF (Manuel) (Paris, 1964).

Hohenberg, P., 'Change in Rural France in the Period of Industrialisation, 1830–1914', in *Journal of Economic History*, vol. 32, no. i (1972).

——'Les migrations dans la France rurale 1836–1901', in *Annales ESC* (mars–avril 1974).

Howorth, Jolyon, *Edouard Vaillant. La création de l'unité socialiste en France* (Paris, 1982).

Huard, Raymond, 'La Préhistoire des partis. Le parti républicain dans le Gard de 1848 à 1851', in *Mouvement social*, no. 107 (1979).

——*Le Mouvement républicain en Bas-Languedoc, 1848–1881* (Paris, 1982).

Hubscher, Ronald, *L'Agriculture et la société rurale dans le Pas de Calais du milieu du dix-neuvième siècle à 1914*, 2 vols. (Arras, 1979).

Hurtig, Christine, *De la SFIO an nouveau Parti Socialiste* (Paris, 1970).

Hurtig, Serge, 'La SFIO face à la Cinquième République', in *Revue française de science politique*, vol. 14, no. iii (1964).

Hutton, Patrick, *The Cult of the Revolutionary Tradition: the Blanquists in French politics, 1864–1893* (Berkeley, 1981).

Hyppolite, Jean, *Introduction à la philosophie de l'histoire de Hegel* (Paris, 1948).

——*Etudes sur Marx et Hegel* (Paris, 1955).

Institut d'Etudes Politiques à Bordeaux, *Les Militants politiques dans trois partis français* (Paris, 1976).

Les Intellectuels, la culture et la révolution, Conseil National du PCF, 9–10 fevrier 1980 (Paris, 1980).

Intervention. 'Les Socialistes croient-ils à leurs mythes?' in nos. 5–6 (août-octobre 1983).

Isambert, F.-A., *Christianisme et classe ouvrière: jalons pour une étude de sociologie historique* (Paris, 1961).

—— *Politique, réligion et science de l'homme chez Philippe Buchez* (Paris, 1967).

—— and Terrenoire, J.-P., *Atlas de la pratique réligieuse des catholiques en France* (Paris, 1980).

Jacobs, Janet, 'Workers in the Stéphanois region 1890–1914' (Univ. of Oxford Ph.D. thesis 1974).

Jaffré, Jérôme, *et al.*, 'La Gauche au Pouvoir', in *Pouvoirs*, no. 20 (1982).

James, Susan D., 'Holism in Social Theory: the case of Marxism' (Univ. of Cambridge Ph.D. thesis 1979).

Jeanneney, Jean-Noel, *Leçon d'histoire pour une gauche au pouvoir: la faillite du Cartel (1924–1926)* (Paris, 1977).

'Jedermann', *La Bolchévisation du PCF, 1923–1928* (Paris, 1971).

Jenson, Jane, 'The French Communist Party and Feminism', in *Socialist Register* (1980).

Johnson, Christopher, *Utopian Communism in France: Cabet and the Icarians, 1839–1851* (Ithaca, NY, 1974).

—— 'Economic Change and Artisan Discontent: The tailors' history 1800–1848', in Roger Price (ed.), *Revolution and Reaction: 1848 and the Second French Republic* (New York, 1975).

Johnson, R. W., *The Long March of the French Left* (London, 1981).

Judt, Tony, *La Reconstruction du parti socialiste 1921–1926* (Paris, 1976).

Julliard, Jacques, 'Jeune et vieux syndicat chez les mineurs du Pas de Calais', in *Mouvement social*, no. 47 (1964).

—— 'Théorie syndicaliste révolutionnaire et pratique gréviste', in *Mouvement social*, no. 65 (1968).

—— *Fernand Pelloutier et les origines du syndicalisme d'action directe* (Paris, 1971).

Kaes, R., 'Mémoire historique et usage de l'histoire chez les ouvriers français', in *Mouvement social*, no. 61 (1967).

Kahan-Rabecq, M., 'Les Réponses havraises à l'enquête sur le travail industriel et agricole de 1848', in *La Révolution de 1848*, vol. 31 (1934–5).

Kakkar, R., *Sociologie, socialisme et internationalisme pré-marxistes: l'influence de St Simon* (Neuchatel, 1968).

Kelly, Michael, *Modern French Marxism* (Oxford, 1982).

Kesler, J.-F., 'Le Communisme de gauche en France, 1927–1947', in *Revue française de science politique*, vol. 28, no. iv (1978).

Kessel, Patrick, *Le Prolétariat français*, vol. 1: *Avant Marx* (Paris, 1968).

Klatzmann, J., 'Comment votent les paysans français', in *Revue française de science politique*, vol. 8, no. i (1958).

—— 'Population ouvrière et vote communiste à Paris', in *Actes de la Recherche en Sciences Sociales*, nos. 36–7 (1981).

Kocka, Jurgen, 'The study of social mobility and the formation of the working class in the nineteenth century', in *Mouvement social*, no. 111 (1980).

Kojève, Alexandre, *Introduction à la lecture de Hegel* (Paris, 1947, collected and pub. by Raymond Queneau).

Kolakowski, Leszek, *The Alienation of Reason* (New York, 1968).

Kriegel, Annie, *Aux origines du communisme français*, 2 vols. (Paris, 1964).

—— *Le Congrès de Tours*, 2 vols. (Paris, 1964).

—— 'L'Historiographie du communisme français', *Mouvement social*, no. 62 (1965).

—— *La Croissance de la CGT 1918–1921* (Paris, 1966).

—— *Les Communistes français* (Paris, 1968).

—— *Le Pain et les roses. Jalons pour une histoire du socialisme* (Paris, 1968).

Kruks, Sonia, *The Political Philosophy of Merleau-Ponty* (Brighton, 1981).

Kurzweil, Edith, 'Louis Althusser: between philosophy and politics', in *Marxist Perspectives*, vol. 2, no. ii (1979).

Labbé, Dominique, *Le Discours communiste* (Paris, 1977).

—— *et al.*, 'Les Elections de 1981', in *Revue française de science politique*, vol. 31, nos. v–vi (1981).

Labrousse, Ernest, *Le Mouvement ouvrier et les théories sociales en France de 1815 à 1848* (Les Cours de la Sorbonne, Paris, 1964).

Lacorne, Denis. 'Analyse et "Reconstruction" de stéréotypes: communistes et socialistes face au socialisme soviétique', in *Revue française de science politique*, vol. 23, no. vi (1973).

—— *Les Notables rouges* (Paris, 1980).

Lagroye, J., and Lord, G., 'Trois fédérations de partis politiques: esquisse de typologie', in *Revue française de science politique*, vol. 24, no. iii (1974).

Lancelot, A., *L'Abstentionnisme électoral en France* (Paris, 1968).

—— 'L'Echec de l'alternance et les chances de renouvellement: les élections des 12 et 19 mars 1978', in *Projet* (juin 1978).

—— and M.-Th., *Atlas des circonscriptions électorales en France depuis 1875* (Paris, 1970).

—— and M.-Th., *Annuaire de la France politique, mai 1981–mai 1983* (Paris, 1983).

Landauer, Carl, *European Socialism* (Berkeley, 1959).

Lanfrey, A., 'Eglise et monde ouvrier: les congréganistes et leurs écoles à Montceau-les-Mines sous le Second Empire et la Troisième République (1875–1903)', in *Cahiers d'histoire*, no. 23 (1978).

Laubier de, Patrick, 'Esquisse d'une théorie du syndicalisme', in *Sociologie du travail*, no. 10 (1968).

Laurens, A., and Pfister, T., *Les Nouveaux Communistes* (Paris, 1973).

Laux, J. M., 'Travail et travailleurs dans l'industrie automobile jusqu'en 1914', in *Mouvement social* (1972).

Lavau, Georges, 'A la recherche d'un cadre théorique pour l'étude du PCF', in *Revue française de science politique*, vol. 18, no. iii (1968).

—— 'Histoire et idéologie dans le discours du parti communiste français', in *International Political Science Association*, 10th World Congress (Edinburgh, 1976).

—— *A Quoi sert le parti communiste français?* (Paris, 1981).

—— 'Le recul du PCF: Péripetie ou déclin historique?', in *Le Débat*, no. 16 (1981).

Lazitch, Branko, 'Les Archives du Komintern et la naissance du Front populaire', in *Contrepoint*, no. 3 (1971).

Lecourt, Dominique, *Marxism and Epistemology* (London, 1975).

Lefebvre, Henri, *Le Matérialisme dialectique* (Paris, 1939).

—— *La Pensée de Lénine* (Paris, 1957).

—— *La Somme et le reste* (Paris, 1959).

—— 'Marxisme et Politique: le marxisme a-t-il une théorie politique?', in *Revue française de science politique*, vol. 11, no. ii (1961).

—— *Au delà du structuralisme* (Paris, 1971).

—— *Une pensée devenue monde . . . faut-il abandonner Marx?* (Paris, 1983).

Lefort, Claude, *Eléments d'une critique de la bureaucratie* (Paris/Geneva, 1971).

—— *Sur une colonne absente* (Paris, 1978).

Lefranc, Georges, *Les Expériences syndicales en France de 1939 à 1950* (Paris, 1950).

—— *Le Mouvement socialiste sous la Troisième République 1875–1940* (Paris, 1963).

—— *Histoire du Front Populaire (1934–1938)* (Paris, 1965).

—— *Le Mouvement syndical sous la Troisième République* (Paris, 1967).

—— *Le Mouvement syndical en France, de la Libération aux événements de mai–juin 1968* (Paris, 1969).

—— 'Le Socialisme français dans l'entre-deux-guerres', in *Information historique*, no. 40 (1978).

Le Gall, G., 'Le Nouvel Ordre électoral', in *Revue politique et parlementaire* (juillet–août 1981).

Legendre, Bernard, *Le Stalinisme français* (Paris, 1980).

Leleu, Claude, *Géographie des élections françaises depuis 1936* (Paris, 1971).

Lemert, Charles, 'Literary Politics and the *champ* of French Sociology', in *Theory and Society*, vol. 10, no. v.

Léon, Pierre, 'Les Grèves de 1867 dans le département de l'Isère', in *Revue d'histoire moderne et contemporaine*, no. 1 (1954).

—— *et al.*, *Histoire économique et sociale de la France*, Tome 111, vols. 1, 2 (Paris, 1976).

Lequin, Yves, *Les Ouvriers de la région lyonnaise*, 2 vols. (Lyons, 1977).

Leroy, Maxime, *Les Précurseurs français du socialisme* (Paris, 1948).

Levasseur, Emile, *Histoire des classes ouvrières et de l'industrie en France de 1789 à 1870*, 2 vols. (Paris, 1904).

——*Questions ouvrières et industrielles en France sous la Troisième République* (Paris, 1970).

Lewisch, Serge, and Roucaute, Yves, 'Histoire des mots', in *Dialectiques*, no. 27.

L'homme, J., 'Le Pouvoir d'achat de l'ouvrier français au cours d'un siècle: 1840–1940', in *Mouvement social*, no. 63 (1968).

L'Huillier, Fernand, *La Lutte ouvrière à la fin du Second Empire* (Paris, 1957).

Lichtheim, George, *Marxism in Modern France* (New York, 1966).

——*A Short History of Socialism* (London, 1970).

——*From Marx to Hegel* (London, 1971).

Ligou, Daniel, *Histoire du socialisme en France 1871–1961* (Paris, 1962).

Lindenberg, Daniel, *Le Marxisme introuvable* (Paris, 1975).

Lolli, M. Larizza, *Il Sansimonismo 1825–1830. Un ideologia per il sviluppo industriale* (Turin, 1976).

Long, R., *Les Elections législatives en Côte d'Or depuis 1870. Essai d'interprétation sociologique* (Paris, 1958).

Lord, J., Petrie, A., and Whitehead, L., 'Political Change in Rural France: the 1967 election in a Communist stronghold', in *Political Studies*, vol. 16, no. ii (1968).

Lorwin, V., *The French Labor Movement* (Cambridge, Mass., 1954).

Loubere, Leo, 'The Intellectual Origins of French Jacobin Socialism', in *International Review of Social History*, no. iv (1959).

——*Louis Blanc: his life and his contribution to the rise of French Jacobin-socialism* (Evanston, Ill., 1961).

Lowy, Michel, *La Théorie de la révolution chez le jeune Marx* (Paris, 1970).

Luciani, Thérèse, 'Candidate féministe en Corse en 1978', in *Questions féministes*, no. 6 (Sept. 1979).

Mabileau, A. (ed.), *Les Facteurs locaux de la vie politique nationale* (Paris, 1972).

Macciocchi, M. A., *Letters from inside the Italian Communist Party to Louis Althusser* (London, 1973).

Machin, Howard, and Wright, Vincent, 'Why Mitterrand won: the French presidential elections of April–May 1981', in *West European Politics*, vol. 5, no. i (1982).

Madjarian, G., *La Question coloniale et la politique du PCF 1944–1947* (Paris, 1977).

Mallet, Serge, *La Nouvelle Classe ouvrière* (Paris, 1963).

——*Le Pouvoir ouvrier: bureaucratie ou démocratie ouvrière* (Paris, 1971).

Mandel, Ernest, *From Stalinism to Eurocommunism* (London, 1978).

Marchais, Georges, *L'Espoir au Present* (Paris, 1980).

Marcou, Lily, *Le Kominform* (Paris, 1977).

—— and Riglet, Marc, 'Du passé font-ils table rase?', in *Revue française de science politique*, vol. 26, no. vi (1976).

Marczewski, J., Toutain, J.-C., and Markovitch, T. J., *Histoire quantitative de l'économie française*, 7 vols. (Paris, 1961–6).

Markovitch, T. J., *Le Revenu industriel et artisanal sous la monarchie de juillet et le Second Empire* (Paris, 1967).

Mayer, Daniel, *Pour une histoire de la gauche* (Paris, 1969).

McBride, Teresa, 'A Woman's World: department stores and the evolution of women's employment, 1870–1920', in *French Historical Studies*, vol. 10, no. iv (1978).

McDougall, Mary L., 'Consciousness and Community: the workers of Lyons, 1830–1850', in *Journal of Social History*, vol. 12, no. i (1978).

Mer, Jacqueline, *Le Parti de Maurice Thorez, ou le bonheur communiste français* (Paris, 1977).

Mercier-Josa, Solange, *Pour lire Marx et Hegel* (Paris, 1980).

Merleau-Ponty, Maurice, *Phénomenologie de la perception* (Paris, 1945).

—— *Humanisme et terreur. Essai sur le probleme communiste* (Paris, 1947).

—— *Les Aventures de la dialectique* (Paris, 1955).

Michaud, René, *J'avais vingt ans. Un jeune ouvrier au début du siècle* (Paris, 1967).

Molinari, J.-P., 'Contribution à la sociologie du PCF', in *Cahiers du Communisme*, no. i (1976).

Le Monde, Elections et Réferendums (octobre 1945 à décembre 1946), 2 vols. (Paris, 1946).

—— *Les Forces politiques et les élections de mars 1973* (Dossiers et Documents, 1973).

—— *L'Election présidentielle de mai 1974* (Dossiers et Documents, 1974).

—— *Les Elections législatives de mars 1978* (Dossiers et Documents, 1978).

—— *L'Election présidentielle du 26 avril–10 mai 1981* (Dossiers et Documents).

—— *Les Elections législatives de juin 1981* (Dossiers et Documents).

Monneta, Jacob, *Le PCF et la question coloniale* (Paris, 1971).

Mony, Adolphe, *Histoire d'une mine: Commentry* (Paris, 1911).

Morin, Edgar, *Autocritique* (Paris 1958, repr. 1975).

—— *Marxisme et sociologie* (Paris, 1963).

—— *Introduction à une politique de l'homme* (Paris, 1965).

Moss, Bernard, *The Origins of the French Labor Movement* (Berkeley, 1976).

Mossuz-Lavau, Janine, and Sineau, Mariette, *Enquête sur les femmes et la politique en France* (Paris, 1983).

Moutet, Aimée, 'Le Mouvement ouvrier à Paris du lendemain de la Commune au premier congrès syndicaliste en 1876', in *Mouvement social*, no. 58 (1967).

Naville, Pierre, *De l'aliénation à la jouissance: la genèse de la sociologie du travail chez Marx et Engels* (Paris, 1957).

—— *L'Entre-deux-guerres (la Lutte de classes en France 1927–1939)* (Paris, 1957).

'*La Nef*', 'Le socialisme français victime du marxisme?' nos. 65–6 (1950).

Noiret, Charles, *Mémoires d'un ouvrier rouennais* (Rouen, 1836).

Ozouf, Mona, 'Fortunes et Infortunes d'un Mot', in *Le Débat*, no. 13 (1981).

Pacquot, Thierry, *Les Faiseurs de nuage: essai sur la genèse des marxismes français, 1880–1914* (Paris, 1980).

Pannequin, Roger, *Adieu, camarades* (Paris, 1977).

Parodi, J.-L., 'L'Echec des gauches', in *Revue politique et parlementaire*, no. 873 (1978).

Parti Communiste français, *Ecarter tout ce qui divise, ne retenir que ce qui unit*, Rapports de Waldeck Rochet et Maurice Thorez à la Conférence du Comité Central, Malakoff (decembre 1962).

—— *Conférence d'Ivry du Comité Central, octobre 1968* (supplément à *l'Humanité*, 23 Oct. 1968).

Peneff, J., 'Autobiographies de militants ouvriers', in *Revue française de science politique*, vol. 29, no. i (1979).

Pennetier, Claude, *Le Socialisme dans le Cher (1851–1921)* (Paris, 1982).

Penniman, H. R. (ed.), *France at the Polls. The Presidential Election of 1974* (Washington, 1975).

—— *The French National Assembly elections of 1978* (Washington, 1980).

Perrot, Michelle, 'Les Guesdistes: controverse sur l'introduction du marxisme en France', in *Annales ESC* (mai–juin 1967).

—— *Les Ouvriers en grève*, 2 vols. (Paris, 1974).

—— and Kriegel, Annie, *Le Socialisme français et le pouvoir* (Paris, 1966).

Petitfils, Christian, *Les Socialismes utopiques* (Paris, 1977).

Peyrefitte, Christel, 'Réligion et Politique', in *SOFRES, l'Opinion française en 1977*.

Philip, André, *Les Socialistes* (Paris, 1967).

Pierrard, Pierre, *La Vie ouvrière à Lille sous le Second Empire* (Paris, 1965).

Pierre, Roger, 'Aux origines du mouvement ouvrier dans le Drôme: les ouvriers chapeliers de Bourg-en-Péage et de Romans', in *Cahiers d'histoire*, (1972).

Pigenet, P., *et al.*, *Terre de luttes: les précurseurs 1848–1939 (Histoire du mouvement ouvrier dans le Cher)* (Paris, 1977).

Pigenet, Michel, 'L'Usine et le village—Rosières 1896–1914', in *Mouvement social*, no. 119 (1982).

Pinset, Jacques, 'Quelques problèmes de socialisme en France vers 1900', in *Revue d'histoire économique et sociale*, vol. 36, no. iii (1958).

Platone, F., and Ranger, J., 'L'Echec du Parti communiste français aux élections du printemps 1981', in *Revue française de science politique*, vol. 31, nos. v–vi (1981).

Portelli, Hugues, *Le Socialisme français tel qu'il est* (Paris, 1980).

—— 'Les Socialistes et l'exercise du pouvoir', in *Projet* (Oct. 1982).

Poster, Mark, *Existential Marxism in post-war France* (Princeton, 1975).

Poulantzas, Nicos, *Pouvoir politique et classes sociales* (Paris, 1968).

—— *Les Classes sociales dans le capitalisme d'aujourd'hui* (Paris, 1974).

—— *L'Etat, le pouvoir, le socialisme* (Paris, 1978).

Power and Opposition in post-revolutionary societies (London, 1979).

Les Principes de la politique du parti communiste français (Paris, 1975).

Problèmes de la révolution socialiste en France (Paris, 1971).

Pronier, Raymond, *Les Municipalités communistes* (Paris, 1983).

Prost, Antoine, *La CGT à l'époque du Front Populaire 1934–1939* (Paris, 1964).

Rabaut, Jean, *Tout est possible; les gauchistes français, 1929–1944* (Paris, 1974).

Rancière, Jacques, *La Leçon d'Althusser* (Paris, 1974).

Ranger, Jean, 'L'Evolution du PCF: organisations et débats idéologiques', in *Revue française de science politique*, vol. 13, no. iv (1963).

—— 'L'Evolution du PCF et ses relations avec la SFIO', in *Revue française de science politique*, vol. 14, no. i (1964).

Rebérioux, Madeleine, 'Les Tendances hostiles à l'Etat dans la SFIO, 1905–1914', in *Mouvement social*, no. 65 (1968).

—— 'Jaurès e il marxismo', in *Annali della Fondazione G. Feltrinelli*, no. 15 (1973).

—— (ed.), *Jaurès et la classe ouvrière* (Paris, 1981).

Reid, Donald, 'The Role of Mine Safety in the Development of Working-Class Consciousness and Organisation: the case of the Aubin coal basin, 1867–1914', in *French Historical Studies*, vol. 12, no. i (1980).

Rémond, René, 'L'Originalité du socialisme français', in *Tendances politiques de la vie française* (Paris, 1960).

Renaud, Marie-Thérèse, *La Participation des femmes à la vie civique* (Paris, 1965).

Renaud, Jean, and Vassart, Albert, 'Quelques documents relatifs à la tactique classe contre classe', in *Mouvement social* (1970).

Reybaud, Louis, *Rapport sur la condition morale, intellectuelle et matérielle des ouvriers qui vivent de l'industrie de fer* (Paris, 1872).

Ridley, F. F., *Revolutionary Syndicalism in France* (London, 1970).

Rigaudias-Weiss, Hilda, *Les Enquêtes ouvrières en France entre 1830 et 1848* (Paris, 1936).

Rioux, J. P., *Révolutionnaires du Front Populaire* (Paris, 1973).

—— 'Les Socialistes dans l'entreprise au temps du Front Populaire:

quelques remarques sur les Amicales Socialistes (1936–1938)', in *Mouvement social*, no. 106 (1979).

Robert, J.-L., *La Scission syndicale de 1921, essai de reconnaissances des formes* (Paris, 1980).

Robrieux, Phillippe, *Histoire intérieure du Parti Communiste*, 4 vols. (Paris, 1980–4).

—— *Maurice Thorez, Vie Secrète et Vie Publique* (Paris, 1975).

Rondeau, Daniel, *Chagrin lorrain: la vie ouvrière en Lorraine, 1870–1914* (Paris, 1979).

Ronsin, Francis, 'La Classe ouvrière et le néo-malthusianisme: l'exemple français avant 1914', in *Mouvement social*, no. 106 (1979).

Ross, George, *Workers and Communists in France* (Berkeley, 1981).

Rossi, A. (pseud. Tasca), *Physiologie du Parti Communiste français* (Paris, 1948).

Roucaute, Yves, *Le PCF et les sommets de l'Etat* (Paris, 1981).

Rougerie, Jacques, *Procès des Communards* (Paris, 1964).

—— 'Remarques sur l'histoire des salaires à Paris au dix-neuvième siècle, in *Mouvement social*, vol. 63 (1968).

—— *Paris Libre, 1871* (Paris, 1971).

—— et al., *1871. Jalons pour une histoire de la Commune (Assen, Neths, 1973).*

Rougeron, Georges, *Le Departement de l'Allier sous la Troisième Republique* (Montluçon, 1965).

Rousseau, A., 'Attitudes politiques des catholiques', in *Projet* (fevrier 1978).

Rudelle, Odile, *La République absolue: Aux origines de l'instabilité constitutionelle de la France républicaine, 1870–1889* (Paris, 1982).

Sagnes, Jean, ' "Parti communiste" et "Parti socialiste": genèse d'une terminologie', in *Revue française de science politique*, no. 32 (1982).

—— *Le Mouvement ouvrier du Languedoc* (Toulouse, 1980).

Salvatti, M., 'Fronte populare e movimenti sociali in Francia', in *Movimento operaio e socialisto*, vol. 1, nos. i–ii (1978).

Saposs, D. J., *The Labor Movement in Post-War France* (New York, 1931).

Sartre, J.-P., *Critique de la raison dialectique* (Paris, 1960).

—— *Situations IV* (Paris, 1964).

—— *Situations VI* (Paris, 1964).

Scott, Joan W., *The Glassworkers of Carmaux* (Cambridge, Mass., 1974).

Semprun, Jorge, 'Rester de gauche', in *Le Débat*, no. 13 (1981).

Sève, Lucien, *La Philosophie française contemporaine et sa genèse de 1789 à nos jours* (Paris, 1962).

—— *Une introduction à la philosophie marxiste* (Paris, 1980).

Sewell, William, 'Social Change and the Rise of Working-Class Politics in Nineteenth-century Marseille', in *Past and Present*, no. 65, (Nov. 1974).

—— *Work and Revolution in France. The language of labor from the Old Regime to 1848* (Cambridge, 1980).

—— La Confraternité des prolétaires: conscience de classe sous la monarchie de juillet', in *Annales ESC* (juillet–août 1981).

Simiand, François, *Le Salaire des ouvriers des mines de charbon en France* (Paris, 1904).

Sokoloff, Sally, 'Peasant Leadership and the French Communist Party, 1921–1940', in *Historical Reflections*, no. 4 (1977).

Soubise, Louis, *Le Marxisme après Marx (1956–1965). Quatre marxistes dissidents français* (Paris, 1967).

Sowerwine, Charles, Sisters or Citizens? Women and Socialism in France since 1876 (Cambridge, 1982).

Stearns, Peter, *Revolutionary Syndicalism and French Labor* (New Brunswick, NJ, 1970).

Stoetzel, Jean, 'Voting behaviour in France', in *British Journal of Sociology*, vol. 6, no. ii (1955).

Subileau, Françoise, 'Les Délégués au 21e Congrès du PCF. Reflexions sur quelques données sociologiques', in *Cahiers du communisme*, no. 51 (1975).

—— 'Les Communistes parisiens en 1977', in *Revue française de science politique*, vol. 29 (1979).

Tartakowsky, Danielle, *Les Premiers Communistes français* (Paris, 1980).

Thompson, E. P., 'The Poverty of theory', in *The Poverty of Theory and Other Essays* (London, 1978).

Thorez, Maurice, *En avant pour l'issue révolutionnaire de la crise, Rapport du Comité Central presenté au 7e Congres du PC(F) (mars 1932)*.

——*Au service du peuple de France*, speech at 11th congress of PCF (Paris, 1947).

——*Défendre la République. Sauvegarder notre indépendance nationale* (Paris, 1947).

—— *La Lutte pour l'indépendance nationale et pour la paix* (Paris, 1950).

Thuillier, Guy, *Aspects de l'économie nivernaise au dix-neuvième siècle* (Paris, 1966).

Tiersky, Ronald, *Le Mouvement communiste en France 1920–1972* (Paris, 1973, English edn., New York, 1974).

Tilly, Charles and Lees, Lynn, 'Le peuple de Juin 1848', in *Annales ESC*, vol. 29 (1974).

Touchard, Jean, 'De l'Affaire Lecœur à l'Affaire Hervé', in *Revue française de science politique*, vol. 6, no. ii (1956).

—— 'Le PCF et ses intellectuels', in *Revue française de science politique*, vol. 17, no. iii (1967).

—— *La Gauche en France depuis* 1900 (Paris, 1977).

Trempé, Rolande, 'Contribution à l'histoire des mineurs sous la Révolution et l'Empire', in *Actes du 83e Congrès Nationale des Sociétés Savantes* (Paris, 1959).

—— *Les Mineurs de Carmaux 1848–1914*, 2 vols. (Paris, 1971).

Truant, Cynthia, 'Solidarity and Symbolism among Journeymen Artisans: the case of compagnonnage', in *Comparative Studies in Society and History*, vol. 21, no. 11 (1979).

Valenta, Jiri, 'Eurocommunism and the USSR', in *Political Quarterly*, vol. 51, no. ii (1980).

Verdès, Jeannine, 'Le Syndicalisme révolutionnaire et le mouvement ouvrier français avant 1914', in *Cahiers Internationaux de Sociologie*, vol. 36 (1964).

Verdès-Leroux, Jeannine, *Au Service du Parti. Le parti communiste, les intellectuels et la culture (1944–1956)* (Paris, 1983).

—— 'Les Invariants du Parti communiste français', in *Actes de la Recherche en sciences sociales*, nos. 36–7 (1981).

Vial, Jean, *L'industrialisation de la sidérurgie française, 1814–1864*, 2 vols. (Paris, 1967).

Viard, Jacques, *Pierre Leroux et les socialistes européens* (Paris, 1983).

Vidal-Nacquet, Pierre, 'L'impossible histoire du PCF', in *Partisans*, no. 20 (1965).

Vidalenc, Jean, *La Société française de 1815 à 1848*, vol. 2: *Le Peuple des villes et des bourgs* (Paris, 1973).

Vincienne, M., and Courtois, J. H., 'Notes sur la situation réligieuse de la France en 1848, d'après l'enquête cantonale ordonnée par le Comité du Travail', in *Archives de sociologie des réligions*, no. 6 (1958).

Viplé, J. F., *Sociologie politique de l'Allier* (Paris, 1967).

Viveret, P., 'La Gauche piègée dans l'Etat', in *Projet* (juin 1982).

Wahl, Alfred, 'Les Députés SFIO de 1924 à 1940: essai de sociologie', in *Mouvement social*, no. 106 (1979).

Walch, Jean, *Bibliographie du Saint Simonisme* (Paris, 1969).

Wall, Irwin, *French Communism in the Era of Stalin* (Westport, Conn., 1983).

Weill, Georges, 'Les Journaux ouvriers à Paris (1830–1870)', in *Revue d'histoire moderne et contemporaine*, vol. 9 (1907–8).

Willard, Claude, *Les Guesdistes* (Paris, 1965).

—— *Socialisme et Communisme français* (Paris, 1967).

Williams, P. M., *French Politicians and Elections, 1951–1969* (Cambridge, 1970).

Williams, Stuart (ed.), *Socialism in France from Jaurès to Mitterrand* (London, 1983).

Wohl, Robert, *French Communism in the Making 1914–1924* (Stanford, 1967).

Worms, J. P., 'The Rise of the French Socialist Party', in *Dissent*, vol. 24, no. iii (1977).

Wright, Vincent, *The Government and Politics of France* (London, 2nd edn., 1983).

Ysmal, Colette, 'Sur la gauche socialiste', in *Revue française de science politique*, vol. 20, no. v (1970).

Ziebura, Gilbert, *Léon Blum et le Parti Socialiste* (Paris, 1967).

Chronology

1803   Reintroduction of workers' *livrets*.

1806   Re-establishment of Conseils de Prud'hommes.

1830   July Revolution.

1831   Silkworkers' uprising in Lyons.

1834   Silkworkers' strike in Lyons, followed by uprisings in Lyons and Paris.
Law against associations.

1839   Insurrection by Blanqui and Société des Saisons.

1848   (February) Revolution in Paris. Proclamation of freedom of association, the right to work. Creation of National Workshops and the Luxembourg Commission.
(March) Establishment of universal male suffrage. Working day reduced to 10 hours in Paris, 11 in the provinces.
(April) Elections to Constituent Assembly.
(June) Abolition of National Workshops. Workers' uprising in Paris.
(November) New Constitution voted. Right to work not included in it.
(December) Louis Napoléon elected President.

1849   (May) Legislative Assembly elected, including 200 'Montagnards'.

1850   (May) Restricted suffrage introduced.

1851   (December) Louis Napoléon's coup. Popular uprising in defence of the Republic.

1852   (March) Sociétés de Secours Mutuels regulated by law
(December) Second Empire inaugurated.

1864   (February) *Manifeste des Soixante*
(May) Law granting right to strike and form coalitions.
(September) Founding of Socialist and Workers' International.

1867   Workers' delegation to Paris Exposition universelle.

1869-71 Numerous strikes. Trials of French sections of the International. Public meetings addressed by Socialists in Paris, Lyons.

1870   (September) Declaration of the Republic.
Formation of Central Committee of Twenty Arrondissements in Paris.

1871   (February) Delegation of Twenty Arrondissements adopts 're-volutionary socialist' declaration of principles.
(March) Election in Paris of Central Committee of National Guard.

Government flees Paris, Central Committee of National Guard proclaims Commune.

Communes established in Lyons, Marseilles, Le Creusot, etc.

(April) Commune promulgates decrees on education, night work, debts; organizes workers' co-operatives and placement offices.

(May) Defeat and overthrow of Commune.

1872 International banned in France.

1874 Creation of Work Inspectorate.

1876 Workers' delegation to Universal Exhibition in Philadelphia. National workers' Congress in Paris.

1877 Jules Guesde founds *l'Egalité*, first socialist newspaper.

1878 Workers' Congress in Lyons.

1879 Amnesty for *communards*. First national syndicalist federation founded (*chapeliers*).

National Congress (at Marseilles) of socialist and professional groups. Establishes Parti Ouvrier Français (POF).

1880 POF Congress in Le Havre—mutualists (anti-collectivists) secede.

1881 Formation of Blanquist Comité révolutionaire central.

1882 POF Congress in St Etienne—'possibilistes', led by Paul Brousse, secede and form Fédération des Travailleurs Socialistes de France.

1883 Foundation of National Federation of Miners.

1884 Law on trade unions grants them legal recognition.

1886 First national trade union congress held at Lyons, establishes Fédération des groupements corporatifs de France.

1887 Congress of Fédération nationale des syndicats at Montluçon.

1888 Third national Congress of Fédération nationale des· syndicats. Votes motion on general strike.

1889 Foundation in Paris of Second International.

1890 First celebration of May Day in France. At Châtellerault Congress of Fédération des travailleurs socialistes de France, scission led by Jean Allemane departs to create Parti socialiste ouvrier revolutionnaire (POSR).

1891 First collective bargaining agreements, in coalmines of Pas de Calais. Fourmies massacre. Establishment of national textile trade union.

1892 First Congress of Fédération nationale des Bourses du travail, in St Etienne.

1893 Fifty Socialists elected at legislative elections.

1894 Fédération des Bourses and Fédération des syndicats adopt the principle of a general strike and no links to political parties.

1895   Joint Congress at Limoges of Bourses and Syndicats Fédérations creates Confédération Générale du Travail (CGT).

1896   Alexandre Millerand, at St Mandé, gives speech outlining 'minimum' socialist programme.

1899   Millerand joins Waldeck–Rousseau's government.

1899   National Congress of socialist organizations held in Paris. Agrees in principle to form common national organization.

1900   Ten-hour day law approved.

1901   Socialist organizations regroup into two umbrella parties: Parti Socialiste de France (comprising POF, POSR, and Blanquists) and Parti Socialiste Française (comprising 'possibilistes' and independent socialists led by Jaurès).

1902   At Montpellier Congress of CGT, Bourses are finally incorporated into federal organization.

1904   Founding of *l'Humanité*. Sixth Congress of Second International condemns divisions in French socialism and blames 'revisionists', recommends unity.

1905   At a Congress in Paris, French Socialists unite and form Parti Socialiste, Section Française de l'Internationale ouvrière (SFIO).

1906   (April) Strikes, government mobilizes army.
        (May) CGT begins general strike for eight-hour day.
        (October) CGT Congress at Amiens votes a 'charter' affirming syndicalists' anti-militarism, independence from political parties, and support for the principle of the general strike.

1907   Strikes and riots in southern vineyards. Mutiny by troops sent to repress strikers.

1908–11 Strikes by postal workers, railway workers, building workers.

1913   Extraordinary CGT Congress votes to oppose call-up in the event of war.

1914   SFIO obtained 1,400,000 votes and 103 seats at legislative elections. Jaurès assassinated 31 July.
        SFIO unanimously votes war credits, two Socialists join government.

1915   (September) Zimmerwald Conference of Socialists for international action against the war.

1916   (April) Second international anti-war conference of Socialists at Kienthal.

1917   (September) SFIO leaves government.

1918   (July) Majority in SFIO moves to the left and urges negotiated peace and support for the Russian Revolution.

1919   (April) Eight-hour day law.
        (May–June) Major strikes by metalworkers, miners, textile workers.

(November) At legislative elections, SFIO obtains 1,700,000 votes, 68 seats.

1920   (February) SFIO Congress at Strasbourg votes to leave Second International.

(February–May) Major series of strikes, culminating in unsuccessful declaration of a general strike by CGT.

(December) SFIO Congress at Tours votes to join Third International. Minority departs to remain in SFIO, majority becomes Parti Communiste (official title: Parti Socialiste, Section Française de l'Internationale Communiste).

1921   (December) Minority in CGT leaves the Confederation, to form CGT-Unitaire (CGTU) and join the Moscow-based Revolutionary Syndicalist International.

1924   (May) Victory of Cartel des Gauches at legislative elections.

1928   (January) PCF adopts tactic of 'class contre classe'.

1930   (October) Maurice Thorez is named Secretary of Bureau Politique of PCF.

1932   (December) 'Neo-socialists' leave SFIO in protest at its refusal to join a Radical government.

1934   (6 February) Extreme right-wing demonstration in Paris;

(12 February) CGT calls general strike in protest, followed by joint SFIO/PCF counter-demonstration.

(April) CGT announces its economic Plan.

(June) PCF proposes a 'unity of action pact' against fascism to SFIO.

(July) PCF and SFIO sign joint pact and create a co-ordinating committee.

(October) CGT and CGTU hold preliminary meeting to discuss syndicalist unity.

Thorez proposes the creation of a 'popular front for work, peace and freedom'.

1935   (July) Bastille Day demonstrations in Paris and elsewhere by Communists, Socialists, and syndicalists together.

1936   (March) CGT and CGTU reunite at national Congress.

(April–May) Legislative elections give 376 seats to Popular Front coalition.

(May–June) Massive wave of strikes and sit-ins.

(June) Formation of Blum government. Major social legislation voted by Chambre.

(December) PCF abstains in vote on foreign policy over support for the republican government in Spain.

1937   (June) Blum resigns after defeat in the Senate.

1938   (March) Second Blum government, again defeated by Senate after three weeks.

(November) CGT calls a general strike against the decree-laws of the Daladier government. The strike is broken by the Radical-led government and the Popular Front coalition definitively destroyed.

1939   (August) Signing of Russo-German non-aggression pact.

(September) Government pronounces dissolution of PCF.

1940   (June) 90 SFIO *députés* vote full powers to Pétain, 36 vote against.

1941   (May–June) Miners' strike in Nord and Pas de Calais.

(June) Hitler invades Russia, PCF commits itself to resistance.

1943   (May) Creation of National Resistance Committee.

1944   (April) PCF representatives enter National Liberation Committee.

(October) Female suffrage instituted.

1945   (October) SFIO and PCF win absolute majority of seats in Constituent Assembly.

(October–December) Social security laws, farm laws and nationalizations voted.

1946   (July) Guy Mollet elected General Secretary of SFIO.

(November) PCF emerges as largest party in France, with 28.6 per cent of the vote.

1947   (January) Vincent Auriol (SFIO) elected first President of the Fourth Republic.

(April) Strikes at Renault works.

(May) SFIO premier Ramadier expels PCF from government.

(November–December) Series of political strikes.

(December) Non-Communist unions leave CGT and form CGT-Force Ouvrière.

1951   (July) Following legislative elections, SFIO leaves government.

1954   (June) Mendès-France government. Settlement of Indo-China war, establishment of collective wage agreements.

(November) Outbreak of revolt in Algeria.

1956   (January) Republican Front victory at legislative elections, Guy Mollet becomes premier.

(February) 20th Congress of Communist Party of Soviet Union secret speech by Khrushchev.

(November) Soviet invasion of Hungary.

1957   (May) Fall of Mollet government.

1958   (June–September) PCF opposes Fifth Republic, SFIO is divided. Socialist opposition leaves to form Parti Socialiste Autonome PSA—later Parti Socialiste Unifié—PSU).

1959   (January) Remaining SFIO ministers leave government.

1962   (November) First SFIO-PCF alliances in some constituencies for legislative elections.

1963   (February–April) Miners' strike.

1964   (July) Death of Maurice Thorez. CFDT (Confédération Française Démocratique du Travail) loses its Christian wing, becomes a secular union movement.

1965   (September) Creation of Fédération de la Gauche Démocrate et Socialiste (FGDS) from electoral alliance of SFIO, Radicals, and left-wing clubs.
       (December) Mitterrand wins 44.8 per cent of votes in second ballot of presidential election.

1966   (December) FGDS and PCF agree on an electoral pact.

1968   (February) PCF and FGDS sign common platform.
       (May) Student 'events' and general strike.
       (November) FGDS dissolved.

1969   (May) At Alfortville Congress, SFIO dissolved and new Parti Socialiste (PS) created.
       (June) In presidential elections, Defferre (PS) obtained 5 per cent of the vote, Duclos (PCF) 22 per cent.
       (July) Issy-les-Moulineaux Congress of PS elects Alain Savary First Secretary.

1970   (February) Georges Marchais becomes General Secretary of PCF.

1971   (June) At Epinay Congress of PS, Mitterrand is elected First Secretary.
       (July) PS and PCF agree to negotiate a common programme of government.

1972   (July) PS and PCF, with Left Radicals, sign *Programme commun*.

1973   (March) Left increases its share of vote at legislative elections.

1974   (April) PCF agrees to back Mitterrand as presidential candidate.
       (May) Mitterrand wins 49.2 per cent of votes in second ballot of presidential elections.
       (October) At Assises Nationales pour le Socialisme, in Paris, PS is expanded to include Michel Rocard (from PSU) and others.

1976   (February) PCF abandons 'dictatorship of the proletariat.'

1977   (March) Major successes for PS at municipal elections.
       (May) PS, PCF, and Radicals begin negotiations to 'update' Common Programme.
       (September) Breakdown of negotiations between Communists and Socialists.

1978   (March) Left defeated in legislative elections, but PS overtakes PCF for first time since 1936.

1979 (June) In first European elections, PS obtains 23.5 per cent of the vote, PCF 20.6 per cent.

1980 (November) Mitterrand announces his candidacy for the presidency.

1981 (April–May) Mitterrand elected President. Marchais, for PCF, obtains only 15.3 per cent of the vote.
(June) In legislative elections, PS wins absolute majority of seats, with 37.6 per cent of the vote.
The PCF obtains 16.2 per cent.
Pierre Mauroy forms a government with four Communist ministers.

1981–2 Major social and economic legislation (nationalizations, decentralization, reform of judiciary, increased workers' say in factory administration, abolition of death penalty).

1983 (March) Serious losses for Left (especially PCF) in municipal elections.
(April) Mauroy government introduces austerity measures.

1984 (June) In European elections, PS vote falls, Communist vote collapses (to 11 per cent of the votes cast).
(June–July) Right mobilizes huge protests at government's bill to reform private education. Mitterrand withdraws the bill and Alain Savary (education minister) resigns, followed by Pierre Mauroy. Mitterrand appoints Laurent Fabius as prime minister. PCF refuses the offer of a place in the new government and abstains in the vote of confidence, opposing government's measures for economic renewal.

Index